FORTRAN
TOOLS

FOR VAX/VMS
AND MS–DOS

FORTRAN TOOLS

FOR VAX/VMS AND MS–DOS

Russell K. Jones

Tracy Crabtree

John Wiley & Sons
New York • Chichester • Brisbane • Toronto • Singapore

This book was prepared using the LATEX documentation system, developed by Leslie Lamport. LATEX is based on the TEX document compiler by Donald Knuth. The camera-ready manuscript was printed on a Talaris T802 laser printer at Talaris Systems, Inc.

TEX is a trademark of the American Mathematical Society. DEC, VAX, and VMS are trademarks of Digital Equipment Corporation. IBM is a trademark of International Business Machines, Inc. MS-DOS is a trademark of the Microsoft Corporation. Fortran is not a trademark of anybody. Tools are the trademark of a good programmer.

Copyright © 1988 by John Wiley and Sons, Inc.

All rights reserved. Published simultaneously in Canada.

Reproduction or translation of any part of this work beyond that permitted by Section 107 or 108 of the 1976 United States Copyright Act without the permission of the copyright owner is unlawful. Requests for permission or further information should be addressed to the Permissions Department, John Wiley and Sons, Inc.

Library of Congress Cataloging in Publication Data:
Jones, Russ. 1957-
    Fortran tools : for VAX/VMS and MS-DOS /
Russ Jones, Tracy Crabtree.
      p. cm.
    Bibliography: p.
    Includes index.
    ISBN 0-471-61976-0;
    1. FORTRAN (Computer program language)
2. VAX/VMS (Computer Operating system)
3. MS-DOS (Computer operating system.
I. Crabtree, Tracy. II. Title.
QA76.73.F25J66   1989
005.13'3—dc19   88-23573
                          CIP

Printed in the United States of America

10 9 8 7 6 5 4 3 2

Contents

Preface

This book is a text on how to write software tools in Fortran. It teaches good programming style by presenting programs and routines that illustrate important design principles and methods. The text is unusual in that it actually contains real, working, tested programs. All too often, programming texts contain few programs, and the programs that are presented are contrived and silly. For instance, a program to compute the payroll expenses of a lumber company with seven employees may be presented in order to illustrate the use of Pascal records or some other syntactic feature of a language. Since very few potential readers are likely to be lumber company owners, the program is essentially useless to them. More importantly, such examples sidestep a critical program design concept, namely, how to write a real program, with a nontrivial purpose, to operate on real input.

The programs in this book are "tools." We prefer this term to the term "utilities" since the connotation of a utility is that of something you call upon for services you can't provide for yourself—much like the electric company. Tools are things that belong to you and make doing a job easier. The tools here are complete; they are tested and useful by themselves or as parts of larger programs. They are also well-written and documented (documentation is an indispensable component of well-written programs), and thus understandable.

Throughout the text, the reader may assume an implicit reference to two excellent texts on the subject of software tools—*Software Tools* (Addison-Wesley, 1976) and *Software Tools in Pascal* (Addison-Wesley, 1981), both by Brian Kernighan and P. J. Plauger. Some of the routines in our text correspond closely to those presented by Kernighan and Plauger, partly because the book began as a project to implement some of their tools in VAX Fortran, and partly because any comprehensive set of tools must include a number of routines to perform simple tasks with the same properties, regardless of the language, environment, or intended application.

The original *Software Tools* contained a language preprocessor called Ratfor (rationalized Fortran) that provided more esthetically pleasing and readable programs, with a syntax and style more closely akin to C than to Fortran. That book was published in 1976, prior to the introduction of Fortran 77, which is now universally available. Some of the changes to the language introduced in Fortran 77 make a revisitation of the design issues in many of the tools worthwhile. In addition, many Fortran implementations support the do...end do and do while constructs, mitigating the need for code generation involving insertion of goto's. The preprocessor presented in this book starts with an extended Fortran language rather than a new syntax and provides code generation for do...end do and do while loops only. It can be easily customized to take advantage of or compensate for characteristics of any given operating environment. We developed the code on a VAX/VMS system, which has a first-rate Fortran compiler with many useful extensions such as long identifier names, lowercase letters, and improved looping constructs. As a result almost none of our code needs preprocessing to compile in VAX/VMS.

The programs in this book are written to be portable. Nonportability due to operating environment differences is dealt with by isolating such dependencies in a small, well defined set of primitive routines. Nonportability due to use of nonstandard extensions is controlled by only using extensions that can easily be preprocessed into Fortran 77 standard form. The usual solution to this problem is to stick to absolutely standard features of the language. Instead, we have tried to show that the programmer need not be forced to adhere to standards such as six-character variables or card format, but can establish his or her own standards by simply preprocessing the source text.

The text has a pragmatic and informal flavor, with brief discussions of the theory behind several advanced programming techniques, and is aimed at readers who are familiar with Fortran but unfamiliar with those techniques. Chapter 1 begins with a broad definition of software tools and presents a summary of the Fortran language. Chapter 2 has the tools to get the ball rolling, with programs for source code management, and a VAX Fortran to Fortran 77 translator is supplied as a "portabilizer," to transform a better human-engineered standard into a more restrictive one.

A comprehensive file I/O system for text processing is presented in Chapter 3 along with a file inclusion routine that provides the first of many examples of implementing recursion cleanly in Fortran (Appendix B describes an implementation of the same functions for MS–DOS Fortran compilers). In Chapter 4 a library of string-handling routines is developed. The programs in these two chapters form a good set of basic tools for a variety of text processing tasks. The reason for focusing on text handling is that it is necessary in designing good user interfaces and useful in the everyday tasks of programming, since source programs are text files too. We feel that Fortran's string manipulation capability is underrated, and this side of Fortran programming has been ignored in all of the books we have seen that contain any source code.

The next four chapters all build on the framework provided by the file system and string library to create a set of powerful tools for program development. Chapter 5 introduces the concept of a hash table for management of symbol tables, and provides routines for table management using direct chaining as well as a generator for preloading hash tables. The hashing routines are in turn used in Chapter 6 to build prep, a preprocessor with macro expansion capabilities. A routine for getting logical lines from the input, with preprocessing, is the finale of Chapter 6, resulting in a self-contained module that is useful in just about any program.

In Chapter 7 a lexical analyzer generator lexgen is developed along with the theory of regular expressions and finite automata. The lexical analyzers made by lexgen are extremely compact and efficient and can be tailored for many applications. Anyone looking for a good practical discussion of table-driven lexical analyzers will find it here in the form of a clearly written generator program. As a sideline a file searching program based on regular expressions is presented.

Chapter 8 presents the spl interpreter, a simple but reasonably complete compiler system. The spl program is simple enough that the entire compiler can be discussed in just one chapter, so it can be easily understood, but complete enough to address some of the practical difficulties in real compilers. The spl compiler will be valuable to all readers interested in learning how to write compilers and interpreters even if their favorite programming language isn't Fortran because spl is methodically developed and fully explained in a down-to-earth style. The obvious application of interpreters to typical Fortran programming is in developing simulation languages, and spl is written to be readily customized for such applications. Studying this small compiler will also help readers understand what real commercial compilers do with their code, which will help them to become better programmers in general.

The spl compiler generates code for a simulated (virtual) machine and interprets the resulting code. The concept of defining a virtual machine to simplify a larger problem is emphasized as a general programming technique. The virtual machine and lexical analyzers produced by lexgen, along with the preprocessor and hash table routines, are major components of the spl compiler. Thus spl ties all of the tools from previous chapters into one program.

The final chapter presents tools for VAX system programming using Fortran. In a sense it goes back to the beginning, by implementing new primitives for VMS logical names and CLI symbols, direct terminal I/O, command line editing and process management. The programs in Chapter 9 are necessarily nonportable because of their inherent system dependencies. The chapter concludes with a command shell that provides transparent I/O redirection and pipelines for DCL, which will be valuable to any VAX/VMS user.

This book is not about the Fortran language per se but rather about its effective use. The only preparation expected of the reader for this book is a knowledge of the Fortran language itself, which can be obtained from any number of introductory textbooks, and some familiarity with the VAX/VMS programming environment. Familiarity with the VAX is not really necessary for understanding any of the programs in the book except for those in Chapter 9.

Fortran Tools is not suitable as a main text for a course in Fortran programming but would make a good supplemental text for a Fortran course at any level because of the practical software it contains. The book shows by example how to write programs that work, how to systematically subdivide a big problem into smaller ones that are easier to solve, and how to design Fortran programs around data structures. The book contains in-depth discussions of file I/O and character data processing in Fortran, subjects that are poorly addressed in most other texts. The main benefit of this book for academic use is its coverage of computer science topics such as hash tables, lexical analyzers, compilers, and machine instruction sets. Since an introductory course in Fortran is the only exposure to computer science for many students, these subjects are a valuable supplement to any Fortran course. *Fortran Tools* will be of greatest value to professionals who program in Fortran and who can benefit from the lessons in program design as well as from the programs themselves.

The writing of this book has had the benefit of help from many sources. We are grateful to Hughes Aircraft Company for providing a work environment that encourages creativity, and to our co-workers at Hughes for their support and encouragement. We would particularly like to thank Jo Anne Jones, John Warner, Adrian Alting-Mees, and Steve McCoy for their helpful comments and suggestions. Steve McCoy drew the cartoons adorning the title page of each chapter, and he and Mr. Alting-Mees helped to write and test several of the routines. Special thanks are due to Tom Morgan and Guy Guzman for careful and comprehensive reviews of the manuscript.

The programs in this book are available in machine-readable form; the software can be ordered using the form at the back of the book or by contacting the authors at P.O. Box 1294, Manhattan Beach, California 90266. The source code media also includes a few programs not listed in the book, such as a larger version of spl supporting functions, local variables, and an assembler for the virtual machine.

Russ Jones
Tracy Crabtree

Manhattan Beach, California
Long Beach, California
October, 1988

FORTRAN TOOLS

FOR VAX/VMS
AND MS–DOS

CHAPTER 1

Introduction

1.1 The Tools Approach

The subject of this book is how to write good programs in Fortran.

But what do we mean by "good"? There are several facets of computer programming that this objective encompasses. A good program must obviously perform a useful function; it should be documented, and the code should be readable and straightforward; and it should be portable to other environments.

Let us consider functionality first. Suppose that you have written a large application program and have just discovered that a variable name you used conflicts with some system-defined symbol (think of any reasonable scenario) and must be changed throughout the program. One possibility is to get a listing of the program, which either you or a junior associate must go through by hand, marking each occurrence in red. This is the method all too often used for lack of a suitable tool. But this is just the kind of tedious assignment for which computers

1

were invented.

Another approach is to write a quick and dirty program to let the computer do the job for you. It might have the file names and text to be found hard-wired into the program, but at least it does the job, and more reliably. Although occasional quick and dirty programs can't be avoided, this is clearly a less than optimum choice as well. A better solution is to write a program to find any text string in any file, and have it also perform the required changes automatically. The requirement for functionality, then, implies both generality and flexibility.

The program to find and change any string of text is a tool—it performs a useful function and is flexible enough to solve the general problem. If written properly, it can also be used as a building block for a larger program, for example, a text editor. But to be a good program, it must also be written well. Programming is as much a literary task as it is a technical one, requiring good organization and clarity of presentation. It is not adequate merely for the program to "work," unless we don't mind throwing it away if it somehow breaks. Of primary concern is the control of complexity: sophisticated programs are necessarily complex, yet to be easily understood, each part must be simple.

Finally, a good program should be portable. Computer technology changes so fast that machines become obsolete about the same time they are designed, so a program that only runs on one machine becomes obsolete just as fast. Programmers may actually use several computer systems on a day-to-day basis for their own tasks or for communicating with other people. It is therefore imperative that programs we intend to use can be made to operate on other systems, without starting over from scratch or rewriting every routine. There are two distinct aspects of portability, each requiring a different solution:

- Differences in the local operating environment and language interface, and

- Differences in "compatible extensions" to some standard language.

We deal with the first issue by confining all operating system dependencies in a set of "primitive" routines upon which the rest of the software is built. Changes in operating environments can then be concealed by only rewriting the primitive routines. Of course, there are some relatively advanced tasks we would like to be able to perform, which rely intimately on operating system details. Programs of this sort have little chance of easy portability without writing most of an operating system ourselves; however, we can still try to define boundaries that minimize the implications for the rest of the program.

The issues of portability and readability seem to be at odds in the Fortran standard. In the prehistoric days of computing, programs were written using a panel of switches and a little red button, and undoubtedly marvelous programs were written using this system. Then a magical device called assembly language was discovered whose translation into the language of switches and the red button was straightforward. The assembler made programs much more readable. The fact that good programs can be written with switches and buttons does not imply that switches and buttons are a good programming language, hence the assembler.

Some people in the software community view Fortran as a dinosaur from ancient times. True, the lack of looping constructs, and the restriction to six-character identifiers are drawbacks, but they do not prevent good programming. In fact, it is relatively easy to write a preprocessor that gives Fortran the features it needs for readability and produces portable code. And Fortran is still evolving—many implementations now support do while and do until loops, and some support structured records à la Pascal. Although the standard implementation lacks some of the niceties of Pascal, such as user-defined data types and records, it is superior to Pascal in several key areas of practical interest to programmers. It supports separate compilation, passed-length arrays, and local data storage, all of which make it a much more modular language. It provides extensive read/write formatting, supports single-precision, double-precision, and complex data types. It has an exponentiation operator, supports complex variable arithmetic, and supplies a rich set of standard scientific functions. This combination of features is not found in any other popular programming language today, and makes Fortran still the language of choice for scientific and engineering applications.

The second of the portability requirements can be satisfied in two ways. One way of ensuring portability is to insist that programs obey the standard of the language in every detail; this necessarily implies some compromise in readability for Fortran. The other approach is the one we have chosen, which we think is much better. We establish our own standards, and where necessary, we preprocess code conforming to our standards into a format acceptable to a "standard" compiler. Regardless of what standards are chosen, the idea of controlling your own programming environment is an important one, which we hope to convey even to readers who are not interested in the programs themselves. The message is that one can and should take matters into one's own hands. Anyone can tailor a programming environment to meet personal needs—it is simply a trade-off between initial effort and continuing effort. Time taken to establish your personal "standard environment" reduces the time you must spend later reinventing the wheel.

The philosophy of developing software tools is an extension of this idea. The size and quality of a programmer's toolbox is in some sense an indicator of experience and productivity, since having tools and knowing how to use them means large parts of just about any program are already written. Developing a general, flexible tool to solve a problem is usually more difficult than developing the same function for the specific problem at hand, but solves the problem once and for all—a trade-off between initial and continuing effort. We believe the effort required to write good tools is repaid many times over by the continuing time savings in writing future programs.

Don't be surprised if you don't understand everything about a program the first time you read it. Programming is not easy—it is hard mental work, requiring concentration, carefull planning, attention to detail, and just plain sweat. The good news is that like any other work, it gets easier with experience. With each new programming task, the number of conceptual breakthroughs needed to arrive at a working design diminishes because of techniques learned in previous programs. By careful study of real programs, you can bypass much of the learning curve.

This book focuses on string handling, file input/output (I/O), and compiler-related tools such as hash tables, lexical analyzers, and preprocessors. The subject matter may seem a bit odd for a book on Fortran, since the primary area of interest for Fortran programming is scientific and engineering number-crunching. Fortran programmers are generally experts in some area of science and technology, and the programs they write are directed at solving specific problems in their line of work. The one common denominator we expect in all potential readers of this book is an interest in computer programming; thus programs that facilitate writing other programs should be of interest to everyone. Real programs are necessarily specialized, and the one specialty all readers are likely to have in common is programming.

Another reason for the focus on compiler-related tools is that the techniques used in compiler design are applicable to any kind of serious programming. Use of interpretive techniques can transform dull and lifeless Fortran application programs into powerful, flexible, and slick "analysis engines," tools that let the user rather than the original programmer specify the problems to be analyzed. Since simulators are the end goal of many Fortran programming projects, application of our tools may be of direct benefit in real situations. Such techniques have rarely been used in Fortran programming, although they are widely used with other languages. Perhaps the reason for this situation is that Fortran programmers have historically been physicists and engineers rather than computer scientists, and thus have never been exposed to computer science topics beyond the fundamentals. If so, this book will help to fill the knowledge gap by providing Fortran users with a down-to-earth discussion of software engineering in their native language—Fortran.

1.2   Fortran Synopsis

This is not a text for the Fortran language itself, but rather for its effective use. The following synopsis of the Fortran language is presented as a refresher course on the most important features of the language and is by no means complete. Readers who are not familiar with the material presented should avail themselves of one of the many textbooks on the Fortran language (some of which are listed at the end of this chapter).

We use an extended Fortran notation that, with a few exceptions, is part of almost every Fortran implementation. The material here describes Fortran as we use it rather than the official Fortran standard. Our usage is more readable and can easily be converted to standard form using the tools in this book.

Character Set and Statement Format

The Fortran character set (the set of characters allowed in programs) consists of uppercase letters A–Z, TAB, BLANK, the digits 0–9, and the following special characters:

$$ \$ \ ' \ (\ ) \ * \ + \ , \ - \ . \ / \ : \ = $$

Other characters may appear within quoted strings.

We use an extended character set throughout this book, which allows lowercase letters and the exclamation mark because it improves readability. We have the convention that all program text is lower case, except for the names of symbolic constants.

Fortran statements consist of sequences of *lexical items*, or pieces of text, and are separated by the end of a physical line unless followed by a continuation line. A line is a continuation line if there is a nonblank character other than the digit 0 in column 6. All statements begin at column 7 or greater. Statements may be given a label by placing any positive integer in columns 1–5.

Comment lines in standard Fortran begin with a C or * in column 1. Comment lines and blank lines are ignored. In our programs, we use ! to mark the beginning of a comment. Comments can begin in any column position, and the remainder of the line after the ! character is ignored. The following are examples:

```
! this is a comment line - ignored

    lval = .false.      !this is a comment - ignored
    call cpu_hog (lval,  !this is a
    &             hours)  !continued statement
```

The lexical items (also called *tokens*) consist of keywords, identifiers, constants, format descriptors, arithmetic and logical operators, and various punctuation characters. The low-level syntax of the tokens is as follows:

Keywords: one of the following:

assign	backspace	block data	call
close	character	common	complex
continue	data	dimension	do
do while	double precision	else	else if
end	end do	end if	endfile
entry	equivalence	external	format
function	goto	if	implicit
include	inquire	integer	intrinsic
logical	open	parameter	pause
print	program	read	real
return	rewind	save	stop
subroutine	write	then	

Identifiers consist of a letter, followed by any number of letters or digits or underscores. We avoid the use of the underscore for the most part, but use it occasionally to improve readability. We have also adopted the additional restriction that an identifier may not be the same as a keyword, that is, keywords are reserved. The Fortran standard requires identifiers to be of length six or less, but most compilers accept much longer names. We use any length identifiers but try to keep them unique to six characters.

Constants have associated data types. The form of a constant for each data type is as follows:

integer: a number (any number of digits) with no decimal point

real: a number with a decimal point, optionally followed by the exponent letter "E" and an optionally signed integer exponent. .1, 0.1, 2., 2.0, 3.E7, 3.E+7 and 3.E-7 are all examples.

logical: the strings .true. and .false.

character: a literal character sequence enclosed in quotes. A quote character is obtained in a character constant by two consecutive quotes. Examples:

```
'this is a string'
'that''s a string, too'
```

complex: two real numbers, enclosed in parentheses and separated by a comma.

Operators: one of the following:

```
arithmetic:    +       -      *       /       **
character:     //
relational:    .eq.   .ne.   .gt.    .ge.    .lt.    .le.
logical:       .and.  .or.   .not.
```

Data Types and Declaration Statements

Fortran programs consist of a main program and a collection of functions, subroutines, and block data subprograms. These entities are called *program units*, each of which has associated with it a number of data items. Data items are, by default, local to a program unit (i.e., unknown outside of it). The same variable name may be used as a local name in more than one program unit. Data can be made available to other program units by means of function or subroutine arguments or by storage blocks known as *common blocks*. Standard Fortran supports the following data types, each of which is a type declaration statement keyword:

```
integer
real
logical
character
double precision
complex
```

We impose the additional requirement that all names used in a program must be explicitly declared in a type statement. Type declaration statements are nonexecutable and must precede any executable statements in a program. The following statement keywords are related to declarations and are also nonexecutable:

```
common
equivalence
save
external
intrinsic
```

Declaration statements declare the existence of symbolic names for constants, data items, or program units. Symbolic constants are declared with parameter statements and have no effect on the output code. Data items can be *scalar items* (single values) or *arrays* (sequences of values). Arrays have subscripts to access individual *array elements*, which are equivalent to scalar data items. Both scalar variables and arrays are declared by a type declaration statement followed by a list of identifiers. Arrays are declared by following an identifier with an *array declarator*, which is an integer or sequence of integers, enclosed in parentheses, denoting the size of the array. The following are examples of type declaration statements:

```
integer  i, j, sp          !three integer scalar items
real     r, stack(MAXSTACK) !scalar real and real array
logical  valid(3,3)         !two-dimensional logical array

integer  MAXSTACK          !symbolic constant type
parameter (MAXSTACK = 32)  !symbolic constant value
```

Arrays can have any number of "dimensions"; the preceding logical array example has two. Arrays are laid out in the computer's memory with the first dimension varying fastest, that is, the array valid(i,j) is laid out in memory as follows:

```
valid(1,1)
valid(2,1)
valid(3,1)
valid(1,2)
valid(2,2)
valid(3,2)
valid(1,3)
valid(2,3)
valid(3,3)
```

Character data has an internal representation and syntax of declaration different from other data types. Character data are organized as strings, whose

length is specified in the `character` declaration statement. Strings are allocated
with fixed length, as in the statement

    character*(10) word

which declares a string variable of length 10 called `word`. We make a somewhat
artificial distinction between character variables and character string variables
in this book. Character variables by our definition are simply a special case in
which the declared length is one. Character arrays are declared in the same way
as for other data types; for example,

    character*(10) name (20)

declares an array of 20 strings, each of length 10.

The `external` and `intrinsic` statements are used to declare names of external or Fortran-supplied intrinsic functions.

Storage Allocation and Association

Every data item in a program or program unit has some name associated with
it. Scalar variables reference a single data item, and the individual scalar items
of arrays are referenced by means of integer subscript expressions. Based on the
example declarations given previously, the following are examples of references
to scalar data items:

    r
    stack(sp)
    value(i,j-1)
    word
    name(i)

The individual characters or substrings of character data are referenced by starting and ending character positions. For example, `word(1:5)` references the first
five characters of the variable `word`, and `word(i:i)` references the ith character
in `word`. Substrings within character arrays are referenced with the array part
first; that is, `name(i)(1:1)` references the first character in the ith array element
of `name`.

Data type declarations generally result in allocation of storage for the named
variables, unless the name is associated with some other name. The Fortran
standard also requires that integer, real, and logical data have the same size in
memory (generally 4 bytes, but not necessarily). Double-precision and complex
data occupy twice the storage size of real, integer, and logical data.

Storage association refers to the existence of two names for the same storage
unit. In a single program unit, two symbolic names can be assigned to the same
storage location via the `equivalence` statement:

    equivalence (r, stack(1))

causes the variable `r` and the array element `stack(1)` to refer to the same memory
location. The statement

```
equivalence (i, r)
```

causes the same memory location to be accessible as either an integer (using variable i) or real (using variable r). The Fortran standard explicitly disallows association of storage for character and noncharacter data.

Names in more than one program unit that reference the same location are considered to be associated, whether they are the same names or not. This type of association occurs in two ways:

- With a common statement, or

- By association of function or subroutine arguments.

The common statement associates a group of variables and allocates consecutive memory locations for the group. The statement

```
common /graphics/ xmin, xmax, ymin, ymax, ndivx, ndivy
```

allocates consecutive storage for the variables listed and gives a name (graphics) to the starting location; the name can be referred to by subprogram units. Within a program unit, the variables in a common block can be renamed, and can be given multiple names via equivalence statements. The statements

```
real             xmin, xmax, ymin, ymax
integer          ndivx, ndivy
common /graphics/ xmin, xmax, ymin, ymax, ndivx, ndivy
integer          ival (6)
real             rval (6)
equivalence      (ival(1), xmin)
equivalence      (rval(1), xmin)
```

causes the variables in /graphics/ to be identified by either their individual names or as elements of either ival or rval. Because common blocks cause storage association, a single common block may not contain both character and noncharacter variables.

Subprograms and Scope of Variables

Fortran provides two distinct types of subprograms: functions, which return a value, and subroutines, which do not. Information is provided to a subprogram via formal arguments, which are associated with actual arguments in the program that invokes it. For example, in the program fragment

```
      .
      .
      .
call sub1 (a, b, c)
      .
      .
      .
```

```
subroutine sub1 (x, y, z)
       .
       .
       .
```

the subroutine formal arguments x, y, and z assume the values of a, b, and c in the calling program. The variables are passed to the subroutine by reference, which means that the address of the value, rather than the value itself, is passed. Therefore, subprograms do not allocate storage for their formal arguments. This feature permits separate compilation and passed-length arrays and character strings. To illustrate,

```
subroutine sub1 (x, y, n)
real x (n), y (n)
```

is legal and dimensions the arrays x and y to the passed length n, whereas the following is not legal:

```
subroutine sub1 (x, y, n)
real x (n), y (n), z (n)
```

Since the variable z is not an argument, its storage is allocated locally at compile time; hence its length cannot be passed. A special syntax is available for dimensioning arguments within subprograms to the same size as in the calling program. The declarations

```
subroutine sub2 (i, s)
integer        i (*)
character*(*)  s
```

specify that i is an integer array of the same length as the corresponding array in the calling program. The string s is also the same length as the corresponding string in the caller.

In general, Fortran allocates no storage to formal arguments and allocates local storage to local variables of a subprogram. The rules for scope of a variable (the region of the program in which a variable is defined) in Fortran are very simple: the scope of a variable is the program unit in which it is declared. Only the names of common blocks are global, and even then the common blocks must be declared in each program unit in which they are used.

According to the Fortran standard, the values of local variables become undefined when a function or subroutine exits. In actual compilers, local variables in subprograms generally are saved from one invocation to the next. This is a natural consequence of the storage allocation rules of the language, although it is not guaranteed. The saving of local variables can be enforced by the programmer, however, using the save statement. Either variable names or common block names can be saved, for example:

```
save   /graphics/, stack, sp
```

Data Statements

Data items may be given an initial value when execution starts by use of the data statement. Data statements are nonexecutable and must follow all declaration statements and precede all executable statements in a program unit (our rule). A data statement has the form

```
data  name / constant /
```

where the constant part is either a literal constant or the name of a symbolic constant that agrees in type with the variable named. Arrays can be initialized with data by a list of values separated by commas, or on a per element basis, or using an *implied do-list*. The following data declarations are equivalent:

```
integer i, a(3)
data      a / 100, 200, 300 /

integer i, a(3)
data      a(1) / 100 /
data      a(2) / 200 /
data      a(3) / 300 /

integer i, a(3)
data      (a(i), i = 1, 3) / 100, 200, 300 /
```

The last case is an example of an implied do-list.

Data statements in a main program, function, or subroutine are only allowed for variables local to the program unit. A special program unit called a *block data subprogram* is required to initialize common block variables. A block data subprogram is nonexecutable and contains only declarative and data statements. The following is an example of a block data subprogram:

```
block data graphics_data

real              xmin, xmax, ymin, ymax
integer           ndivx, ndivy
common /graphics/ xmin, xmax, ymin, ymax, ndivx, ndivy

data    xmin / 0.0 /
data    xmax / 1.0 /
data    ymin / 0.0 /
data    ymax / 1.0 /
data    ndivx / 5 /
data    ndivy / 5 /

end
```

Expressions

Fortran expressions can be of four types—arithmetic, character, relational and logical—and consist of operands, operators and parentheses. Each of the four types of expressions has a set of operators:

```
arithmetic:    +       -      *       /       **
character:     //
relational:    .eq.   .ne.   .gt.    .ge.    .lt.    .le.
logical:       .and.  .or.   .not.
```

The overall precedence relationship between the types of expressions is

Expression Type	Precedence
arithmetic	highest
character	next highest
relational	next lowest
logical	lowest

For all expressions, parentheses can be used to override the default Fortran precedence relationships.

Operands in arithmetic expressions can be

- Arithmetic constants or their symbolic names,

- Arithmetic variable or array element references,

- Arithmetic function references, or

- Arithmetic expressions enclosed in parentheses.

The arithmetic operators have an order of precedence:

Operator	Precedence
**	highest
* and /	intermediate
+ and -	lowest

Operands in character expressions consist of character constants, variables, substrings, or character function results. The only operator allowed in character-valued expressions is concatenation. The expression

```
name(1:k)//'.exe'
```

produces the first *k* characters of name followed by the string .exe as the result.

A relational expression compares the values of two arithmetic expressions or two character expressions and produces a logical result. The relational operators, as listed previously, all have equal precedence.

A logical expression operates on logical operands to produce a logical result. Logical expression operands may be logical constants or variables, logical function results, or relational expressions. There are three logical operators with the following precedences:

Operator	Precedence
.not.	highest
.and. and .or.	lowest

Statement Sequence and Execution Sequence

Program units have the following overall sequence of statements:

```
program unit statement
declarative statements
data statements
executable statements
end statement
```

There is one and only one main program unit, with a declared name given in the program statement. The end statement is the last statement in every program unit. Execution of the program begins with the first executable statement, and statements are executed according to their sequence in the source text, unless the statement causes a *transfer of control*. The following statements can cause transfer of control:

Subprogram invocation: Invoking a subroutine or function transfers control to the first executable statement of the subprogram. Subroutines are invoked with the call statement:

```
call sub (a, b, c)
```

Functions are invoked by use in an expression. For example, the intrinsic function sin is called in evaluation of the expression y = sin(x).

Subprogram termination: A return statement in a subprogram transfers control to the calling program unit (main programs may not contain return statements). For subroutines, control is transferred to the next statement in the calling program; for functions, a function result is returned for use in evaluation of an expression.

Conditional statements: Standard Fortran provides two types of if (conditional) statements. The simple if statement is of the form

```
if (condition) statement
```

where "statement" is almost any single Fortran statement (if(a)if(b) c=d is not legal, nor is if(a) do i=1,10). The block-structured if construct has the syntax

```
if (condition) then
    statements
end if
```

The block-structured if has two variants from the format given above, in that it may also contain else and/or else if clauses:

```
if (condition) then
    statements
else if (condition) then
    statements

        .
        .
        .

else
    statements
end if
```

Note that this is a single block construct containing only one **end if** statement; at most one occurrence of the **else** clause is allowed. The **if...else if...end if** construct is analogous more to the Pascal **case** than to the Pascal **if** construct, which must be nested to extend the construct to test more than one condition.

looping statements: Fortran provides looping on a control variable with the do statement:

```
do i = start_expr, stop_expr, step_expr
    statements
end do
```

where i is any integer variable, and **start_expr**, **stop_expr**, and **step_expr** are integer expressions. The control variable i is initially assigned the value of **start_expr**, and an iteration count c is computed to be

$$c = \max \left[\text{int} \left(\frac{v_2 - v_1 + v_3}{v_3} \right), 0 \right]$$

where v_1, v_2 and v_3 are the values of the expressions **start_expr**, **stop_expr**, and **step_expr**, respectively. The expression **step_value** is optional, and assumed to be 1 if not given. If $c > 0$ then the statements in the body of the loop are executed. After each execution of the loop, the iteration count is decremented, **step_value** is added to the control variable, and the statements in the body of the loop are repeated until the iteration count becomes zero. When loop termination is reached, control is transferred to the statement following **end do**. Note that once a do-loop execution has been initiated, there is no means of causing early termination of the loop except with a **goto** statement.

We also make frequent use of a (nonstandard) conditional do loop construct, the **do while** loop:

```
do while (condition)
  statements
end do
```

The statements within the loop are repeated as long as the conditional part remains true. After each execution of the loop, the conditional expression is tested again; if it is true, all of the statements in the body are executed. Otherwise, control is transferred to the next statement after end do.

goto statements: The statement "goto 100" transfers control to the statement labeled "100." There is also a *computed goto* statement, which has the form

```
      goto (1,2,3,4,5) i
      print*, 'error - i less than 1 or greater than 5'
1 continue        !code for i = 1
      .
      .
      .
5 continue        !code for i = 5
```

Input/output statement error or end-of-file specifiers: certain input and output statements can contain an optional specification of a labeled statement to receive control when an I/O error occurs or when an end-of-file condition results from reading input.

Input/Output Statements

Input/output statements provide the means of transferring data, generally organized as files, to and from external storage media (disk drives, tapes, terminals, etc) or to and from internal files (character strings or character arrays). There are several statements for performing I/O operations:

- inquire—obtain information on file properties,

- open—open a file for reading or writing,

- close—close a file,

- read—read input from file, and

- write—write output to file.

There are others not included in this list.

Read and write operations manipulate complete *records*. A record is a sequence of values or characters and may be unformatted (containing binary values) or formatted (containing characters). Each record is thus considered to be formatted or unformatted. In addition, for read operations there is assumed to be an end-of-file record. File operations have an associated file position, and files themselves have associated allowed access methods. There are two standard access methods: sequential and direct. Internal files may only be accessed sequentially.

File operations are performed on *units*, which are either integer values for external files, asterisk for preconnected files (the standard input and output), or a character variable, substring, or array element for internal files. The open statement has the form

```
open (unit, specifier=value, ... )
```

where unit is an integer constant or expression and is required; all other specifiers are optional. Table 1.1 lists the valid specifiers for the open statement; the close statement is similar:

```
close (unit, specifier=value)
```

where the allowed specifiers are iostat, err and status. The meanings of iostat and err are the same as for open, but the status must be either 'KEEP' or 'DELETE'.

The inquire statement inquires about the properties of a named file or an external unit, usually in preparation for an open statement. Inquiry may be made by file name (file name given) or by unit (unit specifier given). The inquire statement has the same specifiers as open, except that it has no status specifier and has the following additional specifiers:

Table 1.1: Specifiers for the open statement.

Specifier	Meaning
file=string	defines the name of an external file
status=string	defines the status of the file to be opened: 'OLD': the file must already exist 'NEW': the file must not already exist 'UNKNOWN': host system dependent status
iostat=ivar	integer variable to receive status code for I/O operation. the value of the status variable is zero if no error exists, positive otherwise.
err=label	label of statement to receive control if an I/O error occurs
form=string	determines the record formatting of a file: 'FORMATTED' for character records 'UNFORMATTED' for binary records
access=string	determines the type of record access for a file: 'SEQUENTIAL' or 'DIRECT'
recl=ival	determines the record length for direct access files

```
exist = lvar
opened = lvar
number = ival
name = string
```

The inquire statement has additional standard specifiers, and probably some nonstandard ones as well on most systems. There are additional auxiliary I/O statements (backspace, rewind and endfile) not covered here.

Reading from and writing to files is performed using read and write statements. Each read and write statement contains a unit specifier that can be any of the following:

- An integer constant, variable or array element (external files),

- An asterisk (for standard input and output units), or

- A character variable or array element (internal files).

For unformatted file I/O, only the unit number is given as control information:

```
read (u) a, b, c
write (1) x, y, z
```

are examples of unformatted I/O statements.

Formatted read and write statements must contain an additional *format specifier*, which can be a character expression or an integer label of a format statement. Both read and write statements have the iostat and err specifiers of open, and an additional specifier end=label that specifies a labeled statement to receive control when end of file is encountered.

The syntax of read and write statements is

```
read (unit, format, specifier=value, ... ) input_list
write (unit, format, specifier=value, ... ) output_list
```

and is the same with format omitted for unformatted I/O. An input list is a sequence, separated by commas, of names of variables, arrays, array elements, or character substrings. An output list is a sequence of expressions separated by commas. Both input and output lists can contain implied do-loops, as described for data statements.

Format specifiers are sequences of elements called *edit descriptors*, separated by commas and enclosed in parentheses, which specify editing to be performed in an input list or output list. A format specifier can be a character string or character variable or array element; alternatively, Fortran provides a special format statement for assigning integer labels to format specifiers. A format statement may occur anywhere within a program unit. The following are edit descriptors that can be repeated by preceding them with a repeat count (for instance, 4I5 produces four integer fields of width 5):

Iw	Integer field of width w
Fw.d	Floating point number of width w, with d decimal places
Ew.d	Exponential notation of width w, d decimal places
Gw.d	Combination of F and E depending on exponent value
Lw	Logical field of width w
Aw	Character field of width w
A	Character field with width of string in `iolist`

The following edit descriptors are considered nonrepeatable, although any edit descriptor or sequence of edit descriptors can be repeated by enclosing it in parentheses preceded by a repeat count.

nX	Output n blanks on output or skip n chacacters on input
'string'	Literal string
Tc	Tab to column c
/	Skip to next record
:	Skip remainder of format if `iolist` is exhausted

There is a special type of formatting, called *list-directed formatting*, which is indicated by using an asterisk as the format specifier. When list-directed formatting is used, Fortran automatically provides conversion between internal representations and characters in the input or output record. List directed formatting is not allowed on internal files.

When a format specifier other than asterisk is given, the effective number of repeatable edit descriptors must match the number of items in the input list or output list (except when format control is terminated by the colon edit descriptor).

The following are examples of valid `read`, `write` and `format` statements.

```
    read (10, *) a, b, c          !list derected formatting
    write (6, '(''the answer is '', F6.2)') x
    write (u, 100) x, y, z
100 format (4X, 3(10X, '---', 2X, F6.2))
```

Certain processor-dependent units have special carriage control rules intended for printing. On these units a "1" in column 1 of the output causes a page advance (formfeed), a "0" in column 1 causes a linefeed, and a "+" causes overprinting of the previous line.

Intrinsic Functions

A list of the intrinsic or predefined functions used in this text is given in Table 1.2. This is not a complete list of functions, and some of the functions have counterparts with similar names for other data types as arguments or result. Of those listed, `iand` and `ior` are nonstandard.

Table 1.2: Fortran Intrinsic Functions.

Function	Result Type	Argument Type	Definition
int	i	r	integer conversion
real	r	i	real conversion
char	c	i	character conversion
abs	r	r	absolute value
iabs	i	i	absolute value
mod	i	i, i	$a_1 - int(a_1/a_2) \times a_2$
amod	r	r, r	$a_1 - int(a_1/a_2) \times a_2$
sqrt	r	r	square root
exp	r	r	e^a
log	r	r	$\ln(a)$
sin	r	r	$\sin(a)$
cos	r	r	$\cos(a)$
tan	r	r	$\tan(a)$
len	i	c	declared length of string
index	i	c, c	substring position
lge	l	c, c	lexically greater than or equal
lgt	l	c, c	lexically greater than
lle	l	c, c	lexically less than or equal
llt	l	c, c	lexically less than
iand	i	i, i	bitwise and
ior	i	i, i	bitwise or

Data types: i=integer, r=real, l=logical, c=character

1.3 Translation of Extensions

The foregoing synopsis is of the Fortran language as we use it. It is both a superset and subset of standard Fortran since the standard has features we do not use (and which were not discussed), and some of the syntax described is not allowed in standard Fortran. The following are nonstandard features of our peculiar style of Fortran:

- Lowercase letters for keywords and variable names,

- Names longer than six characters,

- Use of ! to delimit comments,

- Long source lines (we use source lines up to 80 characters long, where the Fortran standard allows only columns 7–72 for source text), and

- The constructs do...end do and do while...end do.

Standard Fortran supports only one type of looping construct, with the syntax

```
do <label> ivar = start_val, stop_val, step_val
    statements
<label> statement
```

where `<label>` is an integer statement label. The terminal statement is usually the Fortran `continue` statement, but it is not required by the standard. The VAX Fortran `do--end do` construct translates to this form directly, by simply adding a label in the do statement and replacing the `end do` statement by a labeled `continue` statement. The `do while` loop

```
do while (i .ne. 0)
    i = i - 1
end do
```

can be translated to

```
1 if (.not. (i .ne. 0)) goto 2
    i = i - 1
    goto 1
2 continue
```

which looks a bit goofy at first but shows explicitly the translation that has taken place. An equivalent form, which we prefer, is

```
1 if (i .ne. 0) then
    i = i - 1
    goto 1
  end if
```

since the conditional expression does not have to be negated, and only one label is required.

The summary of Fortran presented here is not a complete description of the language. It fact, what is described is not really Fortran, but instead is the particular subset of VAX Fortran used in this book. Fortunately, many modern Fortran compilers will accept some or all of these deviations from the standard. The VAX/VMS compiler accepts all of our programs without any modification or preprocessing.

Unfortunately, many less than modern Fortran compilers will not accept these extensions. In fact, some of them probably don't accept any. These compilers are no doubt produced by people who don't think you deserve any better, and who think you should thank them for giving you even six characters for variable names. They may even think you should be happy to program with anything other than a switch panel and a red button. It is our position that these compilers, and probably the machines they run on and the companies that make them, should be sent to the scrap heap, but that probably won't happen. For compilers that don't accept our favorite extensions, some rewriting will be necessary.

Most of the nonstandard aspects of our programs can be translated to standard form with very simple tools, which could perform uppercase conversion and delete comments starting with "!". In the following chapter, a translator program that does most of the work necessary to put our source text into standard form will be presented. Meanwhile, it may be necessary to translate a few routines by hand.

Further Reading

The following are all good reference texts for Fortran.

- Meissner and Organick, *Fortran 77 featuring Structured Programming*, Addison-Wesley 1980

- Davis and Hoffman, *Fortran 77: A Structured, Disciplined Style*, McGraw-Hill 1983

- Wagener, *Principles of Fortran Programming*, Wiley 1980

- Middlebrooks, *VAX Fortran*, Reston 1984

- Weinman, *VAX Fortran*, Boyd and Fraser 1986

The last two cover the Fortran language in detail with coverage of the special features of VAX Fortran. The Digital Equipment Corporation manuals *Programming in VAX Fortran* and *Guide to Programming on VAX/VMS (Fortran Edition)* are excellent documentation of the VMS Fortran compiler and of the use of Fortran for VAX system programming.

CHAPTER 2

Getting Started

With any new programming task, it is important to decide on some standards appropriate for the problem. It may be choosing a standard naming convention, or a well-specified and documented data organization, or perhaps a standard file format; getting organized should be the first step of any project. For the case at hand, we assume that we are starting from scratch, so we must first tackle the question of how we will manage our program files. Along the way, we will point out some of the peculiar conventions we use.

The end goal of any new tool we develop is a new command that we can use like other commands. After all, commands are just programs with an ability to read and process command arguments and qualifiers, and we want our programs to behave like any other commands—like tools. One of our conventions concerns the format of commands. VAX/VMS has a fairly uniform convention for command syntax, with qualifiers delimited by slashes:

```
$ command/qualifiers  arguments
```

All of our commands have the same general format:

```
$ command  arguments  -qualifiers
```

with the arguments separated by one or more blank spaces. This is a good choice because it is easy to remember and easy to interpret in programs. It is also the usual format of commands for such popular operating systems as UNIX and MS–DOS. Just how to turn programs into commands will be discussed later.

Throughout the book, examples starting with the $ symbol are examples of commands that can be typed interactively at the terminal; otherwise the examples are programs, routines, or other code fragments. All of the examples, as well as the names of routines or variables in routines are printed in typewriter font as an aid to understanding.

2.1   Basic Housekeeping

How will we compile our programs? This seems like a ridiculously simple question, but there is more to be considered than might appear at first glance. Most compilers have lots of options, and they should be used in an advantageous manner. It turns out that there are enough options needed for the VAX Fortran compiler to make it worth writing a special DCL (DEC Control Language, the command language of the VAX) procedure for compiling, just to avoid the typing. Then, to compile the program calc, we say

```
$ f calc
```

and calc is compiled with default options we choose. We use our command format conventions to enable options other than our defaults. For example, the Fortran compiler has a debug option that is sometimes useful in conjunction with programs that don't work, so the f command has an optional argument:

```
$ f calc -d
```

compiles calc with the debug option enabled. There is also a -l option for producing a listing file. The syntax of the f command, as well as all of the other programs in this book, is documented in the user manual in Appendix C, along with a brief description of its use.

Let's get back to the business of choosing the right default options. The VAX Fortran compiler has options for numeric overflow and array bounds checking, and they should be enabled, at least during the development phases of a program. Numeric overflow occurs when the result of an arithmetic operation is too big to be represented in the computer's floating-point encoding scheme. Array bounds checking means that each time an element of an array is accessed the subscripts are checked to see that they are not before the beginning or beyond the end of the array; for example, if an array is declared integer a(10), then a reference to a(0) or a(11) will be flagged as an error. Both of these options should be enabled as a guard against undetected errors. VAX Fortran optimizes the generated code by default, and we prefer to disable it during the development phase of a program since it slows down compilation. The optimizer can be enabled when the program is complete and ready for a production version. In some cases the numeric and bounds checking can be disabled as well to speed up the final product. We want the default options of the compiler to be those appropriate for development since the vast majority of time spent compiling programs is during development.

We believe that every useful diagnostic of a compiler should be turned on at all times, to head off any potential hidden flaws at compile-time rather than discover them at run-time. We use the VMS Fortran compiler option /warnings to enforce some standards on the source routines. /warnings=(declarations,general) causes the compiler to check for declaration of all identifiers and report general informative diagnostics. Fortran has "default typing rules" in which variables need not be explicitly declared, and the data type of an undeclared variable is determined by the first letter in its name. VAX Fortran has a very important extension, in that it has an implicit none statement, which overrides implicit typing and requires all variables to be explicitly declared. The /warnings=declarations compiler option is equivalent to an implicit none statement in the source file. Fortran programmers may be appalled at the idea of declaring all identifiers, having grown accustomed to being lazy. However, consider the following code fragment:

```
integer keyval, getkey, c, doesc
    .
    .
    .
do while (getkey (keyval) .ne. NEWLINE)
    if (keyval .eq. EOF) then
        return
    else if (keyval .eq. ESCAPE) then
        c = doesc(kryval)
    else if (keyval .eq. DEL) then
        call deletec(keyval)
    else
        continue
    end if
end do
    .
    .
    .
```

If you happened to notice a misspelled variable name, good; please try to imagine a much larger routine where you wouldn't have noticed. With good old implicit typing rules, the program compiles just fine. The new variable kryval is cheerfully accepted and assigned an undefined value without comment from the compiler, and the program eventually crashes in some other routine. After some scratching of heads, we track the problem to the bogus line. If, however, the compiler reports the use of undeclared variables, then the typo is immediately discovered and corrected. The moral of the story is: *let the computer do the work.*

Finally, we want to use compiler options that are less restrictive in source code format than the rules of Fortran 77. We use the VAX Fortran qualifier /extend_source to be able to use lines longer than 72 characters; although long source lines make programs less portable, it also makes them more pleasant to read since continuation lines are needed in fewer instances. Our program v77 can convert VAX Fortran to Fortran 77 source form anyway, so we may as well use the improvements available. Here is our procedure for compiling:

```
$! f   -  invoke VAX Fortran compiler
$!
$!  options:  L - produce listing
$!            O - optimize object code
$!            D - produce debugger object code
$!            P - preprocess source file
$!            S - save preprocessor output
$!            unrecognized options are ignored
$!
$ if p1 .eqs. "" then inquire p1 "source file"
$ if p1 .eqs. "" then exit
$
$! initialize file name
$ filename := 'p1'
$
$! initialize command string
$ cmdstr := fort -
            /nooptimize -
            /check=(bounds, overflow, nounderflow) -
            /extend_source -
            /warnings=(general,declarations)
$
$! delflag = 1 if temporary file is to be deleted
$   delflag = 0
$
$ if p2 .eqs. "" then goto exec
$ length = f$length(p2)
$
$! if L, O or D qualifier is present in p2, append to command string
$   if (f$locate("L",p2) .ne. length) then cmdstr := 'cmdstr'/list
$   if (f$locate("O",p2) .ne. length) then cmdstr := 'cmdstr'/opt
$   if (f$locate("D",p2) .ne. length) then cmdstr := 'cmdstr'/debug
$
$! if -P qualifier is present in p2, output prep to temporary file
$   if (f$locate("P",p2) .eq. length) then goto exec
$   filename := "PREPTEMP"
$   prep 'p1'.for preptemp.for
$   cmdstr := 'cmdstr'/object='p1'.obj
$   if (f$locate("S",p2) .eq. length) then delflag = 1
$
```

```
$ exec:
$    'cmdstr' 'filename'
$    if (delflag .eq. 1) then delete preptemp.for;*
$ exit
```

The procedure, once installed, can be used over and over to compile programs with the defaults chosen by us instead of the compiler writer. It is a tool.

The compiler produces an intermediate *object code module* as output, which we only need in order to link it up with other object modules to make executable programs, also known as *images*. The difference between an object module and an image is essentially that in an object module references to other routines are incomplete. The linker pieces together all of the object modules involved and arranges them in relation to each other to form a complete program. The locations of each of the subroutines in the final program is not known when the program is compiled, hence the intermediate form of an object module.

All practical software development environments provide utilities for management of *libraries* of object code. A library is just a single file containing multiple object modules that can be selectively linked as needed to make an image. Because of the intermediate form of object modules, libraries are the most sensible way to manage object files. Without a library there will be one object file for each source file, and the directory will become hopelessly cluttered. Object libraries provide something like a directory within a file, which is very convenient for stuff that isn't readable by humans anyway. So we need a procedure for inserting object files into libraries. Since the object code is no longer needed after updating the library, we may as well just make the compiling and library insertion one step and delete the object file afterward:

```
$! update  -  compile Fortran source and put output into object library
$!
$! format:  update lib file -options
$! options are passed to f command
$
$ if p1 .eqs. "" then inquire p1 "library"
$ if p1 .eqs. "" then exit
$ if p2 .eqs. "" then inquire p2 "file"
$ if p2 .eqs. "" then exit
$
$! extract file name part from full file specification
$    device    = f$parse("''p2'",,,"DEVICE")
$    directory = f$parse("''p2'",,,"DIRECTORY")
$    filename  = f$parse("''p2'",,,"NAME")
$    name := 'device''directory''filename'
$
$ on error then goto fortran_error
$ f 'name' 'p3'
$ on error then goto library_error
$ library 'p1' 'name'
$
```

```
$ obj := ".obj;"
$ del 'name''obj'
$ exit
$
$ fortran_error:
$ write sys$output "error compiling ''name', update aborted"
$ exit
$
$ library_error:
$ write sys$output "error updating ''name', update aborted"
$ exit
```

The VMS system also has libraries for managing source text. However, text libraries do not support file version numbers, which are very nice for source code management, and we don't use text libraries for this reason.

Putting all of the modules of a program into a single library simplifies linking them into an executable image. The VMS librarian also allows multiple main program modules to reside in a single library (although most others do not). An executable image `calc` is then created with the VAX command

```
$ link /exe=calc tools/lib/include=calc
```

So our third tool is the `image` command, which serves to simplify the syntax and make its user interface similar to that of our other tools:

```
$! image  -  create executable image from library
$!
$! format:  image lib prog  -options
$! options:  -D debug
$!           -M map file
$!           unrecognized options are ignored
$
$ if p1 .eqs. "" then inquire p1 "library"
$ if p1 .eqs. "" then exit
$ if p2 .eqs. "" then inquire p2 "module"
$ if p2 .eqs. "" then exit
$
$ cmdstr := "link"
$ if p3 .eqs. "" then goto skip
$ if f$locate("D",p3) .ne. f$length(p3) then cmdstr := 'cmdstr'"/debug"
$ if f$locate("M",p3) .ne. f$length(p3) then cmdstr := 'cmdstr'"/map=''p2'"
$
$ skip:
$ name = f$parse("''p2'",,,"NAME")
$ 'cmdstr' /exe = 'p2' 'p1'/lib /incl='name'
```

It is an advantage of Fortran, however minor, that programs have names, as opposed to the situation in C where the main program is always called `main`; the VMS librarian can therefore allow the object code for lots of different Fortran programs to be in the same library, whereas the main programs of C programs must be kept around as individual object modules.

These commands (f, update, and image) form a basic code management plan that can be implemented in just about any computer system environment. Because we took control of the process and defined our own conventions and defaults, the compiler interface can be duplicated (or nearly so) on other computers; we have written analogous routines for the IBM-PC for three different Fortran compilers, all with an identical (or nearly identical) user interface. We are almost ready to really get started.

2.2   A Flavor of Things to Come

There is a somewhat embellished version of update that, rather than updating a single file, updates all of the source files named in a *files list*. A files list is simply a list of file names, given one per line; blank lines and comment lines are ignored. We use files lists as a sort of dual-purpose file to describe a complete program, providing both documentation and code management. A files list for a complete program shows what software components it is constructed from, and comments (text beginning with !) can be used to describe how one routine or a group of routines fits into the Big Picture. Indentation can help to show the relationships between routines. The second purpose for files lists is as an easy way to update all of the routines in a big program, which is occasionally necessary when a lot of changes have been made or when common blocks used in many routines have been modified. By convention, files lists have the extension .fil, another example of the up-front standardization we advocate. A files list for the programs in this chapter might be

```
! getting started

! command procedures:
# f.com                !compile
# update.com           !compile and insert into library
# image.com            !link program
# global_update.com    !files list version of update

! Fortran source
pound                  !generate strings from files lists
getargs                !get command line arguments
stdargs                !apply standard defaults to arguments
detab                  !replace tabs by blanks
v77                    !translate VAX Fortran to Fortran 77
fput77                 !output Fortran 77 source lines
```

Files lists are generally used for program files, which have the extension .for, and our convention is to list just the file name part, omitting the .for. The command global_update compiles each source file in the list, so anything other than Fortran source must be listed as a comment. The lines beginning with # are comments as far as global_update is concerned. If the list is in the file start.fil, then the command

```
$ global_update tools start.fil
```

updates the tools library with new versions of all of the Fortran source routines named in the file.

Files lists may also "include" other files lists, so given a list for each chapter, a files list for this book might read

```
#include start.fil
#include prims.fil
#include strings.fil
#include prep.fil
#include lex.fil
#include spl.fil
#include system.fil
#include pctools.fil
```

The include capability is nice for making files lists for really large programs with major subsystems worthy of files lists of their own.

Here is global_update, the fancy model:

```
$! global_update  -  globally compile a list of files and replace
$!                      modules in an object library
$!
$! format:  global_update libname listfile -options
$! options: any option allowed by UPDATE
$
$ if p1 .eqs. "" then inquire p1 "library"
$ if p1 .eqs. "" then exit
$
$ if p2 .eqs. "" then inquire p2 "listfile"
$ if p2 .eqs. "" then exit
$
$ pound "$ write sys$output \h22#\h22\n$ update ''p1' # ''p3'" 'p2' aaa.com
$ @aaa.com
$ del aaa.com;*
```

As each module is updated, its name is written to the terminal so the user can see what's currently being processed, since global updates can take a long time.

Too easy. Obviously, the real work is done by pound, which is written in fabulous Fortran. The pound program is designed to manipulate files lists. It takes a pattern as a command line argument, and each occurrence of the character # in the pattern is replaced by the file names in the list. The command

```
$ pound "$ append #.for calcfiles.for/new" calc.fil aaa.com
```

creates a command procedure aaa.com that concatenates all of the files for the calc program onto the file calcfiles.for, using the DCL append command. The pattern can also contain *escape sequences*, which are prefixed by a special escape character, which in all of our programs is the backslash. Any ASCII code can be generated with escape sequences, and special ones are provided for commonly used special characters, such as \n for newline (a complete list is provided in Chapter 4). Thus the command

```
$ pound "$ copy #.for [-.calc]* \n$ del #.for;" calc.fil aaa.com
```

generates two lines of output for each filename in calc.fil. The escape sequence \h22 used in global_update produces the character with an ASCII code of hexadecimal 22, the quote character. Although most of the time the files lists used are ones we have created, it is possible to create a files list of any VAX directory with the DCL command

```
$ dir/noheader/notrailer/columns=1/versions=1
```

The # character also has a special meaning when it occurs as the first character on a line in a files list. Files lists are generally used to document the organization of a program and show all of its components. The components of programs fall into two categories: source files and other files. The "other" category includes definition files, common block files, or perhaps some documentation. The key attribute of files in the "other" category is that they will evoke nasty messages from the Fortran compiler, so they must not be selected for global updates. On the other hand, they are still part of the program and should be included, for example, for printing. The pound program resolves the problem with an optional command line argument and a special interpretation of lines beginning with #. The commands

```
$ pound "$ print #.for" calc.fil
$ pound "$ print #" calc.fil -p
```

generate print commands for all of the files in calc.fil, first for the Fortran source files (for which the .for extension is given in the pattern argument) and then for the "other" files.

File inclusion, an advertised feature of global_update, is also handled by pound by replacing lines of the form

```
#include  filename
```

with the contents of the named file. Thus the # character is used for three different purposes in pound:

- as a place holder in the pattern which is replaced by a file name in each line of output generated,

- as a flag for #include commands, and

- as a switch to select lines to be ignored and lines to be processed, based on the presence or absence of the -p option.

The different uses must be clearly distinguished to effectively use pound, but at least users should never have trouble remembering which character is special!

We have found pound to be a flexible and convenient way of managing lots of source files for big programs. And it's certainly low budget. Here is the Fortran code for pound:

```
! pound   -   output string and replace '#' by first word of line

   program pound
   include              'global.def'
   integer              argc, u, uin, uout, lp, fopen, i
   character*(MAXSTR)   argv(MAXARGS), pattern, upper, getword, word, line
   character*1          escchar
   logical              finclude, equal, inflag, outflag, pflag, valid

   call ioinit ()
   call getargs (argc, argv)
   if (argc .lt. 1 .or. argc .gt. 4) then
      call fputstr (STDERR,
 &    'syntax: pound "pattern" [infile] [outfile] [-p]'//EOL)
      call fputstr (STDERR,
 &    '        -p: process lines starting with # only'//EOL)
      stop 'argument error - aborted'
   end if
   pattern = argv(1)
   pflag = .false.
   inflag = .false.
   outflag = .false.
   do i = 2, argc
      if (argv(i)(1:1) .eq. QUALIFIER) then
         argv(i) = upper(argv(i))
         pflag = (index(argv(i),'P') .gt. 0)
      else if (.not. inflag) then
         uin = fopen (uin, argv(i), IOREAD)
         inflag = .true.
      else if (.not. outflag) then
         uout = fopen (uout, argv(i), IOWRITE)
         outflag = .true.
      end if
   end do
   if (.not. inflag) uin = STDIN
   if (.not. outflag) uout = STDOUT
   if (uin .eq. IOERROR .or. uout .eq. IOERROR)
 &        stop 'argument error - aborted'


   call inclinit (uin)

   do while (finclude (line))
      lp = 1
      word = getword (word, line, lp)
      valid = .false.
      if (equal(upper(word), '#INCLUDE'//NULL)) then
         word = getword (word, line, lp)
         call fputstr (STDERR, 'error including '//word)
         call fputc (STDERR, NEWLINE)
      else if (word(1:1) .eq. '#') then          !pound line
         if (pflag) then
            valid = .true.
```

```
                word = getword(word,line,lp)
             end if
          else if (word(1:1) .eq. COMMENT) then   !skip comment
             continue
          else if (word(1:1) .eq. NEWLINE) then   !skip blank lines
             continue
          else                                    !un-pound line
             if (.not. pflag) valid = .true.
          end if
          if (valid) then                         !substitute pattern
             i = 1
             do while (pattern(i:i) .ne. NULL)
                if (pattern(i:i) .eq. '#') then
                   call fputstr (uout, word)
                   i = i + 1
                else if (pattern(i:i) .eq. ESCAPE) then
                   call fputc (uout, escchar(pattern,i))
                else
                   call fputc (uout, pattern(i:i))
                   i = i + 1
                end if
             end do
             call fputc (uout, NEWLINE)
          end if
       end do

       call fclose (uin)
       call fclose (uout)
       call iofinit ()
       end
```

Because it makes use of a collection of other tools, pound is a short program. It calls on these routines:

- ioinit and iofinit for initiating and terminating I/O,

- fopen and fclose for opening and closing files,

- finclude for reading from the main input file or files it has included (the main input file is set up by inclinit),

- fputstr and fputc for writing output,

- getword to get the next word from a line,

- upper for converting strings to upper case,

- equal for comparing strings,

- getargs for obtaining command line arguments, and

- escchar for handling escape sequences.

This same toolbox is used by lots of other programs as well. All of these routines will be presented in the next two chapters.

The pound program reveals some of the standards adhered to in our programs. By convention, everything is typed in lower case, except for symbolic constants such as COMMENT or NEWLINE, which are defined in the file global.def. Symbolic parameters are capitalized to distinguish them clearly from variables and are used to attach an obvious meaning to otherwise meaningless codes — if (c .eq. NEWLINE) is certainly a clearer way to express checking for end of line than if (c .eq. char(10)). There is also another, more important reason for using symbolic names for constants. At some later date, we may decide that it would be better to use some other character as the COMMENT character. If all of the code uses the literal string '!' for comments, then we must find and change every occurrence, and if any occurrence is missed, strange bugs may arise. But with a symbolic constant, defined in a central location, the character can be changed in just one place, and all of the affected routines recompiled. Symbolic constants aren't just more readable, they are also more convenient and reliable.

We always make a special effort to make the code as direct and clear as possible. We restrict the "header" commentary part of our source files to only a few lines at most; we used to write longer ones, but found that keeping the comments up to date was harder than managing the code itself. Programmers often overcomment code with the goal of making it easier to understand, but with the end effect of making it hard to even find the code, much less understand it.

While comments can provide documentation of a program, they are a poor excuse for real documentation, and some less entangled method (such as a manual, or a book like the one you are reading) is much better. Programs that document themselves by being well-written reduce the need for comments, and an occasional "trailing comment" (using the VAX Fortran ! comment delimiter after a source line) is unobtrusive and effective.

Throughout the text, we have tried to keep the variable names short and unique in the first six characters. We don't have to, of course, since nearly all compilers accept longer ones; the VAX Fortran compiler accepts 31-character identifiers. We use shorter names partly to make programs more portable, but also because unnecessarily long variable names seem to be more of a distraction than an aid to understanding. Both unreasonably long and unreasonably short names are common sins found in programs (depending on the inclinations of the programmer), and we have tried to choose a happy medium. The important thing in choosing variable names is to give them mnemonic value, and it isn't necessary to use mile-long names to make them understandable. The name lp is just as good as the name line_pointer for a variable used as a line pointer, if we are consistent in our naming conventions. While lp is less explicit, it is also shorter, and use of a longer name without a real need for it leads to excessive continuation lines, which are equally unreadable.

All of the input to pound is obtained through the function finclude, which handles all of the details of including files; as far as pound is concerned, it gets input from only one source. This is an example of perhaps the most important principle of good software design: concealing complexity. As we shall see in the next chapter, finclude is a fairly complicated routine, about as complicated as pound; yet it has a simple interface and performs a function that is conceptually simple, even if the implementation isn't. Likewise, the details of how escape sequences are interpreted are completely hidden in the escchar routine; pound doesn't need to know such details in order to use the capability.

Another expression of the same principle is the routine getargs, which provides the interface between the command interpreter and all of our programs. It accesses the command line and separates it into words (delimited by one or more blanks), returning the words in the array argv and the count in argc. If it is enclosed in double quotes, an argument can have embedded blanks; then the entire quoted string, minus the quotes, is returned as one argument. Putting an argument in quotes is also the only way to keep DCL from converting it to uppercase. When the command

```
$ pound "$ append #.for calcfiles.for/new" calc.fil aaa.com
```

is entered, getargs returns argc=3 and the arguments in argv(1)–argv(3).

```
! getargs  -  get command line arguments and argument count

        subroutine getargs(argc,argv)
        integer         argc            !argument count
        character*(*)   argv(*)         !array of arguments
        include         'global.def'
        include         '($clidef)'
        character*(MAXSTR) line         !local string for parsing
        integer*2       length          !total length of command line
        integer         i,k

        call cli$get_value('$LINE',line,length)
        i = 1
        argc = 0

        do while (line(i:i) .ne. BLANK)  !skip the command invocation
          i = i + 1
        end do
        i = i + 1                       !skip the space after command

        do while (i .le. length)

          k = i

          if (line(i:i) .eq. DQUOTE) then
            argc = argc + 1
            i = i + 1                   !skip the quote mark
```

```
        k = i
        do while (i .ne. length .and. line(i:i) .ne. DQUOTE)
          i = i + 1
        end do
        argv(argc) = line(k:(i-1))//NULL    !skip trailing quote
        i = i + 1                           !move past quote
      else if (line(i:i) .eq. BLANK) then
        i = i + 1
      else
        argc = argc + 1
        do while (i .le. length .and. line(i:i) .ne. BLANK)
          i = i + 1
        end do
        argv(argc) = line(k:i-1)//NULL
      end if

    end do

    return
    end
```

In general, the convention regarding the order of declarations in our routines is
to declare all of the function or subroutine arguments first, followed by include
statements, followed by declarations for local variables and external functions.
There is no language requirement for any particular order, but our convention
helps to set the interface specifications apart from the rest of the code.

getargs calls a VAX-specific routine to retrieve the command line; it is known
as a *primitive* because of its inherent system dependency. We try to isolate all
such dependencies in a limited number of routines with well-defined interfaces,
and then write all other programs in terms of the primitives. This preserves
portability—if only the primitives can be implemented for some particular environment, then all of the programs will work. Thus the real task of getting started
is to define and implement these primitives, the subject of the next chapter.

The statement

```
        character*(*) argv (*)
```

causes argv to assume the dimensions of the caller's array. In general we try
to push decisions about storage sizes to the highest level since that's where the
requirements are known—getargs will be used by many different programs. The
elements of argv are *null-terminated* strings, meaning that the special ASCII
character code zero is appended to the end. This is unconventional in Fortran
programs and is another of our standards throughout the code. The purpose
is to eliminate the need to carry the length around with the string as useless
baggage and thus simplify the interfaces to routines that deal with strings (this
topic discussed more fully in Chapter 4).

For all of the work it does, pound is a short program, and took all of about
an hour to write and debug. In fact, nearly half of the source text is the code
required to interpret command line arguments. With finclude and getargs, it is

seldom necessary to use `assign` statements or other operating-system-dependent methods to get information into programs (none of the programs in this book do). Instead, we can provide the names of the files to be used as command arguments, and with a little code to interpret the arguments we can make the file connections directly.

In fact, a surprising percentage of programs read from one input file and write to one output file, and of those that meet this criterion, most can adhere to a uniform interpretation of file names. Our standard syntax for commands is

```
$ command infile outfile -options
```

where the special dash symbol denotes an optional argument and distinguishes options from file names. It has a symbolic name (QUALIFIER) and is defined in global.def. Both file names are optional and are interpreted as follows:

- If two file names are provided on the command line, the first is taken as the input file, and the second is taken as the output.

- If only one file name is provided, it is taken to be the input file name, and the output is assumed to be the standard output device (usually the terminal screen).

- If no file names are given, the input is read from the standard input unit STDIN and output is written to the standard output unit STDOUT.

This interpretation is used widely enough to rate a special routine:

```
! stdargs  -  connect input files to units with standard defaults

        subroutine stdargs (argc, argv, uin, uout)
        character*(*)  argv (*)
        integer        argc, uin, uout
        include        'global.def'
        integer        a, fopen

        if (argc .eq. 0) then
           a = 0
        else if (argc .gt. 0) then
           a = 1
           do while (a .le. argc .and. argv(a)(1:1).ne. QUALIFIER)
              a = a + 1
           end do
           a = a - 1
        else
           call fputstr (STDERR, 'ERROR: argc < 0 in STDARGS'//EOL)
           stop ' '
        end if

        if (a .eq. 0) then
           uin  = STDIN
           uout = STDOUT
```

```
      else if (a .eq. 1) then
         uin  = fopen (uin, argv(1), IOREAD)
         uout = STDOUT
      else if (a .ge. 2) then
         uin  = fopen (uin, argv(1), IOREAD)
         uout = fopen (uout, argv(2), IOWRITE)
      end if

      return
      end
```

The pound program adheres to the standard interpretation for file names but does not use stdargs because its required pattern argument is not delimited by the QUALIFIER character. Nevertheless, stdargs is adequate for many programs and can be used in those cases to hide the details of argument interpretation from the main program.

Here are the definitions for the symbolic parameters used so far, excerpted from global.def (a complete listing of global.def is given in Appendix A):

```
      integer     MAXSTR
      parameter   (MAXSTR = 255)
      character*1 NULL
      parameter   (NULL = char(0))
      character*1 NEWLINE
      parameter   (NEWLINE = char(10))
      character*2 EOL
      parameter   (EOL = NEWLINE//NULL)

      character*1 QUALIFIER
      parameter   (QUALIFIER = '-')
      character*1 COMMENT
      parameter   (COMMENT = '!')
      character*1 ESCAPE
      parameter   (ESCAPE = '\')
      integer     MAXARGS
      parameter   (MAXARGS = 10)

      integer     STDIN, STDOUT, STDERR
      parameter   (STDIN = 5)
      parameter   (STDOUT = 6)
      parameter   (STDERR = 7)
      integer     IOREAD, IOWRITE, IOERROR
      parameter   (IOREAD = 1)
      parameter   (IOWRITE = 2)
      parameter   (IOERROR = -1)
```

pound is a tool: it performs a useful function, does it in a general way, and simplifies the creation of other tools. It solves the general problem of "doing stuff" with files lists by providing users the flexibility of deciding what needs to be done and specifying the commands to be generated for themselves.

pound is the basic component of a collection of programs we have to work with files lists, all implemented as command procedures. One of those programs is concat, which uses pound and the DCL append command to concatenate all of the files named in a files list onto a single output stream. It adheres to the standard argument interpretation, and has one option -f, which puts a form feed character between files. The concat command is useful for printing files lists, with each file beginning on a fresh page:

```
$ concat tools.fil tools.txt -f
$ print tools.txt
$ delete tools.txt;
```

How much nicer it would be to eliminate the need for the temporary file, by connecting the output of concat directly to the print command. This is possible with the UNIX or MS–DOS systems using a *pipe*. The command

```
$ concat tools.fil -f | print
```

is the equivalent of the DCL version. Both UNIX and MS–DOS also support *I/O redirection*, or assigning the standard input or output (usually the terminal) to a file:

```
$ concat -f <tools.fil >tools.txt
```

would cause tools.fil and tools.txt to be the standard input and output for concat as if they were the terminal. Then, concat would be oblivious to the redirection and just receive -f as its only argument.

The DCL interpreter (along with many other operating system command interpreters) unfortunately doesn't support either I/O redirection or pipes. The equivalent DCL commands for I/O redirection are more verbose:

```
$ assign tools.fil sys$input
$ assign tools.txt sys$output
$ concat -f
$ deassign sys$input
$ deassign sys$output
```

This is a lot more typing (72 characters more) to express the same idea. In chapter 9, we will present a program that provides I/O redirection and pipelines as a "shell" over DCL. Meanwhile, we can avoid the need for such lengthy definitions by providing the file names as arguments.

The final piece of the basic system interface, for VMS, is the definition of commands to the DCL interpreter. In MS–DOS, there is no such facility; instead, commands are made known to the interpreter by putting them on the "path" (this is also the case for UNIX). For DCL, definition of all your favorite commands in your login file is the ticket. We have a central directory for all of our own programs, and assign a logical name to it:

```
$ assign/nolog dual:[tools.cmd] toolscmd
```

We then assign DCL "global symbols" to each command:

```
$ f                  :== @toolscmd:f
$ update             :== @toolscmd:update
$ image              :== @toolscmd:image
$ global_update      :== @toolscmd:global_update
$ concat             :== @toolscmd:concat
$ pound              :== $toolscmd:pound
```

All of these commands can be placed in your login file, so that they become defined and ready to use whenever you log in to the VAX. Note the difference in the definition of pound from the others, with a $ instead of a @ as the first character. The pound command is an executable image, and definitions of this form are known as *foreign commands*. The full path name to the image (disk and directory) must be specified in the definition. Foreign commands are required in order for a program to make use of getargs.

This will be the last mention of DCL commands until the final chapter of this book. We won't need DCL command procedures much since we have the ability to create our own commands in Fortran. We are now ready to create programs that work like tools.

2.3   Nice to Ugly Conversion

As promised in Chapter 1, a translator that converts our style of Fortran into standard form is presented here. Our particular flavor of Fortran is just VAX Fortran, and no preprocessing is required for our programs on VAX/VMS systems. However, the do...end do and do while...end do constructs used everywhere are nonstandard, and many compilers do not permit them. The ! comment delimiter is also nonstandard, as is the use of lower case letters, identifiers longer than six characters, and source lines extending beyond column 72.

Before plunging into the problem of translation, it should be noted that tab characters are considered illegal, both in our programs and in the Fortran standard. In fact, none of our programs ever test for tabs, so tabs are never treated as equivalent to blanks as one might expect. The problem with tabs, aside from the nuisance of extra code to check for them, is that they never seem to be treated the same way on any two devices. A terminal may treat tabs as equivalent to eight spaces and a printer may simply ignore them, so a nice table that looks fine on the screen becomes garbage when printed. We have learned from bitter experience to never use tabs.

Unfortunately, many VAX Fortran programmers use nonstandard VAX tab formatting in their programs, and such programs will not work with v77. The problem arises often enough to rate a special program for converting tabs to blanks:

```
! detab  -  replace tabs with blanks

      program detab
      include            'global.def'
```

```
integer          argc, uin, uout, ntab, i, atoi
character*(MAXSTR) argv (MAXARGS)
character*1       fgetc, c

call ioinit ()
call getargs (argc, argv)
call stdargs (argc, argv, uin, uout)
ntab = 8
do i = 1, argc
   if (argv(i)(1:1) .eq. QUALIFIER) then
      ntab = atoi(argv(i)(2:))
   end if
end do

i = 0
do while (fgetc (uin, c) .ne. EOF)
   if (c .eq. NEWLINE) then
      call fputc (uout, NEWLINE)
      i = 0
   else if (c .eq. TAB) then
      call fputc (uout, BLANK)
      i = i + 1
      do while (mod(i, ntab) .ne. 0)
         call fputc (uout, BLANK)
         i = i + 1
      end do
   else
      call fputc (uout, c)
      i = i + 1
   end if
end do

call iofinit ()
end
```

This works fine for text files, but it is not quite what is needed for tab-formatted VAX Fortran continuation lines; some additional effort is needed to get continuation characters into column 6.

The v77 program is designed to process Fortran as we write it and will produce correct results on all of the programs in this book. It is not designed to process all standard-conforming programs. It requires source files that adhere to Fortran rules for statement labels and continuation characters, without tabs. It accepts source lines longer than 72 characters and is kind enough not to trash files that have things such as labeled do statements, which we never use. It can, however, trash files with "continued character contexts," that is, programs with quoted character strings extending over more than one source line. Such problems can be avoided by using the concatenation operator or by using multiple assignment statements of substrings when a string is too long to fit on a single source line. v77 won't work on tab-formatted programs, programs that regard blanks as

insignificant, or programs that use the keyword do as a variable, and can overflow
the 19 continuation line limit of Fortran 77.

```
! v77  -  convert VAX Fortran extensions to Fortran 77 equivalents

         program  v77
         include            'global.def'
         integer            argc, uin, uout, u, i, length, lp, lbl, plevel
         integer            atoi, fopen, qindex
         logical            equal, finclude, isletter, inclflag
         character*(MAXSTR) argv(MAXARGS), line, word, getword, upper, itoa
         integer            WHILESTMT, DOSTMT, STACKSIZE
         parameter          (WHILESTMT = 1)
         parameter          (DOSTMT = 2)
         parameter          (STACKSIZE = 16)
         integer            stack(STACKSIZE), label(STACKSIZE), sp, ilabel
         data               sp, ilabel  / 0, 7701 /

         call ioinit ()
         call getargs (argc, argv)
         call stdargs (argc, argv, uin, uout)
         do i = 1, argc
           if (argv(i)(1:1) .eq. '-') then
             inclflag = (index(upper(argv(i)),'I') .gt. 0)
           end if
         end do
         call inclinit (uin)

         do while (finclude (line))
           length = index (line, EOL)
           lp = qindex (line(1:length), COMMENT)
           if (lp .ge. 2) then               !trailing comment
             line = line(1:lp-1)//EOL
             length = lp - 1
           else if (lp .eq. 1) then          !full line comment
             line(1:2) = EOL
             length = 1
           else
             length = length - 1
           end if
           line = upper (line)
           if (line(1:1) .ne. '*' .and. line(1:1) .ne. 'C') then
             if (length .gt. 6 .and. line(1:5) .ne. '    ') then
               lbl  = atoi (line(1:5)//NULL)     !get existing label
             end if
             lp = 7
             if (equal (getword (word,line,lp), 'DO'//NULL)) then
               if (equal (getword (word,line,lp), 'WHILE'//NULL)) then
                 sp         = sp + 1
                 stack(sp)  = WHILESTMT
                 if (lbl .eq. 0) then
                   label(sp) = ilabel
                   ilabel    = ilabel + 1
```

```
                else
                  label(sp) = lbl
                end if
                call fput77 (uout, ' '//itoa(label(sp)))
                call fput77 (uout, ' IF'//NULL)
                do while (line(lp:lp) .eq. BLANK)
                   lp = lp + 1
                end do
                lp = lp + 1                        !skip past opening parenthesis
                call fput77 (uout, '('//NULL)
                plevel = 1
                do while (plevel .ne. 0)       !find closing parenthesis
                   if (line(lp:lp) .eq. '(') then
                      plevel = plevel + 1
                      call fput77 (uout, line(lp:lp)//NULL)
                      lp = lp + 1
                   else if (line(lp:lp) .eq. ')') then
                      plevel = plevel - 1
                      call fput77 (uout, line(lp:lp)//NULL)
                      lp = lp + 1
                   else if (line(lp:lp) .eq. NEWLINE) then   !continued
                      if (finclude(line)) then
                         lp = 7                     !skip past continuation
                         line = upper(line)
                         do while (line(lp:lp) .eq. ' ')
                            lp = lp + 1
                         end do
                      else
                         call fputstr (STDERR,
   &                     'unexpected eof on while stmt expression'//EOL)
                         stop ' '
                      end if
                   else
                      call fput77 (uout, line(lp:lp)//NULL)
                      lp = lp + 1
                   end if
                end do
                call fput77 (uout, ' THEN'//EOL)
             else if (isletter (word(1:1))) then       !VAX do stmt
                sp        = sp + 1
                stack(sp) = DOSTMT
                label(sp) = ilabel
                ilabel    = ilabel + 1
                call fput77 (uout, '      DO '//itoa (label(sp)))
                call fput77 (uout, ' '//word(1:index(word,NULL)-1)//line(lp:))
             else                                       !Fortran 77 do stmt
                call fput77 (uout, line)
             end if
          else if (equal (word, 'END'//NULL)) then
             if (equal (getword (word, line, lp), 'DO'//NULL)) then
                if (sp .le. 0) then
                   call fputstr (STDERR, 'END DO without DO'//EOL)
                else if (stack(sp) .eq. WHILESTMT) then
```

```
              call fput77 (uout, '        GOTO '//itoa (label(sp)))
              call fput77 (uout, EOL)
              call fput77 (uout, '        END IF'//EOL)
            else if (stack(sp) .eq. DOSTMT) then
              call fput77 (uout, ' '//itoa (label(sp)))
              call fput77 (uout, ' CONTINUE'//EOL)
            end if
            sp = sp - 1
          else
            call fput77 (uout, line)
          end if
        else if (equal (word, 'INCLUDE'//NULL)) then !get filename
          if (inclflag) then
            word = getword (word,line,lp)
            word = word(2:index(word(2:),QUOTE))//NULL !strip quotes
            if (fopen (u, word, IOREAD) .eq. IOERROR) then
              call fputstr (STDERR, 'file include failed, file:'//word)
              call fputc (STDERR, NEWLINE)
              call fput77 (uout, line)
            else
              call pushincl (u)       !push u onto finclude unit stack
            end if
          else                      !not processing includes - output to file
            call fput77 (uout, line)
          end if
        else                                          !all other lines
          call fput77 (uout, line)
        end if
      end if
    end do
    if (sp .ne. 0) then
      call fputstr (STDERR, 'Unclosed DO or DO WHILE statement'//EOL)
    end if

    call iofinit ()
    end
```

The output of v77 looks like the kind of code many Fortran programmers write: no indentation, no comments, no blank lines (except there are too many declarations and not enough goto's). As far as we are concerned, it may as well be machine code; the source code is VAX Fortran, which v77 makes available on every machine. If you are working with a compiler that doesn't accept end do, do while, or lowercase letters, then you should make v77 a built-in part of your f command. The improvement in readability and understandability is well worth the penalty of longer compile times.

The v77 program uses the same library of tools that pound uses and consequently is also a short program. It has a few extras as well: qindex performs the same function as the Fortran intrinsic function index, except it ignores substring matches enclosed in quotes. The functions itoa and atoi convert integer values into ASCII digit strings and vice versa. There is also one subroutine, fput77, which is not used by any program except v77. It has the job of buffering output lines and then outputting them in columns 1–72, creating a continuation line if necessary.

```
! fput77  -  output source lines in Fortran 77 format

      subroutine fput77 (u, str)
      integer       u
      character*(*)     str
      include       'global.def'
      character*(MAXSTR) buffer
      integer       bp, i, j, k
      save          buffer, bp
      integer       MAXSOURCE
      parameter     (MAXSOURCE = 66) !# columns for source text
      data    bp      / 1 /

      i = 1
      do while (str(i:i) .ne. NULL)
         buffer(bp:bp) = str(i:i)
         if (str(i:i) .ne. NEWLINE) then
            bp = bp + 1
         else
            if (bp .gt. 1) then    !not a blank line - output it
               buffer(bp+1:bp+1) = NULL
               call fputstr (u, buffer(1:6)//NULL)
               j = 7
               do while (buffer(j:j) .eq. BLANK)   !discard indentation
                  j = j + 1
               end do
               if ((bp-1-j) .le. MAXSOURCE) then   !line fits
                  call fputstr (u, buffer(j:))
               else                                !continuation required
                  k = j + MAXSOURCE - 1
                  if (index(buffer(k:),QUOTE) .gt. 0) then
                     do while (buffer(k:k) .ne. QUOTE)
                        k = k - 1
                     end do
                     k = k - 1
                  end if
                  call fputstr (u, buffer(j:k)//EOL)
                  call fputstr (u, '     &'//buffer(k+1:))
               end if
            end if
            bp = 1
         end if
         i = i + 1
      end do

      return
      end
```

The save statement causes buffer and bp to retain their values after fput77 exits so that an output line can be built in chunks, with no output actually occurring until a NEWLINE character is seen. The somewhat involved task of constructing legal output lines is hidden from the main program, which appears to just be writing output as it goes.

---

v77 is the tool needed to get our programs running on any system. Here is a complete files list for it:

```
! v77.fil  -  files list for v77 translator

    # global.def    !global parameter declarations
    # iox.cmn       !I/O primitives common block
    # include.cmn   !unit stack for finclude

    v77             !main program
      ioinit        !initialize I/O system
      getargs       !get command line arguments
      stdargs       !apply standard filename defaults
      fopen         !open a file
        falloc      !allocate a unit number
        freset      !reset I/O buffer
        ioerr       !report file open/close error
      inclinit      !initialize unit stack for finclude
      finclude      !get line from (possibly included) file
        fgetline    !get line from file
        fclose      !close a file
            fdealloc !deallocate a unit number
            fflush   !flush I/O buffer
      pushincl      !push file unit onto include stack
      equal         !compare strings for equality
      getword       !get next word from line
      upper         !convert string to uppercase
      itoa          !convert integer to ASCII digit string
      atoi          !convert ASCII digit string to integer
        isdigit     !test character to see if it's a digit
      isdigit       !test character to see if it's a letter
      qindex        !find substring index outside quotes
      fput77        !output string in Fortran 77 source format
        fputstr     !output string to file
      fputc         !output character to file
      iofinit       !close all files and flush buffers
```

There are quite a few routines required to get v77 working, but all are standard or nearly standard Fortran and can be adapted easily to run on any machine.

v77 translates all of the nonstandard syntax used regularly in this book to standard form, except for long variable names. This is a more difficult task than the translation of looping constructs, but it is still easy given the right tools for the job (which will be presented in Chapter 5). The few other nonstandard extensions we use are isolated in "primitive" routines, the subject of the next chapter.

Exercises

1. Write a version of global_update in the command language of your computer. Can you get it to accept blank lines? comments? include files?

2. What other commands for doing useful things with files lists can you think of?

3. Modify detab to accept a list of tab stops instead of a single tab width as an option.

4. Write a program entab to replace sequences of blanks with tabs wherever possible. Write it to allow the tab width as an optional argument.

5. Write a special program to convert VAX Fortran tab-formatted files to standard form, with continuation characters in column 6.

6. Comment on the merits and drawbacks of writing software that cannot deal intelligently with tabs.

CHAPTER 3

I/O Primitives

The primary motivation for developing software tools is to provide mechanisms to perform commonly needed functions. Where the underlying language has some deficiency, tools can sometimes be used to overcome the shortcomings, either by hiding the difficulty in some primitive routine or by short-circuiting the problem completely by some ingenious device. At the beginning, it pays to examine the language and its deficiencies so that they can be mitigated as early as possible.

I/O operations are a main source of nonportability in many programs. This is partly due to the fact that different operating systems provide differences in I/O facilities at a lower level, and these differences result in idiosyncrasies in the interface to a programming language. In the case of Fortran programming, the language itself has aspects that lead to inherent nonportability and some inconvenience. We therefore set out in this chapter to develop a set of "primitive" routines for performing I/O operations to some standard that we define. Then this aspect of portability, at least, can be dealt with by limiting all I/O operations

49

to these routines.

There are two features of Fortran concerning I/O operations that warrant special consideration at the outset, namely:

- Record-oriented input and output and

- Special carriage control rules.

It behooves us to decide what to do about these "features" (a software term roughly synonymous with "bugs") before writing tons of code, since a uniform methodology leads to consistent and compatible programs. This chapter and the next deal with these choices.

In many respects, Fortran has outstanding input/output capabilities compared to other languages: it supports an extensive set of formatting edit descriptors unequaled by any other language, as well as a mechanism of writing numeric data in a compact binary form; it permits a wide latitude in file characteristics including direct-access files and even sports a standard means of determining the properties of a file before performing operations on it. Fortran also possesses excellent string processing capabilities. The built-in multicharacter data type, coupled with the ability to pass assumed-length strings to subprograms and obtain their declared lengths at run-time with the standard len function, makes Fortran much better suited to character processing than Pascal, for instance, which is widely used for such applications.

One might ask then, why is Pascal preferred by many programmers for applications involving character processing? The answer is that there are unfortunate mistakes in the Fortran language specification that largely negate the benefits of these features and make it difficult to write portable code in Fortran if the I/O processing is beyond the idiotically simple.

Ample proof of this assertion is the fact that a standard conforming Fortran program cannot be written which exactly copies an ASCII text file; indeed, there is not even a way to read the exact contents of a line of input. Nor can a program be written to output a line with any guarantee of its exact content, even for simple ASCII text, unless the particulars of the local operating environment are specified (i.e., no guarantee that the program will work on any system). This is surely a ridiculous situation, but unfortunately true.

The first problem (inability to faithfully read text) is due to lack of a format edit descriptor to obtain the length of a line read. Upon reading, a character buffer must be provided to receive the input text, read using the A edit descriptor. The following is an example:

```
character*80 buffer
      .
      .
      .
read (u, '(A)') buffer
```

The buffer must be big enough to hold the longest expected input line, otherwise data may be lost. If buffer is longer than the input line, it is padded with blanks. It is therefore impossible to determine the exact contents of the input line since it may have had some trailing blanks.

We could write a function to remove trailing blanks, which would be nice to have anyway, but it doesn't solve the real problem. One might argue that trailing blanks are insignificant, but a programming language should not arbitrarily decide what is significant and what is not.

An additional edit descriptor, the 'Q' descriptor, is available in VAX Fortran and does solve the problem. The Q edit descriptor causes an integer variable to be assigned the length of the input line:

```
character*80 buffer
integer     length
      .
      .
      .
read (u, '(Q,A)') length, buffer
```

causes the variable length to contain the length of what was actually read, discounting carriage control characters. The Q descriptor is easily implemented in any Fortran compiler, since the length must be determined anyway in conforming to the requirements of the A descriptor. However, if your compiler doesn't support it, you will have to find some other means, such as with a nonstandard "binary" or "transparent" file format, or if all else fails, by removing trailing blanks.

Given that the problem of reading input is solved, one still cannot be assured that a file can be copied exactly because of the phenomenon of "Fortran carriage control." Fortran carriage control is an extremely archaic method of controlling paper advance on printers, devised before bona fide standards for such things were invented.

The Fortran standard makes the situation even worse by specifying that the carriage control characters are to be obeyed only on "certain devices determined by the processor," and that "the PRINT statement does not imply that printing will occur, and the WRITE statement does not imply that printing will not occur."

Indeed, the "standard" allows no control over the appearance of output on a single processor since processors are allowed to make any assumption regarding the interpretation of carriage control characters. The VAX implementation of Fortran carriage control is unusual in that it tags files with a carriage control attribute and thus indirectly makes all output files "printing devices." Older CDC machines use Fortran carriage control on all printed output, even if the origin of the data is not Fortran, and provide special utilities to prepare files for the printer. Both implementations conform to the so-called standard.

Consider a program that is intended to copy a Fortran source from one file to another. Further, assume that the source file contains a statement label beginning with the digit '1' in column 1. On one processor, it may be necessary to precede the output format with a 1X edit descriptor, while on another it may not. In one case, the copied program may be compilable, while in the other it is not (continuation characters are in column 7); in one case the statement label may be corrupted, while in the other it is not. In either case, an attempt to print the copied program may or may not result in a formfeed when the '1' in column 1 is encountered. There is no requirement, of course, that the processor consider a printer to be a printing device. In summary, the wording of the present standard can be paraphrased as "there is no standard" regarding carriage control.

VAX Fortran has an optional carriagecontrol specifier for the open statement, with a default of carriagecontrol='fortran'. carriagecontrol='list' indicates that the first character on an output line has no special significance.

It is very desirable at times to be able to access the input to a program one character at a time and to write the output one character at a time. Fortran provides no facility to access a single record (line) of the input with two separate read or write statements—it is a record-oriented language. It is certainly possible to access each individual character with something like

```
1    read (5, 10) line
10   format (A80)

     if (line(i:i) .eq. 'z') then ...
        etc.
     goto 1
```

in which the characters are read a line at a time and then accessed by string subscripting. But what a pain in the caboose to have to keep doing this throughout a large program wherever we need it, especially if the line structure of the input file is unimportant. For the sake of generality we want to be able to read and write not only a line at a time but also a character at a time. Our first tools, then, are programs that allow us to read a single character from the input and write a single character to the output.

3.1   iox

Since we can't just read a character from the input, we read an entire line at a time. The line is stored in a buffer, so that input doesn't get lost, and then just one character is returned to the calling program. Here is the program to get just one character from the input:

```
! fgetc  -  get character from file

     character*1 function fgetc (u, c)
     integer    u
     character*1 c
     include    'global.def'
     include    'iox.cmn'

     bp(u) = bp(u) + 1
```

```
      if (bp(u) .eq. 1) then
         read (u, ' (Q,A) ',end=10) length(u), buffer(u)
         if (length(u) .eq. 0) then
            c = NEWLINE
            bp(u) = 0
         else
            c = buffer(u)(bp(u):bp(u))
         end if
      else if (bp(u) .eq. length(u)+1) then
         c = NEWLINE
         bp(u) = 0
      else
         c = buffer(u)(bp(u):bp(u))
      end if
      fgetc = c
      return

10    c = EOF
      fgetc = c
      return
      end
```

The definitions of NEWLINE, EOF, and MAXLINE are provided by the parameter file global.def. The buffer and length arrays are defined in the include file iox.cmn. We use the standard file extensions def and cmn to denote parameter definition and common block definition files, respectively. The reason for having length and buffer in a common block will be apparent soon.

The design of fgetc may seem a bit odd at first glance. fgetc is a character function, and the character is returned both as the function result and in the argument c. This is a useful design choice, however, because the function can be used to simultaneously assign a variable to c and test its value:

```
      if (fgetc(u,c) .eq. AFLAG) then
         do this
      else if (c .eq. BFLAG) then
         do that
      else
         do nothing
      end if
```

Note also that fgetc returns a special character called EOF, which indicates end of file. This allows a simple looping through all input:

```
      do while (fgetc(u,c) .ne. EOF)
         process c
      end do
```

The buffers are necessary for three reasons. First, the only way within the constraints of the Fortran standard to implement access by character is to use a buffer for complete records. Second, by defining the buffers in a common block, the data in them can be shared by other cooperating routines. Third, by

associating the buffers with file unit numbers and providing special file open and
close routines the buffer system becomes a complete and reasonably portable file
I/O system.

The `fgetline` routine is one of the cooperating routines: it returns the next
line of text from an input file:

```
! fgetline  -  get line from file (VMS file system)

      logical function fgetline (u, line)
      character*(*) line
      integer      u
      include      'global.def'
      include      'iox.cmn'
      integer      lp, i

      bp(u) = bp(u) + 1
      if (bp(u) .eq. 1) then
         read (u, ' (Q,A) ', end=10) length(u), line
         if (length(u) .eq. 0) then
            line(1:1) = NEWLINE
            line(2:2) = NULL
         else
            line(length(u)+1:length(u)+1) = NEWLINE
            line(length(u)+2:length(u)+2) = NULL
         end if
      else
         lp = 0
         do i = bp(u),length(u)
            lp = lp + 1
            line(lp:lp) = buffer(u)(i:i)
         end do
         line(lp+1:lp+1) = NEWLINE
         line(lp+2:lp+2) = NULL
      end if
      bp(u) = 0
      buffer(u)(1:1) = NULL

      fgetline = .true.
      return

10    fgetline = .false.
      line(1:1) = EOF
      line(2:2) = NULL

      return
      end
```

The routine returns the remainder of the buffer filled by `fgetc` up to the
NEWLINE or gets a new line of input if the buffer is empty. Unlike `fgetc`, `fgetline`
is a logical function, always returning true until the end of file is encountered,
and as an extra courtesy, returns EOF in the first position of the line on end of
file. This construction also allows simple looping over all input:

```
do while (fgetline(u, line))
    process line
end do
```

There are two analogous routines, fputc and fputstr, that perform buffered output to files. Here is fputc:

```
! fputc  -  output character to file

    subroutine fputc (u, c)
    integer     u, i
    character*1 c
    include     'global.def'
    include     'iox.cmn'

    bp(u) = bp(u) + 1
    if (c .eq. NEWLINE) then
        write (u,'(<MAXLINE> A1:)') (buffer(u)(i:i),i= 1,bp(u)-1)
        bp(u) = 0
    else if (bp(u) .eq. MAXLINE) then
        buffer(u)(MAXLINE:MAXLINE) = c
        write (u,'(<MAXLINE> A1:)') (buffer(u)(i:i),i= 1,MAXLINE)
        bp(u) = 0
    else
        buffer(u)(bp(u):bp(u)) = c
    end if

    return
    end
```

The format specifier (<MAXLINE>A1:) causes the line to be written out exactly "as is." The colon is a standard Fortran edit descriptor, causing remaining format items to be ignored if the input list is exhausted. The <> are a VAX extension for run-time format control. In all of the tools, fputc and fputstr are the only places where run-time format control is used. If standard Fortran rules are followed, parameters may not appear in format statements, and these would be the only routines where the actual code would require modification to change MAXLINE and MAXSTR. This nonstandard code allows them to be changed everywhere by simply changing global.def.

fputstr cooperates with fputc the same way that fgetline does with fgetc. There is no fputline routine, since a line is just a special type of string, and sometimes we want to write just part of a line; fputstr is more general. Since no return value is required from either fputc or fputstr, they are subroutines.

```
! fputstr  -  output string to file

    subroutine fputstr (u, string)
    character*(*) string
    integer       u, i, j
```

```
include        'global.def'
include        'iox.cmn'

i = 1

do while (string(i:i) .ne. NULL)
   bp(u) = bp(u) + 1
   if (bp(u) .eq. MAXLINE) then
      write (u, '(<MAXLINE>A1:)') (buffer(u)(j:j), j=1,MAXLINE)
      bp(u) = 0
   else if (string(i:i) .eq. NEWLINE) then
      write (u, '(<MAXLINE>A1:)') (buffer(u)(j:j), j=1, bp(u)-1)
      i = i + 1
      bp(u) = 0
   else
      buffer(u)(bp(u):bp(u)) = string(i:i)
      i = i + 1
   end if
end do
return
end
```

Both fgetc and fgetline must follow the same rules for updating the buffer, and the same applies to fputc and fputstr; clearly, the routines are intimately connected. This is somewhat bad since in general interdependencies among routines should be avoided. On the other hand, routines that use them do not need to know that the buffers even exist, and that is good since, in general, complexity should be concealed. The only restriction is that all I/O should be performed through these routines, rather than with direct read and write statements. The formatting capabilities of Fortran can still be used by writing to a string buffer with a Fortran write statement, a Fortran 77 feature.

We could have implemented fgetline in terms of fgetc, or vice versa, and the routines would be less connected, although they would also be less efficient (more subroutine calls). We usually consider efficiency to be of secondary importance compared to clarity and mutual independence, but since we must filter all I/O through these routines, their speed will be the controlling factor in the speed of many other programs. We could write them in assembly language to make them faster, but as is they are nearly portable code.

3.2   iof

The buffers and their lengths were put in a common block so that the iox routines can communicate; they are organized as arrays so that each open file unit has its own private buffer. This is necessary to keep from getting alphabet soup when more than one file is opened for reading or writing at the same time. It could be left up to the programmer to keep track of which units are in use, except that we would then need to dimension buffer to as many Fortran unit numbers as are allowed by the language (too many).

The iox system needs more help to control allocation of buffers to units, and indeed is not too useful without it. That help is provided by another set of routines, collectively called iof. The iox routines govern the contents of the buffers, while the iof routines control their allocation and deallocation. The status of each unit allowed is stored in the common block arrays alloc and access. Here is the underlying data structure of iox and iof, stored in file iox.cmn:

```
! iox  -  common block for I/O primitives (VMS file system)

      logical    alloc (MAXOPEN)         !allocation flag array
      integer    access(MAXOPEN)         !access type array

      character*(MAXSTR)  buffer(MAXOPEN)  !i/o line buffer array
      integer             bp(MAXOPEN)      !buffer pointer array
      integer             length(MAXOPEN)  !lengths of line buffers

      common /iof/    alloc, access
      common /iox/    buffer
      common /ioxptr/ bp, length
      save    /iof/, /iox/, /ioxptr/
```

VAX Fortran include statements are always used to define common blocks in our routines. Using include statements, with the common block in a separate file, ensures that all the routines using the common block have the same definitions (even though they all must be recompiled if the common block is changed).

The separate iox and ioxptr blocks are not required in VAX Fortran, but in the ANSI Fortran 77 standard, mixing character and noncharacter data in a single common block is prohibited. The parameter MAXOPEN, contained in global.def, is the maximum number of open files a program may have, which is dependent on the local system setup. The array alloc contains true if a unit (which is just a subscript into any of the arrays) is presently allocated and false if it is not. The access array specifies the type of access for which a unit is opened (read or write).

Likewise, the save statement is not required in VAX Fortran. Many Fortran programs are written with the implicit requirement that the values of variables will be remembered the next time a routine is called, and for the most part Fortran compilers allocate storage in a way that the requirement is met. However, Fortran 77 does not gaurantee that values in common blocks are saved when control passes to a routine in which the common block is undeclared. The routines that call the I/O primitives never need access to the underlying common blocks and should never include iox.cmn, so per the Fortran standard the save statement should be used to ensure that the values in the arrays are retained. It is a good practice in general to use the save statement wherever an algorithm depends on values being saved, both as clear documentation of your intentions and as an aid to portability.

Given this organization of iox and iof, it is necessary for the file management routines to manage the assignment of files to buffers. It would be possible to devise a pointer system in which the unit number is associated with its buffer indirectly, and let the programmer use whatever unit numbers he chooses. However, there is no fundamental reason why the programmer must choose unit numbers if the I/O routines can choose them automatically. Most programs have their I/O units hard-wired in the main program, or even worse, hard-wired in the I/O statements themselves. This arrangement is inconvenient because it makes it harder to reuse pieces of the program in new programs, which is after all the purpose of software tools. Some more sophisticated programs associate units with "logical names," which are assigned to actual files at run-time. Although better, this method is still inconvenient, because it is an extra step to go through to run the program; if nothing else, it is something else to have to remember.

Given the existence of a getargs routine to pass parameters to a program at run-time, it is simpler to connect a file for I/O directly, rather than through a logical name. To open a file for reading, we simply say

```
u = fopen (u, filename, IOREAD)
```

where fopen is an integer function that returns the unit number to be used for the file, and once again, the same value is returned in the argument u and in the function value itself, allowing a file to be opened while simultaneously checking that it was opened successfully. On failure to open the named file, a special code IOERROR is returned, an integer such as -1, which could never be returned by a successful operation. The access codes allowed by fopen are

```
IOREAD    -  read only access
IOWRITE   -  write access with ASCII carriage control
IOAPPEND  -  write access with append to existing file
IOFORTRAN -  write access with Fortran carriage control
```

By keeping a record of the status of each file, fopen and its friends can allocate, deallocate, and reuse Fortran file units. It is possible to handle hundreds of files by a program using iof, so long as no more than MAXOPEN are ever used at once:

```
! fopen  -  open file and assign unique unit number

      integer function fopen (u, filename, mode)
      character*(*) filename
      integer       u, mode, falloc
      include       'global.def'
      include       'iox.cmn'
      integer       flength, ios

      flength = index(filename, NULL) - 1
```

```
      u = falloc (u)
      fopen = u

      if (u .eq. IOERROR) then
         continue
      else if (mode .eq. IOREAD) then
         open (unit = u,
&              file = filename(1:flength),
&              status = 'OLD',
&              iostat = ios,
&              readonly,
&              err = 10)
         access(u) = IOREAD
         bp(u) = 0
         length(u) = 0

       else if (mode .eq. IOWRITE) then
         open (unit = u,
&              file = filename(1:flength),
&              status = 'NEW',
&              iostat = ios,
&              carriagecontrol = 'LIST',
&              err = 10)
         access(u) = IOWRITE
         bp(u) = 0
         length(u) = 0

       else if (mode .eq. IOAPPEND) then
         open (unit = u,
&              file = filename(1:flength),
&              status = 'OLD',
&              iostat = ios,
&              access = 'APPEND',
&              carriagecontrol = 'LIST',
&              err = 10)
         access(u) = IOWRITE
         bp(u) = 0
         length(u) = 0

       else if (mode .eq. IOFORTRAN) then
         open (unit = u,
&              file = filename(1:flength),
&              status = 'NEW',
&              iostat = ios,
&              err = 10)
         access(u) = IOFORTRAN
         bp(u) = 0
         length(u) = 0

       else
         call fdealloc (u)
         call fputstr (STDERR,'fopen: Illegal access mode'//EOL)
         fopen = IOERROR
```

```
      end if

      return

10    call fdealloc (u)
      fopen = IOERROR
      call fputstr(STDERR,'fopen: '//NULL)
      call ioerr(ios)

      return
      end
```

When a file is opened the buffer pointer and length for the corresponding unit
are reset so that the first call to fgetc or fgetline causes the first record to be
read. The dynamic assignment of unit numbers for use by fopen and its callers
is handled by the function falloc:

```
! falloc  -  allocate a unit number for I/O

      integer function falloc (u)
      integer u
      include 'global.def'
      include 'iox.cmn'

      u = 1
      do while (u .le. MAXOPEN .and. alloc(u))
         u = u + 1
      end do

      if (u .gt. MAXOPEN) then
         u = IOERROR
         call fputstr
     &   (STDERR,'FALLOC: Exceeded open file limit'//EOL)
      else
         alloc (u) = .true.
      end if

      falloc = u

      return
      end
```

Isolation of the unit allocation in a routine that does nothing else allows fopen
to be used in Fortran programs with other types of I/O operations, such as
unformatted or direct I/O. One can just say

```
if (falloc(u) .ne. IOERROR) then
    open (unit=u, file='xyz.dat', form='UNFORMATTED', status='OLD')
end if
```

and be assured of getting a unit number that doesn't conflict with any others in the program.

Files are closed by the cooperating routine fclose, which does the opposite of fopen:

```
! fclose  -  deallocate a file

    subroutine fclose (u)
    integer  u, ios
    include  'global.def'
    include  'iox.cmn'
    if (u .le. 0 .or. u .gt. MAXOPEN) then
        call fputstr (STDERR,'fclose: Illegal unit number'//EOL)
    else
        if (access(u) .ne. IOREAD) then
            call fflush(u)
        end if
        close (unit = u, iostat = ios, err = 10)
        call fdealloc (u)
    end if
    return

10  call fputstr (STDERR,'fclose: '//NULL)
    call ioerr(ios)
    return
    end
```

When a file is closed, its unit number should be deallocated for later use if needed. The fdealloc routine does the opposite of falloc:

```
! fdealloc  -  deallocate a unit

    subroutine fdealloc (u)
    integer  u
    include  'global.def'
    include  'iox.cmn'

    if (u .le. 0 .or. u .gt. MAXOPEN) then
        call fputstr (STDERR,'FDEALLOC: Illegal unit number'//EOL)
    else
        alloc(u) = .false.
    end if

    return
    end
```

fclose must flush any characters remaining in an output buffer, put there
after the last NEWLINE was received. A separate routine fflush is provided to do
this housekeeping:

```
! fflush  -  dump buffer associated with unit u

        subroutine fflush(u)
        integer u, i
        include 'global.def'
        include 'iox.cmn'

        if (bp(u) .gt. 0) then
            write(u,'(<MAXLINE> A1:)') (buffer(u)(i:i),i= 1,bp(u))
        end if

        return
        end
```

fflush is a separate routine rather than in-line code because some applications
might need to flush a buffer without closing the file. The buffer can always be
emptied by sending a NEWLINE, but if the buffer is already empty then NEWLINE
would produce an unwanted blank line.

The flexibility of iox is illustrated by the error handling of iof. When an error
occurs in either fopen or fclose, it puts its name onto the standard error stream,
without a NEWLINE, and calls the error message routine ioerr. Then ioerr just
outputs the message corresponding to ios and returns, so the complete error
message is printed on one line.

```
! ioerr  -  writes appropriate I/O error message to STDERR

        subroutine ioerr(ios)
        integer    ios
        include    '($foriosdef)'
        include    'global.def'

        if (ios.eq.FOR$IOS_CLOERR) then
            call fputstr(STDERR,'File close error'//EOL)
        else if (ios.eq.FOR$IOS_FILNOTFOU) then
            call fputstr(STDERR,'File not found'//EOL)
        else if (ios.eq.FOR$IOS_OPEFAI) then
            call fputstr(STDERR,'File open failure'//EOL)
        else if (ios.eq.FOR$IOS_MIXFILACC) then
            call fputstr(STDERR,'Mixed file access modes'//EOL)
        else if (ios.eq.FOR$IOS_UNIALROPE) then
            call fputstr(STDERR,'Unit already opened'//EOL)
        else if (ios.eq.FOR$IOS_NO_SUCDEV) then
            call fputstr(STDERR,'No such device'//EOL)
        else if (ios.eq.FOR$IOS_FILNAMSPE) then
            call fputstr(STDERR,'File name specification error'//EOL)
        else if (ios.eq.FOR$IOS_WRIREAFIL) then
            call fputstr(STDERR,'Attempt to write to READONLY file'//EOL)
```

```
      else
          call fputstr(STDERR,'VAX FORTRAN I/O error'//EOL)
      end if

      return
      end
```

The name $foriosdef refers to a standard include module provided by VAX
Fortran for iostat symbolic names; other standard modules are provided for
system programming applications. Some of the other modules are discussed in
Chapter 9.

Neither fopen nor fclose attempts to recover from an error, but fopen
returns an unmistakable error signal when one does occur. They also do not stop
the program since the assumption that a file open error is fatal is unjustified for
these low level routines. For similar reasons, the routines that actually do the
input and output—fgetc, fgetline, fputc and fputstr—do not trap errors on
Fortran read and write statements. The VAX Fortran run-time environment
knows as well or better than we do whether an I/O error is fatal and will provide
an informative traceback message on any I/O error. However, if the primitives
are to run on a system without such first-class error handling, the code to trap
errors can be readily added.

This completes the code necessary for management of all file I/O in our programs except for a means of initializing everything, which we will return to. Although it is seldom necessary, provisions for use with more conventional Fortran
I/O are possible. As for opening and closing files, fopen can be used for files with
Fortran carriage control by specifying IOFORTRAN as the access code. For reading
and writing, direct read and write statements can be used with care. After any
execution of fgetline or after fgetc has returned a NEWLINE, the buffer for a
file is empty, and the file can be read directly without losing any input. Direct
output via a Fortran write statement can be performed just after a NEWLINE has
been sent. Alternatively, formatted I/O can be performed indirectly by using
"internal files." The statements

```
      character*(MAXSTR) mybuf
      real               x
           .
           .
           .
      write (mybuf, '('' The answer is '',f5.2,a2)') x, EOL
      call fputstr (u, mybuf)
```

would do the trick. The system cannot be used for unformatted I/O as implemented since iox uses formatted I/O statements. However, falloc can allocate
a unit number to use without conflict if unformatted I/O is desired. Even if
the complete system is not used, falloc and fdealloc can be used to manage
unit numbers, which is an improvement over the method (or lack of one) in most
programs. As a final remark, note that if a unit number is not obtained with

falloc, it can cause fopen to fail unexpectedly if its unit number conflicts with
one used by fopen. On the other hand, if a unit number outside the range of
those used by falloc is used, then file I/O can be carried out independently of
iof and iox, as long as the number of files opened does not exceed the true limit.

The standard units STDIN, STDOUT, and STDERR are special in that they are
supposed to be preconnected (they are already defined when the program starts
without opening them). However, we need to take special action to prevent the
Fortran carriage control phenomenon from occurring on STDOUT and STDERR. In
addition, since they need buffers too, they either need extra buffers or fopen
will have to know about them. We chose the latter method since then STDIN,
STDOUT and STDERR are treated like any other file, as they should be, and there
are no "special cases" (read: "bad design") introduced in any of the routines.

All implementations of Fortran have an implicit standard input and output,
its unit number specified as * in read and write statements. Although not
guaranteed, nearly all have standard unit numbers as well. On the VAX, they
are 5 for STDIN, and 6 for STDOUT. However, there is no standard number for
STDERR. We explicitly open all three in the initialization routine ioinit, called
at the beginning of every program.

```
! ioinit  -  initialize file system and connect standard units

        subroutine ioinit()
        integer   i, ios
        include   'global.def'
        include   'iox.cmn'

        do i = 1, MAXOPEN      !initalize i/o buffers
          bp(i)     = 0
          length(i) = 0
          alloc(i)  = .false.
          access(i) = 0
        end do

        do i = 5, 7
          alloc(i) = .true.
        end do

        access(5) = IOREAD
        access(6) = IOWRITE
        access(7) = IOWRITE

        open (unit = 5,
     &        status = 'OLD',
     &        iostat = ios,
     &        err = 10)

        open (unit = 6,
     &        status = 'NEW' ,
     &        iostat = ios,
     &        carriagecontrol = 'LIST',
```

```
&        err = 10)

 open (unit = 7,
&        file = 'SYS$ERROR',
&        status = 'NEW',
&        iostat = ios,
&        carriagecontrol = 'LIST',
&        err = 10)

 return

10 call ioerr (ios)
   return
   end
```

This routine could also be implemented with calls to fopen, in which case the unit numbers would be 1, 2, and 3, the first three returned by fopen. A routine is also provided to shut everything down in an orderly fashion at the end of a program:

```
! iofinit  -  deallocate and flush any open write-enabled buffers

      subroutine iofinit()
      include 'global.def'
      include 'iox.cmn'
      integer   i

      do i = 1, MAXOPEN
         if (alloc(i)) then
            if (access(i).ne.IOREAD) then
               call fflush(i)
            end if
            close (unit = i, err = 10)
10          alloc(i) = .false.
            access(i) = 0
         end if
      end do

      return
      end
```

3.3   The Acid Test

Now that we have a complete I/O system to work with, let's do something interesting and useful with it. We need some good way to test the I/O routines anyway, before going too much further. The simplest test routines we could write are routines to copy files, either by lines or by individual characters. Here is a complete test program for copying files:

```
! ccopy  -  copy a file by character

      program ccopy
      include          'global.def'
      integer          argc, uin, uout
      character*(MAXSTR) argv(MAXARGS)
      character*1      fgetc, c

      call ioinit ()
      call getargs (argc, argv)
      call stdargs (argc, argv, uin, uout)

      do while (fgetc(uin,c) .ne. EOF)
         call fputc (uout, c)
      end do

      call iofinit ()
      end
```

This is a good test, but not good enough by itself. A more comprehensive test
routine should also test the interaction between character and line I/O and should
excercise the system with more files to make sure that the iof routines are really
working as advertised. We have a routine called finclude, the routine used
by pound in the previous chapter to take care of including files. The function
finclude is not a primitive like the other routines in this chapter, but it exercises
the primitives (at least the line-oriented ones) rather thoroughly, and we consider
it something of an "acid test" of the iox system. finclude looks for lines of the
form

      #include filename

and when they are found, opens the named file and begins reading from it. When
the end of the file is found, it is closed, and reading of the first file resumes at
the next line following the #include statement. A good example of where file
inclusion could be used is in writing program documentation with source listings.
A text file with prose descriptions of programs could serve as the "master" file,
and a #include statement could be used wherever a program listing is desired,
so that the listings are always up-to-date. The capability of including files makes
it convenient to merge all input to a program into a single input stream, while
simultaneously giving users the flexibility of organizing their input into files any
way they like. For example, if you are writing a plotting program that requires
some instructions such as the type of axes to be used or the color of each curve,
as well as sets of x-y coordinate pairs to be plotted, you can require all input to
come from a single input file, and give that file the capability to include other
files. Then users will be able to put everything in one file if they like, to put all
of the instructions in one file and all of the data in another, or to put the data
for each curve in a separate file. By using finclude you can give users a choice
about the organization of input to your program instead of making the decision
for them.

We want included files to be able to include files themselves to any nesting depth. This problem is essentially recursive in nature—the operation is defined partially in terms of itself. To illustrate, here is a rough cut at the problem:

```
! finclude  -  process include files (pseudocode version)

    subroutine finclude (uin, uout)

    do while (fgetline(uin, line))
        if (line begins with "#include") then
            get filename
            u = fopen (u, filename, IOREAD)
            call finclude (u, uout)
        else
            call fputstr (uout, line)
        end if
    end do
    return
    end
```

Some details have been skipped over, like variable declarations and just how to get and compare strings. finclude can be viewed as a *filter*, a program that copies input to output with some transformation between. In an environment that supports pipelines, we could say

```
$ include <myfile.txt | pound "$ type #.for" | @sys$input
```

and pound (or any other program, such as "@") could make use of files with include statements in them without being aware that the include operation exists.

Better yet, if finclude is designed properly, it can be used by any program to retrieve input one line at a time from a single apparent input source, which is in fact a collection of files linked together by include statements. finclude can still be thought of as a filter, but one that filters lines rather than entire files. This is a far more useful design since the inclusion capability can be built into any program, so users needn't be bothered with a separate include command. In addition, a routine that handles include statements by line can be used in a very simple main program to implement the file filter. The organization suggested above for finclude processes the entire input stream without any chance for the caller to regain control, so we would like to redesign it for including a line at a time.

There is another major reason for discarding the approach outlined, however: it requires a recursive subroutine call, which is explicitly disallowed in Fortran. This must be viewed as one of the most serious drawbacks of the Fortran language since many important problems in computer programming are essentially recursive in nature. In the dim ancient past of computing, when Fortran was born and the business of programming language and compiler design was not understood too well, implicitly recursive programs were viewed as inefficient and unnecessary. This is essentially a true statement, at least in theory, since recursive algorithms could still be written explicitly in Fortran with reduced storage, and in those days efficiency was an overriding concern. Nowadays, a smart programmer should realize that while efficiency is important, clarity in the source code is even more important; after all, computers aren't getting any slower—they get faster every year.

The advantage of using recursion is that it often makes the solution to a problem much simpler and thus easier to understand. A favorite example of the use of recursion in computer science texts is evaluation of the Fibonacci series

$$F_{n+2} = F_{n+1} + F_n, \qquad n \geq 0$$

with $F_0 = 0$ and $F_1 = 1$. This is probably a bad choice for illustrating recursion as a useful technique since the recursive version is much slower than its iterative counterpart and is more difficult to understand. The original implementers of Fortran undoubtably read some of these books and decided recursion was worthless. Our recursive outline for finclude does illustrate the simplicity of some recursive algorithms, and we will see that a nonrecursive implementation does require more code.

Fortran programmers can take heart, however. The lack of recursion in Fortran can be a real nuisance at times, but recursion can always be transformed to iteration, and the transformation should always result in routines that are more efficient. Recursion can be implemented directly in Fortran by making use of a stack, and often the resulting code is clean and straightforward. Some recursive algorithms are easier to implement in Fortran than others, and unfortunately, some cases lead to real difficulty. But at least the effort required does lead to programs that are faster.

Our implementation of finclude implements recursion by use of a stack to store file unit numbers, so that when EOF is found on the current file, reading resumes from the file unit on top of the stack. The stack is declared in a common block:

```
! include.cmn  -  common block for finclude file stack

        integer   MAXINCLUDE
        parameter (MAXINCLUDE = 10)

        integer unit (MAXINCLUDE), isp
        common /inclstack/ unit, isp
        save   /inclstack/
```

It is best for finclude to keep track of the stack itself, rather than the calling program. This conceals the existence of the stack from routines that use finclude, making it appear to them that finclude is reading from a single file (which may or may not be true). So finclude has no unit number argument, just the returned line. Otherwise, it behaves like fgetline, returning false when the end of all input is reached. An important decision to be made is what to do when, for some reason, the file named in an include statement cannot be opened.

Rather than throw up its hands and quit, finclude just returns the #include line unprocessed and a true result. After all, fopen will still report whatever error message is appropriate on STDERR, and the calling program can always explicitly look for lines beginning with #include returned from finclude if some special action is required. This keeps finclude looking like fgetline, and preserves the ability to test for EOF and retrieve lines of input in one statement.

Since finclude has no unit number argument, we need some means of setting the initial unit number to read from in the common block, and we don't want the caller to have to access the common block to do it, so we provide an initialization routine:

```
! inclinit  -  make u the main input file for finclude

        subroutine inclinit (u)
        integer u
        include 'global.def'
        include 'include.cmn'

        unit(1) = u
        isp = 1

        return
        end
```

This way, the existence of the common block is concealed from the calling routine. Finally, here is finclude:

```
! finclude  -  get line from a (possibly included) file

        logical  function  finclude (line)
        character*(*)       line
        include             'global.def'
        include             'include.cmn'
        character*(MAXSTR)  getword, word, upper
        integer             lp, fopen
        logical             fgetline, equal, done

        done = .false.
        do while (.not. done)
          if (fgetline (unit(isp), line)) then
            lp = 1
            if (equal (upper (getword (word,line,lp)),'#INCLUDE'//NULL)) then
              isp = isp + 1
              unit(isp) = fopen (unit(isp),getword(word,line,lp),IOREAD)
              if (unit(isp) .eq. IOERROR) then !return "#" line
                call fputstr (STDERR, 'include failure, file = '//word)
                call fputc   (STDERR, NEWLINE)
                isp = isp - 1
                done = .true.
                finclude = .true.
              end if
```

```
      else                 !finished reading unit(i)
        done = .true.
        finclude = .true.
      end if
    else
      if (isp .gt. 1) then    !resume processing of previous file
        call fclose (unit(isp))
        isp = isp - 1
      else                    !end of all input
        done = .true.
        finclude = .false.
      end if
    end if
  end do

  return
  end
```

The routines equal, upper, and getword will be presented in the next chapter. We also have a program that does the job of finclude on entire files instead of individual lines, so that file inclusion can be used with any program that reads files. Even though we have a better line-based version, we still need the file-based version for programs we didn't write.

```
! doinclude  -  process a file with #include <file> replaced by contents

      program doinclude
      include            'global.def'
      integer            argc, uin, uout
      character*(MAXSTR) argv(MAXARGS)
      character*(MAXLINE) line
      logical            finclude

      call ioinit()
      call getargs (argc, argv)
      call stdargs (argc, argv, uin, uout)

      if ((uin .eq. IOERROR) .or. (uout .eq. IOERROR)) stop ' '

      call inclinit (uin)

      do while (finclude (line))
         call fputstr (uout, line)
      end do

      call iofinit()
      end
```

It is possible on the VAX to say

```
#include TT
```

to direct the input stream to the terminal, and then revert to reading from wherever the previous source was by typing C T R L / Z on the terminal. On other systems this might not be possible, depending on the implementation of the I/O primitives, in which case there would be no way to get input from a terminal via finclude if it was initiated with a file. In any case, it is occasionally useful to be able to fool finclude into reading from some other input source without using a #include statement. The routine pushincl does this by simply pushing a new unit number onto the include stack:

```
! pushincl - push (preopened) unit onto include stack

      subroutine pushincl (u)
      integer    u
      include    'include.cmn'

      isp        = isp + 1
      unit(isp)  = u

      return
      end
```

The file should already be open before calling pushincl. Our only use so far for this trick is in v77, to get finclude to process Fortran include statements. It could, however, be used in other circumstances where more than one input stream is needed and the file inclusion functionality is desired.

We have done a lot in this chapter, and it is worth a moment to contemplate what, exactly, has been accomplished. We have implemented a complete system for handling character input and output in an unconventional way. As you can probably guess, this organization has some advantages for writing programs that are text oriented. More importantly, however, we have created a set of routines with well-defined behavior that handle tasks involving details of the local environment. Several nonstandard features of the VAX/VMS implementation of Fortran have been used (namely the Q edit descriptor, the CARRIAGECONTROL='LIST' open specifier, and the run-time format syntax) to get the desired behavior. While these features might not be found elsewhere, it is certainly possible to implement the same functions on any other system. While all of the routines in iox and iof are interlinked and manipulate a common data set, the underlying complexity is concealed from programs that use them.

Rather than propagate the idiosyncrasies of the local environment throughout programs, they are completely contained in the iox and iof routines. These are thus "primitives" that differ from one system to the next. It is important to isolate system dependencies in this way as much as possible, and to keep the number of such routines to a bare minimum. Each such routine is considered a primitive. If only these routines can be implemented on a target system, then all programs using them can also be made to work, creating a sort of "virtual operating system." These are the most basic tools.

Exercises

1. Make iox and iof work on your system.

2. What are the relative merits and demerits of rewriting iox in assembly language?

3. Write a program wc that counts characters, words, and lines in its input.

4. Write a program head that prints the first 10 lines in its input.

5. Write a program tail that prints the last 10 lines of input.

6. What character signals EOF when typed from the keyboard on your system?

7. (VAX lovers) Why does the EDT editor display the message "input file does not have standard text format" when a Fortran output file is edited?

Further Reading

Kernighan and Plauger present a similar set of primitive I/O routines in their books *Software Tools* and *Software Tools in Pascal*; they also present a recursive version of finclude that processes entire files in *Software Tools in Pascal* and a nonrecursive version in *Software Tools*.

There are many textbooks that discuss recursive algorithms, their uses, and their relationship to nonrecursive ones. The monograph by D. W. Barron, *Recursive Techniques in Programming* (American Elsevier, 1968) deals exclusively with this topic in a down-to-earth way. Robert Sedgewick, *Algorithms*, and Wirth, *Algorithms + Data Structures = Programs*, present many practical algorithms that are recursive in nature.

The widespread use of the Fibonacci series to illustrate recursion is partly because the problem is so simple that it is easy to illustrate how recursion is implemented at the machine level. Tannenbaum, *Structured Computer Organization*, presents a good illustration of recursive subroutine calls at the machine level with another well-known example of recursive algorithms, the "Towers of Hanoi."

CHAPTER 4

String Manipulation

The tools in this book employ a rather unconventional method of describing strings, at least by Fortran standards. The representation of strings we use has already been illustrated in Chapter 2 and in the construction of the I/O primitives, without much discussion or justification. We have deferred this discussion to the present chapter in order to present a more complete explanation.

4.1   Character and String Representation

Strings are sequences of characters. So before getting into the representation of strings, a consideration of the more fundamental question of how to represent characters is in order. There is more to the question than might appear at first glance. There are some good reasons why a representation of characters as integers, rather than as Fortran character data, is desirable. An integer representation has the advantage of permitting a much wider range of values than a single byte character code, and special characters such as the EOF character returned by fgetc and fgetline could be given values outside the range of other valid characters. For instance, EOF could be given the value -1, so that it could never occur in a valid character sequence. An integer representation is also advantageous for certain special applications, where characters are intermixed with pointers or special codes, or where character codes are to be used for array addressing.

The advantages of integer representation must be weighed against the disadvantages. One obvious disadvantage is storage space, which is typically four times greater per element of a string than for Fortran character strings. Less obvious is the disadvantage of not being able to generate the EOF character from the keyboard, since almost all of our programs are designed to read from a file or the keyboard. The Fortran language provides convenient facilities for manipulation of the built-in character type. For instance, there is a special concatenation operator "//" and a function index that locates characters or substrings in strings. More importantly, it provides a means of writing perfectly general string handling routines that can operate on strings of any length. The declarations

```
character*(*) function getword (word, line, lp)
character*(*) word, line
```

cause word, line, and the function result all to assume the length specified by the caller, and that length, in the rare instances where it is required, can be obtained with the Fortran intrinsic len function. The same function can thus be used for words of length 10 or length 1000 in the same program, and without the need for a length argument. Note that integer arrays can be declared as assumed length in subprograms, as in

```
integer table (*)
```

but there is no way to recover the size of the array if it is not passed as a separate argument.

Fortran does not provide the luxury of user-defined data types, and Fortran programmers must choose between the alternative representations. We have chosen to use the intrinsic Fortran character type for its greater flexibility, although both choices have their merits. Pascal provides for derived types, but has no special intrinsic string type or string operators; a Pascal string is simply an array of characters. An integer representation in Pascal is as good a choice as a char representation, except for the storage, since string functions must be provided by the programmer in either case.

We regard the data type character*1 as a character, different from character*10, which is a string. Fortran, of course, makes no such distinction, but we make one in our own conventions. Character functions always have their length explicitly declared, as in

```
character*1 function fgetc (u, c)
```

while string functions are uniformly declared as character*(*). We use the character ASCII value 26 as EOF since this is recognized as end of file by the VMS operating system. It can be generated from the keyboard by typing CON-TROL/Z (on most keyboards the nonprintable ASCII characters can be generated by typing CONTROL and the letter corresponding to the number, i.e. CONTROL/A generates an ASCII value of 1 and CONTROL/Z generates 26).

The length of almost all of our strings is MAXSTR which has the value 255 in our system. This is long enough that very few instances of actual strings exceeding this length ever occur, at the expense of wasted space. It is better not to worry too much about wasted space until you actually run out of it, a situation that doesn't happen too much in modern computer systems (ones with virtual memory). Being overly concerned with string lengths tends to lead to many special length specifiers hard-coded into various subprograms. This can at least be saved for the very end if storage space becomes an issue.

The len function only provides the declared maximum length of a string, and generally the actual string stored is shorter than the maximum length. We use a special termination character, ASCII value 0, as the last character in all strings. Such strings are called *null-terminated* strings. This is hardly the norm in Fortran code, but is the most common method of string representation in assembly language programming and in some high-level languages such as C. The advantage of this convention is the elimination of any need for carrying around a length variable for each string. The length of a null-terminated string is given by the expression index(string,NULL) - 1, where NULL is a symbolic name for ASCII 0.

The use of null-terminated strings has some drawbacks and some trade-offs to consider. The use of the standard character representation means that the string termination character must be a valid character (that is, it can't be -1 or some other value outside the range of character values) and therefore any strings that need to contain this termination character literally will be troublesome. Fortunately, the ASCII null character is so widely used as a string termination character that it is rarely used for anything else. In our code, the termination character could be changed in exactly one place, in global.def, to fix the code everywhere if the choice of a particular termination character ever became a problem.

Fortran has an intrinsic method of string comparison in which the strings can be of different lengths; if the longer string matches the shorter string exactly up to its length, and contains only blanks beyond, then the strings are equal. This means, however, that strings must be padded with blanks before comparison. Use of a termination character will cause the standard Fortran string comparison method to fail on strings that should be considered identical, if any garbage characters are present in either string beyond the termination character. The use of a termination character eliminates the need for blank padding strings but also demands that a special string comparison routine be used to compare strings. An advantage of null termination is that there is no need to search for the end of a string before doing something with it, or any need to clear character buffers before use. The price we must pay is the development of tools to support null-terminated strings. The simplification in code and especially in interfaces between routines is worth the price.

4.2   A String-Handling Library

Our choice for string termination leads to an immediate requirement for at least a small set of low-level string functions to do common operations not provided for by the language. For starters we need a function equal to compare null-terminated strings for equality up to the NULL character, returning true only if both are identical and the same length. We always use equal rather than Fortran comparison for strings, thus eliminating the need to clear (fill with blanks) a string buffer prior to use.

```
! equal  -  compare two strings for equality

      logical function equal(s,t)
      character*(*) s,t
      include      'global.def'
      integer      i

      i = 1
      do while (s(i:i) .ne. NULL)
         if (s(i:i) .ne. t(i:i)) then
            equal = .false.
            return
         end if
         i = i + 1
      end do

      if (t(i:i) .eq. NULL) then
         equal = .true.
      else
         equal = .false.
      end if

      return
      end
```

We can easily form null-terminated strings using the concatenation operator:

```
call fputstr(STDERR,'this is a literal string'//NULL)
```

However, we occasionally want to concatenate two string variables; this operation can be done in a single Fortran statement, but is worthy of its own library routine:

```
! cat  -  concatenate two null-terminated strings
```

```
      character*(*) function cat (str1, str2)
      character*(*) str1, str2
      include       'global.def'
      integer       i1, i2

      i1 = index(str1,NULL) - 1
      i2 = index(str2,NULL) - 1
      cat = str1(1:i1)//str2(1:i2)//NULL

      return
      end
```

We can also immediately see the possibility of having to make the null-terminated string scheme interface with other Fortran programs or operating system routines that require blank-padded strings. We have two routines to convert formats, one for each direction: fortstr converts its null-terminated argument into a blank-padded result, and nullstr converts a grungy old Fortran string to our form.

```
! fortstr  -  pad string buffer with spaces from null byte to end

      character*(*) function fortstr (string)
      character*(*) string
      integer i, p, length
      include 'global.def'

      p = index (string,NULL)
      length = len (fortstr)
      if (p .eq. 1) then
         fortstr = ' '
      else if (length .lt. p) then
         call fputstr (STDERR, 'fortstr: output string truncated'//EOL)
         fortstr(1:length) = string(1:length)
      else
         fortstr = string(1:p)
      end if

      return
      end
```

```
! nullstr  -  null-terminate an unterminated string

      character*(*) function nullstr (str)
      character*(*) str
      include       'global.def'
      integer       i

      i = len(str)
      do while (i .gt. 0 .and. str(i:i) .eq. BLANK)
         i = i - 1
```

```
      end do
      if (i .eq. 0) then
         nullstr = NULL
      else
         nullstr = str(1:i)//NULL
      end if

      return
      end
```

These are about the only routines in our library that will have anything to do with strings that are not null-terminated. All of the others demand strings to be null-terminated, and generally will crash the program or at least produce weird bugs if given a string with a missing NULL. The only exception to the rule is qindex, which is designed to be just like the Fortran index function except that it will not report a match of a substring if it is protected by quotes.

```
! qindex  -  get index of substring if outside of quotes

      integer function qindex (s1, s2)
      character*(*) s1, s2
      include       'global.def'
      integer       i
      logical       inquote

      if (index(s1,s2) .gt. 0) then
         inquote = .false.
         do i = 1, len(s1) - len(s2)
            if (s1(i:i) .eq. QUOTE) then
               inquote = (.not. inquote)
            else if (.not. inquote) then
               if (index(s1(i:),s2) .eq. 1) then
                  qindex = i
                  return
               end if
            end if
         end do
      end if
      qindex = 0

      return
      end
```

Another string manipulation tool we often need is a routine to get the next word from a string, starting at some initial position. The function getword does this, returning the next word both as the function result and as the argument word. getword does almost the same thing as getargs, but returns each word on a separate call, automatically updating the line pointer to the start of the next word. The complicated looking code in the loop

```
lp = 1
do while (.not. equal(getword(word,line,lp), EOL))
    if (equal(word, 'hello'//NULL)) then
        . . .
    else if (equal(word, 'goodbye'//NULL)) then
        . . .
    else
        . . .
    end if
end do
```

would scan through all of the words in line, comparing them with a list of things to be recognized, and properly terminating the loop when the whole line has been processed. The same design principle as in fgetc and fopen is used in getword, namely that the function returns the same information in the function result and in one of its arguments to facilitate using the function in conditional expressions.

```
! getword  -  get word from line at lp and increment lp

    character*(*) function getword (word, line, lp)
    character*(*) word, line
    integer       lp, wp, L
    include       'global.def'

    L = len(word)
    do while (line(lp:lp) .eq. BLANK) !skip blanks
        lp = lp + 1
    end do

    if (line(lp:lp) .eq. NEWLINE) then
        word = NEWLINE//NULL
    else
        wp = 1
        do while (wp .ne. L .and.
    &              line(lp:lp) .ne. BLANK .and.
    &              line(lp:lp) .ne. NEWLINE)
            word(wp:wp) = line(lp:lp)
            wp = wp + 1
            lp = lp + 1
        end do
        word(wp:wp) = NULL

    end if
    getword = word
    return
    end
```

getword has a naive definition of "word" as any sequence of nonblanks; it is even less intelligent than getargs in this respect since getargs returns any quoted string as a single argument, even with embedded blanks. The getword function makes no such distinctions.

The tool nextc does by character what getword does by string; nextc returns the next nonblank character from a string, skipping blanks in the process. As in getword, the line pointer is left pointing just past the character returned:

```
! nextc  -  get next nonblank character from line

        character*1 function nextc (c, line, lp)
        character*1   c
        character*(*) line
        integer       lp
        include       'global.def'

        do while (line(lp:lp) .eq. BLANK)
           lp = lp + 1
        end do
        c = line(lp:lp)
        nextc = c
        lp = lp + 1

        return
        end
```

Classifying Characters

It is convenient to have some tools that determine membership of a character in a set, such as the set of letters or digits. There are several useful character sets we can identify immediately:

Character Set	Function
Letters	isletter
Uppercase letters	isupper
Lowercase letters	islower
Digit	isdigit
Hex digit	ishex
Letter or digit	isalpha

and here are the corresponding functions:

```
! isletter  -  true if character is a letter

        logical function isletter(c)
        character*1 c
        isletter = ((lge(c,'a') .and. lle(c,'z'))
     &       .or.  (lge(c,'A') .and. lle(c,'Z')))
        return
        end
```

```
! isupper  -  true if character is uppercase letter

        logical    function isupper(c)
        implicit   none
        character*1 c

        isupper = (lge(c,'A') .and. lle(c,'Z'))
        return
        end


! islower  -  true if character is lowercase letter

        logical    function islower(c)
        character*1 c
        islower = (lge(c,'a') .and. lle(c,'z'))
        return
        end


! isdigit  -  return true if character is a digit

        logical function isdigit (c)
        character*1 c

        isdigit = (lge(c,'0') .and. lle(c,'9'))
        return
        end


! ishex  -  test character for hex digit

        logical function ishex(c)
        character*1 c
        ishex = ((lge(c,'0') .and. lle(c,'9'))
     &    .or.  (lge(c,'a') .and. lle(c,'f'))
     &    .or.  (lge(c,'A') .and. lle(c,'F')))
        return
        end


! isalpha  -  true if character is any letter or digit

        logical    function isalpha(c)
        character*1 c

        isalpha = ((lge(c,'0') .and. lle(c,'9'))
     &     .or.  (lge(c,'a') .and. lle(c,'z'))
     &     .or.  (lge(c,'A') .and. lle(c,'Z')))
        return
        end
```

We can use these character classification functions for a variety of useful string operations; uppercase conversion is straightforward.

```
! upper  -  convert string to uppercase except where enclosed in quotes

        character*(*) function upper(string)
        character*(*) string
        include      'global.def'
        integer      i

        i = 1
        do while (string(i:i) .ne. NULL)
           if (string(i:i) .eq. QUOTE) then
              upper(i:i) = QUOTE
              i = i + 1
              do while (string(i:i) .ne. QUOTE .and. string(i:i) .ne. NULL)
                 upper(i:i) = string(i:i)
                 i = i + 1
              end do
              upper(i:i) = string(i:i)
              if (string(i:i) .ne. NULL) i = i + 1
           else
              if (llt(string(i:i),'a') .or. lgt(string(i:i),'z')) then
                 upper(i:i) = string(i:i)
              else
                 upper(i:i) =
     &           char (ichar('A') - ichar('a') + ichar(string(i:i)))
              end if
              i = i + 1
           end if
        end do

        upper(i:i) = NULL
        return
        end
```

Portions of the input string enclosed in quotes are undisturbed. The upper routine simply loops through the input string performing an arithmetic conversion on lowercase letters.

There are a few things to watch out for in our string-handling library concerning character sets. In the preceding routines, we have used the Fortran intrinsic functions lle and lge to guarantee the comparison is made according to the ASCII collating sequence. These character classifications are thus independent of the host machine's character set and can be expected to work on any system. equal didn't concern itself with the character set at all because it only tests for equality. But we must beware that not all machines use the ASCII character set, and that the Fortran ichar function doesn't necessarily use ASCII. Thus upper can be expected to fail on systems that don't use ASCII since it relies on the fact that ASCII uppercase and lowercase letters have an uninterrupted sequence of character codes so that ichar('A')-ichar('a') is the distance between an uppercase letter and its lowercase equivalent. Anywhere the integer value of a character code is used, a special primitive aichar could replace the Fortran ichar function and remap the host computer character set onto the ASCII set. Otherwise, routines needing integer codes for characters must be viewed as primitives if the algorithms depend in any way on the ordering of character codes.

String Conversions

Since we have implemented a portable replacement of Fortran I/O that accepts only character strings, we need a set of conversion routines which translate numbers from character strings to their internal representations and vice versa. Here is a list of the conversion routines:

Conversion	Function
ASCII to integer	atoi
Integer to ASCII	itoa
ASCII to floating	atof
Floating to ASCII	ftoa
Integer to hex	itoh
Hex to integer	htoi

These routines do the job usually handled by the Fortran format statement, but they do not put the output in fixed-width fields.

atoi scans through the input string and multiplies the accumulated value by ten for each new decimal digit:

```
! atoi  -  convert ascii string to integer

        integer function atoi (string)
        character*(*)  string
        include    'global.def'
        integer    i, sign
        logical    isdigit

        atoi = 0
        i. = 1
        do while (string(i:i) .eq. ' ')
           i = i + 1
        end do
        sign = 1
        if (string(i:i) .eq. '+' .or. string(i:i) .eq. '-') then
           if (string(i:i) .eq. '-') sign = -1
           i = i + 1
        end if
        do while (isdigit (string(i:i)))
           atoi = 10 * atoi + ichar (string(i:i)) - ichar ('0')
           i = i + 1
        end do
```

```
atoi = atoi * sign
return
end
```

The itoa function performs the conversion in reverse:

```
! itoa  -  convert integer to string

      character*(*) function itoa (ival)
      integer      ival
      include      'global.def'
      character*16 buffer
      integer      i, n, sign

      if (ival .eq. 0) then
         itoa = '0'//NULL
         return
      else if (ival .lt. 0) then
         sign = -1
      else
         sign = 1
      end if

      n = abs(ival)
      buffer(16:16) = NULL
      i = 16
      do while (n .gt. 0)
         i = i - 1
         buffer(i:i) = char(mod(n,10) + ichar('0'))
         n = n / 10
      end do
      if (sign .eq. -1) then
         i = i - 1
         buffer(i:i) = '-'
      end if

      itoa = buffer(i:16)
      return
      end
```

The atof function performs a more complicated conversion since it must deal with decimal points and an optional power of 10.

```
! atof  -  convert string to floating point number

      real function atof (str)
      character*(*)  str
      include        'global.def'
      real           val, power
      integer        exponent, sign, esign, i
      logical        isdigit
```

```
      sign = 1
      val = 0.
      power = 1.
      exponent = 0
      esign = 1
      i = 1
      do while (str(i:i) .eq. ' ')
         i = i + 1
      end do
      if (str(i:i) .eq. '+' .or. str(i:i) .eq. '-') then
         if (str(i:i) .eq. '-') sign = -1
         i = i + 1
      end if
      do while (isdigit(str(i:i)))
         val = 10.*val + ichar(str(i:i)) - ichar('0')
         i = i + 1
      end do
      if (str(i:i) .eq. '.') then
         i = i + 1
         do while (isdigit(str(i:i)))
            val = 10.*val + ichar(str(i:i)) - ichar('0')
            i = i + 1
            power = 10. * power
         end do
      end if
      if (str(i:i) .eq. 'e' .or. str(i:i) .eq. 'E') then
         i = i + 1
         if (str(i:i) .eq. '+' .or. str(i:i) .eq. '-') then
            if (str(i:i) .eq. '-') esign = -1
            i = i + 1
         end if
         do while (isdigit(str(i:i)))
            exponent = 10*exponent + ichar(str(i:i)) - ichar('0')
            i = i + 1
         end do
      end if

      atof = (sign * val / power) * 10.**(esign * exponent)
      return
      end
```

Experienced Fortran programmers are no doubt chuckling at this point about our use of complicated routines to do what can be accomplished with a few statements using internal files. atoi could be written

```
      write (buffer, '(i15)') ival
      i = 1
      do while (buffer(i:i) .eq. BLANK)
         i = i + 1
      end do
      atoi = buffer(i:15)//NULL
```

In fact, in VAX Fortran we could just say write(buffer,*) using list-directed formatting, but this is disallowed for some obscure reason in standard Fortran 77. The reason for not using internal files is mainly to avoid using Fortran I/O if possible on microcomputers with limited memory, with the hope that the host compiler won't include Fortran I/O in the executable image; it is also kind of nice to be able to do it on your own. In our tests of IBM-PC programs that do not use Fortran I/O in the primitives, replacing versions of itoa and atoi using internal files with the ones shown here reduced the size of executable programs by 21K bytes. However, the conversion logic is more difficult for ftoa than for the others, and we are not gluttons for punishment, so ftoa uses an internal file:

```
! ftoa  -  return ascii string from floating point input

        character*(*) function ftoa (rval)
        real    rval
        include 'global.def'
        integer i

        write (ftoa, '(1P,G13.6)') rval
        i = 1
        do while (ftoa(i:i) .eq. BLANK)
           i = i + 1
        end do
        ftoa = ftoa(i:)
        i = len (ftoa)
        do while (ftoa(i:i) .eq. BLANK .or. ftoa(i:i) .eq. '0')
           i = i - 1
        end do
        if (ftoa(i:i) .eq. '.') i = i + 1

        ftoa = ftoa(1:i)//NULL
        return
        end
```

htoi does the same thing as atoi except it multiplies each digit by 16 instead of 10 and has to do more work to decode the letters a–f.

```
! htoi  -  convert a hexadecimal string to integer

        integer function htoi (string)
        character*(*) string
        include     'global.def'
        integer     i
        logical     done

        i = 1
        do while (string(i:i) .eq. BLANK)
           i = i + 1
        end do
```

```
      htoi = 0
      done = .false.
      do while (.not. done)
         if (lge(string(i:i), '0') .and. lle(string(i:i), '9')) then
            htoi = htoi * 16 + ichar(string(i:i)) - ichar('0')
         else if (lge(string(i:i), 'A') .and. lle(string(i:i), 'F')) then
            htoi = htoi * 16 + 10 + ichar(string(i:i)) - ichar('A')
         else if (lge(string(i:i), 'a') .and. lle(string(i:i), 'f')) then
            htoi = htoi * 16 + 10 + ichar(string(i:i)) - ichar('a')
         else
            done = .true.
         end if
         i = i + 1
      end do

      return
      end
```

The last one is itoh:

```
! itoh  -  convert integer value to hexadecimal string

      character*(*) function itoh (ival)
      integer     ival
      include     'global.def'
      character*16 buffer
      integer     i, j, n, sign

      if (ival .lt. 0) then
         call fputstr (STDERR, 'itoh: negative value not allowed'//EOL)
         itoh = '0'//NULL
         return
      end if

      n = ival
      buffer(16:16) = NULL
      i = 16
      do while (n .gt. 0)
         i = i - 1
         j = mod(n,16)
         if (j .le. 9) then
            buffer(i:i) = char(j + ichar('0'))
         else
            buffer(i:i) = char(j-10 + ichar('A'))
         end if
         n = n / 16
      end do

      itoh = buffer(i:16)
      return
      end
```

The restriction of the I/O primitives to deal with only character strings forces some means of character conversion on us, and the preceding routines are the basic string tools for building up a line of text containing numbers; however, they do not make printing of tables with aligned columns very easy. This would be a major drawback if it weren't for internal files, which can always be used for formatting numbers in columns prior to output. Code something like

```
do i = 1, 10
    write (line(1:78), '(3(I10))') a(i), b(i), c(i)
    call fputstr (uout, line(1:78)//EOL)
end do
```

can be used to get columns of numbers and still retain the flexibility of the primitives. Null-terminated strings can also be output in columns with something like

```
write (line(1:78), '(2(4x,A16))') fortstr(s1), fortstr(s2)
```

Internal files make our new tools tolerable for use in the number-crunching programs that are the domain of most Fortran programmers. At the same time, the conversion routines in our tools library make Fortran tolerable for string processing applications, giving us the best of both worlds.

The Escape Character

We are now going to introduce a special routine that adds a useful extension to any program that performs character manipulation. It causes a special interpretation of the characters at the current input position. The routine is called escchar; in the calling program it is used in a loop of the form

```
do while (line(lp:lp) .ne. NULL)
    if (line(lp:lp) .eq. ESCAPE) then
        c = escchar (line, lp)
    else
        c = line(lp:lp)
        lp = lp + 1
    end if
    . . .
end do
```

The routine looks for an ESCAPE character and, if present, does some special interpretation of the characters following it. In our version, the backslash is the escape character, defined in global.def. The C language has an escape convention like this one, and also uses the backslash character. We have already seen some examples of strings using escape sequences in Chapter 2.

escchar recognizes special codes for the most common nonprintable characters, and a means of specifying any 8-bit unsigned integer value for a character.

Character	Escape Sequence
Blank	\b
Tab	\t
Null	\0
Newline	\n
Backslash	\\
Decimal encoded	\d000–\d255
Hex encoded	\h00–\hFF

Thus the string "hello, world\h07\n" would be transformed to the string "hello, world" followed by ASCII character 07 (which should ring the terminal bell) followed by NEWLINE.

```
! escchar  -  interpret escaped characters

      character*1 function escchar (line, lp)
      character*(*) line
      integer       lp
      include       'global.def'
      character*1   c
      logical       isdigit, ishex, valid
      integer       atoi, htoi, k

      lp = lp + 1
      if (line(lp:lp) .eq. 'n') then
         c = NEWLINE
         lp = lp + 1
      else if (line(lp:lp) .eq. 't') then
         c = TAB
         lp = lp + 1
      else if (line(lp:lp) .eq. 'b') then
         c = BLANK
         lp = lp + 1
      else if (line(lp:lp) .eq. '0') then
         c = NULL
         lp = lp + 1
      else if (line(lp:lp) .eq. 'f') then
         c = FORMFEED
         lp = lp + 1
      else if (line(lp:lp) .eq. ESCAPE) then
         c = ESCAPE
         lp = lp + 1
      else if (line(lp:lp) .eq. 'd') then              !decimal
         valid = isdigit(line(lp+1:lp+1)) .and.
     &           isdigit(line(lp+2:lp+2)) .and.
     &           isdigit(line(lp+3:lp+3))
         if (valid) then
            k = atoi(line(lp+1:lp+3)//NULL)
            valid = ((k .ge. 0) .and. (k .le. 255))
         end if
         if (valid) then
```

```
         c = char(k)
         lp = lp + 4
      else
         c = 'd'
         lp = lp + 1
      end if
   else if (line(lp:lp) .eq. 'h') then            !hexadecimal
      valid = ishex(line(lp+1:lp+1)) .and.
   &              ishex(line(lp+2:lp+2))
      if (valid) then
         k = htoi(line(lp+1:lp+2)//NULL)
         valid = ((k .ge. 0) .and. (k .le. 255))
      end if
      if (valid) then
         c = char(k)
         lp = lp + 3
      else
         c = 'h'
         lp = lp + 1
      end if
   else                                           !unrecognized
      c = line(lp:lp)
      lp = lp + 1
   end if

   escchar = c
   return
   end
```

Any other character following ESCAPE just returns the character itself. This is a reasonable default action and can be used to advantage for programs that use special "metacharacters," characters that have a special meaning. If the character & means something special to a program, and the program filters its input through escchar, the special meaning can be overridden by preceding it with backslash.

escchar has a companion routine called doescape that processes an entire input string for escaped characters. doescape is dead simple:

```
! doescape  -  replace escape sequences in string

      character*(*) function doescape (string)
      character*(*) string
      include      'global.def'
      integer      i, j
      character*1  escchar

      i = 1    !input pointer
      j = 1    !output pointer
      do while (string(i:i) .ne. NULL)
         if (string(i:i) .eq. ESCAPE) then
            doescape(j:j) = escchar(string,i)
```

```
        j = j + 1
      else
        doescape(j:j) = string(i:i)
        i = i + 1
        j = j + 1
      end if
    end do
    doescape(j:j) = NULL

    return
    end
```

In most applications of the escape mechanism, doescape is useless. A primary use of escchar is to escape metacharacters in some input language, and processing the escapes before scanning the string removes the backslashes in front of any characters other than the built-in sequences given in the table, which defeats the purpose as far as metacharacters are concerned. In applications for which only the built-in sequences are needed, however, doescape is convenient.

Classifying Tokens

The getword routine is a convenient tool for dividing an input line into smaller pieces. The smaller pieces can be used to ascertain the meaning of each line of input, providing a very simple form of *parsing*. Parsing is associated with the idea of language recognition, usually in connection with what compilers do, or what your brain does in reading this sentence. However, any computer program that reads input could be considered to be parsing a language. We might view finclude as parsing the language

$$
\begin{aligned}
S &::= A|B \\
A &::= \text{``#include''} word \\
B &::= \; < \text{other} > \\
word &::= \; < \text{any except BLANK} >
\end{aligned}
$$

A data file is the simplest computer language. It has just one possible sentence form, differing only by the values in the data fields, and is correspondingly easy to "parse."

Parsing methods range from the very simple to the very sophisticated, depending on the language to be parsed. A discussion of some of the more advanced parsing methods is provided in Chapter 8. Meanwhile, we will use a simple ad hoc method of interpreting input that is not very sophisticated but is adequate for many useful mini-languages. We need something a little better than getword. Instead of looking for words separated by blanks, our ad hoc routines test the current input position for *tokens* of a given class. They are logical functions, returning true if the input matches the token class and false if it doesn't. If true, the token in the input is *accepted*, meaning that the literal string matched is returned and the line pointer is advanced to just past it. If the input does not match what the function requires, the line pointer is not disturbed (except to skip blanks) so that another tokenizing routine can be called to test for the next alternative in the grammar of the language. To illustrate, here is the routine to recognize integers:

```
! is_ival  -  get integer from input text

        logical    function    is_ival (ival, line, lp)
        include               'global.def'
        integer               ival, lp
        character*(*)         line
        integer               i, atoi
        logical               isdigit

        do while (line(lp:lp) .eq. BLANK)
           lp = lp + 1
        end do
        i = lp
        if (line(i:i) .eq. '+' .or. line(i:i) .eq. '-') then
           i = i + 1
        end if
        if (isdigit(line(i:i))) then
           do while (isdigit(line(i:i)))
              i = i + 1
           end do
           ival = atoi(line(lp:i-1)//NULL)
           lp = i
           is_ival = .true.
        else
           is_ival = .false.
           ival = 0
        end if

        return
        end
```

Note that `is_ival` doesn't need a blank to delimit an integer like `getword` does; any character other than digit marks the end, and `is_ival` only needs one character of lookahead.

There is a methodical and practically bullet-proof way to write recognizers for just about any kind of token, using a *state transition diagram*. The diagram is an efficient way to describe the recognition problem and is easily translated to code. As an example, figure 4.1 is a state transition diagram for signed real values.

The numbers in circles represent states, and the arcs represent transitions to other states when the corresponding character is seen in the input. The states in double circles are accepting states, meaning that the characters seen so far make a valid real number token. If an input character does not match any of the transitions for that state, the recognizer terminates. As an example, the character string

```
0.5e-5 is a real number
```

is recognized as a real number, starting at state 1 and passing through the sequence of states 1–4–6–6–7–9–10. When the blank space after the number is read, there is no transition in the diagram, so the match terminates.

The translation to code is straightforward. A node with more than one branch out translates to an if...else if...end if construct; a node containing a branch that loops back into itself is represented by a while construct. Each time an input character causes a transition to an accepting state (the states in double circles), a token pointer is advanced to save that position so that the routine doesn't fail on an input like

```
3.47error
```

This string must be scanned past the e to find out that there is no exponent part, and the valid real number 3.47 must be recognized and the position of the last digit remembered. Here is the resulting routine for recognizing real numbers:

```
! is_rval  -  get a real number from input text

        logical function is_rval (rval, line, lp)
        real            rval
        character*(*)   line
        integer         lp, tp, i
        include         'global.def'
        real            atof
```

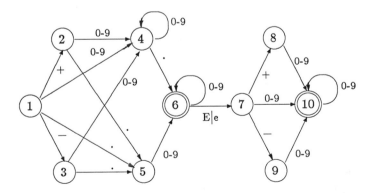

Figure 4.1: State transition diagram for real numbers.

```
logical            matched, isdigit

do while (line(lp:lp) .eq. BLANK)
   lp = lp + 1
end do
i = lp
if (line(i:i) .eq. '+' .or. line(i:i) .eq. '-') i = i + 1
if (isdigit(line(i:i))) then
   do while (isdigit(line(i:i)))
      i = i + 1
   end do
   if (line(i:i) .eq. '.') then
      i = i + 1
      do while (isdigit(line(i:i)))
         i = i + 1
      end do
      matched = .true.
   else
      matched = .false.
   end if
else if (line(i:i) .eq. '.') then
   i = i + 1
   if (isdigit(line(i:i))) then
      do while (isdigit(line(i:i)))
         i = i + 1
      end do
      matched = .true.
   else
      matched = .false.
   end if
else
   matched = .false.
end if
! get optional exponent
tp = i - 1       !set temporary pointer to last digit or decimal point
if (matched) then
   if (line(i:i) .eq. 'e' .or. line(i:i) .eq. 'E') then
      i = i + 1
      if (line(i:i) .eq. '+' .or. line(i:i) .eq. '-') i = i + 1
      if (isdigit(line(i:i))) then
         do while (isdigit(line(i:i)))
            i = i + 1
         end do
         rval = atof (line(lp:i-1)//NULL)
         lp = i
      else
         rval = atof (line(lp:tp)//NULL)
         lp = tp + 1
      end if
   else
      rval = atof (line(lp:tp)//NULL)
      lp = tp + 1
   end if
```

```
else
   rval = 0.0
end if

is_rval = matched
return
end
```

For completeness, there are routines for recognizing integers, reals, logicals, quoted strings, and identifiers as tokens; the others are simple enough to write without the aid of a diagram. The is_lval function recognizes Fortran-style logical constants:

```
! is_lval  -  test for logical constant

      logical function is_lval (lval, line, lp)
      character*(*)      line
      integer           lp, i, j
      logical           lval, found, equal
      include           'global.def'
      character*(MAXSTR) upper

      i = lp
      do while (line(i:i) .eq. BLANK)
         i = i + 1
      end do
      j = index (line, NULL) - 1
      found = .false.
      if (j-i .ge. 6) then
         if (equal(upper(line(i:i+6)//NULL),'.FALSE.'//NULL)) then
            found = .true.
            lval = .false.
            lp = i + 7
         else if (equal(upper(line(i:i+5)//NULL),'.TRUE.'//NULL)) then
            found = .true.
            lval = .true.
            lp = i + 6
         end if
      else if (j-i .ge. 5) then
         if (equal(upper(line(i:i+5)//NULL),'.TRUE.'//NULL)) then
            found = .true.
            lval = .true.
            lp = i + 6
         end if
      else
         lp = i
      end if

      is_lval = found

      return
      end
```

This can easily be extended to deal with fuzzy logic operations or political debate simulations by adding code to recognize .maybe. as a logical constant.

The string recognition accepts two successive quote characters as a single literal quote in a string, just like Fortran does.

```
! is_sval  -  get quoted string from input text

        logical    function   is_sval (string, line, lp)
        integer               lp, i, p
        character*(*)         line, string
        include               'global.def'

        do while (line(lp:lp) .eq. BLANK)
          lp = lp + 1
        end do
        i = lp
        if (line(i:i) .eq. QUOTE) then
          i = i + 1
        else
          is_sval = .false.
          string(1:1) = NULL
          return
        end if
        p = 1
        do while (line(i:i) .ne. QUOTE .and. line(i:i) .ne. NULL)
          string(p:p) = line(i:i)
          p = p + 1
          i = i + 1
          if (line(i:i) .eq. QUOTE .and. line(i+1:i+1) .eq. QUOTE) then
            string(p:p) = QUOTE
            p = p + 1
            i = i + 2       !bump past literal quote
          end if
        end do
        if (line(i:i) .eq. QUOTE) then
          is_sval = .true.
          string(p:p) = NULL
          lp = i + 1
        else
          is_sval = .false.
          string(1:1) = NULL
        end if

        return
        end
```

is_sval processes the string into its internal form by removing the outer quotes and converting two successive quote characters to a single literal quote.

Our routine for recognizing identifiers accepts dollar signs and underscores, as does VAX Fortran, but also allows dollar or underscore as the first character in an identifier, which Fortran does not allow:

```
! is_ident  -  get identifier from input text

      logical function is_ident (ident, line, lp)
      include       'global.def'
      character*(*) ident, line
      integer       i, lp
      logical       isletter, isdigit, isalpha

      do while (line(lp:lp) .eq. BLANK)
         lp = lp + 1
      end do

      i = lp
      if (line (i:i).eq.'$' .or. line (i:i).eq.'_'
     &   .or. isletter (line(i:i))) then
         is_ident = .true.
         i = i + 1
         do while (line(i:i) .eq. '$' .or. line(i:i) .eq. '_'
     &               .or. isalpha (line(i:i)))
            i = i + 1
         end do
         ident = line (lp:i-1) // NULL
         lp = i
      else
         is_ident   = .false.
         ident(1:1) = NULL
      end if

      return
      end
```

All of the token classification routines are designed to recognize Fortran style tokens, so they can be used either for processing Fortran source code or for designing mini-languages.

Wildcard Matching

We wrap up this chapter with some routines for pattern matching with wildcard characters. Most computer operating systems provide some means of performing operations on multiple files specified with wildcard characters, but the interpretation of the wildcard characters may be different on different systems. For instance, VAX DCL accepts multiple wildcard characters in a file specification; a * can match zero or more characters in a file name, and a % matches exactly one character. The MS–DOS wildcard matching algorithm cannot handle more than one * in the name part and one in the extension part of a filename; the specification *abc*.* matches all files in a directory, not just ones containing abc as a substring. DOS uses a question mark to match exactly one character, rather than %.

There are three good reasons for writing our own wildcard matching routines:

- Programs can be made more uniform on multiple host computers by using the same wildcard matching routine rather than relying on the facilities of the host computer. A wildcard matching routine supplemented by a primitive for retrieving directory entries is all that is needed, and would allow programs to process command line arguments with wildcards.

- The wildcard matching algorithm can be used for operations other than filename matching, since wildcard handling is useful for any text searching application.

- We can access the substrings matched by each wildcard character and perform pattern substitution, as in the change program presented later.

The function wcmatch performs wildcard pattern matching and returns an array w containing the substrings matched by each wildcard character; it returns true if the input string matches the wildcard pattern. The * character is the only wildcard and recognizes zero or more characters. The pattern

```
*abc*
```

matches any of the following strings:

```
thisisabc
abcisthis
isabcthis?
```

In the first case, the first wildcard matches "thisis" and the second wildcard matches the "empty string." The routine has no restrictions on the characters in the string to be searched, which can even contain blanks; however the pattern must match the entire string. The pattern can have the escape character to specify nonprintable characters or the wildcard character itself.

wcmatch will only match the shortest possible string in the input for each wildcard character, even though longer matching sequences may exist. For example, the pattern

```
aa*bb*xyz
```

matches

```
aa@bb@xyz
```

but not

```
aa@bb@xyz@bb@xyz
```

even though the pattern does match the string. Properly handling pathological cases would be nice but would also complicate the program, and such cases rarely occur in practice. In most instances the pattern can be specified differently to avoid the problem altogether, so to keep life simple we just won't worry about it.

```
! wcmatch  -  match string and pattern with wildcards

    logical function wcmatch (string, pattern, w)
    character*(*)      string, pattern, w (*)
    include            'global.def'
    integer            i, j, k, n, L, i2, count
    character*(MAXSTR) substr
    character*1        escchar
    logical            done

    done = .false.
    L = index (string, NULL)
    i = 1                   !string pointer
    j = 1                   !pattern pointer
    count = 0               !wildcard count
    do while (.not. done)
       if (string(i:i) .eq. NULL .and. pattern(j:j) .eq. NULL) then
          wcmatch = .true.
          done = .true.
       else if (pattern(j:j) .eq. WILDCARD) then
          count = count + 1
          if (pattern(j+1:j+1) .eq. NULL) then   !match to end
             w(count) = string(i:index(string,NULL))
             wcmatch = .true.
             done = .true.
          else
             j = j + 1
             k = j
             n = 0
             do while ((pattern(j:j) .ne. WILDCARD) .and.
   &                   (pattern(j:j) .ne. NULL))  !find literal substring
                n = n + 1
                if (pattern(j:j) .eq. ESCAPE) then
                   substr(n:n) = escchar(pattern,j)
                else
                   substr(n:n) = pattern(j:j)
                   j = j + 1
                end if
             end do
             i2 = index (string(i:L), substr(1:n))
             if (i2 .eq. 0) then
                wcmatch = .false.
                done = .true.
             else
                if (i2 .eq. 1) then
                   w(count) = NULL
                else
                   w(count) = string(i:i+i2-2)//NULL
                end if
                i = i + i2 + j - k - 1
             end if
          end if
       else if (pattern(j:j) .eq. ESCAPE) then
```

```
            if (string(i:i) .eq. escchar(pattern,j)) then
               i = i + 1
            else
               wcmatch = .false.
               done = .true.
            end if
         else if (string(i:i) .eq. pattern(j:j)) then !ordinary character
            i = i + 1
            j = j + 1
         else               !ordinary character and failed
            wcmatch = .false.
            done = .true.
         end if
      end do

      return
      end
```

The routine works by looking beyond each wildcard character for a substring of literal characters to be matched. The remainder of the input string is searched for a match to this literal character sequence, and the wildcard is used to match all of the intervening text. The wildcard strings are returned null-terminated in array w, whose size is determined by the calling program.

We can use wcmatch for file searching, and have a program find to do it. find searches through a file one word at a time looking for a match with the specified pattern; any lines containing a match are copied to the output. It has an option -u to perform the search ignoring case. The case conversion is only performed temporarily, so that the input case is preserved.

```
! find   -   search file for pattern and print matching lines

      program find
      include           'global.def'
      integer           argc, nargs, uin, uout, fopen, lp, i
      character*(MAXSTR) argv (MAXARGS), w (10), line, pattern, word
      character*(MAXSTR) getword, upper
      logical           fgetline, wcmatch, caseflag, done

      call ioinit ()
      call getargs (argc, argv)
      if (argc .lt. 1 .or. argc .gt. 4) then
         call fputstr (STDERR, 'syntax: find pat [file1] [file2] [-u]'//EOL)
         stop ' '
      else
         nargs = 0
         caseflag = .false.
         uin = STDIN
         uout = STDOUT
         do i = 1, argc
            if (argv(i)(1:1) .eq. QUALIFIER) then
               argv(i) = upper(argv(i))
```

```
          caseflag = (index(argv(i),'U') .gt. 0)
       else
          nargs = nargs + 1
          if (nargs .eq. 1) then
             pattern = argv(i)
          else if (nargs .eq. 2) then
             if (fopen(uin,argv(i),IOREAD) .eq. IOERROR) stop ' '
          else if (nargs .eq. 3) then
             if (fopen(uout,argv(i),IOWRITE) .eq. IOERROR) stop ' '
          end if
       end if
    end do
end if

if (caseflag) pattern = upper(pattern)
do while (fgetline (uin, line))
   done = .false.
   lp = 1
   do while (.not. done)
      word = getword (word, line, lp)
      if (caseflag) word = upper(word)
      if (word(1:1) .eq. NEWLINE) then
         done = .true.
      else if (wcmatch(word, pattern, w)) then
         call fputstr (uout, line)
         done = .true.
      end if
   end do
end do

call fclose (uin)
call fclose (uout)
call iofinit ()
end
```

The wildcard string array returned by wcmatch can be used to perform text substitutions. The change command can do substitution operations with more flexibility than the corresponding function in many good text editors because of wildcards, and in addition is more convenient to use than a full-blown editor for some applications just because it is a single command. Like find, change searches through the input text by words and therefore cannot do substitutions on strings containing blanks. This enables it to perform multiple substitutions on a line while preserving the ability of wcmatch to be used for file name matching— a file name matching application would be pretty useless if a match was indicated on a pattern that only matched part of a file name. The actual reason that find searches by word is so that it matches the same strings as does change.

In the substitute pattern, wildcard characters have a one-to-one correspondence with the wildcards in the search pattern. Thus the command

```
$ change "abc*123*xyz" "abc*xyz"
```

and the input line

```
abcppp123qqqxyz
```

produces

```
abcpppxyz
```

In order to selectively use the strings matched by any wildcard character in the search pattern, some means must be provided to skip over any wildcards that aren't wanted in the substituted string. The tilde character in the substitute pattern in effect deletes the text of the corresponding wildcard in the search pattern. For example, the following command (using the shell in Chapter 9) makes a files list of a VAX directory:

```
$ dir/nohead/notrail/col=1 | change "*[*]*;*" "~~*" > dir.fil
```

In this case the third wildcard matches the file name and extension. Tildes and asterisks can be obtained in the output string by escaping them.

```
! change  -  substitute matched pattern with wildcards

        program change
        include          'global.def'
        integer          MAXWILD
        parameter        (MAXWILD = 10)
        integer          argc, uin, uout, fopen, lp, count, i
        character*(MAXSTR) argv (MAXARGS)
        character*(MAXSTR) srcpat, subspat, line, getword, word
        character*(MAXSTR) w (MAXWILD)   !wildcard match strings
        character*1      escchar
        logical          fgetline, wcmatch, done

        call ioinit ()
        call getargs (argc, argv)
        if (argc .lt. 2 .or. argc .gt. 4) then
            call fputstr (STDERR,
     &     'syntax: change pat1 pat2 [file1] [file2]'//EOL)
            stop ' '
        else
            srcpat = argv(1)
            subspat = argv(2)
            if (argc .ge. 3) then
                if (fopen(uin,argv(3),IOREAD) .eq. IOERROR) stop ' '
            else
                uin = STDIN
            end if
            if (argc .eq. 4) then
                if (fopen(uout,argv(4),IOWRITE) .eq. IOERROR) stop ' '
            else
                uout = STDOUT
```

```
         end if
      end if

      do while (fgetline (uin, line))
         done = .false.
         lp = 1
         do while (line(lp:lp) .ne. NEWLINE)
            if (line(lp:lp) .eq. BLANK) then
               call fputc (uout, BLANK)
               lp = lp + 1
            else
               word = getword (word, line, lp)
               do i = 1, MAXWILD
                  w(i) = NULL
               end do
               if (wcmatch(word, srcpat, w)) then
                  i = 1
                  count = 0
                  do while (subspat(i:i) .ne. NULL)
                     if (subspat(i:i) .eq. WILDCARD) then
                        count = count + 1
                        call fputstr (uout, w(count))
                        i = i + 1
                     else if (subspat(i:i) .eq. SKIPCARD) then
                        count = count + 1
                        i = i + 1
                     else if (subspat(i:i) .eq. ESCAPE) then
                        call fputc (uout, escchar(subspat,i))
                     else
                        call fputc (uout, subspat(i:i))
                        i = i + 1
                     end if
                  end do
               else
                  call fputstr (uout, word)
               end if
            end if
         end do
         call fputc (uout, NEWLINE)
      end do

      call fclose (uin)
      call fclose (uout)
      call iofinit ()
      end
```

Fortran is often maligned for its lack of facilities for character-oriented processing. This chapter has hopefully shown that this conception is wrong. The apparent deficiency of Fortran for string manipulation is primarily because of the methods traditionally used rather than because of a shortcoming of the language itself. The main shortcoming of Fortran for string handling is the lack of a standard library of routines for often-needed functions. As Fortran programmers we are faced with a choice: we either invest the up-front effort required to create our own standard library or we live with the continuing effort of hacking together a solution each time we are presented with similar problems.

We think the up-front effort has a favorable return on investment. The find and change commands are the only complete programs in this chapter, but there are dozens of other useful programs that can be built from this library at the drop of a hat. A good library goes a long way toward the goal of reusable software.

Exercises

1. Discuss the relative merits of a design for getargs similar to that used for getword, that is, arguments would be retrieved by a loop of the form

   ```
   do while (getarg (argv) .ne. EOL)
       if (equal (argv, 'STRING_A'//NULL)) then
           .
           .
           .
   ```

2. Discuss the relative merits of a design for getword similar to that used for getargs, that is, the line would be divided up into words in a single call:

   ```
   call getwords (wordcount, wordval, line)
   ```

   where wordval is an array of strings.

3. Write a version of ftoa that does not use internal files to perform the conversion.

4. Write a routine ftab for output of aligned columns, that is,

   ```
   call ftab (u, 20, '10.0'//NULL)
   ```

   writes "10.0" into the output buffer for unit u starting at character position 20. Make sure that intervening space is filled with blanks when writing past the end of the buffer. What other alternatives exist for implementing aligned columns of numbers?

5. Add an option -n in find to find all lines in a file that do *not* match the specified pattern.

6. Write a new version of change that performs its substitutions on lines rather than words so that the patterns may include blanks. How can you handle multiple occurrences of a pattern on a single line?

7. Write a program that does wildcard substitution of identifiers only.

8. Write a file filter to do uppercase conversion. Write another for lowercase conversion.

9. Is it worthwhile to write a routine fputesc that outputs a string containing escape characters to a file? For example,

```
call fputesc (u, 'This is a line of text\n\0')
```

outputs a line properly terminated with NEWLINE//NULL to unit u. Is the convenience worth the overhead?

Further Reading

Several of the routines in this chapter are essentially the same as those presented in Kernighan and Plauger in *Software Tools in Pascal*. Comparison of our versions with theirs might be an interesting juxtaposition of Fortran and Pascal for character handling. The C language uses null-termination of strings, and any C string-handling routine could be a good model for a Fortran implementation for our system. The standard libraries supplied with any good C compiler have lots of good functions for string operations and thus can be a source of ideas for additional routines for our library. One of the reasons that C is so popular these days is that there are so many good tools available for program development. One of the reasons for this book is to make many of the same ones available for Fortran.

CHAPTER 5

Hash Tables

The tools we have discussed so far are bits and pieces that may be used to build bigger programs. Now we are going to develop a more substantial tool, one that will help efficiently create and manage tables of strings. Such tables are widely used for applications such as symbol tables and reserved word lists; we now present a set of tools to greatly simplify their construction and use.

There are numerous algorithms available for searching tables of strings. The simplest (and slowest) is a linear search from the beginning to end; another possibility is a binary search on a table that has been sorted in lexicographic (alphabetic) order. Table searching methods have been extensively analyzed by a great many authors; the interested reader will find references to some of these analyses at the end of this chapter. The subject of table searching algorithmns will not be reviewed here; we shall just pick a good method and run with it.

It turns out that one of the simplest table searching methods is also one of the most efficient. The thrust of the idea is: instead of finding an entry by comparison with other table elements, use some arithmetic function to compute its location directly. This is called *hashing*, and the arithmetic function used is called a *hash function*. The function result is used as a direct index into a table of symbols. Tables organized in this manner are called *hash tables*. Before worrying about the organization of the table, we will first examine the characteristics required of a good hash function.

5.1 Hash Functions

Let S be a character string to be located, and let $h(K)$ be the hash function for a *key* K. The key is some integer value derived from the string S; for example, a formula for K could be

$$K = \sum_{i=1}^{\text{len}(s)} \text{ichar}(S(i : i)),$$

just the sum of the character codes of the characters in S. Some other formula for the key might be better since this one will produce the same key value for strings that have the same characters in different orders. For instance, the strings xy and yx will produce the same value, and we would like each string to produce a distinct value.

Given a key value, the hash function must return values in the range

$$0 < h(K) \leq \text{HASHSIZE},$$

that is, the function should return positive integer values between 1 and some maximum size, known as the *hash size*, for all possible input strings. Obviously, mapping all possible strings to HASHSIZE integers means that many distinct input strings must produce the same value. If two strings have the same hash value, it is said to be a *collision*, and some provision must be made for *collision resolution*. A hash function should also satisfy two other requirements, in addition to the mapping to HASHSIZE: its computation should be fast, and it should minimize collisions. Another description of the second requirement is that the distribution of values produced by the hash function for the keyword set of interest should be uniform. One simple hash function that approaches these criteria is

$$h(K) = K \bmod(\text{HASHSIZE}) + 1.$$

This hash function falls into a category generally referred to as a division method, in reference to the use of the mod operator; for hash functions of this type it turns out that the hash size should be a prime number in order to get an even distribution. The routine hash1 is an implementation of this function.

```
! hash1  -  compute hash value of name

    integer function hash1 (name, hashsize)
    character*(*)  name
    integer        hashsize
    include        'global.def'
    integer        i, k

    k = 0
    i = 1
    do while (name(i:i) .ne. NULL)
       k = k + ichar (name(i:i))
       i = i + 1
    end do
    hash1 = mod (k, hashsize) + 1

    return
    end
```

A variant of the method of hash1 that uses a modified key computation is embodied in hash2:

```
! hash2  -  compute hash value of name

    integer function hash2 (name, hashsize)
    character*(*)  name
    integer        hashsize
    include        'global.def'
    integer        i, k

    k = 0
    i = 1
    do while (name(i:i) .ne. NULL)
       k = mod ((3*k + ichar (name(i:i))), hashsize)
       i = i + 1
    end do
    hash2 = k + 1

    return
    end
```

The key computation is equivalent to the formula

$$K = \sum_{i=1}^{n} 3^{n-i}\text{ichar}[S(i:i)],$$

where $n = \text{len}(S)$. This key computation weights each character in S by a different value so that strings differing only in the order of the characters will hash to different values. Even though overflow detection can be disabled with a compiler option, we want to prevent integer overflows from happening so that we don't have to remember to compile the function differently from all of the others.

While hash1 can be expected to generate keys no larger than a few thousand, the modified key formula is guaranteed to produce overflow in strings longer than 19 characters with a 32-bit signed integer key $(3^{19} \simeq 2^{31})$, hence the mod operation is inside the loop. Thus, while hash2 may produce better keys, hash1 has the advantage of taking less time to compute a hash value.

Another possibility for good hash functions is related to the linear congruential method often used for generating random numbers, with the form

$$h(K) = AK \bmod(\text{HASHSIZE}) + 1.$$

Hash functions of this type are referred to as multiplicative, even though they look almost exactly like the division method. The differences are in the multiplier A and the choice of HASHSIZE. The hash size for this method must be a power of 2, and the choice of A is based on black magic (a layman's term for mathematics). If HASHSIZE is 2^n, the function result is the least significant n bits of the product AK.

A great deal of research has been done by smart people on this type of function, and the evidence indicates that for a good pseudo-random distribution A should be a number ending in "$x21$," with x even, and should have one less digit than HASHSIZE. The smallest A that meets these criteria is 21 (zero is even), and the smallest hash size to go with it is 128 (three digits). Since we don't know beforehand how large HASHSIZE will be, we could use a formula like

$$A = \left(\frac{\text{HASHSIZE}}{100}\right) \times 10 + 21,$$

but to keep the same interface as in hash1 and hash2 A would have to be computed internally in hash3 on each call. A hash function is supposed to be a simple, quick computation, so we just use the value 21 with the expectation that it will work well for most applications.

```
! hash3  -  compute hash value of name

      integer function hash3 (name, hashsize)
      character*(*)  name
      integer        hashsize
      include        'global.def'
      integer        k, i

      k = 0
      i = 1
      do while (name(i:i) .ne. NULL)
         k = k + ichar (name(i:i))
         i = i + 1
      end do
      hash3 = mod (21*k, hashsize) + 1

      return
      end
```

Note that the rule of thumb dictating the number of digits in A restricts the hash size that can be used but doesn't limit the number of strings that can be stored in a table since some provision for collision resolution is needed anyway.

As with hash1, hash3 has a simple variant in which the mod operation is performed inside the loop:

```
! hash4  -  compute hash value of name

      integer function hash4 (name, hashsize)
      character*(*)  name
      integer        hashsize
      include        'global.def'
      integer        k, i

      k = 0
      i = 1
      do while (name(i:i) .ne. NULL)
         k = mod (21*k + ichar (name(i:i)), hashsize)
         i = i + 1
      end do
      hash4 = k + 1

      return
      end
```

Each intermediate value of k in this version is like a number in a pseudorandom sequence produced with a random number generator, with the increment in the seed being the character code of the next letter in the string being hashed.

In both hash2 and hash4 it was necessary to perform the mod operation inside the loop to prevent overflows, because each successive result was multiplied by a constant k, giving rise to a series of the form $k^n c_n + k^{n-1} c_{n-1} + \cdots + k c_1$, which can grow to be very large. However, there are lots of series that grow with n much more slowly than k^n, and this observation suggests a whole class of hash functions that could be based on series of multipliers for the characters in the string. Here is one that uses the Fibonacci series:

```
! hash5  -  compute hash value of name (Fibonacci hash)

      integer function hash5 (name, hashsize)
      character*(*)  name
      integer        hashsize
      include        'global.def'
      integer        i, k
      integer        f(25)   !Fibonacci series values
      data   f /
     & 1, 1, 2, 3, 5, 8, 13, 21, 34, 55, 89, 144, 233, 377, 610,
     & 987, 1597, 2584, 4181, 6765, 10946, 17711, 28657, 46368,
     & 75025 /

      k = 0
```

```
i = 1
do while (name(i:i) .ne. NULL .and. i .le. 25)
   k = k + (ichar(name(i:i)) * f(i))
   i = i + 1
end do
hash5 = mod (k, hashsize) + 1

return
end
```

There is no added overhead in using any series if the values are preassigned with a data statement.

5.2   Table Organization

The preceding hash functions are all written with the same interface, and any one of them could be selected interchangeably for use in a hash table storage scheme. It is easy to make new hash functions that are minor variations of these themes and the possibilities for such functions are endless (Knuth says there are 10^{43} functions to map 31 keys into 41 hash values, and $10^{43} \simeq \infty$ in our book). If the table is to be used for a predetermined list of words (like a keyword list) and speed is important, then it might be worthwhile to experiment with new functions; otherwise one of the functions hash1–hash5 is probably as good as any.

As a practical matter, it is impossible to find hash functions that do not produce any duplicate values (collisions) if the input strings are not known beforehand. The table organization must therefore provide some means of resolving collisions. Once again, there are many alternate methods of doing this. One simple method is called *chaining* in which each hash entry points to the head of a linked list of all entries with the same hash value. This list is then searched sequentially since it is expected to be short. Each element of a linked list consists of a pointer to the string and a pointer to the next element in the list. A value of zero as the next pointer signifies the end of the list.

Figure 5.1 illustrates the linked list structure used in our hash routines. The tildes in Figure 5.1 represent NULL. We use a large, amorphous buffer, imaginatively named buffer, to store the actual strings instead of storing them as an array of strings. This conserves space since there is no wasted space between names.

The hash table management routines are written to manage any number of tables in a single program. This management is accomplished by passing a lot of arguments to the subroutines, which is usually a bad idea. An attempt should always be made to draw the dividing lines between program units in a way that minimizes the number of data paths at the interfaces. However, minimizing data connections in Fortran is generally achieved by maintaining local data structures, and in this instance would require the hashing routines to contain the hash table

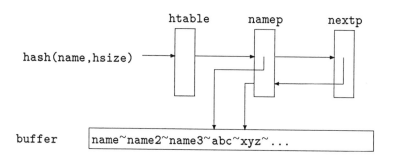

Figure 5.1: Linked list table structure.

itself as a local data structure. Instead, the organization of these routines is such that "encapsulation routines" can easily be written to manage a particular table, and routines that manage different tables in a program can use the same underlying search and insert routines. Their purpose is to separate the logic of how to store and look up strings from the logic of when and why, in tested and proven routines. The three basic hash table operations provide a slightly higher level description of hash tables to programs that use them.

Here are the arguments for the hash table manager routines:

name	Name to be installed in hash table
buffer	Character storage buffer for name
bufp	Pointer to name in buffer
namep	Array of pointers to names in buffer
nextp	Array of pointers to next name in list
tabp	Array subscript to be used for namep and nextp
htable	Main hash table pointer array
hsize	Size of htable pointer array

The generalized hash table manager consists of three routines: hinstall, hlookup, and hremove. The function hlookup searches for a name in the table, and if found returns its index into namep or zero if the name is not found. This permits other information about the name such as its data type or storage address to be stored in arrays parallel to namep.

```
! hlookup  -  look up name in hash table

      integer function hlookup (name, buffer, namep, nextp, htable,
     &                          hash, hsize)
      character*(*)  name, buffer
      integer        namep(*), nextp(*), htable(*), hash, hsize
      external       hash
```

```
      include      'global.def'
      integer      p
      logical      equal

      p = htable (hash (name, hsize))

      do while (p.ne.0 .and. .not. equal (name, buffer(namep(p):)))
         p = nextp(p)
      end do

      hlookup = p

      return
      end
```

Subroutine `hinstall` installs a name in the table. The name to be installed is put at the head of the linked list so that if the same name is installed twice only the most recent definition is found.

```
! hinstall  -  install a new entry into hashtable

      subroutine hinstall (name, buffer, bufp, namep, nextp, tabp,
     &                     htable, hash, hsize)
      character*(*)  name, buffer
      integer        bufp, tabp, hsize, hash
      integer        namep(*), nextp(*), htable(*)
      external       hash
      include        'global.def'
      integer        h, l

      h = hash (name, hsize)
      l = index (name, NULL)

      nextp(tabp) = htable(h)
      htable(h)   = tabp
      namep(tabp) = bufp
      buffer(bufp:bufp+l) = name(1:l)//NULL

      return
      end
```

The calling routines are completely responsible for storage allocation, providing the hash function to be used, and maintaining the table and buffer pointers; any suitable combination of hash function, hash size, and table size can be chosen for the application at hand.

`hremove` removes a name from the table by relinking the chain to bypass it; it is a logical function and returns false if the name is not found. No attempt is made to recover its space in `buffer`; every new string added to the table is added at the end.

```
! hremove  -  remove a name from hash table
```

```
      logical function hremove (name, buffer, namep, nextp, htable,
     &                          hash, hsize)
      character*(*)  name, buffer
      integer        namep(*), nextp(*), htable(*), hash, hsize
      external       hash
      include        'global.def'
      integer        h, p, prevp
      logical        equal

      prevp = 0
      h = hash (name, hsize)
      p = htable (h)

      do while (p.ne.0 .and. .not. equal (name, buffer(namep(p):)))
         prevp = p
         p = nextp(p)
      end do

      if (p .eq. 0) then
         hremove = .false.
      else
         hremove = .true.
         if (prevp .eq. 0) then
            htable(h) = nextp(htable(h))
         else
            nextp(prevp) = nextp(p)
         end if
      end if

      return
      end
```

5.3 Fortran Name Translation

Now that we have a firm grasp of the workings of a hash table, let's apply it to a practical problem. One improvement that v77 could use is the automatic translation of long identifiers into standard-conforming six-character names. The hash table routines provide the tools to do this in a self-contained filter called f77name that takes a line at a time and shortens all long names. Since the output line can never be longer than the input line, the conversion is performed in place with no temporary string.

f77name doesn't try to be too smart. It doesn't resolve conflicts between names that aren't unique in the first 6 characters, but it does report them. It also cannot know whether subroutines and functions processed separately have names unique to 6 characters, so even if all modules of a big program are processed separately with no reported conflicts the program might not link correctly. A program that deals with such problems would be most of a Fortran compiler, and we aren't ready for that yet. Instead, the human user must make sure that program unit names are unique to six characters.

Identifiers in the hash table are given a classification of LONG, SHORT, or KEY-WORD. f77name scans the input line for identifiers, and each one is classified as either KEYWORD or LONG (SHORT is only used for shortened names). Keywords are output immediately; identifiers are looked up and put in the symbol table if not already present. If a new identifier is longer than six characters, it is truncated to six and the shorter name is looked up. If the shortened name is found, then there is a name conflict. Otherwise the shortened name is stored with the attribute SHORT. Conversely, when a name shorter than six characters is encountered, it is looked up and stored as a LONG name if not present. If it is present in the table with the attribute SHORT, a name conflict is detected. If any name conflict is found it is reported to the user with no attempt to correct it.

```
! f77name  -  truncate long identifiers to 6 characters

       subroutine f77name (line)
       character*(*)        line
       include             'global.def'
       include             'forttable.cmn'
       integer              KEYWORD, SHORT, LONG
       parameter            (KEYWORD = 1)
       parameter            (SHORT = 2)
       parameter            (LONG = 3)
       integer              i, lp, op, p, shortp, idlen, hlookup
       logical              is_ident, inquote
       character*(MAXSTR)   id, shortid
       integer              hash3
       external             hash3, f77data

       lp = 1
       op = 1
       do while (line(lp:lp) .ne. NEWLINE)
          do while (line(lp:lp) .eq. BLANK)
             line(op:op) = BLANK
             lp = lp + 1
             op = op + 1
          end do
          if (line(lp:lp) .eq. NEWLINE) then
             continue
          else if (is_ident (id, line, lp)) then
             idlen  = index (id, NULL) - 1
             if (idlen .gt. 6) then
                do i = 1, 6              !replace dollar and underscore
                   if (id(i:i) .eq. '_' .or. id(i:i) .eq. '$') then
                      shortid(i:i) = 'X'
                   else
                      shortid(i:i) = id(i:i)
                   end if
```

```
         end do
         shortid(7:7) = NULL
         p = hlookup (id,buffer,namep,nextp,htable,hash3,hashsize)
         if (p .eq. 0) then      !not found - install in table
            call hinstall (id,buffer,bufp,namep,nextp,tabp,
   &                       htable,hash3,hashsize)
            type(tabp) = LONG
            tabp = tabp + 1
            bufp = bufp + idlen + 1
            shortp = hlookup (shortid,buffer,namep,nextp,
   &                          htable,hash3,hashsize)
            if (shortp .eq. 0) then
               call hinstall (shortid,buffer,bufp,namep,nextp,tabp,
   &                          htable,hash3,hashsize)
               type(tabp) = SHORT
               tabp = tabp + 1
               bufp = bufp + 7
            else
               call fputstr (STDERR, 'f77name: name conflict:'//EOL)
               call fputstr (STDERR, buffer(namep(tabp-1):))
               call fputstr (STDERR, '  '//buffer(namep(shortp):))
               call fputc (STDERR, NEWLINE)
            end if
            line(op:op+5) = shortid(1:6)
            op = op + 6
         else if (type(p) .eq. KEYWORD) then    !leave it alone
            line(op:op+idlen-1) = id(1:idlen)
            op = op + idlen
         else               !found and not keyword - use short name
            line(op:op+5) = shortid(1:6)
            op = op + 6
         end if
      else if (idlen .eq. 6) then              !check for conflicts
         p = hlookup (id,buffer,namep,nextp,htable,hash3,hashsize)
         if (p .eq. 0) then
            call hinstall (id,buffer,bufp,namep,nextp,tabp,
   &                       htable,hash3,hashsize)
            type(tabp) = LONG
            tabp = tabp + 1
            bufp = bufp + idlen + 1
         else if (type(p) .eq. SHORT) then
               call fputstr (STDERR, 'f77name: name conflict:'//EOL)
               call fputstr (STDERR, buffer(namep(p):))
               call fputstr (STDERR,
   &               ' conflicts with previously shortened name'//EOL)
         end if
         line(op:op+5) = id(1:6)
         op = op + 6
      else               !name shorter than 6 chars - use as is
         line(op:op+idlen-1) = id(1:idlen)
         op = op + idlen
      end if
   else if (line(lp:lp) .eq. QUOTE) then    !skip quotes
```

```
line(op:op) = QUOTE
lp = lp + 1
op = op + 1
do while (line(lp:lp) .ne. QUOTE .and. line(lp:lp) .ne. NEWLINE)
    line(op:op) = line(lp:lp)
    op = op + 1
    lp = lp + 1
end do
line(op:op) = QUOTE
op = op + 1
if (line(lp:lp) .eq. NEWLINE) then
    call fputstr (STDERR, 'f77name: missing quote'//EOL)
else
    lp = lp + 1
end if
    else
        line(op:op) = line(lp:lp)
        lp = lp + 1
        op = op + 1
    end if
end do
line(op:op+1) = EOL

return
end
```

Identifiers containing $ or _ are modified by replacing these characters with X, since standard Fortran allows only letters and digits in identifiers. f77name has an internal common block declared in the file forttable.cmn, and the Fortran keywords are defined in data statements in the file f77data.def. A common block can always be used for a local data structure, although it is never required if its data is strictly local to one routine. Its easier to use a common block in f77name simply because we have a generator program that can generate hash table common blocks, automating the tedious part of using a hash table. Note also that while f77name contains a fairly complex internal data structure, its interface to the outside world is extremely simple. The complexity of the hash table is completely concealed within f77name.

5.4   hashgen

The only problem with f77name is how to get those keywords into the table. A valuable tool for programs employing hash tables is one that simplifies their definition and initialization, for use in programs like f77name where a predefined list of words is needed. In this section we will present hashgen, a general-purpose hash table generation tool. hashgen generates both a common block file and a series of data statements to initialize the common block from a simple description of the required table. The symbol tables generated by hashgen are useful not only for lists of reserved words as in f77name but also can be used to write flexible and powerful interpreters for Fortran application programs.

The input to hashgen consists of a series of statements that define the hash table array sizes and the names of any other arrays needed to store information related to each name. For example, in a compiler symbol table each name would have an associated data type and storage address that must be retrieved each time the name is looked up. The keywords recognized by hashgen are

maxsymbol	Maximum number of names in symbol table
maxbuffer	Maximum number of characters in symbol table
hashsize	Size of main hash table
hashfunction	Hash function selector (1–5)
array	Array declaration for a symbol table attribute

All of the hash functions presented earlier are built-in to hashgen. Once the table parameters have been declared, the names and associated attributes are defined in a series of statements consisting of the name followed by the attributes in the order declared. Here is an example of a complete hashgen input file:

```
! thag.hsh  -  hash table declaration file

    hashfunction = 3
    hashsize = 128
    maxsymbol = 1024      !big enough
    maxbuffer = 4096      !ditto

    array integer num
    array logical defined
    array real    value
    array string  synonym

    !name     #    defined    value    synonym
    !----    ---   -------    -----    -------
    Mighty    1       T        1.2     'super'
    Thag      2       F        2.1     'caveman'
    meets     3       T        5.5     'encounters'
    hungry    4       T       19.0     'ravenous'
    dinosaur  5       T       11.9     'reptile'
```

All arrays must be declared before data begins. Comment lines are ignored. Obviously, routines using the generated table must use the same hash function as that specified in the input file.

hashgen has one optional argument -u that causes the names to be converted to uppercase before they are hashed. The input file name is used to create names for the common block and block data files, respectively. For example

```
$ hashgen thag.hsh thag.rpt
```

would produce a common block file name of thagtable.cmn and a data file name of thagdata.def. A summary of the hash table performance, with information

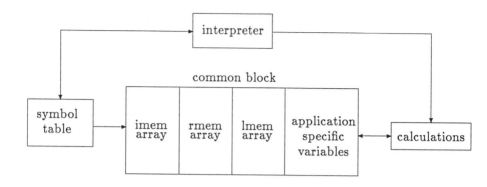

Figure 5.2: Table-driven simulation language interpreter.

such as the total number of collisions, is written to thag.rpt; if no output file is named, the report is written on STDOUT.

hashgen can make Fortran programs more flexible and works well with the kind of analysis and modeling software that is the bread and butter of Fortran programmers. The main intended use of hashgen is with Fortran application programs to generalize the access to variables in common blocks via a symbol table. The locations of individual variables within the common block are stored in the symbol table as "addresses;" these addresses are simply offsets from the start of the common block. The symbol table can thus supply names accessible to the user for the variables in the common block. The symbol table can then be used as part of an interpreter to provide a flexible, convenient, and powerful human interface.

To see how to apply the idea behind hashgen to a real program we must first consider the anatomy of a typical Fortran program. Fortran programs for scientific and engineering applications are usually organized around a common block; there is a routine for reading an input file to load the common block, various subroutines for performing calculations that access the common block, and one or more routines that print results stored in common blocks. hashgen can be used to make the variables in the common block accessible in a symbol table so that an interpreter serving as the user interface to the program can deal with data manipulation in a generalized fashion while the computations in the program are performed in a specific fashion applicable to the problem. Figure 5.2 is a picture of how the high-level organization of such a program might look.

The symbol table accesses program variables as locations in some amorphous array mem, while the underlying analysis program uses meaningful variable names suitable to a specific engineering or scientific analysis. For example, a circuits analysis program could have variables in the common block describing the circuit devices, node voltages, and branch currents, while the interpreter, with its abstract representation of the common block, could provide a flexible means of describing the circuit and its components using names meaningful to the user. The Fortran equivalence statement is what makes the scheme illustrated in Figure 5.2 possible. The Fortran standard guarantees that the integer, real, and logical data types occupy the same number of bytes in memory, so the scheme used here is portable to any Fortran 77 installation.

To illustrate the implementation, the following common block file might be used with a hashgen-based interpreter for an engineering graphics program:

```
!  graphics.cmn  -  common block for graphics routines

      logical                 sflag, lflag, gxflag, gyflag
      integer                 layout, plot_type
      real                    thickness (50)
      integer                 curve_fit (50), line_type (50)

      common  / gwiz /
     &          plot_type,    !axis system code
     &          layout,       !page layout code
     &          sflag,        !manual scaling flag
     &          gxflag,       !x grid flag
     &          gyflag,       !y grid flag
     &          lflag,        !autolabel flag
     &          thickness,    !line thickness for each curve
     &          curve_fit,    !type of interpolation for each curve
     &          line_type     !line pattern code for each curve

      character*(255)         xtitle, ytitle, caption
      common  / gstring /
     &          xtitle,       !x-axis title
     &          ytitle,       !y-axis title
     &          caption       !plot caption

! equivalence to hash table addresses
      integer      imem (156)           ! 156 = length of /gwiz/
      logical      lmem (156)
      real         rmem (156)
      equivalence  (ival(1), plot_type)
      equivalence  (ival(1), lval(1))
      equivalence  (ival(1), rval(1))

      character*(255) cmem (3)          ! 3 = length of /gstring/
      equivalence  (cval(1)(1:1), xtitle(1:1))
```

This looks like a garden-variety common block declaration file except for the equivalence statements. The length of the imem, lmem, and rmem arrays is equal to the sum of the lengths of all the variables in the common block, that is, equal to the length of the gwiz common block. Likewise, the length of the cmem array is equal to the length of the gstring common block.

The symbol table associated with the common block is initialized with the type and location of each variable. The location is the offset in Fortran storage units (usually 4 bytes each) to each variable. Here is the hashgen input to do it:

```
! graphics.hsh - hashgen input for graphics program symbol table

    hashfunction = 1
    hashsize     = 19
    maxsymbol    = 64
    maxbuffer    = 1024
    array integer  addr     !offset from start of common block
    array integer  type     !1 = integer
                            !2 = logical
                            !3 = real
                            !4 = character*255
    array integer  size

    ! name         addr       type      size
    !--------      ------     ------    ------
    plot_type        1          1         1
    layout           2          1         1
    sflag            3          2         1
    gxflag           4          2         1
    gyflag           5          2         1
    lflag            6          2         1
    thickness        7          3        50
    curve_fit       57          1        50
    line_type      107          1        50
    xtitle           1          4         1
    ytitle           2          4         1
    caption          3          4         1
```

With this arrangement, the following code could be used to process assignments.

```
if (refsymbol (ident, attr)) then
    if (attr(IDSIZE) .gt. 1) then
        if (line(lp:lp) .eq. '(') then
            lp = lp + 1
            if (is_ival (ival, line, lp)) then
                if (line(lp:lp) .eq. ')') then
                    lp = lp + 1
                    idx = ival
                else
                    call fputstr (STDERR, 'missing )'//EOL)
                end if
            else
                call fputstr (STDERR, 'integer index required'//EOL)
            end if
        else
            call fputstr (STDERR, 'missing ('//EOL)
        end if
```

```
      else
         idx = 0
      end if
      addr = attr(IDADDR) + idx
      do while (line(lp:lp) .eq. ' ' .or. line(lp:lp) .eq. '=')
         lp = lp + 1
      end do
      if (attr(IDTYPE) .eq. ITYPE) then
         if (is_ival(ival, line, lp) then
            imem(addr) = ival
         else
            call fputstr (STDERR, 'integer required'//EOL)
         end if
      else if (attr(IDTYPE) .eq. LTYPE) then
         if (is_lval(lval, line, lp) then
            lmem(addr) = lval
         else
            call fputstr (STDERR, 'logical required'//EOL)
         end if
      else if (attr(IDTYPE) .eq. RTYPE) then
         if (is_rval(rval, line, lp) then
            rmem(addr) = rval
         else
            call fputstr (STDERR, 'real required'//EOL)
         end if
      else if (attr(IDTYPE) .eq. CTYPE) then
         if (is_sval(sval, line, lp) then
            cmem(addr) = sval
         else
            call fputstr (STDERR, 'integer required'//EOL)
         end if
      end if
   else
      call fputstr (STDERR, 'unknown identifier'//EOL)
   end if
```

It is assumed here that a routine refsymbol has been provided to encapsulate the symbol table and return an array of attributes for the referenced symbol: IDTYPE, IDADDR, and IDSIZE, corresponding to the parallel arrays declared in the hashgen input. An example of such a routine can be found in Chapter 8.

The amount of code required to handle assignments in this new design method is less than would be needed to do the same job by brute force:

```
      if (equal (ident, 'plot_type'//NULL)) then
         do while (line(lp:lp) .eq. ' ' .or. line(lp:lp) .eq. '=')
            lp = lp + 1
         end do
         if (.not. is_ival (plot_type, line, lp)) then
            call fputstr (STDERR, 'integer required'//EOL)
         end if
      else if (equal (ident, 'layout'//EOL)) then
         . . .
      end if
```

Although for this small example the savings in code is small, the second brute force method grows linearly as the number of variables increases. More importantly, the use of a symbol table means that the interpreter needn't be changed when the underlying graphics program is changed—only the hashgen input for initializing the symbol table must be changed if the common block is changed. hashgen can thus make programs more maintainable.

Now that we know where we are going, let's figure out how to get there. The hashgen program maintains an internal hash table that gets loaded with the data found in the input. When all input has been processed, the contents of the common block are written to the data file as a bunch of data statements. The internal table is defined in hashgen.cmn:

```
! hashgen.cmn  -  hash table generator common block

      integer            MAXTABLE, MAXSYM, MAXBUF
      parameter          (MAXTABLE = 1024)
      parameter          (MAXSYM = 1024)
      parameter          (MAXBUF = 25000)
      integer            htable(MAXTABLE), hcount(MAXTABLE)
      integer            namep(MAXSYM), nextp(MAXSYM), tabp, bufp
      integer            hashfunction, hashsize, maxbuffer, maxsymbol
      character*(MAXBUF) buffer, name

      common  /tabvals/  htable, hcount, namep, nextp, tabp, bufp,
     &                   hashfunction, hashsize, maxbuffer, maxsymbol
      common  /tabchars/ buffer, name

      integer            BOGUSTYPE, ITYPE, RTYPE, LTYPE, STYPE, MAXARR
      parameter          (BOGUSTYPE = -1)
      parameter          (ITYPE = 1)
      parameter          (RTYPE = 2)
      parameter          (LTYPE = 3)
      parameter          (STYPE = 4)
      parameter          (MAXARR = 10)
      logical            ldata(MAXSYM,MAXARR)
      real               rdata(MAXSYM,MAXARR)
      integer            idata(MAXSYM,MAXARR)
      integer            acount, atype(MAXARR)
      character*(MAXSTR) aname(MAXARR)

      equivalence        (idata, ldata)
      equivalence        (idata, rdata)

      common  /arrayvals/  acount, atype, idata
      common  /arraychars/ aname
```

The hashgen.cmn file declares a set of arrays in parallel with namep, the name pointer array, and hashgen uses the arrays to store attribute data declared in the input file.

The equivalence statement is used to make all of the parallel arrays for different data types start at the same address in memory. Since all of the arrays start at the same place and their elements have the same size, the same subscript counter can be used to access all data types; by using the equivalence statement, the data access is generalized.

hashgen simply processes the declaration file on a line-by-line basis, getting the first identifier from each line and comparing it to a short internal list of hard-coded "directives." If one of the directives is found as the first item on a new line, the relevant information is extracted for later use; if the first item is not a directive to the program, then the line is treated as a data input statement and the name is installed in the hash table for later output. Here is the main program for our hash table generator:

```
! hashgen  -  hash table generator

        program hashgen
        include         'global.def'
        include         'hashgen.cmn'
        integer         argc, uin, uout
        logical         finclude, equal, is_ident, upflag
        logical         is_ival, errflag
        integer         lp, i, j
        character*(MAXSTR) argv(MAXARGS), upper
        character*(MAXSTR) line, ident, type

        call ioinit ()
        call getargs (argc, argv)
        call stdargs (argc, argv, uin, uout)
        upflag = .false.
        name(1:1) = NULL
        do i = 1, argc
            if (argv(i)(1:1) .eq. QUALIFIER) then
                argv(i) = upper (argv(i))
                j = index(argv(i),NULL)
                if (index(argv(i)(1:j),'U') .gt. 0) upflag = .true.
            else                      !define prefix for output file names
                if (name(1:1) .eq. NULL) then
                    j = index(argv(i)(1:index(argv(i),NULL)), '.')
                    if (j .eq. 0) then
                        name = argv(i)
                    else
                        name = argv(i)(1:j-1)//NULL
                    end if
                end if
            end if
        end do
        if (uin .eq. IOERROR .or. uout .eq. IOERROR) stop 'hashgen aborted'

        call inclinit (uin)
        call hashinit ()          !provide defaults and initialize table
        errflag = .false.
```

```
do while (finclude (line))
  lp = 1
  if (is_ident (ident, line, lp)) then
    ident = upper (ident)
    do while (line(lp:lp).eq.' ' .or. line(lp:lp).eq.'=')
      lp = lp + 1
    end do
    if (equal (ident, 'HASHFUNCTION'//NULL)) then
      if (.not. is_ival (hashfunction, line, lp)) then
        call fputstr (STDERR, 'integer value required'//EOL)
        call fputstr (STDERR, line)
        errflag = .true.
      end if
    else if (equal (ident, 'HASHSIZE'//NULL)) then
      if (.not. is_ival (hashsize, line, lp)) then
        call fputstr (STDERR, 'integer value required'//EOL)
        call fputstr (STDERR, line)
        errflag = .true.
      end if
    else if (equal (ident, 'MAXSYMBOL'//NULL)) then
      if (.not. is_ival (maxsymbol, line, lp)) then
        call fputstr (STDERR, 'integer value required'//EOL)
        call fputstr (STDERR, line)
        errflag = .true.
      end if
    else if (equal (ident, 'MAXBUFFER'//NULL)) then
      if (.not. is_ival (maxbuffer, line, lp)) then
        call fputstr (STDERR, 'integer value required'//EOL)
        call fputstr (STDERR, line)
        errflag = .true.
      end if
    else if (equal (ident, 'ARRAY'//NULL)) then
      acount = acount + 1
      if (is_ident (type, line, lp)) then
        type = upper (type)
        atype(acount) = BOGUSTYPE
        if (equal (type, 'INTEGER'//NULL)) atype(acount) = ITYPE
        if (equal (type, 'REAL'//NULL)) atype(acount) = RTYPE
        if (equal (type, 'LOGICAL'//NULL)) atype(acount) = LTYPE
        if (equal (type, 'STRING'//NULL)) atype(acount) = STYPE
        if (atype(acount) .eq. BOGUSTYPE) then
          call fputstr (STDERR, 'invalid ARRAY type: '//EOL)
          call fputstr (STDERR, line)
          errflag = .true.
        end if
        if (.not. is_ident (aname(acount), line, lp)) then
          call fputstr (STDERR, 'invalid ARRAY name'//EOL)
          call fputstr (STDERR, line)
          errflag = .true.
        end if
      else
        call fputstr (STDERR, 'invalid ARRAY statement'//EOL)
        call fputstr (STDERR, line)
```

```
                    errflag = .true.
                  end if
            else                          !data input
                  if (upflag) ident = upper (ident)
                  if (.not. errflag) call hashident (ident, line, lp)
            end if
         else
            if (line(lp:lp).ne.NEWLINE .and. line(lp:lp).ne.COMMENT) then
                  call fputstr (STDERR, 'hashgen: unrecognized keyword:'//EOL)
                  call fputstr (STDERR, line)
                  errflag = .true.
            end if
         end if
      end do

      call hashrpt   (uout)   !write collision report
      call hashcmn   ()       !write common block file
      call hashdata  ()       !write block data file

      end
```

The internal hash table is initialized by hashinit:

```
! hashinit  -  initialize hashgen tables

      subroutine hashinit ()
      include           'global.def'
      include           'hashgen.cmn'
      integer           i

      hashfunction = 1
      hashsize   = 53
      maxsymbol = 250
      maxbuffer = 5000
      bufp = 1
      tabp = 1
      acount = 0
      do i = 1, MAXTABLE
         htable(i) = 0
         hcount(i) = 0
      end do
      do i = 1, MAXSYM
         namep(i) = 0
         nextp(i) = 0
      end do

      return
      end
```

The main program handles all of the keywords for hashgen; all of the identifiers and their associated attributes are installed in the table by hashident. If the first word on an input line is not a keyword, it is assumed to be an identifier to be installed in the table; a side effect of this assumption is that the hashgen keywords cannot be used as identifiers to be hashed; they are "reserved words."

```
! hashident  -  process hashgen user data input

    subroutine hashident (ident, line, lp)
    character*(*)      ident, line
    integer            lp
    include            'global.def'
    include            'hashgen.cmn'
    logical            lval, is_rval, is_ival, is_lval, is_sval
    integer            ival, i, h, idlen
    real               rval
    character*(MAXSTR) sval
    integer            hash1, hash2, hash3, hash4, hash5
    external           hash1, hash2, hash3, hash4, hash5

    idlen = index (ident, NULL)
    if (bufp+idlen .gt. maxbuffer) stop 'buffer overflow'
    if (tabp .gt. maxsymbol) stop 'symbol table overflow'
    if (hashfunction .eq. 1) then
       call hinstall (ident, buffer, bufp, namep,
&                      nextp, tabp, htable, hash1, hashsize)
       h = hash1 (ident, hashsize)
    else if (hashfunction .eq. 2) then
       call hinstall (ident, buffer, bufp, namep,
&                      nextp, tabp, htable, hash2, hashsize)
       h = hash2 (ident, hashsize)
    else if (hashfunction .eq. 3) then
       call hinstall (ident, buffer, bufp, namep,
&                      nextp, tabp, htable, hash3, hashsize)
       h = hash3 (ident, hashsize)
    else if (hashfunction .eq. 4) then
       call hinstall (ident, buffer, bufp, namep,
&                      nextp, tabp, htable, hash4, hashsize)
       h = hash4 (ident, hashsize)
    else if (hashfunction .eq. 5) then
       call hinstall (ident, buffer, bufp, namep,
&                      nextp, tabp, htable, hash5, hashsize)
       h = hash5 (ident, hashsize)
    else                          !unknown hash function
       h = 1
       nextp(tabp) = htable(1)
       htable(1)   = tabp
       namep(tabp) = bufp
       buffer(bufp:) = ident(1:idlen)//NULL
    end if
    bufp = bufp + idlen
```

```
hcount(h) = hcount(h) + 1
do i = 1, acount                    !read parallel array values
   do while (line(lp:lp) .eq. ' ')
      lp = lp + 1
   end do
   if (atype(i) .eq. ITYPE) then
      if (is_ival (ival, line, lp)) then
         idata(tabp,i) = ival
      else
         call fputstr (STDERR, 'integer value required'//EOL)
         call fputstr (STDERR, line(lp:))
      end if
   else if (atype(i) .eq. RTYPE) then
      if (is_rval (rval, line, lp)) then
         rdata(tabp,i) = rval
      else
         call fputstr (STDERR, 'real value required'//EOL)
         call fputstr (STDERR, line(lp:))
      end if
   else if (atype(i) .eq. LTYPE) then
      if (line(lp:lp).eq.'T' .or. line(lp:lp).eq.'t') then
         ldata(tabp,i) = .true.
         lp = lp + 1
      else if (line(lp:lp).eq.'F'.or.line(lp:lp).eq.'f') then
         ldata(tabp,i) = .false.
         lp = lp + 1
      else if (is_lval (lval, line, lp)) then
         ldata(tabp,i) = lval
      else
         call fputstr (STDERR, 'logical value required'//EOL)
         call fputstr (STDERR, line(lp:))
      end if
   else if (atype(i) .eq. STYPE) then
      if (is_sval (sval, line, lp)) then
         idata(tabp,i) = bufp
         buffer(bufp:) = sval
         bufp = bufp + index (sval, NULL)
      else
         call fputstr (STDERR, 'string data required'//EOL)
         call fputstr (STDERR, line(lp:))
      end if
   end if
end do
tabp = tabp + 1

return
end
```

To conserve space, `string` array types are implemented by storing the (null-terminated) string value in `buffer` and assigning the array name to an array of integer string pointers.

Once the entire input has been processed, the only remaining task is to write out the results. The common block file is produced by hashcmn:

```
! hashcmn  -  generate hash table common block file

      subroutine hashcmn ()
      include              'global.def'
      include              'hashgen.cmn'
      integer              u, fopen, i
      character*(MAXSTR)    itoa, cmnfile

      cmnfile = name(1:index(name,NULL)-1)//'table.cmn'//NULL
      if (fopen (u, cmnfile, IOWRITE) .eq. IOERROR) then
         stop 'Error opening common block file'
      end if

      call fputstr (u, '! '//cmnfile)
      call fputstr (u, '  -  hash table common declaration'//EOL)
      call fputstr (u, EOL)
      call fputstr (u, '      integer   HASHSIZE'//EOL)
      call fputstr (u, '      parameter (HASHSIZE = '//itoa(hashsize))
      call fputstr (u, ')'//EOL)
      call fputstr (u, '      integer   MAXSYMBOL'//EOL)
      call fputstr (u, '      parameter (MAXSYMBOL = '//itoa(maxsymbol))
      call fputstr (u, ')'//EOL)
      call fputstr (u, '      integer   MAXBUFFER'//EOL)
      call fputstr (u, '      parameter (MAXBUFFER = '//itoa(maxbuffer))
      call fputstr (u, ')'//EOL)
      call fputstr (u, '      integer   htable(HASHSIZE)'//EOL)
      call fputstr (u, '      integer   namep(MAXSYMBOL)'//EOL)
      call fputstr (u, '      integer   nextp(MAXSYMBOL)'//EOL)
      call fputstr (u, '      character*(MAXBUFFER)  buffer'//EOL)
      call fputstr (u, EOL)
      call fputstr (u, '      integer   tabp'//EOL)
      call fputstr (u, '      integer   bufp'//EOL)
      call fputstr (u, EOL)
      call fputstr (u, '      common   '//'/'//name)
      call fputstr (u, 'table/  htable, namep, nextp, tabp, bufp'//EOL)
      call fputstr (u, '      common   '//'/'//name)
      call fputstr (u, 'buffer/  buffer'//EOL)
      call fputstr (u, EOL)
      do i = 1, acount
         if (atype(i).eq.ITYPE .or. atype(i).eq.STYPE) then
            call fputstr (u, '      integer    '//aname(i))
         else if (atype(i) .eq. RTYPE) then
            call fputstr (u, '      real       '//aname(i))
         else if (atype(i) .eq. LTYPE) then
            call fputstr (u, '      logical    '//aname(i))
         end if
         call fputstr (u, '(MAXSYMBOL)'//EOL)
      end do
      call fputstr (u, EOL)
      if (acount .gt. 0) then
```

```
          call fputstr (u, '       common  /'//name)
          call fputstr (u, 'arrs/'//EOL)
          call fputstr (u, '      &        '//aname(1))
          call fputstr (u, EOL)
      end if
      do i = 2, acount
          call fputstr (u, '      &        ,'//aname(i))
          call fputstr (u, EOL)
      end do

      call fclose (u)

      return
      end
```

The data file is written by hashdata.

```
! hashdata  -  write data statements for hash table

      subroutine hashdata ()
      include           'global.def'
      include           'hashgen.cmn'
      integer           i, j, k, n, u, fopen
      character*(MAXSTR) itoa, datfile

      datfile = name(1:index(name,NULL)-1)//'data.def'//NULL
      if (fopen (u, datfile, IOWRITE) .eq. IOERROR) then
          stop 'Hashgen: Error opening data file'
      end if

      call fputstr (u, '      data   tabp  /'//itoa(tabp))
      call fputstr (u, '/'//EOL)
      call fputstr (u, '      data   bufp  /'//itoa(bufp))
      call fputstr (u, '/'//EOL)

      n = 10
      i = 1
      do while (i .lt. hashsize-n)
          call mk_idata (u, n, 'htable'//NULL, htable(i), i)
          i = i + n
      end do
      call mk_idata (u, hashsize-i+1, 'htable'//NULL, htable(i), i)
      call fputstr (u, EOL)

      i = 1
      do while (i .lt. tabp-n)
          call mk_idata (u, n, 'namep'//NULL, namep(i), i)
          i = i + n
      end do
      call mk_idata (u, tabp-i, 'namep'//NULL, namep(i), i)
      call fputstr (u, EOL)

      i = 1
```

```
do while (i .lt. tabp-n)
   call mk_idata (u, n, 'nextp'//NULL, nextp(i), i)
   i = i + n
end do
call mk_idata (u, tabp-i, 'nextp'//NULL, nextp(i), i)
call fputstr (u, EOL)

call mk_sdata (u, 'buffer'//NULL, buffer, bufp)
call fputstr (u, EOL)

do i = 1, acount
   j = 1
   do while (j .lt. tabp-n)
      if (atype(i).eq.ITYPE) call mk_idata(u,n,aname(i),idata(j,i),j)
      if (atype(i).eq.LTYPE) call mk_ldata(u,n,aname(i),ldata(j,i),j)
      if (atype(i).eq.RTYPE) call mk_rdata(u,n,aname(i),rdata(j,i),j)
      if (atype(i).eq.STYPE) call mk_idata(u,n,aname(i),idata(j,i),j)
      j = j + n
   end do
   k = tabp-j
   if (atype(i).eq.ITYPE) call mk_idata (u,k,aname(i),idata(j,i),j)
   if (atype(i).eq.LTYPE) call mk_ldata (u,k,aname(i),ldata(j,i),j)
   if (atype(i).eq.RTYPE) call mk_rdata (u,k,aname(i),rdata(j,i),j)
   if (atype(i).eq.STYPE) call mk_idata (u,k,aname(i),idata(j,i),j)
   call fputstr (u, EOL)
end do

call fclose (u)

return
end
```

Whenever initial values are needed for variables in common blocks, the Fortran standard requires the use of a block data subprogram. VAX Fortran allows data statements for common blocks anywhere, but as usual we stick to the standard when there is no good reason not to. In fact, block data routines really should be used on the VAX anyway because strange debugging problems can arise when data statements for common block variables are put into an include file and seen by more than one program unit. The block data subprogram must be referenced (via a Fortran external statement) in at least one program unit to inform the linker of its existence.

hashgen has a subroutine just for printing performance statistics: hashrpt prints input parameters for verification and then prints a collision map along with a summary of table usage.

```
! hashrpt  -  generate hash table collision report

      subroutine hashrpt (u)
      integer          u
      include          'global.def'
```

```
include          'hashgen.cmn'
integer          i, j, lp, rows, columns, excess
integer          used, unused, tabcol, keycol
character*(MAXSTR) itoa, line

call fputstr (u, 'Input Summary:'//EOL)
call fputstr (u, 'hashsize:      '//itoa(hashsize))
call fputstr (u, EOL)
call fputstr (u, 'maxsymbol:     '//itoa(maxsymbol))
call fputstr (u, EOL)
call fputstr (u, 'maxbuffer:     '//itoa(maxbuffer))
call fputstr (u, EOL)
call fputstr (u, 'hashfunction: '//itoa(hashfunction))
call fputstr (u, EOL)
call fputstr (u, EOL)

call fputstr (u, 'Collision Map:'//EOL)
rows    = hashsize/10 + 1
columns = 10
excess  = mod (hashsize, 10)
if (excess .eq. 0) rows = rows - 1
do i = 1, rows
   line = itoa (10*(i-1)+1)
   if (i.eq.rows .and. excess.ne.0) columns = excess
   do j = 1, columns
      line(index(line,NULL):) = ' '
      lp = 7*j + 3
      line(lp:) = itoa (hcount(10*(i-1)+j))
   end do
   call fputstr (u, line(1:index(line,NULL)-1)//EOL)
end do
call fputstr (u, EOL)

call fputstr (u, 'Output Summary:'//EOL)
used   = 0
unused = 0
tabcol = 0
keycol = 0
do i = 1, hashsize
   if (hcount(i) .eq. 0) then
      unused = unused + 1
   else
      used = used + 1
      keycol = keycol + hcount(i) - 1
      if (hcount(i) .gt. 1) tabcol = tabcol + 1
   end if
end do
call fputstr (u, 'total symbols:     '//itoa(tabp-1))
call fputstr (u, EOL)
call fputstr (u, 'buffer length:     '//itoa(bufp))
call fputstr (u, EOL)
call fputstr (u, 'empty entries:     '//itoa(unused))
call fputstr (u, EOL)
```

```
      call fputstr (u, 'active entries:     '//itoa(used))
      call fputstr (u, EOL)
      call fputstr (u, 'overactive entries: '//itoa(tabcol))
      call fputstr (u, EOL)
      call fputstr (u, 'keyword collisions: '//itoa(keycol))
      call fputstr (u, EOL)

      return
      end
```

A few new tools were developed to make the job of writing the data statements a little less tedious. These routines, mk_idata, mk_rdata, and mk_ldata simplify the job by wrapping up the logic of outputting one data statement at a time and let the calling routine just dump arrays in a loop of calls to the appropriate routine.

```
! mk_idata  -  make data statement from integer array

      subroutine mk_idata (uout, n, aname, array, s)
      integer             uout, n, array(n), s
      character*(*)       aname
      include             'global.def'
      integer             i
      character*(MAXSTR)  itoa

      call fputstr (uout, '      data '//'('//aname)
      call fputstr (uout, '(i),i='//itoa(s))
      call fputstr (uout, ','//itoa(s+n-1))
      call fputstr (uout, ') /'//itoa(array(1)))
      do i = 2, n
         call fputstr (uout, ','//itoa(array(i)))
      end do
      call fputstr (uout, '/'//EOL)

      return
      end


! mk_rdata  -  make data statement for real array

      subroutine mk_rdata (uout, n, aname, array, s)
      integer             uout, n, s
      real                array(n)
      character*(*)       aname
      include             'global.def'
      integer             i
      character*(MAXSTR)  itoa, ftoa

      call fputstr (uout, '      data ('//aname)
      call fputstr (uout, '(i),i='//itoa(s))
      call fputstr (uout, ','//itoa(s+n-1))
      call fputstr (uout, ') /'//ftoa(array(1)))
```

```
      do i = 2, n
         call fputstr (uout, ','//ftoa(array(i)))
      end do
      call fputstr (uout, '/'//EOL)

      return
      end
```

```
! mk_ldata  -  make data statement from logical array

      subroutine mk_ldata (uout, n, aname, array, s)
      integer              uout, n, s
      logical              array(n)
      character*(*)        aname
      include              'global.def'
      integer              i
      character*(MAXSTR) itoa

      call fputstr (uout, '      data ('//aname)
      call fputstr (uout, '(i),i='//itoa(s))
      call fputstr (uout, ','//itoa(s+n-1))
      if (array(1)) then
         call fputstr (uout, ') /.true.'//NULL)
      else
         call fputstr (uout, ') /.false.'//NULL)
      end if
      do i = 2, n
         if (array(i)) then
            call fputstr (uout, ',.true.'//NULL)
         else
            call fputstr (uout, ',.false.'//NULL)
         end if
      end do
      call fputstr (uout, '/'//EOL)

      return
      end
```

The mk_sdata subroutine is a little different. It writes out an entire packed character buffer containing multiple strings in one call. Fortran has definite limitations when it comes to writing out character data in data statements because concatenation is illegal in data statements, and the only reliable way to put control characters in is with parameters. mk_sdata is equipped to handle only NEWLINE and NULL as special characters; any others will be written into a literal character string with possibly erroneous results.

```
! mk_sdata  -  make data statement from string buffer

      subroutine mk_sdata (uout, name, buffer, endp)
      integer              uout, endp
```

```
character*(*)      name, buffer
include            'global.def'
integer            lp, i, j, L
character*(MAXSTR) itoa, line, string

L = 55 - index (name, NULL) - 2 * (index (itoa(endp),NULL) - 1)

i = 1
do while (i .le. endp)
   line(1:11) = '        data '
   line(12:) = name
   lp = 11 + index (name, NULL)
   line(lp:) = '('//itoa(i)
   lp = lp + index (itoa(i), NULL)
   line(lp:lp) = ':'
   lp = lp + 1
   if (buffer(i:i) .eq. NEWLINE) then
      string = 'NEWLINE'//NULL
      i = i + 1
   else if (buffer(i:i) .eq. NULL) then
      string = 'NULL'//NULL
      i = i + 1
   else
      string(1:1) = QUOTE
      j = 2
      do while (buffer(i:i).ne.NEWLINE .and.
&                buffer(i:i).ne.NULL .and. j.le.L)
         string(j:j) = buffer(i:i)
         i = i + 1
         j = j + 1
      end do
      string(j:j+1) = QUOTE//NULL
   end if
   line(lp:) = itoa(i-1)
   lp = lp + index(itoa(i-1),NULL) - 1
   line(lp:lp+3) = ')/'//NULL
   call fputstr (uout, line)
   call fputstr (uout, string)
   call fputstr (uout, '/'//EOL)
end do

return
end
```

hashgen is a simple program, although its usefulness is with more sophisticated programs. Here is the files list for hashgen:

```
! hashgen.fil  -  files list for hash table generator
    # hashgen.cmn    !common block
    hashgen          !main program
      hashinit       !initialize hash table
      hashident      !process user identifiers
      hashcmn        !write common block
```

```
        hashdata        !write block data
        hashrpt         !write collision report

! hash table primitives
        hash1           !division method 1
        hash2           !division method 2
        hash3           !multiplication method 1
        hash4           !multiplication method 2
        hash5           !fibonacci method
        hinstall        !install name in hash table
        hlookup         !lookup name in hash table
        hremove         !remove name from hash table

! data statement generators
        mk_idata        !integer
        mk_ldata        !logical
        mk_rdata        !real
        mk_sdata        !character
```

Several of these routines will come in handy later; the hash table management routines are used by the preprocessor in Chapter 6 and by the spl compiler in Chapter 8. The data statement generators are useful for any kind of generator program used in automatic Fortran software construction. They are used again in chapter 7 to make data tables for lexical analyzers.

Since f77name wouldn't be complete without it, here is the input file for Fortran keywords:

```
! fort.hsh   -   f77name hash table description

hashfunction 3  !hash function
hashsize  256   !hash table size
maxsymbol 512   !symbol table size
maxbuffer 4096  !hash buffer size

array integer type   !KEYWORD type

!keyword     type
!-------     ----
backspace    1
character    1
complex      1
continue     1
endfile      1
equivalence  1
external     1
function     1
include      1
inquire      1
integer      1
intrinsic    1
logical      1
parameter    1
```

```
precision     1
program       1
subroutine    1
formatted     1
sequential    1
unformatted   1
nextrec       1
```

Only the keywords with length greater than 6 are listed since shorter names are never modified by f77name. The name of this file is fort.hsh, and the common block generated from it is used directly in f77name.

```
! FORTtable.cmn  -  hash table common declaration

        integer   HASHSIZE
        parameter (HASHSIZE = 256)
        integer   MAXSYMBOL
        parameter (MAXSYMBOL = 512)
        integer   MAXBUFFER
        parameter (MAXBUFFER = 4096)
        integer   htable(HASHSIZE)
        integer   namep(MAXSYMBOL)
        integer   nextp(MAXSYMBOL)
        character*(MAXBUFFER)  buffer

        integer   tabp
        integer   bufp

        common    /FORTtable/   htable, namep, nextp, tabp, bufp
        common    /FORTbuffer/  buffer

        integer   type(MAXSYMBOL)

        common /FORTarrs/
     &          type
```

The data statements are included in a block data subprogram f77data:

```
! f77data  -  block data definition for f77name

        block data f77data
        include   'global.def'
        include   'forttable.cmn'   !hashgen-generated common block
        integer   i
        include   'fortdata.def'    !hashgen-generated data statements
        end
```

hashgen could produce a complete block data routine instead of just a sequence of data statements, so the user wouldn't have to bother with writing the block data routine. On the other hand, it is easy to envision applications in which things other than the hash table need to be initialized, so a "boilerplate" block data routine would not be appropriate, and the user would have to cut and paste the data statements into some larger block data routine. There is a trade-off here, and we have opted for the less automatic but more flexible approach.

We did some experimenting on hash function performance for kicks. The file we used had identifiers consisting of the names of all the routines in this book, all the identifiers in global.def, and some of our favorite variable names, like line, buffer, bp, and lp. There were 252 names in all. The results are shown in Table 5.1.

Table 5.1: Hash function performance

Hash Function	Hash Size	Unused Entries	Entries with Collisions	Total Number of Collisions	Maximum Number of Collisions
hash1	211	91	65	132	6
	251	95	62	96	5
	307	157	57	102	5
hash2	211	51	69	92	6
	251	98	74	99	5
	307	138	57	83	5
hash3	128	20	78	144	6
	256	102	65	98	5
	512	337	53	77	4
hash4	128	16	80	140	6
	256	93	62	89	4
	512	314	47	54	4
hash5	100	8	72	160	8
	200	54	72	106	5
	300	133	63	85	4

We were able to get good performance with the hash functions on hand, and could probably find a function with perfect performance if we were willing to spend some time looking (a hash function is said to be perfect if it maps a given set of keys onto an equal number of hash values with no collisions). However, we will see in Chapter 7 that there is a method even faster than hashing for recognizing keywords, and what we have here is good enough for now. Hash functions are best used for long lists of keywords or symbol tables in which at least some of the keys are not known beforehand, although they are often used for reserved word lists as well.

It would not be wise to take these numbers too seriously because the performance is highly data-dependent and because the goal of hashing is, after all, to randomize the names. Note, for instance, that in two cases (one each for hash1 and hash2) increasing the hash size increased, rather than decreased, the number of collisions. However, there is one general observation from the data that is worth notice. As the hash size is increased, one would expect the number of collisions to go down in proportion. The number does indeed go down, but not in direct proportion to the hash size. This is an illustration of the so-called birthday paradox: with any group more than 23 people, the likelihood that two will have the same birthday is greater than 50%.

hashgen is different from the other tools we have studied; rather than a hunk of code to be used as is, hashgen is a generator—it generates hunks of code that would otherwise be tedious to create by hand. There are many good applications for hash functions—symbol tables and keyword lists are present in one form or another in just about any real program. Any place you find yourself with a page or two of code with statements like

```
else if (str .eq. 'A') then
   . . .
else if (str .eq. 'B') then
   . . .
```

is a good candidate for using a hash table to speed things up, as well as to make a more elegant program.

Exercises

1. A perfect hash function maps all input strings (from a predefined list) onto an equal number of hash values with no collisions. How would you go about finding such a function? What's the closest you can come for Fortran keywords, using the hash functions provided?

2. A variation of the direct chaining method used for collision resolution employs *self-organizing lists*. A self-organizing list takes advantage of the "clustering" of references to a name in most computer programs. Whenever a name is looked up, it is moved to the head of the linked list, so the list becomes organized in order of most to least recently used.

   (a) Implement self-organizing lists in hlookup.

   (b) How much performance improvement do you expect?

3. When names are removed from a hash table, hremove removes the pointer to the name and does nothing to recover the storage; text associated with

a name that has been redefined also becomes unreachable. The process of recovering this space is known as *garbage collection*.

(a) How can you locate strings in buffer that no longer have pointers to them?

(b) Write a garbage collection routine to work with hinstall, hremove, and hlookup.

4. What additional statistics about a preloaded hash table could be reported by hashgen? Can you devise a "performance index" that summarizes the overall performance?

5. Most languages have scope rules to determine where identifiers are defined and where they are not. Pascal, for instance, is a block-structured language, and an identifier can be declared in the current block or any enclosing block. How would you design a hash table for symbol table management for a Pascal compiler?

6. Write a program that generates a hashgen input file from a Fortran common block declaration file.

Further Reading

Donald Knuth provides a definitive treatment of hashing, hash functions, and collision resolution in Volume 3 of *The Art of Computer Programming*, published by Addison-Wesley, as well as a definitive treatment of the related subject of random number generation in Volume 2. It is, however, probably too intense for most readers. A source for a simplified discussion of hashing and random numbers is *Algorithms* by Robert Sedgewick (Addison-Wesley). "Hashing for High Performance Searching" by Edwin T. Floyd in *Dr. Dobbs Journal* (Feb. 1987) is a good introductory article on hash functions, and also discusses self-organized lists. "Look it up Faster with Hashing" by Jon C. Snader in *Byte* (Jan. 1987) is a good introduction to collision resolution methods. Berman, et al. (*SIAM Journal of Computing*, Vol 15 #2, pp. 604–618, May 1986) and Sebesta and Taylor (*SIGPLAN Notices*, Vol 20 #12, pp. 47–53, December 1985) investigate perfect hash functions and how to automate the process of finding them.

CHAPTER 6

Preprocessing

We have developed a modest set of low-level routines in the preceding chapters, which allow other programs efficient file I/O and string operations. We essentially have stockpiled routines for future use. While such stockpiling is useful and necessary, it doesn't result in many complete or sophisticated programs. Top-down program design, on the other hand, may result in code that is complete or sophisticated but is difficult to apply to other programs directly. Both bottom-up and top-down design are necessary to achieve both objectives. In this chapter, we will create a simple computer language preprocessor with macro capabilities and conditional processing control. We begin with a specification of the program and design top-down code to meet the requirements. The result is prep, a preprocessor language similar to the standard C preprocessor language.

The v77 preprocessor in chapter 2 was used to standardize Fortran, making VAX Fortran flow control constructs available on any machine. The prep preprocessor, on the other hand, is generally applicable to any text file processing application, although it is best used in conjunction with a programming language like Fortran. We use it to extend Fortran, to add features that even VAX Fortran doesn't have such as macro processing and conditional compilation. Having a preprocessor written in Fortran means that we can use it to process input to our own programs as well as to process Fortran code, so we can write programs that are, in effect, extensions of Fortran. We use prep in the lexgen program in Chapter 7 to allow the user to define symbolic names for the integer codes returned by the lexical analyzer; these same symbolic names can be used in a Fortran program by preprocessing the code with prep, so that lexgen, by virtue of prep, becomes an integral part of the Fortran programming environment. In the interpreter in Chapter 8, we use prep and the logical line buffering routine getlogline at the end of this chapter as the front end of the interpreter, thus making the features of prep an integral part of the spl language. Thus prep is a flexible tool.

6.1　a text processor

To design top-down code for prep we must first have a definition of what it is supposed to do. Writing a specification is perhaps the most important step in developing a large program since having a clear idea of what the final product is supposed to do generally points the way toward a solution. The statements to be recognized by the preprocessor are

```
#include filename
#define   NAME   replacement_string
#define   NAME(arg1,...argn)   replacement_string(arg1,...argn)
#undef    NAME
#clear
#quote    quote_char
#ifdef    NAME
#ifndef   NAME
#elsifdef NAME
#else
#endif
```

All of the preprocessor statements begin with the pound symbol, and all other input lines are scanned for macros specified in #define statements. The first form of #define is actually the same as the second form with no arguments; it can be used to declare symbolic constants as in

```
#define   NEWLINE  char(10)
#define   NULL     char(0)
```

which is similar to the Fortran parameter declaration, but foregoes all type checking. It also allows definitions such as

```
#define BETA     rval(4)
```

where `rval` is an array, something not allowed in a Fortran parameter statement. The #undef statement removes a macro definition; the #clear statement undefines everything.

The second form of #define is more powerful. It is something like a one line function definition, with arguments. It is different from a function, however, in that it is repeated in code for each time it is used. The overhead of a procedure call is eliminated but at the expense of more redundant code. For example,

```
#define incr(x)  x = x + 1
incr(i)
incr(stack(sp+OFFSET))
```

produces the output

```
i = i + 1
stack(sp+OFFSET) = stack(sp+OFFSET) + 1
```

It is different from a Fortran statement function in that it can generate multiple lines of replacement text and has the significant advantage of being useful in places other than Fortran programs. Since the preprocessor is intended to be useful for applications like text processing, blanks in the input are preserved. The replacement of a defined name by its corresponding definition is called *macro expansion*. Special characters such as NEWLINE can be included in a macro definition by using the escape mechanism introduced in Chapter 4, and macro definitions can be extended over one physical line by placing an ampersand at the end of a line. This allows multiple Fortran output lines from a macro expansion, as in

```
#define skipblank(line,lp)  &
do while (line(lp:lp) .eq. BLANK) \n&
   lp = lp + 1 \n&
end do
```

To distinguish between the two forms of #define, no intervening spaces are allowed between the macro name and the opening parenthesis of its arguments. There is a special quote character that can be used to prevent the expansion of a macro. By default, the character is the double quote character, so that

```
the "skipblank(line,lp)" macro is real handy.
```

comes out literally as shown, except that the quotes are removed. The quote character can be changed with the #quote statement. If #quote is entered without any quote character, then quoting is disabled altogether.

The #if-related statements control the inclusion of lines in the output and processing of define statements. For example,

```
#define   BIGSTRINGS
#ifdef BIGSTRINGS
    #define   MAXSTR   255
    !big strings enabled
#else
    #define   MAXSTR   134
    !small strings enabled
#endif
```

would define MAXSTR to be 255, and the text comment "!big strings enabled"
to appear in the output. The conditional processing capability is often used
to make code with machine or language implementation dependencies more
portable. Here is an example:

```
#ifdef _VAX
    #define MAX_STR_LEN   65535
#end if
#ifdef _PC
    #define MAX_STR_LEN   32767
#end if
```

Another possibility for using the conditional capability is to define code generation macros that produce different code depending on the setting of some flag:

```
#ifdef (BIGBUFFER)
    ! macros for character*1 buffer (BUFSIZE)
    #define sccopy(buffer,bp,string) &
    do i = 1, index(string,NULL) \n &
       buffer(bp) = string(i:i) \n &
       bp = bp + 1 \n &
    end do
    #define cscopy(string,buffer,bp) &
    i = 1 \n &
    do while (buffer(bp) .ne. NULL) \n &
       string(i:i) = buffer(bp) \n &
       bp = bp + 1 \n &
       i = i + 1 \n &
    end do \n &
    string(i:i) = NULL
#else
    ! macros for character*(BUFSIZE) buffer
    #define sccopy(buffer,bp,string) &
       buffer(bp:bp+index(string,NULL)) = string(1:index(string,NULL))
    #define cscopy(string,buffer,bp) &
       string(1:index(string,NULL)) = buffer(bp:bp+index(string,NULL))
#end if
```

An additional specification for the preprocessor concerns its overall organization from a programming standpoint. We would like the preprocessor to be
written as a line filter that looks something like a souped-up version of finclude,
so that it can be easily built into any program. A program using the preprocessor
might look something like

```
...
call ppinit (uin)
...
do while (ppline(line))
   process line
   ...
end do
...
```

The preprocessor should provide its own error handling but should also make an error status available to the calling program so that it can determine whether errors have occurred.

Now that we have a pretty good idea of what the problem is we are ready to begin solving it. We already have the #include statement and need to implement the other preprocessor statements. We already have many of the parts on hand, and already know some of the things to be done. For example, we know that macros can be defined to produce multiple lines of output, and buffers large enough to handle long macros will be needed in various places in the program. To make sure the whole program is singing from the same sheet of music, a parameter PPLINESIZE needs to be placed in global.def to define the maximum buffer size for macros to expand into (currently set to 2048). Since error reporting will occur in just about every routine, it would be nice to have some centralized error handler that takes care of incrementing the error count. We can and should write that routine as a first step:

```
! pperror  -  error handler for preprocessor

        subroutine pperror (msg, line)
        character*(*)  msg, line
        include        'global.def'
        include        'pperror.cmn'

        call fputstr (STDERR, 'PREPROCESSOR:'//NULL)
        call fputstr (STDERR, msg)
        call fputc (STDERR, NEWLINE)
        call fputstr (STDERR, line)
        pperrcount = pperrcount + 1

        return
        end
```

This will be used for all of the error reporting in the preprocessor routines, although errors in the I/O system or finclude will not get counted. The error count is made available to the caller via a common block:

```
!pperror.cmn  -  common block for preprocessor error count

        integer        pperrcount
        common /pperr/ pperrcount
        save   /pperr/
```

Routines that call the preprocessor can include this common block to be able to detect preprocessor errors, or they can ignore pperror.cmn altogether if they don't care.

Here is a first cut at what our main routine will look like:

```
do while (finclude (line))
    lp = 1
    if (ifclause (line, lp, ppjunk)) then
        if (.not. ppjunk) ppjunk = macro (line, lp, quotec)
        if (.not. ppjunk) ppjunk = setquote (line, lp, quotec)
        if (.not. ppjunk) call fputstr (uout, line)
    end if
end do
```

The main components of the preprocessor are finclude, ifclause to handle conditional statements, and macro to handle macro processing. The variable ppjunk is a flag that becomes true when a preprocessor statement is recognized, and these statements are not copied to the output. The ifclause routine will return true whenever the conditional processing is in the "on" state, and the others will return true whenever they recognize a statement. This outline isn't really right because the loop here will process all of the input instead of just one line; logic must be devised that does line buffering and returns one line at a time to the caller in case a macro generates multiple lines of output. We don't have enough details yet to write the real code for ppline. It is a strange but true fact that even when programs are designed from the top down, they usually are written from the bottom up.

Macro Processing

The most important rule in top-down programming is to define the data structure first and then write the program around it. The pieces tend to come together more naturally with this procedure than with the opposite procedure of designing the data around the code. There has to be some feedback, of course, between program and data design.

For the case at hand, we can break the problem down into two smaller problems—reading and storing macro definitions, and expanding macros when they occur in the text. The first problem is easier to solve, so we will tackle it first. We need a table organization to store the macro names along with the corresponding replacement text, and the hash table tools in Chapter 5 are perfect for the job. We don't need hashgen since all of the macros are user-defined, but we need three routines, mkdef, finddef, and rmdef to create, find, and remove macro definitions from the table, and these routines will all have access to a common block containing the hash table and associated variables. This will encapsulate the complexity of the hash table in three cooperating routines with simple interfaces.

What's in a name? A macro argument by any other name would smell as sweet. The names of arguments in a macro definition are simply for the user's

convenience since during macro expansion the actual arguments occurring in
the text are substituted for the dummy arguments in the definition anyway.
Therefore the dummy arguments will be changed to a simple internal code in
the replacement text when the definition is installed since the dummy names
have no significance themselves. The internal code is simply an "argument flag"
followed by a digit, so that, for example if ARGFLAG is "%," then the first argument
is represented in the replacement text as "%1." For example, for the macro
definition

```
#define  incr(i)   i = i + 1
```

we will install the macro name incr and the replacement text %1 = %1 + 1. The
representation chosen cannot deal with more than 10 arguments, but this limi-
tation is really a minor problem. The fact that the argument flag is a character
is a more serious problem, so to keep the preprocessor as general as possible, a
means of handling a literal occurrence of the argument flag should be provided.

We have enough of the details now to start implementing some of the code.
The macro table structure is just like that of the hash tables discussed in Chapter
5; in this case the names are macro names, and the data associated with each
name is its replacement text. An additional data item we can easily obtain for
each name is the number of arguments it has, and the number of arguments can
be used to do argument checking during macro expansion.

```
! macro.cmn  -  declarations for macro processor hash table

        integer           HASHSIZE
        parameter         (HASHSIZE = 256)      !number of linked lists
        integer           BUFSIZE
        parameter         (BUFSIZE = 5000)      !total # chars in macro def
        integer           MAXSYMBOL
        parameter         (MAXSYMBOL = 512)     !maximum # macros

!permanent local data
        character*(BUFSIZE) buffer              !name/definition table
        integer           hashtable(HASHSIZE)   !pointers to linked lists
        integer           nextfree              !next free position in buffer
        integer           nextsymbol            !next subscript in symbol table

!linked list data components
        integer           namepos(MAXSYMBOL)    !ptr to table pos: name
        integer           defpos(MAXSYMBOL)     !ptr to table pos: definition
        integer           nargs(MAXSYMBOL)      !# arguments in definition
        integer           nextptr(MAXSYMBOL)    !ptr to next list element

        common /mactables/ hashtable, nextfree, nextsymbol,
       &                   namepos, defpos, nargs, nextptr
        common /macbuffer/ buffer
        save   /mactables/, /macbuffer/
```

Each of the routines mkdef, finddef, and rmdef calls the corresponding hash table management routine (hinstall, hlookup, and hremove) while providing a simple interface to the rest of the preprocessor.

```
! mkdef  -  install new macro definition in hash table

        logical function mkdef (name, definition, argcount)
        character*(*) name, definition
        integer      argcount
        include      'global.def'
        include      'macro.cmn'
        integer      L, hash3
        external     hash3

        L = index(name, NULL) + index(definition, NULL)

        if ((nextfree+L .le. BUFSIZE).and.(nextsymbol .le. MAXSYMBOL)) then
           call hinstall (name, buffer, nextfree,
     &                    namepos, nextptr, nextsymbol,
     &                    hashtable, hash3, HASHSIZE)
           nextfree = nextfree + index(name, NULL)
           buffer(nextfree:nextfree+index(definition,NULL)) = definition
           defpos(nextsymbol) = nextfree
           nextfree = nextfree + index(definition, NULL)
           nargs(nextsymbol) = argcount
           nextsymbol = nextsymbol + 1
           mkdef = .true.
        else
           mkdef = .false.
        end if

        return
        end




! finddef  -  find replacement text for macro

        logical function finddef (name, definition, argcount)
        character*(*) name, definition
        integer      argcount
        include      'global.def'
        include      'macro.cmn'
        integer      hlookup, hash3, deflen, p
        external     hash3

        p = hlookup (name,buffer,namepos,nextptr,hashtable,hash3,HASHSIZE)
        if (p .ne. 0) then
           deflen = index(buffer(defpos(p):),NULL)
           definition = buffer(defpos(p):defpos(p)+deflen)
           argcount = nargs(p)
           finddef = .true.
        else
```

```
        definition = NULL
        finddef = .false.
      end if

      return
      end


! rmdef  -  remove macro definition

      logical function rmdef (name)
      character*(*) name
      include       'macro.cmn'
      logical       hremove
      integer       hash3
      external      hash3

      rmdef = hremove (name, buffer, namepos, nextptr,
     &                 hashtable, hash3, HASHSIZE)
      return
      end
```

We have enough information about the routines above and below it to write the main routine, macro, now. macro processes #define, #undef and #clear statements and scans for macros on all other statements. It relies on two subroutines dodef and macscan to do the hard parts, namely installing names and scanning ordinary lines for macros, respectively. macro handles the details of statement continuation in #define statements so that dodef doesn't need to read input. As indicated in the outline for the main routine of the preprocessor, macro is a logical function and returns true when a macro processor statement is recognized.

```
! macro  -  macro processor with arguments

      logical function macro (line, quotec)
      character*(*)     line
      character*1       quotec
      include           'global.def'
      logical           is_ident, equal, rmdef, finclude, done
      character*(MAXSTR) name, getword, word, upper, cat, tmpline
      integer           lp, i, j

      lp = 1
      word = upper (getword (word, line, lp))

      if (equal(word, '#DEFINE'//NULL)) then
                                        !install macro definition
          macro = .true.
          i = index (line, NEWLINE) - 1
          do while (line(i:i) .eq. BLANK)
              i = i - 1
```

```
         end do
         if (line(i:i) .eq. '&') then     !get continuation line
            done = .false.
            do while (.not. done)
               if (finclude(tmpline)) then
                  j = index (tmpline, NEWLINE) - 1
                  do while (tmpline(j:j) .eq. BLANK .and. j .gt. 1)
                     j = j - 1
                  end do
                  if (tmpline(j:j) .eq. '&') then
                     line(i:i+j-1) = tmpline(1:j-1)
                     i = i + j - 1
                  else
                     done = .true.
                     line(i:i+j+2) = tmpline(1:j)//EOL
                  end if
               else
                  call pperror
&                    ('unexpected EOF in DEFINE statement'//NULL, line)
               end if
            end do
         end if
         call dodef (line, lp)

      else if (equal(word, '#UNDEF'//NULL)) then
                                           !remove macro definition
         macro = .true.
         if (.not. is_ident(name, line, lp)) then
            call pperror
&           ('object of UNDEFINE must be an identifier'//NULL, line)
         else if (.not. rmdef(name)) then
            call pperror (cat(name,' was not defined'//NULL), line)
         end if

      else if (equal (word, '#CLEAR'//NULL)) then
         macro = .true.
         call initmacro ()                !reset hash table

      else                                !scan line and expand macros
         macro = .false.
         call macscan (line, quotec)

      end if

      return
      end
```

The initialization routine for macro initializes all of the hash table pointers; the #clear statement just calls initmacro again.

```
   ! initmacro  -  initialize macro symbol table

      subroutine initmacro ()
```

```
include   'macro.cmn'
integer   i

nextsymbol = 1
nextfree = 1
do i = 1, HASHSIZE
   hashtable(i) = 0
end do
return
end
```

Macro expansion is handled by the as yet unspecified routine macscan. We know what dodef needs to do and can implement it now. dodef performs the argument substitution before installing a macro definition. It first builds a miniature symbol table from the arguments and then searches the replacement text for the argument identifiers. The argument symbol table is simply a linear list of names, since there will never be more than 10 anyway. dodef handles literal occurrences of the argument flag by encoding it like an argument, using zero as the argument number. With this scheme it is possible to use any character for the argument flag except a digit.

```
! dodef   -   get macro name and replacement text

        subroutine dodef (line, lp)
        character*(*)       line
        integer             lp
        include             'global.def'
        include             'macscan.cmn'
        character*(MAXSTR)  name, def, ident
        character*(MAXSTR)  nametable                !storage for argument names
        integer             nameptr (MAXARGS) !pointers to argument names
        integer             ntp                      !next free loc in nametable
        integer             endp, defp, argno, argcount, i
        logical             is_ident, done, found, equal, mkdef
        character*1         escchar, c

! get name and arguments
        argcount = 0
        ntp = 1
        if (is_ident(name, line, lp)) then
            if (line(lp:lp) .eq. '(') then   !collect argument names
                lp = lp + 1
                done = .false.
                do while (.not. done)
                    if (is_ident (ident, line, lp)) then
                        argcount = argcount + 1
                        nametable(ntp:) = ident(1:)
                        nameptr(argcount) = ntp
                        ntp = ntp + index (ident, NULL)
                    else if (line(lp:lp) .eq. ')') then
                        done = .true.
```

```
              else if (line(lp:lp) .eq. ',') then
                 lp = lp + 1
              else if (line(lp:lp) .eq. NEWLINE) then
                 call pperror
   &             ('missing right parenthesis in argument list'//NULL, line)
                 done = .true.
              else if (line(lp:lp) .eq. '(') then
                 call pperror
   &             ('illegal parentheses in argument list'//NULL, line)
                 done = .true.
              else                !all other characters are illegal
                 call pperror
   &             ('argument must be an identifier'//NULL, line)
                 done = .true.
              end if
           end do
           if (line(lp:lp) .eq. ')') then
              lp = lp + 1
           else
              call pperror ('statement ignored'//NULL, line)
              return
           end if
        else                                   !no arguments
           continue
        end if
     else                                   !no identifier after #DEFINE
        call pperror
   &    ('object of DEFINE must be an identifier'//NULL, line)
        return
     end if

! get definition
     do while (line(lp:lp) .eq. BLANK)       !skip leading blanks
        lp = lp + 1
     end do
     if (line(lp:lp) .ne. NEWLINE) then
        i = lp
        endp = lp
        do while (line(i:i) .ne. NEWLINE)    !find last nonblank
           if (line(i:i) .ne. BLANK) endp = i
           i = i + 1
        end do
        line(endp+1:endp+2) = EOL            !effectively deletes
     end if                                  !trailing blanks

! scan the definition and encode arguments
     done = .false.
     defp = 1
     do while (.not. done)
        if (line(lp:lp) .eq. NEWLINE) then
           done = .true.
        else if (line(lp:lp) .eq. BLANK) then !save blanks from is_ident
           def(defp:defp) = BLANK
```

```
        defp = defp + 1
        lp = lp + 1
    else if (is_ident (ident, line, lp)) then   !lookup name
        found = .false.
        argno = 1
        do while ((.not. found) .and. (argno .le. argcount))
            if (equal (ident, nametable(nameptr(argno):))) then
                found = .true.
            else
                argno = argno + 1
            end if
        end do
        if (found) then                    !substitute arg flag for ident
            def(defp:defp) = ARGFLAG
            def(defp+1:defp+1) = char(argno + ichar('0'))
            defp = defp + 2
        else
            i = 1
            do while (ident(i:i) .ne. NULL)
                def(defp:defp) = ident(i:i)
                defp = defp + 1
                i = i + 1
            end do
        end if
    else if (line(lp:lp) .eq. ESCAPE) then !special character
        c = escchar (line, lp)
        if (c .eq. ARGFLAG) then
            def(defp:defp+1) = ARGFLAG//'0'
            defp = defp + 2
        else
            def(defp:defp) = c
            defp = defp + 1
        end if
    else                                   !ordinary character
        if (line(lp:lp) .eq. ARGFLAG) then
            def(defp:defp+1) = ARGFLAG//'0'
            defp = defp + 2
        else
            def(defp:defp) = line(lp:lp)
            defp = defp + 1
        end if
        lp = lp + 1
    end if
end do
def(defp:defp) = NULL

if (.not. mkdef (name, def, argcount)) then
    call pperror ('symbol table overflow'//NULL, line)
end if

return
end
```

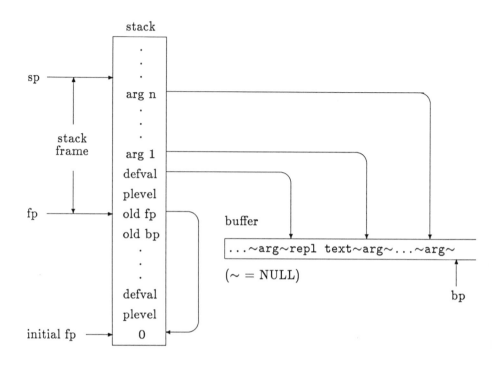

Figure 6.1: Macro call stack and replacement text expansion buffer.

Now for the problem of macro expansion. We have two main issues to resolve before trying to write any code. One is that we need to allow macros to be used as arguments for other macros; the other is that we need to allow macro definitions to be made in terms of other macros. Let's address the first issue first: during expansion we must be able to handle nested macro calls. The nature of the beast suggests a stack organization, and that is what will be used. Each recognition of a macro name will result in the creation of a stack frame, consisting of pointers to the replacement text and actual arguments of the macro. This is similar to the run-time stack organization of a programming language procedure call and requires a stack pointer sp pointing to the top of the stack and a frame pointer fp pointing to the bottom of the current call frame. The value at the bottom of each frame (pointed to by fp) is the frame pointer for the previous (outer) frame.

Figure 6.1 shows the organization of the stack and macro expansion buffer for a case in which a macro has invoked another macro as one of its arguments, in an expression such as

```
macro1(arg1, macro2(arg1, ... , argn), ... , argn)
```

`plevel` keeps track of the nesting of parentheses following a macro call. All of the other stack entries are pointers into the macro expansion buffer, which contains the text strings corresponding to the macro definition and the actual arguments. When one of the arguments is a macro, a new stack frame is created, and its replacement text and arguments are pushed onto the stack for evaluation. When the end of an argument list is encountered (signaled by the closing parenthesis), the stack frame is popped, meaning the frame pointer `fp` is set to the value at `stack(fp)`, and expansion of the outer macro resumes. When the outermost macro call has been expanded, the resulting replacement text is shifted to the output. Arguments are pushed onto the stack as they occur in the input, and if one of the arguments is a macro it is expanded immediately. What gets left on the stack after the inner macro expansion is completed is its replacement text, which becomes the corresponding argument for the outer macro.

The `macscan` data structure uses a character buffer to hold the replacement text and argument text. The buffer actually is used like a stack. The buffer pointer `bp` is incremented by the length of each string, so that the first characters in the buffer represent text and arguments of the outermost macro, and the last charracters are from the innermost macro, in a nested macro call. The storage in `buffer` occupied by an inner macro is recovered when all pointers to it are removed, when a stack frame is popped.

This data structure is defined by a common block, containing the stack and its pointers, as well as codes for locating elements within a stack frame, given as offsets from the frame pointer `fp`. Using symbolic codes for these offsets rather than hard-wired constants means that the stack frame can be reorganized easily by just changing the common block file.

```
! macscan.cmn  -  data structure for macscan

        integer             STACKSIZE
        parameter           (STACKSIZE = 64)
        integer             stack (STACKSIZE)
        character*(PPLINESIZE) buffer
        integer             fp, sp, bp

        character*1         ARGFLAG
        parameter           (ARGFLAG = '%')

! stack organization parameters - offsets from current fp

        integer             PLEVEL, DEFVAL, ARGVAL
        parameter           (PLEVEL = 1)
        parameter           (DEFVAL = 2)
        integer             FRAMESIZE     !size of fixed part of frame
        parameter           (FRAMESIZE = 3) !excludes bp at top of frame

        common /scanvalue/ stack, sp, bp, fp
        common /scanbuffer/ buffer
        save    /scanvalue/, /scanbuffer/
```

The second question to be answered before committing ourselves to code is how to handle macro definitions that themselves contain macro calls and ensure that all macros get fully expanded. Consider the following definitions:

```
#define  incr(i)    i = i + 1
#define  push(val,stack,sp)   stack(sp) = val \n incr(sp)
```

When a call to the push macro occurs, it will expand into text that contains a call to the incr macro and must be scanned again to find and expand the incr macro. In general it is necessary to scan the replacement text for every expanded macro over and over until no further macro calls are encountered. Furthermore, since the replacement text of a macro is generally longer (i.e., it has more characters) than the name and arguments, we need to make provision for the expanded line to grow as needed.

Both requirements can be implemented by putting the input onto a stack; then we can read input from the stack and push expanded macros back onto the stack to be read again. The stack allows the length of the input string to grow as necessary and gives macscan recursive input reading implicitly, while the recursion in nested macro calls is handled explicitly via stack frames. A collection of routines, which we call the "putback system," will be needed for reading from the stack and for pushing text back onto it. The putback system is hidden from macscan by use of a private stack and routines to push or pop it. macscan just keeps reading from the putback buffer as if it were reading from a line, until the stack is exhausted and NULL is returned.

```
! putback.cmn  -  common block for putback system

      character*(PPLINESIZE)  buffer
      integer                 bp
      common /pbbuffer/       buffer
      common /pbpointer/      bp
      save   /pbpointer/, /pbbuffer/
```

This is starting to sound complicated. We have two logically distinct stacks: the input stack managed by the putback system routines and the expansion stack holding replacement text and arguments of macros presently being expanded. The following is a pseudocode outline of macscan, the main macro scanner routine called by macro:

```
! macscan  -  pseudocode outline of macro scanner

      subroutine macscan (line, quotec)

      push input line onto putback stack
      do while (next token on putback stack .ne. NULL)
         if (token is identifier) then
            if (identifier is a macro name) then
               make stack frame
            else
```

```
            copy identifier to output
        end if
    else if (token is quotec) then
        copy quoted string to output
    else if (fp = 0) then   !not in any macro
        copy token to output
    else if (token is '(') then
        if (plevel for current stack frame > 0) then
            copy '(' to output    !part of argument
        end if
        plevel = plevel + 1
    else if (token is ')') then
        plevel = plevel - 1
        if (plevel for current stack frame > 0) then
            copy ')' to output    !part of argument
        else
            expand macro
            push replacement text onto putback stack
            pop expansion stack frame
        end if
    else if (plevel of current frame = 1 and token = comma) then
        mark end of previous argument and
            begin collecting next argument
    else
        copy token to output
    end if
end do
```

The conditional tests in this outline need to occur in the order given since for instance we don't want to take any special action on parentheses if fp = 0, that is, if we are not evaluating a macro. An additional fine point about the pseudocode concerns the meaning of the word "output." When we are not expanding any macro, "output" really is the output (the string that will eventually be returned to the caller). But when we are in the process of collecting arguments for a macro, the output is the macro expansion buffer since the replacement text for an inner macro forms an argument of an outer macro.

Now that we have the overall organization spelled out clearly, we are ready to start writing the code. The putback system is relatively self-containded and independent so we will write it first. The putback system has a simple initialization routine:

```
! pbinit  -  initialize putback buffer

        subroutine pbinit()
        include    'global.def'
        include    'putback.cmn'

        bp = 0
        return
        end
```

There is no reason why the initialization cannot be performed with a data statement, but doing so requires a separate block data routine since bp is in a common block. The use of an executable routine instead preserves the flexibility of resetting the putback buffer at any time.

The getpbc and putback routines perform operations analogous to fgetc and fputc, with getpbc returning NULL when the buffer is empty:

```
! getpbc  -  get a character from putback buffer

        character*1 function getpbc (c)
        character*1 c
        include    'global.def'
        include    'putback.cmn'

        if (bp .gt. 0) then
          c = buffer(bp:bp)
          bp = bp - 1
        else
          c = NULL
        end if
        getpbc = c

        return
        end
```

```
! putback  -  put character onto putback buffer

        subroutine putback (c)
        character*1 c
        include    'global.def'
        include    'putback.cmn'

        if (bp .ge. PPLINESIZE) then
            call fputstr (STDERR,'PUTBACK: buffer overflow'//EOL)
            stop ' '
        else
            bp = bp + 1
            buffer(bp:bp) = c
        end if

        return
        end
```

The subroutine pbstr puts back a whole string at once:

```
! pbstr  -  put a string onto putback buffer

        subroutine pbstr (string)
        character*(*) string
        include       'global.def'
        include       'putback.cmn'
```

```
      integer      i

      i = index(string,NULL) - 1
      do while (i .gt. 0)
         if (bp .ge. PPLINESIZE) then
            call fputstr(STDERR,'PBSTR:buffer overflow'//EOL)
         else
            bp = bp + 1
            buffer(bp:bp) = string(i:i)
            i = i - 1
         end if
      end do

      return
      end
```

Likewise, pb_ident does the task analogous to is_ident.

```
! pb_ident  -  get identifier from putback buffer

      logical function pb_ident (ident)
      character*(*) ident
      include       'global.def'
      logical       isletter, isalpha
      character*1   getpbc, c
      integer       i

      if (isletter(getpbc(c)) .or. c .eq. '$' .or. c .eq. '_') then
         pb_ident = .true.
         ident(1:1) = c
         i = 2
         do while (isalpha(getpbc(c)) .or. c .eq. '$' .or. c .eq. '_')
            ident(i:i) = c
            i = i + 1
         end do
         ident(i:i) = NULL
      else
         pb_ident   = .false.
         ident(1:1) = NULL
      end if
      call putback (c)

      return
      end
```

macscan doesn't use pb_ident directly, but rather, uses the character*1 function getpbtoken. The only purpose of getpbtoken is to classify input tokens as identifier or "other" and to always consume at least one character of input. The return value is just the first letter of the token, so that it can be checked to classify the token.

```
! getpbtoken  -  get identifier or single character from putback buffer
```

```
character*1 function getpbtoken (ident)
character*(*) ident
include      'global.def'
logical      isletter, isalpha
character*1   getpbc, c
integer       i

if (isletter(getpbc(c)) .or. c .eq. '$' .or. c .eq. '_') then
   ident(1:1) = c
   i = 2
   do while (isalpha(getpbc(c)) .or. c .eq. '$' .or. c .eq. '_')
      ident(i:i) = c
      i = i + 1
   end do
   ident(i:i) = NULL
   call putback(c)
else
   ident(1:1) = c
   ident(2:2) = NULL
end if
getpbtoken = ident(1:1)


return
end
```

We are ready to write the real version of macscan now. It simply has to loop
through the input with getpbtoken, searching for macros and creating stack
frames when they are found. If quotes are found, then the quoted text is copied
to the output without scanning, and the quotes are removed. macscan must
keep track of the parentheses after a macro name so that it knows when all of the
arguments have been collected, and when the final closing parenthesis is seen,
the macro is expanded in subroutine expand.

```
! macscan  -  scan line for macro calls and expand

subroutine macscan (line, quotec)
character*(*)     line
character*1       quotec
include          'global.def'
include          'macscan.cmn'
include          'pperror.cmn'
character*1       c, getpbc, getpbtoken
integer           optr, i, argcount
logical           pb_ident, isletter, finddef
character*(MAXSTR) ident, def

call pbstr (line)
optr = 1
fp = 0
sp = 1
bp = 1
```

```
do while (getpbtoken(ident) .ne. NULL)
  c = ident(1:1)

  if (isletter(c) .or. c .eq. '$' .or. c .eq. '_') then
    !check for macro
    if (finddef (ident, def, argcount)) then !make new stack frame
      call mkframe (def)
      if (argcount .eq. 0) then   !no args - expand immediately
        call expand ()
        sp = fp - 1                !pop stack frame
        fp = stack (fp)
        bp = stack(sp)
      end if
    else                          !finddef failed - not a macro
      i = 1
      do while (ident(i:i) .ne. NULL)
        call putchr (ident(i:i), line, optr)
        i = i + 1
      end do
    end if

  else if (c .eq. quotec) then        !skip quote
    do while ((getpbc(c) .ne. quotec) .and. (c .ne. NULL))
      call putchr (c, line, optr)
    end do
    if (c .eq. NULL) then
      call pperror ('missing quote'//NULL, line)
    end if

  else if (fp .eq. 0) then            !not in any macro
    call putchr (c, line, optr)

  else if (c .eq. '(') then
    if (stack(fp+PLEVEL) .gt. 0) then !part of argument - keep it
      call putchr (c, line, optr)
    end if
    stack(fp+PLEVEL) = stack(fp+PLEVEL) + 1

  else if (c .eq. ')') then
    stack(fp+PLEVEL) = stack(fp+PLEVEL) - 1
    if (stack(fp+PLEVEL) .gt. 0) then !part of argument - keep it
      call putchr (c, line, optr)
    else                              !end of argument list
      call putchr (NULL, line, optr)
      call expand ()     !expand macro and put back onto input
      sp = fp - 1        !pop stack frame
      fp = stack(fp)
      bp = stack(sp)
    end if

  else if ((c .eq. ',') .and.
&         (stack(fp+PLEVEL) .eq. 1)) then   !new argument
```

```
            call putchr (NULL, line, optr)
            if (sp .gt. STACKSIZE) then
                call pperror ('stack overflow'//NULL, line)
            else
                stack(sp) = bp
                sp = sp + 1
            end if

        else                                    !everything else
            call putchr (c, line, optr)

        end if
    end do

    if (fp .gt. 0) then
        call pperror ('line ended during expansion of macro'//NULL, line)
    end if
! empty putback buffer in case of error
    do while (getpbc(c) .ne. NULL)
        continue
    end do
    line(optr:optr) = NULL

    return
    end
```

Although macscan has intimate knowledge of the structure of a stack frame, the details of creating stack frames are handled by mkframe:

```
! mkframe  -  create new stack frame entry for macscan

    subroutine mkframe (def)
    character*(*)    def
    include          'global.def'
    include          'macscan.cmn'
    include          'pperror.cmn'

    if ((sp + FRAMESIZE + 2) .ge. STACKSIZE) then
        call fputstr (STDERR, 'PREPROCESSOR: stack overflow'//EOL)
        pperrcount = pperrcount + 1
    else
        stack(sp) = bp                  !push bp
        sp = sp + 1
        stack(sp) = fp                  !update fp
        fp = sp
        stack (fp + PLEVEL) = 0         !initialize parenthesis counter
        stack (fp + DEFVAL) = bp        !set pointer to def
        sp = sp + 3
        buffer(bp:) = def(1:)
        bp = bp + index (def, NULL)
        stack(sp) = bp                  !preset pointer to first argument
        sp = sp + 1
    end if
```

```
      return
      end
```

Since mkframe doesn't have access to the input line, the pperror common block
is included and the error message is written directly to STDERR.

putchr keeps track of where to put output characters. Since the input is
pushed onto the putback stack to begin macro scanning, the input string is
available for use as the output string for putchr. If fp is greater than zero, then
we are in a macro evaluation and output characters are put in the macro buffer
for the outer macro. If fp = 0, then we are not in any macro call, and output is
copied to the output string.

```
! putchr  -  put character into scan buffer or output line

      subroutine putchr (c, line, optr)
      character*1    c
      character*(*) line
      integer       optr
      include       'global.def'
      include       'macscan.cmn'

      if (fp .eq. 0) then
         if (optr .ge. PPLINESIZE) then
            call pperror ('output overflow'//NULL, line(1:optr-2)//EOL)
         else
            line(optr:optr) = c
            optr = optr + 1
         end if
      else if (fp .gt. 0) then
         if (bp .ge. PPLINESIZE) then
            call pperror ('buffer overflow'//NULL, line)
         else
            buffer(bp:bp) = c
            bp = bp + 1
         end if
      else
         call pperror ('fatal error in PUTCHR'//NULL, line)
      end if

      return
      end
```

Macros without arguments in their definitions (signaled by argcount=0 returned from finddef) are expanded immediately when they are encountered, so
that macros without arguments will not swallow anything in parentheses following them. For macros with arguments, there is no check to ensure that actual
arguments are present in the input text. The lack of argument checking has
the somewhat freaky side effect of causing any intervening characters between
the macro name and the first argument in parentheses all to be counted as the

first argument. Although this handling can cause an erroneous output (defined as other than that intended) without any error message, it is probably a pretty harmless bug (call it a "feature"). In fact, there is never any check to see that the number of arguments supplied is the same as the number in the definition. However, if too few are supplied then the error will be caught when the macro is expanded, and if none are supplied at all then the error message "string ended during expansion of macro" will be produced.

expand searches the replacement text backwards, looking for ARGFLAG and substituting the appropriate argument when ARGFLAG is found. Everything is pushed back onto the input as it is expanded.

```
! expand   -   expand macro into replacement text with argument substitution

        subroutine expand ()
        include  'global.def'
        include  'macscan.cmn'
        include  'pperror.cmn'
        integer  i, j, k1, k2, argcount, argno

        argcount = sp - fp - FRAMESIZE
        j = stack(fp+DEFVAL)                !pointer to start of defining text
        i = j
        do while (buffer(i:i) .ne. NULL)    !find end of replacement text
           i = i + 1
        end do
        i = i - 1                           !last char of replacement text

        do while (i .gt. j)
           if (buffer(i-1:i-1) .eq. ARGFLAG) then
              argno = ichar(buffer(i:i)) - ichar('0')
              if (argno .gt. 0 .and. argno .le. argcount) then
                 k1 = stack(fp+DEFVAL+argno)
                 k2 = k1 + index(buffer(k1:),NULL) - 2
                 do while (k2 .ge. k1)
                    call putback (buffer(k2:k2))
                    k2 = k2 - 1
                 end do
              else if (argno .eq. 0) then
                 call putback (ARGFLAG)
              else
                 call fputstr (STDERR, 'PREPROCESSOR: missing argument'//EOL)
                 pperrcount = pperrcount + 1
              end if
              i = i - 2
           else
              call putback (buffer(i:i))
              i = i - 1
           end if
        end do

        if (i .eq. j) call putback (buffer(i:i))
```

```
      return
      end
```

The macro processing portion of our preprocessor is now complete, except for the #quote statement to change the quote character. So here it is, to wrap up the macro processor. setquote checks for the presence of any nonblank character before the end of the line and sets it to be the quote character. If no nonblank character is present, then the quote character is set to NULL, effectively disabling quotes.

```
! setquote  -  set preprocessor quote character

      logical function setquote (line, quotec)
      character*(*)      line
      character*1        quotec
      include            'global.def'
      character*(MAXSTR) upper, getword, word
      integer            lp
      logical            equal

      lp = 1
      if (equal(upper(getword(word,line,lp)), '#QUOTE'//NULL)) then
         setquote = .true.
         do while (line(lp:lp) .eq. BLANK)
            lp = lp + 1
         end do
         if (line(lp:lp) .eq. NEWLINE) then
            quotec = NULL
         else
            quotec = line(lp:lp)
         end if
      else                           !none of my business
         setquote = .false.
      end if

      return
      end
```

Conditional Output

Now we are ready to turn our attention to the conditional processing portion of the preprocessor. All of the if-related statements are handled by a single routine ifclause, which just returns true or false to the main program. This allows a rather simple organization for the main program in which ifclause "masks" the execution of all of the macro processor routines. So the ifclause routine needs to keep track of whether the current line is in the true or false part of an if clause. It also must deal with nested if clauses, and for this purpose the simplest means is with a stack; each stack entry corresponds to a nesting level, and the current state (true or false) is pushed onto the stack whenever a new nesting level begins:

```
! ifclause.cmn  -  common variable declarations for ifclause

     logical state, stack (10)
     integer sp
     common  /ifdata/ state, stack, sp
     save    /ifdata/
```

The algorithm for ifclause is quite simple. Each time an if-related clause is encountered, one of two things happens: if the statement results in a false state, the current state is set to false. If, however, the condition has a true result, the state is set to true only if the state on top of the stack is true (meaning this statement is within the true part of an outer nesting level). For this reason, the initial stack position is set to true since at the start all lines are processed.

```
! ifclause  -  set state for conditional output

     logical function ifclause (line, ppjunk)
     character*(*)    line
     logical          ppjunk
     include          'global.def'
     include          'ifclause.cmn'
     character*(MAXSTR) getword, word, upper, name, def
     integer          lp, a
     logical          equal, finddef, is_ident

     lp = 1
     word = upper (getword (word, line, lp))
     if (ppjunk) then                         !ignore this line
        continue
     else if (equal(word, '#IFDEF'//NULL)) then
        ppjunk = .true.
        sp = sp + 1                           !increment nesting level
        stack(sp) = state
        if (is_ident(name,line,lp)) then
           state = (finddef(name,def,a) .and. stack(sp))
        else
           state = .false.
           call pperror
   &        ('object of #IFDEF must be an identifier'//NULL, line)
        end if
     else if (equal(word, '#IFNDEF'//NULL)) then
        ppjunk = .true.
        sp = sp + 1                           !increment nesting level
        stack(sp) = state
        if (is_ident(name,line,lp)) then
           state = ((.not. finddef(name,def,a)) .and. stack(sp))
        else
```

```
               state = .false.
               call pperror
&              ('object of #IFDEF must be an identifier'//NULL, line)
            end if
         else if (equal (word, '#ELIFDEF'//NULL)) then
            ppjunk = .true.
            if (sp .lt. 2) then
               call pperror ('#ELSE without #IF'//NULL, line)
            end if
            if (state) then
               state = .false.
               stack(sp) = .false.
            else
               if (is_ident(name,line,lp)) then
                  state = (finddef(name,def,a) .and. stack(sp))
               else
                  state = .false.
                  call pperror
&                 ('object of #IFDEF must be an identifier'//NULL, line)
               end if
            end if
         else if (equal (word, '#ELSE'//NULL)) then
            ppjunk = .true.
            if (sp .lt. 2) then
               call pperror ('#ELSE without #IF'//NULL, line)
            end if
            if (state) then
               state = .false.
            else
               state = stack(sp)
            end if
         else if (equal (word, '#ENDIF'//NULL)) then
            ppjunk = .true.
            sp = sp - 1                       !decrement nesting level
            if (sp .lt. 1) then
               call pperror ('#ENDIF without #IF'//NULL, line)
            end if
            state = stack(sp)
         else                                 !none of my business
            continue
         end if

         ifclause = state

         return
         end
```

The stack and stack pointer are initialized with initif:

```
! initif  -  initialize data for ifclause

         subroutine initif ()
         include 'ifclause.cmn'
```

```
state = .true.
stack(1) = .true.
sp = 1
return
end
```

We are finally ready for the main routine of the preprocessor. The outline for the main routine presented earlier can be modified to allow the preprocessor to act as a line filter rather than as a file filter, like the include processor before it. This allows programs to get lines from a file with preprocessing, oblivious to the fact that it is taking place. The variable ppjunk is a flag that is true whenever the current line is a preprocessor line and is not to be returned to the calling program; ppline continues to process lines of input until a line that is not ppjunk is found before returning.

```
! ppline  -  get preprocessed input line

      logical function ppline (line)
      character*(*)        line
      include              'global.def'
      include              'ppline.cmn'
      character*(MAXSTR)   upper, getword, word
      integer              lp
      logical              equal, finclude, setquote, macro, ifclause
      logical              ppjunk, done, state

      done = .false.
      do while (.not. done)
         if (buffer(bp:bp) .eq. NULL) then      !refill buffer
            ppjunk = finclude (buffer)
            bp = 1
            if (.not. ppjunk) then
               done = .true.
               ppline = .false.
            else if
     &      (equal(upper(getword(word,buffer,bp)), '#INCLUDE'//NULL)) then
               call fputstr (STDERR, getword(word, buffer, bp))
               call fputc (STDERR, NEWLINE)
            else                                !successful finclude
               bp = 1
               ppjunk = .false.
               state = ifclause (buffer, ppjunk)
               if (state) then
                  if (.not. ppjunk) ppjunk = setquote (buffer, quotec)
                  if (.not. ppjunk) ppjunk = macro (buffer, quotec)
               end if
               if (ppjunk .or. (.not. state)) then
                  bp = index (buffer, NULL)
               else
                  bp = 1
```

```
            end if
         end if
      else
         lp = 1
         do while (buffer(bp:bp) .ne. NEWLINE)
            line(lp:lp) = buffer(bp:bp)
            bp = bp + 1
            lp = lp + 1
         end do
         line(lp:lp+1) = EOL
         bp = bp + 1
         done = .true.
         ppline = .true.
      end if
   end do

   return
   end
```

Because they must be initialized before use, buffer and bp are stored in a common block.

```
! ppline.cmn  -  declarations for ppline buffer

      character*(PPLINESIZE) buffer
      integer                bp
      character*1            quotec
      common /ppchar/ buffer, quotec
      common /ppint/  bp
      save   /ppchar/, /ppint/
```

The initialization is performed at run-time by ppinit, which initializes everything needed for the preprocessor.

```
! ppinit  -  initialization for preprocessor

      subroutine ppinit (u)
      integer  u
      include  'global.def'
      include  'ppline.cmn'
      include  'pperror.cmn'

      call initif ()
      call initmacro ()
      call inclinit (u)
      quotec = DQUOTE
      bp = 1
      buffer(1:1) = NULL
      pperrcount = 0

      return
      end
```

For use as a stand-alone program, the main program just loops through the input using ppline. Our main program allows one optional argument to pre-define a macro (with no replacement text) for conditional processing. Thus the command line

```
$ prep abc.txt xyz.txt -d:QWERTY
```

would use abc.txt as input and xyz.txt as output, and would define the macro QWERTY.

```
! prep  -  general-purpose preprocessor

    program prep
    include           'global.def'
    integer           argc, uin, uout
    character*(MAXSTR) argv(MAXARGS), line, word, upper
    logical           ppline, mkdef, junk
    integer           i

    call ioinit ()
    call getargs (argc, argv)
    call stdargs (argc, argv, uin, uout)
    if (uin .eq. IOERROR .or. uout .eq. IOERROR) stop ' '
    do i = 1, argc                !check for define's on command line
        if (argv(i)(1:1) .eq. QUALIFIER) then
            argv(i) = upper(argv(i))
            if (argv(i)(2:3) .eq. 'D:') then
                word = argv(i)(4:index(argv(i),NULL))
                junk = mkdef (word, NULL)
            else
                call fputstr (STDERR, 'PP: unrecognized option '//argv(i))
                call fputc (STDERR, NEWLINE)
            end if
        end if
    end do

    call ppinit (uin)

    do while (ppline (line))
        call fputstr (uout, line)
    end do

    call iofinit()
    end
```

All said and done, this is a fairly involved program, enough so that a diagram showing (roughly) the routines used and their relationships is needed to see the whole picture. Here is such a list, with the standard I/O and string-handling tools omitted:

```
! prep  -  software organization
```

```
! common blocks
        # ifclause.cmn    !current state and stack for nested #IF's
        # macro.cmn       !hash table data structure for macro processor
        # macscan.cmn     !data structure for recursive macro expansion
        # include.cmn     !unit stack for include processor
        # ppline.cmn      !buffer and bp for ppline
        # pperror.cmn     !preprocessor error count


        prep
             ppinit        !initialization
                ioinit
                inclinit
                initif
                initmacro
                pbinit


             pperror       !error handler


             ppline
                finclude
                ifclause
                setquote
                macro
                    dodef     !collect name, replacement text and args
                    mkdef     !install name in tables
                    finddef   !lookup name in tables
                    rmdef     !remove name from tables
                macscan       !scan line and expand macros
                    mkframe   !make new stack frame
                    expand    !expand macro and substitute arguments
                    putchr    !put character into scan buffer or output string

! putback buffer management
        #  putback.cmn    !buffer and bp for putback system
           getpbc         !get c from putback buffer
           getpbtoken     !get token from putback buffer
           putback        !put back 1 char
           pbstr          !put back string
           pb_ident       !put back identifier
```

6.2   Processing Logical Lines

The preprocessor is written as a general-purpose tool for processing text files. It preserves blanks in the input, and aside from discarding its own instructions, also preserves the physical line structure of its input. This makes it useful for other applications besides program preprocessing, such as in text processing.

The idea of a "logical line" of input is generally restricted to programming languages. It is easy to imagine applications where a single input statement takes more than 80 characters to specify, so that some means of continuing a logical line over more than one physical line of input is required. We have a routine for buffering logical lines of input, so that programs using it don't have to deal with the logic of figuring out whether to continue reading or not while doing whatever else they do. The logical line buffering routine conceals the complexity of the problem, making it appear to the caller that logical lines are just physical lines. It also conceals the complexity of the preprocessor, which is built in to it.

The Fortran language itself provides an obvious example of a convention for continuation lines, but not the only one. For instance, the SPICE circuit simulation program has an input language in which a + in column 1 indicates that a line is a continuation of the previous line. Both languages have a "postcontinuation" convention, in which the continuation line, rather than the continued line, has a special character (or character position) to indicate continuation. The postcontinuation convention of Fortran 77 has one serious drawback: it is unsuitable for interactive programs. Imagine how it would work: the user would type in a command; nothing happens. The user types in a second command; then the first is executed! The need to see the beginning of a new logical line before completing the old gives rise to this situation, and the only way to eliminate it is to have the continuation indicated at the end of the first line rather than at the beginning of the second, or else to have a special character to mark the end of a statement and ignore the physical line structure altogether.

The routine `getlogline` follows a "precontinuation" convention and is useful as a general-purpose logical line buffering routine. It replaces any series of multiple blanks in the input with a single blank, to preserve space in the output line. Since it has no lookahead line, it doesn't need an initialization routine. It does a few extra things, like providing a means of continuing a character context (i.e., a quoted string) and the recognition of the semicolon as a statement separator for multiple logical lines on a single physical line. The following are some examples of lines it will accept:

```
call xyz (a, b, c)              !this is a comment

call fputstr (STDOUT, 'now is the time for all good men to &
              &come to the aid of their country'//EOL)
status = sys$lotsof (arg1,   &   !sys$lotsof is a system routine
              arg2,   &   !with lots of arguments
              arg3,   &   !some of which are optional
              ,,,,,,)
i = 0 ; j = 0 ; k = 0           !three logical lines
```

The ampersands are required (cannot be any other character). The following is a formal specification of the rules for logical lines:

Character context: A character appears in a character context if it is between the delimiters of a literal string, which are apostrophes (single quote marks).

Comments: The character ! indicates a comment except where it occurs in a character context. The comment extends to the end of the physical line. A comment is processed as though it were an end-of-line character.

Logical line separation: The character ; separates logical lines on a single physical line. Otherwise, the end-of-line character separates logical lines.

Logical line continuation: The character & as the last nonblank character of a line signifies that the logical line is continued on the next physical line. If a character context is being continued, the & may not be followed by a comment, and the first nonblank character of the next physical line determines the character position at which the continuation begins: if the first nonblank character is &, then the continuation begins at the character position immediately following the &; otherwise, it begins in column 1.

Blank lines: Blank lines between logical lines are ignored. Blank lines may not occur between physical lines of a logical line.

This is a pretty complicated prescription, and the code is correspondingly long. However, it's worth the trouble since getlogline provides a reliable means of continuing long quoted strings and can be used in interactive systems. The logic can be worked out more easily by making use of a state transition diagram, incorporating actions to be taken at various points. Figure 6.2 is such a diagram, showing the characters on which state transitions occur and the actions to be taken upon entering a new state. This doesn't say everything necessary to do the job, but it does provide a guide for writing the actual code.

The code uses an integer variable *s* that takes on the state numbers in the diagram. One difference between the diagram and the real code is that we don't want getlogline to ever return an empty line to the caller, so special action is required on semicolons.

```
! getlogline  -  get logical line of input

      logical function getlogline (logline)
      character*(*)      logline
      include            'global.def'
      character*(MAXSTR) line
      logical            ppline, done, gotline
      integer            s, lp, llp, tp, i
      character*1        c
      data gotline / .false. /
      save gotline, lp, line

      if (.not. gotline) then
         done = .false.
         do while (.not. done)              !get first line
            if (ppline(line)) then
               lp = 1
               do while (line(lp:lp) .eq. BLANK .or. line(lp:lp) .eq. ';')
                  if (line(lp:lp) .eq. ';') line(lp:lp) = BLANK
                  lp = lp + 1
               end do
               if (line(lp:lp) .ne. NEWLINE .and.
```

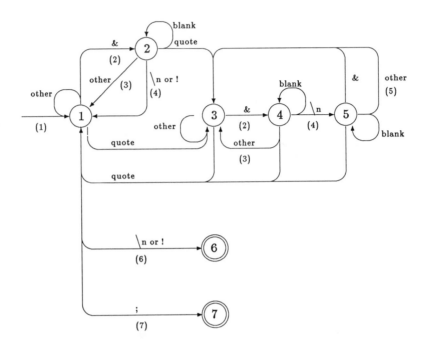

Actions: (1) if (.not. gotline) get next nonblank line
(2) set pointer to &
(3) copy from & to current position
(4) read next line
(5) copy from column 1 to current position
(6) gotline = false
(7) gotline = true

Figure 6.2: State diagram for recognizing logical lines.

```
&                   line(lp:lp) .ne. COMMENT) then
                    done = .true.
                end if
            else
                getlogline = .false.
                return
            end if
        end do
        lp = 0
    end if

    done = .false.
```

```
llp = 1
s = 1
do while (.not. done)
   lp = lp + 1
   c = line(lp:lp)
   if (s .eq. 1) then          !initial state
      if (c .eq. NEWLINE .or. c .eq. COMMENT) then
         logline(llp:llp+1) = EOL
         getlogline = .true.
         gotline = .false.
         done = .true.
      else if (c .eq. ';') then
         logline(llp:llp+1) = EOL
         getlogline = .true.
         i = lp + 1
         do while (line(i:i) .eq. BLANK .or. line(i:i) .eq. ';')
            if (line(i:i) .eq. ';') line(i:i) = BLANK
            i = i + 1
         end do
         if (line(i:i) .eq. NEWLINE .or. line(i:i) .eq. COMMENT) then
            gotline = .false.
         else
            gotline = .true.
         end if
         done = .true.
      else if (c .eq. '&') then
         tp = lp
         s = 2
      else if (c .eq. QUOTE) then
         logline(llp:llp) = QUOTE
         llp = llp + 1
         s = 3
      else if (c .eq. ' ') then          !crunch blanks
         if (lp .eq. 1) then
            continue
         else if (line(lp-1:lp-1) .eq. ' ') then
            continue
         else if (line(lp-1:lp-1) .eq. ';') then
            continue
         else
            logline(llp:llp) = ' '
            llp = llp + 1
         end if
      else
         logline(llp:llp) = c
         llp = llp + 1
      end if
   else if (s .eq. 2) then     !seen & outside of character context
      do while (line(lp:lp) .eq. ' ')
         lp = lp + 1
      end do
      if (line(lp:lp) .eq. NEWLINE .or. line(lp:lp) .eq. COMMENT) then
         if (ppline(line)) then
```

```
            lp = 0
          else
            call fputstr (STDERR,
  &         'unexpected EOF after continuation'//EOL)
            getlogline = .false.
            done = .true.
          end if
        else
          lp = tp
          logline(llp:llp) = '&'
          llp = llp + 1
        end if
        s = 1
      else if (s .eq. 3) then    !in character context
        if (c .eq. QUOTE) then
          logline(llp:llp) = QUOTE
          llp = llp + 1
          s = 1
        else if (c .eq. '&') then
          tp = lp
          s = 4
        else
          logline(llp:llp) = c
          llp = llp + 1
        end if
      else if (s .eq. 4) then    !seen & within character context
        do while (line(lp:lp) .eq. ' ')
          lp = lp + 1
        end do
        if (line(lp:lp) .eq. NEWLINE) then
          if (ppline(line)) then
            lp = 0
            s = 5
          else
            call fputstr (STDERR,
  &         'unexpected EOF in character context'//EOL)
            getlogline = .false.
            done = .true.
          end if
        else
          logline(llp:llp+(lp-tp)) = line(tp:lp)
          llp = llp + lp - tp
          if (line(lp:lp) .eq. QUOTE) then
            s = 1
          else
            s = 3
          end if
        end if
      else if (s .eq. 5) then    !new line in continued character context
        do while (line(lp:lp) .eq. ' ')
          lp = lp + 1
        end do
        if (line(lp:lp) .eq. '&') then
```

```
          s = 3
      else
          logline(llp:llp+lp) = line(1:lp)
          llp = llp + lp
          if (line(lp:lp) .eq. QUOTE) then
              s = 1
          else
              s = 3
          end if
      end if
  else
      call fputstr (STDERR, 'cannot happen in GETLOGLINE'//EOL)
  end if
end do

return
end
```

No initialization routine is needed, but some initial values are required the first time getlogline is called; the data statements provide all of the initialization required. Because of the possibility of more than one logical line per physical line, getlogline needs to remember the line pointer and whether it is already working on a physical line when it is called.

The responsibility for deciding how large logical lines may be is left completely to the calling routine. The maximum line length is typically quite large; for pseudo-Fortran logical lines, for instance, it should be 1320 characters ($(72 - 6) \times 20$).

The astute reader may have noticed that all of this preprocessing has added a substantial overhead to the simple process of reading input. Indeed, just the buffers used to hold input take a lot of memory; if MAXOPEN is, say, 20, then the input buffers of iox, ppline, and getlogline occupy $(20 \times 255) + 2048 + 1320 = 8468$ bytes. The hash tables for the macro processor alone require 11K bytes, and all of the local variables associated with the preprocessor routines take up roughly another 9.5K bytes (although all of the local storage can be allocated each time a routine is called and deallocated when it exits by a smart compiler). Thus the total memory requirements for getlogline are about 29K bytes for data only, not counting the code itself.

On the other hand, memory is cheap and getting cheaper all the time. 29K is a trivial amount of memory for just about any computer system, at least for any that supports Fortran. For computer systems with virtual memory like the VAX this is even more insignificant; 29K represents about one-millionth of the total address space of a VAX. For a computer without virtual memory and supporting a maximum memory of 1 megabyte, 29K is only 0.3% of the available memory. ppline and getlogline embody a significant capability, and are worth the penalty in overhead. A little preprocessing has enormous payoffs in reduced complexity of programs using it and in the "power" of the resulting programs. At the same time, everything has been written to be useful in pieces. The macro processor can be used without the rest of the preprocessor, and by changing getlogline to use finclude or even fgetline, all of the overhead of the preprocessor can be avoided while retaining the benefits of filtering logical lines for the calling program.

We have reached something of a turning point in this book. The preprocessor is a fairly powerful minilanguage and we intend to use it heavily in later chapters. The things it can do are useful as extensions to Fortran, although this aspect is not developed much. The real usefulness of the preprocessor for our purposes lies in its ability to be used in both Fortran source code and in special languages of our own design. prep thus opens a whole new realm of possibilities, allowing our own programs to be mated smoothly to the Fortran language itself.

Exercises

1. Modify the macro processor so that it checks to make sure that the number of actual arguments in a macro call agrees with the number of arguments in its definition.

2. Write a preprocessor for Fortran that uses getlogline to get source lines and outputs lines in Fortran 77 standard format. How much do you have to write from scratch?

3. Extend your Fortran preprocessor by incorporating the translations performed by v77.

4. Write a routine f77logline that gets logical lines in postcontinuation format.

5. Add an option -s to prep to print statistics of the macro hash table usage.

Further Reading

Although the overall organization is different, the macro expansion algorithm embodied in macscan is essentially the same as the one presented by Kernighan and Plauger in *Software Tools in Pascal*, which in turn is based on one written by D. M. Ritchie at Bell Laboratories. The macro processor of Kernighan and Plauger is considerably more powerful than ours because of the ability to evaluate arithmetic expressions and because the conditional testing occurs during macro expansion. The macro processing facilities of TEX, the program used to typeset this book, are even more powerful, enough so that it is possible to write real programs in TEX (even if you can't make sense of them when you are done).

The specification for logical lines was adapted from the draft Fortran 8X standard, X3J3/S8.103, February 1987. Our syntax is only slightly less permissive than that of the Fortran standard in that ours does not allow blank lines in the middle of logical lines.

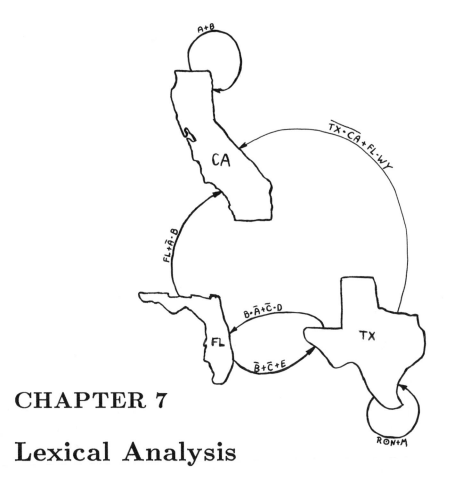

CHAPTER 7

Lexical Analysis

The input to most programs is a sequence of characters, and the actions taken by the program depend in some way on the specific sequence of input characters. The analysis of the input can be subdivided into two phases, at least conceptually, called *lexical analysis* and *parsing*. The lexical analysis phase consists of the grouping of individual characters into meaningful, possibly multicharacter "tokens" such as numbers, identifiers, operators, or punctuation. The parsing phase refers to the analysis of these tokens for correct syntax and associated meaning. In this chapter and the next, we will develop tools for the automatic generation of lexical analyzers and parsers.

In previous chapters, we developed an ad hoc method for performing lexical analysis and parsing. The is_rval, is_ival, and is_ident routines from Chapter 4 actually do a little of both—they check for a sequence of characters matching the desired token class, and if the characters are recognized as belonging to that class, the line pointer is advanced (lexical analysis); by returning a Boolean result

they facilitate syntax checking (parsing). For example, a statement with several
alternative forms might be parsed with the code

```
if (is_ival (ival, line, lp)) then
   do this
else if (is_rval (rval, line, lp)) then
   do that
else if (is_ident (ident, line, lp)) then
   do something else
else
   call fputstr (STDERR, 'OOPS!')
end if
```

We can write relatively bullet-proof code by always including the else clause
for every if statement; each part of the syntax is checked by calling an is_xxx
routine in an if statement, and each else clause then represents a distinct error
for which a meaningful message (something more than "oops") can be given.
The ad hoc method with ready-made tools lets you write code just about as fast
as you can type and lets programs deal with input errors intelligently instead of
silently going crazy.

Recall the *state transition diagram* for recognition of real numbers shown in
Figure 4.1. It is quite possible and easy to merge the recognition of integers and
reals into one transition diagram and to return a code as to which was found.
For a complete lexical analyzer we merge the logic for recognition of all possible
tokens into a single transition diagram. A real lexical analyzer has a known set
of tokens with which to compare the input and returns a code according to what
it found (including the catch-all OTHER). It always advances the input pointer by
at least one character, as opposed to is_ival, which doesn't go anywhere unless
an integer is found.

However, the ad hoc method is far from optimal for speed of recognizing
tokens because a single input character may be subjected to several comparisons
before it is "accepted" as part of a token. The fastest possible method is to
avoid comparisons entirely, via a table that implements the transition diagram
directly, so that in any state the next state is stored in a transition array; that is,
there is an array next such that the next state on an input character c is found
by the assignment state = next(ichar(c), state). For lexical analyzers with
large token sets, this direct lookup results in a huge table (say 200 states and
128 characters, which requires 25,600 integers or 100K bytes); nevertheless, some
form of table-driven recognizer is what we are after. Since construction of even
a small table by hand is unacceptably boring and error-prone, it is clear that
a tool for generating the required tables from some higher-level specification is
required. Such a tool is presented in this chapter.

7.1 Regular Expressions and Finite Automata

As an overview of what we are about to do, we need the bare essential facts of the theory behind it. The kind of state diagram we used for real numbers is known as a *finite state machine* or *finite automaton*, a kind of specialized conceptual "machine" for recognizing some pattern. Furthermore, it is deterministic in that there is no ambiguity as to which state to enter next on any input character. More precisely, a deterministic finite automaton (DFA) is distinguished from a nondeterministic one (an NFA) by the following properties:

- For each state, there is at most one transition to another state on each input character

- There are no transitions on the empty string.

The *empty string* is a useful concept that means, in effect, state transitions on no input. An empty string transition is represented in our diagrams as a branch from one state to another labeled ϵ. An NFA is broadly defined as any set of states with transitions between states on instances of characters in the input sequence.

The high-level input to our table generator will be based on *regular expressions*. A regular grammar is a restricted class of mathematical grammars, and a sentence in such a grammar is a regular expression. Let A be the input alphabet, or the set of all allowed input characters. Then each element of A is a regular expression. If r and s are regular expressions, then the following are also:

$$rs \qquad r \text{ followed by } s$$
$$(r|s) \qquad r \text{ or } s$$
$$\{r\} \qquad \text{closure of } r \text{ (zero or more occurrences of } r)$$

These rules can be applied to individual characters in the alphabet or to expressions built up from previous applications of the rules. We extend the notation above to include a range of characters of the form $[c_1 - c_2]$, which is just shorthand for $(c_1 | \ldots | c_2)$. Here are some examples:

$$
\begin{aligned}
&\text{unsigned integer:} && [0-9]\{[0-9]\} \\
&\text{signed integer:} && (+|-|)[0-9]\{[0-9]\} \\
&\text{decimal number:} && (+|-|)([0-9]\{[0-9]\} . \{[0-9]\} | \\
&&& \{[0-9]\} . [0-9]\{[0-9]\})
\end{aligned}
$$

The last example accepts signed decimal numbers provided they have at least one digit, either before or after the decimal point. The expression $\{[0-9]\}$ accepts zero or more digits; the expression $[0-9]\{[0-9]\}$ accepts one or more digits.

The reason for using regular expressions as the input language for our scanner generator is that the tokens for practically all computer languages can be described as regular expressions. What we need is a method of converting the input regular expressions to deterministic state tables so that an efficient driver routine can be used to interpret the tables and thus recognize the input expressions. The theory of grammars and finite automata provides two theorems that guarantee that suitable tables can be generated from the input expressions:

- For any regular expression, there exists an NFA that recognizes it.

- For any NFA, there is a DFA that accepts the same language.

The interested reader can find proofs of these and other useful related theorems in more formal texts on compiler construction, a few of which are listed at the end of the chapter. Our intent here is to write software, not prove theorems. There are known algorithms for both translation steps; thus a general outline of the scanner generator is as follows:

1. Read input regular expressions and translate into an NFA state table.

2. Transform NFA to corresponding DFA state table.

3. Optimize and compact the DFA state table.

The final state table is then used in conjunction with a prewritten driver routine as part of a larger program.

Note that the generator could just perform steps 1 and 2, and a driver that works with the (huge) intermediate form of the DFA table could be used. This intermediate form is useful for file searching since the search pattern typically doesn't have many states, so that an efficient table storage mechanism is not critical. This is the first program we will develop in this chapter. It will let us get something working and debugged before tackling step 3. It is also possible to stop after step 1 if we are willing to sacrifice the efficiency of the driver routine by making it simulate an NFA instead of a DFA (simulation of an NFA requires the ability to backtrack in the input sequence to test multiple possible transition paths on the same input sequence). This approach is suitable for the kind of pattern matching in interactive text editors, and many editors do support at least a limited type of regular expression syntax for text searching using NFAs. These ideas will be made more clear in the following section.

7.2   Constructing an NFA

The transition diagram corresponding to recognition of a single character a is and the transition diagram for the string ab (a followed by b) is just

That is, the transition diagram is formed by simply linking the component diagrams end to end. More generally, if r and s are any regular expressions (with any number of states in their respective transition diagrams), then the transition diagram corresponding to rs is formed by making the initial state of s the same state as the final state of r. The usefulness of empty string transitions in an NFA lies in the fact that it is very easy to generate a state diagram employing them from a regular expression. The empty string transitions facilitate the automatic generation of transition diagrams for $(r|s)$ and $\{r\}$ expressions. Figure 7.1 shows the state diagrams constructed automatically for the three rules allowed in building regular expressions.

The rules for regular expressions are recursive, and each box in Figure 7.1 could be any complex NFA state diagram. The NFA constructed for closure may look like overkill at first, and indeed, only two states are really needed with ϵ transitions in either direction to implement closure. However, all of these diagrams have the useful property that none of the terminal states have any transitions leaving them. While not required, this property simplifies translation of a regular expression into an NFA by a computer program since ϵ transitions never have to be remembered from one construct to the next (e.g. one closure followed by another). A further simplification is the fact that by design choice, each literal character accepted causes a transition to the next state in numerical order; the next state is implied.

Our representation of the NFA therefore consists of a set of characters accepted for each state, along with a list of ϵ transitions. The list of ϵ transitions is actually stored in a secondary table epstab to save space, with a pointer to the appropriate place in the table stored along with each state in the epsset array. The character set for each state is encoded in the chrset array to determine the interpretation of the values in cval1 and cval2, which contain the integer codes for the characters themselves.

```
! nfa.cmn  -  declaration of structure for NFA representation
!
! representation of NFA states:
!   chrset(s) - character set for transitions out of s:
!               NONE (no transitions), LITCHAR, or RANGE
!   epsset(s) - set of states that can be reached on empty string
!   nfatoken(s) - token value of accepting state (0 = nonaccepting)

      integer   MAXNFA              !max number of NFA states
      parameter (MAXNFA = 4096)
```

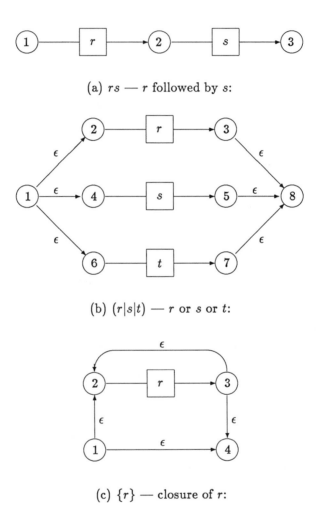

(a) rs — r followed by s:

(b) $(r|s|t)$ — r or s or t:

(c) $\{r\}$ — closure of r:

Figure 7.1: Nondeterministic state diagrams for regular expressions.

```
integer   MAXEPS                !size of epsset table
parameter (MAXEPS = 4096)

integer   chrset (MAXNFA)       !character set for state
integer   cval1 (MAXNFA)        !character or beginning of range
integer   cval2 (MAXNFA)        !end of range
integer   epsset (MAXNFA)       !ptr to list of transitions
                                !out of s on empty string
integer   nfatoken (MAXNFA)     !token value (0 = none)

integer   epstab (MAXEPS)       !storage for list table
integer   epstabp               !pointer to next free location

integer   NONE, LITCHAR, RANGE
parameter (NONE = 0)
parameter (LITCHAR = 1)
parameter (RANGE = 2)

common /nfatable/ chrset, cval1, cval2, epsset, nfatoken,
&                 epstab, epstabp
save    /nfatable/
```

The lists in epstab are terminated by a special code called ENDLIST, which is just an integer expected never to occur in a list. It is set to the magic value $-(2^{31})$ in global.def, although for our purposes any negative integer would do.

Like most programs dealing with nesting, our NFA generator mknfa uses a stack to keep track of the nesting levels of closures and OR operators. The stack also keeps track of the start state and end state of whatever has been generated between opening and closing delimiters, so that the necessary ϵ transitions can be added at the beginning and end. mknfa uses the same syntax as used in all of our discussion so far, and allows the special characters to be escaped via the escchar routine. Blanks are ignored, except when explicitly specified by \b.

```
! mknfa  -  make an NFA from regular expression

        subroutine mknfa (s, line, lp)
        character*(*) line
        integer     lp, s
        include     'global.def'
        include     'nfa.cmn'
        integer     MAXEMPTY
        parameter   (MAXEMPTY = 20)
        integer     tmpset1 (MAXEMPTY), tmpset2 (MAXEMPTY)
        integer     i
        logical     done
        character*1 c, escchar, nextc

        integer     MAXSTACK
        parameter   (MAXSTACK = 32)
        integer     type (MAXSTACK)     !stack entry type
```

```
      integer      startstate (MAXSTACK) !start end end states for
      integer      endstate (MAXSTACK)   !generation of epsset entries
      integer      sp

! stack entry types
      integer      CLOSURE, ALT, OR
      parameter    (CLOSURE = 1)
      parameter    (ALT = 2)
      parameter    (OR = 3)

      sp = 0
      do while (nextc (c, line, lp) .ne. NEWLINE .and. c .ne. COMMENT)
         if (c .eq. ESCAPE) then                      !literal escaped char
            chrset(s) = LITCHAR
            lp = lp - 1                               !point to ESCAPE
            cval1(s) = ichar(escchar(line, lp))
            tmpset1(1) = ENDLIST
            epsset(s) = epstabp
            call ascopy (tmpset1, epstabp, epstab)
            s = s + 1
         else if (c .eq. '[') then                    !range
            chrset(s) = RANGE
            if (nextc(c, line, lp) .eq. ESCAPE) then
               lp = lp - 1
               cval1(s) = ichar(escchar(line, lp))
            else
               cval1(s) = ichar(c)
            end if
            if (nextc(c, line, lp) .ne. '-') then
               call fputstr (STDERR, 'invalid range syntax'//EOL)
               call fputstr (STDERR, line)
            end if
            if (nextc(c, line, lp) .eq. ESCAPE) then
               lp = lp - 1
               cval2(s) = ichar(escchar(line, lp))
            else
               cval2(s) = ichar(c)
            end if
            tmpset1(1) = ENDLIST
            epsset(s) = epstabp
            call ascopy (tmpset1, epstabp, epstab)
            s = s + 1
            if (nextc(c, line, lp) .ne. ']') then
               call fputstr (STDERR, 'invalid range syntax'//EOL)
               call fputstr (STDERR, line)
            end if
         else if (c .eq. '{') then                    !begin closure
            sp = sp + 1
            type(sp) = CLOSURE
            startstate(sp) = s
            s = s + 1
         else if (c .eq. '}') then                    !end closure
            if (type(sp) .ne. CLOSURE) then
```

```
              call fputstr (STDERR, 'closure delimiter mismatch'//EOL)
              call fputstr (STDERR, line)
           else
              tmpset1(1) = startstate(sp) + 1
              tmpset1(2) = s + 1
              tmpset1(3) = ENDLIST
              epsset(s) = epstabp
              call ascopy (tmpset1, epstabp, epstab)
              chrset(s) = NONE
              tmpset1(1) = s + 1
              tmpset1(2) = startstate(sp) + 1
              tmpset1(3) = ENDLIST
              epsset(startstate(sp)) = epstabp
              call ascopy (tmpset1, epstabp, epstab)
              chrset(startstate(sp)) = NONE
              sp = sp - 1
              s = s + 1
           end if
        else if (c .eq. '(') then                  !begin alternative
           sp = sp + 1
           type(sp) = ALT
           startstate(sp) = s
           sp = sp + 1
           type(sp) = OR
           startstate(sp) = s + 1
           s = s + 1
        else if (c .eq. '|') then                  !delimit alternative
           endstate(sp) = s
           sp = sp + 1
           type(sp) = OR
           startstate(sp) = s + 1
           s = s + 1
        else if (c .eq. ')') then                  !end alternative
           endstate(sp) = s
           s = s + 1
           i = 1
           done = .false.
           do while (.not. done)
              if (type(sp) .eq. OR) then
                 tmpset1(i) = startstate(sp)
                 tmpset2(1) = s
                 tmpset2(2) = ENDLIST
                 epsset(endstate(sp)) = epstabp
                 call ascopy (tmpset2, epstabp, epstab)
                 chrset(endstate(sp)) = NONE
                 sp = sp - 1
                 i = i + 1
              else if (type(sp) .eq. ALT) then
                 done = .true.
                 tmpset1(i) = ENDLIST
                 epsset(startstate(sp)) = epstabp
                 call ascopy (tmpset1, epstabp, epstab)
                 chrset(startstate(sp)) = NONE
```

```
                            sp = sp - 1
                          else
                            call fputstr (STDERR, 'or delimiter mismatch'//EOL)
                            call fputstr (STDERR, line)
                          end if
                        end do
                      else                                  !literal character
                        chrset(s) = LITCHAR
                        cval1(s) = ichar(c)
                        tmpset1(1) = ENDLIST
                        epsset(s) = epstabp
                        call ascopy (tmpset1, epstabp, epstab)
                        s = s + 1
                      end if
                    end do

            ! give final state an epsset
                    epsset(s) = epstabp
                    call ascopy (ENDLIST, epstabp, epstab)

                    return
                    end
```

From the regular expression

$$([0-9]\{[0-9]\} \cdot \{[0-9]\}|\{[0-9]\} \cdot [0-9]\{[0-9]\}),$$

which specifies an unsigned decimal number, the reader should verify that the NFA in Figure 7.2 is constructed. Note that mknfa does not know anything about token values or accepting states; therefore, the marking of a state as accepting and assignment of a token value must be performed by the calling routine. The caller has the information necessary since it passes the start state to mknfa and is returned the end state.

7.3   Constructing a DFA

We now have a nondeterministic state table representation of a regular expression and need to convert it to a deterministic form. What makes the NFA nondeterministic is that there are transitions on ϵ, the empty string, so that the NFA can be in many different states for a single input string. Since our NFAs have no more than one transition on any real character, we need only consider ϵ transitions to find all of the states the NFA could be in for a given input string. To do this we will need what is known as the ϵ-closure of each state. For state s, ϵ-closure(s) is the set of all states that can be reached from s on ϵ transitions alone. Thus, for the NFA for unsigned decimal numbers, ϵ-closure(1) is $\{1, 2, 11, 12, 14\}$. The set ϵ-closure(s) always includes s; the ϵ-closure of a set of states is just the union of the ϵ-closures of each of the individual states in the set.

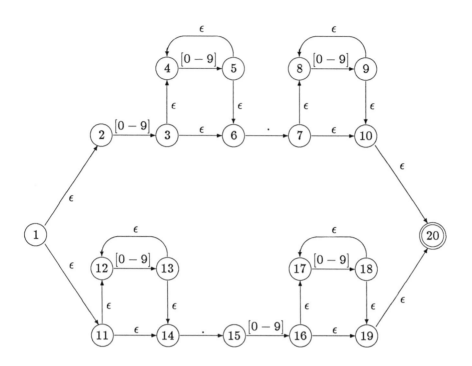

Figure 7.2: NFA for unsigned decimal number.

To convert the NFA into a DFA, we must make a list of all states the NFA could be in for all possible input strings. This set of NFA states for a given input string is a unique state of the DFA. Thus each DFA state is some subset of all NFA states, representing all possible configurations of the NFA upon reading some input string. The algorithm that computes these subsets to construct a DFA representation is called the *subset construction*. A pseudocode version of the algorithm is

```
{M} = eps_closure of NFA state 1
DFA state 1 = {M}
push {M}
do while (stack not empty)
   pop {M}
   do for each input character i
      {P} = set of states reachable from {M} on input i
      if ({P} is the empty set) then
         do nothing
      else
         {N} = eps_union ({P})
```

```
              if ({N} already exists as a DFA state) then
                 do nothing
              else
                 push {N}
              end if
              add a transition from {M} to {N} labeled i
           end if
        end do   !over input character set
     end do      !until every DFA state has been considered
```

The notation {M} means that M is a set, in this case a set of states in the NFA. As in the case of the NFA construction, our implementation will make use of pointers to sets stored in a secondary table. The function eps_union is just eps_closure with a set of states as input, rather than an individual state. The stack is not really necessary because it doesn't matter what order the DFA states are considered in (the last-in, first-out nature of the stack is not essential to the algorithm). The stack is just a convenient way of storing the DFA states for later use.

To see how the subset construction works, apply it to the NFA for decimal numbers. Figure 7.3 is a blow-by-blow description of what happens. The DFA constructed for decimal numbers has 9 states:

```
DFA state 1 = NFA subset {1,2,11,12,14}
DFA state 2 = NFA subset {15}
DFA state 3 = NFA subset {3,4,6,12,13,14}
DFA state 4 = NFA subset {7,8,10,15,20}
DFA state 5 = NFA subset {4,5,6,12,13,14}
DFA state 6 = NFA subset {8,9,10,16,17,19,20}
DFA state 7 = NFA subset {8,9,10,17,18,19,20}
DFA state 8 = NFA subset {16,17,19,20}
DFA state 9 = NFA subset {17,18,19,20}
```

The transition diagram for the resulting DFA is given in Figure 7.4.

The DFA states whose subsets contain NFA state 20 are marked as accepting states, since NFA state 20 is the final state constructed for recognizing the given regular expression. When we construct a full lexical analyzer, we will simply mark the final NFA state for each token as an accepting state, and link the start states of all token NFAs together with ϵ transitions.

The routine implementing the subset construction follows the pseudocode algorithm closely, with modifications necessary for a practical program. The compact storage of the NFA is replaced by a huge array dfanext to store all of the DFA state transitions, since the restrictions in the NFA of only one character or character range accepted per state are no longer guaranteed. The common block declaration for the DFA is

```
! dfa.cmn  -  common block for DFA representation

      integer   MAXCHAR                    !maximum character code used
      parameter (MAXCHAR = 255)
```

Outer Loop		Inner Loop
stack: 1	".":	{P} = {15}
pop 1		{N} = {15}
		push {N} = DFA state 2
	[0-9]:	{P} = {3,13}
		{N} = {3,4,6,12,13,14}
		push {N} = DFA state 3
stack: 2,3	".":	{P} = {7,15}
pop 3		{N} = {7,8,10,15,20}
		push {N} = DFA state 4
	[0-9]:	{P} = {5,13}
		{N} = {4,5,6,12,13,14}
		push {N} = DFA state 5
stack: 2,4,5	".":	{P} = {7,15}
pop 5		{N} = {7,8,10,15,20}
		{N} exists as DFA state 4
	[0-9]:	{P} = {5,13}
		{N} = {4,5,6,12,13,14}
		{N} exists as DFA state 5
stack: 2,4	".":	{P} = {empty set}
pop 4	[0-9]:	{P} = {9,16}
		{N} = {8,9,10,16,17,19,20}
		push {N} = DFA state 6
stack: 2,6	".":	{P} = {empty set}
pop 6	[0-9]:	{P} = {9,18}
		{N} = {8,9,10,17,18,19,20}
		push {N} = DFA state 7
stack: 2,7	".":	{P} = {empty set}
pop 7	[0-9]:	{P} = {9,18}
		{N} = {8,9,10,17,18,19,20}
		{N} exists as DFA state 7
stack: 2	".":	{P} = {empty set}
pop 2	[0-9]:	{P} = {16}
		{N} = {16,17,19,20}
		push {N} = DFA state 8
stack: 8	".":	{P} = {empty set}
pop 8	[0-9]:	{P} = {18}
		{N} = {17,18,19,20}
		push {N} = DFA state 9
stack: 9	".":	{P} = {empty set}
pop 9	[0-9]:	{P} = {18}
		{N} = {17,18,19,20}
		{N} exists as DFA state 9
stack: empty (algorithm terminates)		

Figure 7.3: Conversion of decimal number NFA to corresponding DFA.

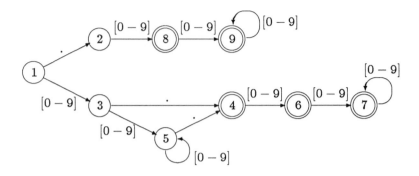

Figure 7.4: DFA for unsigned decimal number.

```
integer   MAXDFA                       !max number of DFA states
parameter (MAXDFA = 512)

integer   dfanext (0:MAXCHAR, MAXDFA)  !state transition matrix
integer   dfatoken (MAXDFA)            !DFA token values (0 = none)
integer   d                            !actual number of DFA states

common /dfatable/ dfanext, dfatoken, d
save   /dfatable/
```

Each state of the DFA corresponds to a column of the dfanext matrix, so that the transition from state s on character c is given by dfanext(ichar(c),s). Multidimensional arrays in Fortran are laid out in memory with elements for the first subscript sequentially in memory. Thus dimensioning dfanext(0:255,MAXDFA) makes the subscript denoting the input character start at zero (so regular expressions can contain NULL characters) and span all possible 8-bit character codes sequentially.

The integer value d is the actual number of DFA states, so MAXDFA−d states are allocated storage but unused. The subset construction routine is called mkdfa. d is initialized to 1 and used as a counter that gives the last used DFA state number; it is incremented each time a new subset is identified.

```
! mkdfa   -   construct dfa from nfa

      subroutine mkdfa ()
      include  'global.def'
      include  'nfa.cmn'
      include  'dfa.cmn'
      integer  M               !DFA state currently being considered
      integer  P (16)          !set of states reachable from {M} on i
```

```
      integer  N (64)              !eps_closure({P}) = dfanext(i,M)
      integer  subset (MAXDFA)     !set of NFA states in each DFA state
      integer  subtab (8*MAXDFA)   !storage table for subset lists
      integer  subp                !pointer to next available entry in subtab
      integer  stack (64)          !list of DFA states to be considered
      integer  sp
      integer  i, j, k, smin
      logical  found, eqvset

! initialize DFA tables
      do i = 1, MAXDFA
         do j = 0, MAXCHAR
            dfanext(j,i) = 0
         end do
         dfatoken(i) = 0
      end do

! compute subset of first NFA state and store it as first DFA subset
      call eps_closure (N, 1, epsset, epstab)
      subp = 1
      subset(1) = subp
      call ascopy (N, subp, subtab)

      d = 1
      sp = 1
      stack(1) = 1
      do while (sp .gt. 0)
         M = stack(sp)
         sp = sp - 1
         do i = 0, MAXCHAR
            j = subset(M)
            k = 1
            do while (subtab(j) .ne. ENDLIST)  !see if transition exists
               if (chrset(subtab(j)) .eq. LITCHAR) then
                  found = (cval1(subtab(j)) .eq. i)
               else if (chrset(subtab(j)) .eq. RANGE) then
                  found = (i .ge. cval1(subtab(j)) .and.
     &                     i .le. cval2(subtab(j)))
               else
                  found = .false.
               end if
               if (found) then                 !add to {P}
                  P(k) = subtab(j) + 1          !next state always s + 1
                  k = k + 1
               end if
               j = j + 1
            end do
            P(k) = ENDLIST
            if (k .eq. 1) then                  !{P} is empty
               continue
            else
               !compute eps_closure of {P}
               call eps_union (N, P, epsset, epstab)
```

```
                    ! see if {N} is already a state of the DFA
                    call bubblesort (N)    !sort N before comparing
                    j = 0
                    found = .false.
                    do while (.not. found .and. j .lt. d)
                       j = j + 1
                       found = eqvset (N, subset(j), subtab)
                    end do
                    if (found) then  !add a transition to existing state
                       dfanext(i,M) = j
                    else              !create state and add transition
                       d = d + 1
                       sp = sp + 1
                       stack(sp) = d
                       !store subset for new state
                       subset(d) = subp
                       call ascopy (N, subp, subtab)
                       dfanext(i,M) = d
                    end if
                 end if
              end do                 !over all input characters
           end do                    !until all dfa states have been constructed

      ! set token values -
      ! if two or more NFA states in subset have token values, the token value
      ! of the smallest NFA state number is accepted

           do i = 1, d
              j = subset(i)
              smin = MAXNFA
              k = 0
              ! find min nfa state # with non-zero token value
              do while (subtab(j) .ne. ENDLIST)
                 if (nfatoken(subtab(j)) .ne. 0) then
                    if (subtab(j) .lt. smin) then
                       k = nfatoken (subtab(j))
                       smin = subtab(j)
                    end if
                 end if
                 j = j + 1
              end do
              dfatoken(i) = k
           end do

           return
           end
```

The mkdfa subroutine follows the pseudocode outline closely, with the additional action of setting DFA token return values. A DFA state is an accepting state if its subset contains any NFA accepting state (e.g. state 20 in the NFA for decimal numbers). It is possible for a DFA state to include more than one NFA accepting state in its subset, and some means of resolving this conflict is required. The method used here is to select the lowest numerical NFA state number if more than one possibility exists.

To compute ϵ-closure(s), we initially push all of the states in epsset(s) onto a stack, and initialize ϵ-closure(s) to s. Then we pop each state from the stack and push its epsset onto the stack. If the popped state is already a member of ϵ-closure(s), it is discarded; else it is added to ϵ-closure(s).

```
! eps_closure  -  find set of states that can be reached on empty string

        subroutine eps_closure (clset, s, epsset, epstab)
        integer   clset (*)     !return array containing eps_closure(s)
        integer   s             !input state
        integer   epsset (*)    !ptrs to epsilon transition lists for states
        integer   epstab (*)    !list table
        include   'global.def'
        integer   MAXSTACK
        parameter (MAXSTACK = 256)
        integer   stack (MAXSTACK), sp
        integer   i, j, k
        logical   found

! add all epsilon transitions of s to clset
        clset(1) = s            !eps_closure(s) always includes s
        j = 2                   !pointer to next element of clset
        sp = 0
        i = epsset(s)
        do while (epstab(i) .ne. ENDLIST)
          sp = sp + 1
          stack(sp) = epstab(i)
          clset(j) = epstab(i)
          i = i + 1
          j = j + 1
        end do

! add epsilon transitions from states in clset to clset
        do while (sp .gt. 0)
          i = epsset(stack(sp))
          sp = sp - 1
          do while (epstab(i) .ne. ENDLIST)
            found = .false.          !see if state is already in closure
            k = 1
            do while (.not. found .and. k .lt. j)
              if (clset(k) .eq. epstab(i)) found = .true.
              k = k + 1
            end do
            if (.not. found) then    !add it and its epsset to closure
              sp = sp + 1
              stack(sp) = epstab(i)
              clset(j) = epstab(i)
              j = j + 1
            end if
```

```
            i = i + 1
          end do
        end do

        clset(j) = ENDLIST
        return
        end
```

eps_union computes ϵ-closure for a set of states by simply calling eps_closure for each state in the set and finding its union with the ϵ-closure of all of the states previously considered.

```
! eps_union  -  compute eps_closure for a set of states

        subroutine eps_union (clset, P, epsset, epstab)
        integer    clset (*)   !return array with eps_union({P})
        integer    P (*)       !input set of states
        integer    epsset (*)  !ptrs to epsilon transitions of states
        integer    epstab (*)  !list table
        include    'global.def'
        integer    tmpset1 (256), tmpset2 (256)
        integer    i, j, k

        i = 1                  !find number of states in {P}
        do while (P(i) .ne. ENDLIST)
          i = i + 1
        end do
        clset(1) = ENDLIST

        if (i .eq. 1) then     !{P} is empty
          continue
        else                   !get union of eps_closure(P(i)) for all i
          do k = 1, i - 1
            call eps_closure (tmpset1, P(k), epsset, epstab)
            j = 1              !make temp copy of clset
            do while (clset(j) .ne. ENDLIST)
              tmpset2(j) = clset(j)
              j = j + 1
            end do
            tmpset2(j) = ENDLIST
            call union (tmpset1, tmpset2, clset)
          end do
        end if

        return
        end
```

7.4   File Searching

Once the DFA has been constructed, it is simple to use it to scan text for the tokens it recognizes. It never needs to compare an input character with a set of possibilities for a given state; instead, because of the direct table storage scheme, it can simply look up its next state. The function dfascan is a driver routine that uses the DFA table to scan for tokens starting at the current line pointer. If a match with a pattern of the DFA is found, the token value is returned and the line pointer is advanced to the character after the token; otherwise, the token value returned is zero, and the line pointer is advanced by one.

```
! dfascan  -   scan for DFA pattern match at lp

        integer function dfascan (token, line, lp)
        character*(*) token, line
        integer       lp
        include       'global.def'
        include       'dfa.cmn'
        integer       t, s, ip, tp
        logical       done

        t = 0                              !token value
        s = 1                              !current state
        ip = lp                            !input pointer
        done = .false.
        do while (.not. done)
           if (line(ip:ip) .eq. NULL) then
              done = .true.
           else if (dfanext (ichar(line(ip:ip)), s) .eq. 0) then
              done = .true.
           else
              s = dfanext (ichar(line(ip:ip)), s)
              if (dfatoken(s) .ne. 0) then
                 t = dfatoken(s)
                 tp = ip
              end if
           end if
           ip = ip + 1
        end do

        if (t .ne. 0) then
           token = line(lp:tp)//NULL
           lp = tp + 1
        else
           token = NULL
           lp = lp + 1
        end if
        dfascan = t

        return
        end
```

dfascan just keeps on moving until there is no transition on the next character; each time it passes through an accepting state, it sets a token value and pointer to the input position. Then when failure finally occurs, the last accepting state visited is the one returned.

We are now just about ready to test this much of the lexical analyzer generator. Our test program is called match, and is useful in its own right. The command

```
$ match "([a-z]|[A-Z]|$|_)*{(([a-z]|[A-Z]|$|_|[0-9])*}" abc.txt
```

causes all identifiers in file abc.txt to be listed on STDOUT.

The match command will also accept an option -u, which causes the input file's lines and all characters in the regular expression to be converted to uppercase before searching, a conversion that makes the search case-insensitive. The command

```
$ match "hello" xyz.txt -u
```

degenerates to the level of most file searching programs.

```
! match  -  search file for specified regular pattern

        program match
        include          'global.def'
        include          'nfa.cmn'
        integer          argc, uin, uout
        character*(MAXSTR) argv(MAXARGS)
        character*(MAXSTR) line, uline, pattern, token, cat, upper
        integer          dfascan, lp, s, t, fopen, nargs, i
        logical          fgetline, done, caseflag

        caseflag = .false.
        nargs = 0
        uin = STDIN
        uout = STDOUT
        call ioinit ()
        call getargs (argc, argv)
        do i = 1, argc
          if (argv(i)(1:1) .eq. QUALIFIER) then
            argv(i) = upper(argv(i))
            if (index(argv(i), 'U') .gt. 0) caseflag = .true.
          else
            nargs = nargs + 1
            if (nargs .eq. 1) then
              pattern = cat(argv(i), EOL)
            else if (nargs .eq. 2) then
                if (fopen (uin, argv(i), IOREAD) .eq. IOERROR) stop ' '
            else if (nargs .eq. 3) then
                if (fopen (uout, argv(i), IOWRITE) .eq. IOERROR) stop ' '
            end if
          end if
        end if
```

```
      end do
      if (nargs .lt. 1 .or. nargs .gt. 3) then
         call fputstr (STDERR,
      &    'syntax: match "pattern" [infile] [outfile]'//EOL)
         stop 'argument error - aborted'
      end if
      if (caseflag) pattern = upper(pattern)

      s = 1
      epstabp = 1
      lp = 1
      call mknfa (s, pattern, lp)   !build NFA transition diagram
      nfatoken(s) = 1               !mark end state as accepting
      call mkdfa ()                 !convert to DFA

      do while (fgetline (uin, line))
         if (caseflag) then
            uline = upper(line)
         else
            uline = line
         end if
         lp = 1
         done = .false.
         do while (.not. done)
            if (uline(lp:lp) .eq. NULL) then
               done = .true.
            else
               t = dfascan(token, uline, lp)
               if (t .ne. 0) then
                  done = .true.
                  call fputstr (uout, line)
               end if
            end if
         end do
      end do

      end
```

The routines for NFA and DFA construction make use of a number of lower-level tools for mundane operations involving set manipulation; now it is time to spell these out. All of these routines are written for sets consisting of integers and terminated by ENDLIST. For the case of the algorithms in this chapter, all sets consist of small positive integers. The routines ascopy and sacopy are used to copy a set (terminated by ENDLIST) from an array to a list table and vice versa.

```
! ascopy  -  copy integer array to settab, update setp

      subroutine ascopy (a, setp, settab)
      integer a (*), setp, settab (*)
      include 'global.def'
      integer i
```

```
call bubblesort (a)
i = 1
do while (a(i) .ne. ENDLIST)
   settab(setp) = a(i)
   i = i + 1
   setp = setp + 1
end do
settab(setp) = ENDLIST
setp = setp + 1

return
end
```

A side effect of ascopy is that the input array is returned sorted. ascopy sorts the set into ascending order before installing it in the table via the routine bubblesort:

```
! bubblesort  -  sort integer set terminated by ENDLIST

   subroutine bubblesort (set)
   integer    set (*)
   include    'global.def'
   integer    i, j, k

   i = 1
   do while (set(i) .ne. ENDLIST)
      i = i + 1
   end do
   i = i - 1
   do while (i .ge. 2)
      do j = 1, i - 1
         if (set(j) .gt. set(j+1)) then
            k = set(j)
            set(j) = set(j+1)
            set(j+1) = k
         end if
      end do
      i = i - 1
   end do

   return
   end
```

bubblesort uses the simplest exchange sort algorithm known to man. It is also one of the poorest in performance but is adequate when the number of items to be sorted is small. The performance gain of even an inefficient sort is significant if the sets are compared much more often than they are stored, as is the case in mkdfa.

The sacopy subroutine is not used by any of the routines in this chapter, but it is the natural complement to ascopy:

```
! sacopy - copy set starting at settab to integer array

      subroutine sacopy (set, settab, a)
      integer  set, settab (*), a (*)
      include  'global.def'
      integer  i, j

      i = 1
      j = set
      do while (settab(j) .ne. ENDLIST)
        a(i) = settab(j)
        j = j + 1
        i = i + 1
      end do
      a(i) = ENDLIST

      return
      end
```

The simplest set operation is to see if an integer is a member of a set. is_element doesn't mess with setp, so it can be called with a constant as the actual argument for setp (if setp were modified in the subroutine, then attempting to return to a routine that called is_element with a constant argument would cause an access violation error on the VAX).

```
! is_element - determine membership in a set

      logical function is_element (element, set, setp)
      integer  element, set (*), setp
      include  'global.def'
      integer  i
      logical  found

      i = setp
      found = .false.
      do while ((.not. found) .and. (set(i) .ne. ENDLIST))
        if (set(i) .eq. element) found = .true.
        i = i + 1
      end do

      is_element = found
      return
      end
```

A basic operation needed for sets is the ability to compare two sets for equality. eqvset is the only routine that requires the sets to be sorted on input to work correctly. It is worth sacrificing a little generality in this case, since eqvset gets called by mkdfa about 10 million times for a typical lexical analyzer. The routine is more general if it can compare an array with either another array or with a set already stored in a table. It is actually only called from one place, but nevertheless can be called either way, with 1 as the set pointer to compare two arrays.

```
! eqvset  -  compare set with settab starting at p for equivalence

        logical function eqvset (set, p, settab)
        integer set (*), p, settab (*)
        include 'global.def'
        integer i, j
        logical equiv

        i = 1
        j = p
        equiv = .true.
        do while (equiv .and. set(i) .ne. ENDLIST)
           equiv = (set(i) .eq. settab(j))
           i = i + 1
           j = j + 1
        end do
        if (equiv .and. settab(j) .eq. ENDLIST) then
           eqvset = .true.
        else
           eqvset = .false.
        end if

        return
        end
```

Set union and intersection are also fundamental set operations that should be provided. We have thus far had no need for the intersection operation, but it is included anyway for completeness.

```
! union  -  find the union of two sets

        subroutine union (set1, set2, uset)
        integer set1 (*), set2 (*), uset (*)
        include 'global.def'
        integer i,j
        logical is_element

        i = 1
        j = 1
        do while (set1(i) .ne. ENDLIST)
           if (is_element (set1(i), set2, 1)) then
              continue                    !skip duplicated elements
           else
              uset(j) = set1(i)         !add to union set
              j = j + 1
           end if
           i = i + 1
        end do
```

```
      i = 1                        !copy set 2 to union set
      do while (set2(i) .ne. ENDLIST)
         uset(j) = set2(i)
         i = i + 1
         j = j + 1
      end do
      uset(j) = ENDLIST

      return
      end


! intersection  -  find the intersection of two sets

      subroutine intersection (set1, set2, iset)
      integer   set1 (*), set2 (*), iset (*)
      include   'global.def'
      integer   i, j
      logical   is_element

      i = 1
      j = 1
      do while (set1(i) .ne. ENDLIST)
         if (is_element (set1(i), set2, 1)) then
            iset(j) = set1(i)
            j = j + 1
         end if
      end do
      iset(j) = ENDLIST

      return
      end
```

This is a bare-bones DFA generator and is about half of a lexical analyzer generator. Since it takes time to generate the DFA, match is best used for long file searches. Here is a files list for the match program:

```
! match  -  software organization

! common blocks
      # nfa.cmn
      # dfa.cmn

      match
         mknfa
            ascopy
         mkdfa
            eps_union
               union
                  eps_closure
            eqvset
            is_element
         dfascan
```

7.5   Optimization

The DFA created by the subset construction algorithm can be used to efficiently search for occurrences of the text patterns it represents, but it is not necessarily optimal. For example, states 8 and 9 in the DFA for decimal numbers are obviously identical since for all input characters they go to the same state (state 9). The same can be said for states 6 and 7, and for states 3 and 5. After these reductions, it becomes clear that state 4 and the state representing 6 and 7 combined are also identical. It is less obvious that the combined states 8,9 and 4,6,7 are the same. The optimal DFA for recognizing decimal numbers has just four states, while that constructed by mkdfa has nine, over twice as large. This is no big deal for match, which only searches for one regular expression at a time. Note that the extra states have no impact on search time, but only on overall table size. match has to allocate enough storage for the largest table it might ever see anyway, so there is no reason to optimize the DFA. For a full lexical analyzer, however, the table size can be very large, and a 50% size reduction can be a substantial savings. Anyway, a lexical analyzer table once generated can then be used zillions of times, so it's worth spending extra time to make it as small as possible.

Fortunately, there is an algorithm (called the *Mealy-Huffman* algorithm) that can reduce any DFA to the fewest possible states. The idea is to start with the most optimistic assumption possible, which is to mark all nonaccepting states as the same, and all states returning the same token as the same. Then every possible input character is applied to every state in each group to see if they really are the same. If they are, then the grouping of the original DFA states is unchanged; if they aren't, then the group is subdivided and the process is repeated. The algorithm terminates when no further subdivision is required.

Specifically, the Mealy-Huffman algorithm is as follows:

```
let G be a group of states in the current partition; each DFA state
    is a member of some group
let n be the number of states in some group G

set the initial partition to consist of:
    one group for all nonaccepting states
    one group for each token value, such that all states with the same
        token value are in the same group G
    one group representing state 0 (no transition)


do
    for each group G                    !determine new partition
        do i = 2, n
            do j = 1, i - 1
                if (for every input a, states
                    i and j go to the same group) then
                    states i and j are in the same group
                end if
            end do
```

```
                    if (no state j was found to be
                        in the same group as state i) then
                        make state i a new group
                    end if
                end do
                replace G in next partition by the set of subgroups formed
            end for
        until new partition is the same as the previous partition

        each remaining group is a single state of the reduced DFA
```

The algorithm is difficult to explain in words; it is best illustrated with an example. Figure 7.5 shows how the Mealy-Huffman algorithm is applied to our decimal number DFA shown in Figure 7.4. The entries in each column are filled in by reference to the transition diagram and the current grouping of states. For instance, for state 1 in partition 1, the target states for "." and $[0 - 9]$ are DFA states 2 and 3, respectively, as indicated in the transition diagram. Both of these states are in group 1 in the initial partition. The new transition diagram can be deduced from the final partition and is illustrated in Figure 7.6. The state diagram in Figure 7.6 is clearly the minimal number of states required, at least in this case. It can be proven, in fact, that the algorithm produces the minimal number of states for any DFA.

All said and done, mkrfa is pretty complicated. The heart of the algorithm is two nested do loops which compare the states within a group for equivalence. The variable r is used as a counter for the next available group number, like n in mknfa and d in mkdfa. Although there is much work to be done for each iteration, generally only a few iterations are required for the Mealy-Huffman algorithm to terminate, so overall the run time is not too long.

```
! mkrfa  -  minimize DFA state transition table (Mealy-Huffman algorithm)

        subroutine mkrfa ()
        include 'dfa.cmn'
        integer G (0:MAXDFA)            !current group of each DFA state
        integer Gtoken (MAXDFA)         !token value for group
        integer oldG (0:MAXDFA)         !previous group of each state
        integer nextG(0:MAXCHAR, MAXDFA) !next group for each input character
        integer group (MAXDFA)          !list of states in current group
        integer r                       !next available group number
        integer i, j, k, c, n
        logical eqvarray, same, found

! initialize groups
        r = 1                           !r=1 for nonaccepting states
        G(0) = 0                        !bogus dead state
        do i = 1, d
            G(i) = 0
            oldG(i) = 0
        end do
        do i = 1, d
```

partition 1:	group 0 = {0}									
	group 1 = {1,2,3,5}									
	group 2 = {4,6,7,8,9}									

	{0}	{1	2	3	5}	{4	6	7	8	9}
".":	0	1	0	2	2	0	0	0	0	0
[0-9]:	0	1	2	1	1	2	2	2	2	2

partition 2:	group 0 = {0}									
	group 1 = {1}									
	group 2 = {4,6,7,8,9}									
	group 3 = {2}									
	group 4 = {3,5}									

	{0}	{1}	{2}	{3	5}	{4	6	7	8	9}
".":	0	3	0	2	2	0	0	0	0	0
[0-9]:	0	4	2	4	4	2	2	2	2	2

no new groups:	algorithm terminates; states {3,5} and {4,6,7,8,9} are identical

Figure 7.5: Optimization of the unsigned decimal number DFA.

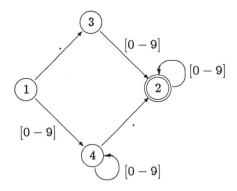

Figure 7.6: Optimized DFA for unsigned decimal numbers.

```
        if (G(i) .ne. 0) then          !group already set
          continue
        else
          if (dfatoken(i) .eq. 0) then  !nonaccepting state
            G(i) = 1
          else                          !accepting state
            r = r + 1
            G(i) = r
            do j = i, d               !find other states with same token
              if (dfatoken(i) .eq. dfatoken(j)) then
                G(j) = G(i)
                end if
              end do
            end if
          end if
        end do


! subdivide groups until termination
! terminate when two consecutive partitions are identical

      do while (.not. eqvarray (G, oldG, d))
        !record target groups of all states and update oldG
        do i = 1, d
          oldG(i) = G(i)
          do j = 0, MAXCHAR
            nextG(j,i) = G(dfanext(j,i))
            end do
          end do

        !check states in each group for equivalence
        do k = 1, r
          n = 0
          do j = 1, d              !make list of states in group k
            if (G(j) .eq. k) then
              n = n + 1
              group(n) = j
              end if
            end do
          do i = 2, n
            j = 0
            found = .false.
            do while ((j .lt. i-1) .and. (.not. found))
              j = j + 1
              same = .true.
              c = 0
              do while (c .le. MAXCHAR .and. same)
                if (nextG(c,group(j)) .ne. nextG(c,group(i))) then
                  same = .false.
                  end if
                c = c + 1
                end do
              if (same) found = .true.
              end do
```

```
            if (.not. found) then        !create new group
               r = r + 1
               G(group(i)) = r
            else                         !make same as matched group
               G(group(i)) = G(group(j))
            end if
          end do
        end do                           !for all groups
      end do                             !until partition does not change

! reduced table is contained in nextG - copy to common block
    do i = 1, r
      do j = 1, d
        if (G(j) .eq. i) then            !state j is in group i
           Gtoken(i) = dfatoken(j)       !adopt the token value of state j
           do k = 0, MAXCHAR             !use group transitions of state j
              dfanext(k,i) = nextG(k,j)
           end do
        end if
      end do
    end do

! set token values for reduced table
    do i = 1, r
       dfatoken(i) = Gtoken(i)
    end do
    d = r

    return
    end
```

The routine eqvarray is used to provide a convenient termination condition for
the main loop of mkrfa. The eqvarray routine is dead simple, just looping
through the arrays and comparing each element:

```
! eqvarray  -  check two integer arrays for order-dependent equivalence

    logical function eqvarray (a1, a2, n)
    integer a1(*), a2(*), n
    integer i
    logical ok

    ok = .true.
    do i = 1, n
       if (a1(i) .ne. a2(i)) ok = .false.
    end do

    eqvarray = ok
    return
    end
```

Even after minimizing the number of states in the DFA, the resulting table can still be expected to be very large with its present organization since 256 array elements are needed for each state. Some means of compacting the table without much adverse effect on speed is highly desirable.

Our first improvement takes advantage of the fact that most states will have transitions on only a small number of characters, with all other characters causing failure (termination). Table size can be conserved by making the table entries for different states overlap, so that the same table entries can be addressed by more than one state. The price we must pay for this savings is indirect addressing, rather than direct addressing, so that the storage for each state can start at an arbitrary location. Additionally, we need some means of verifying, for each table entry, whether the entry belongs to the current state. The scheme is illustrated in Figure 7.7. For state s_1, the next state is given by s_2 in the next array for input character c. In this way, the entries in the next array for different states may overlap, only requiring the range of values of valid input characters for each state in the next array. For states with only one valid input character, only one location in next is consumed.

For the entry in next to be regarded as valid, the state value in the check array must be equal to the current state. If the entry is found to be invalid, termination is reached. The code for choosing the next state is something like

```
if (check (base(s) + ichar(c)) .eq. s) then
    s = s2
else
    return token value
end if
```

The check array must be the same size as the next array, so the net reduction in entries must be at least 50% to gain any advantage at all (neglecting the storage for the base array). However, as a worst case estimate, assume each state has valid transitions on all of the uppercase and lowercase letters and the digits; each state would therefore span 74 locations in next, the difference between ichar('z') = 122 and ichar('0') = 48. The net savings would then be $256 - 74 \times 2$ or 108 storage units, neglecting the base array. This 42% savings can be expected to be much greater in practice since usually many states will have valid transitions on only a few characters. If the input is restricted to uppercase letters, the worst case savings estimate becomes $256 - 42 \times 2 = 172$ locations, or 67%.

The second improvement we can make to reduce the table size is suggested by considering the recognition of keywords. Keywords usually have the same general form as identifiers and make up half to two-thirds of the total number of tokens to be recognized. Suppose one of the keywords is then, and we have just seen the in the input. If the next character is n, then the next state will be the accepting state for the keyword then; if it is any other letter or digit, then the next state will be the accepting state for identifiers. The current state must therefore store transitions for all letters and digits, all of which go to the

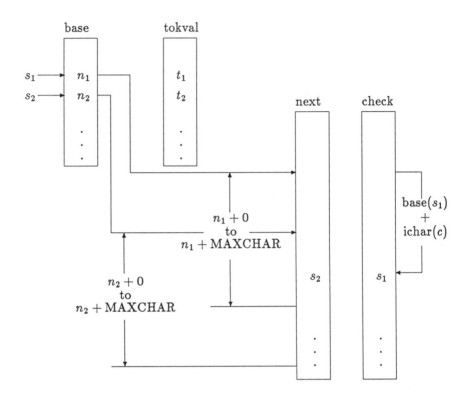

Figure 7.7: Compacted state transition table with overlapping entries for states.

same state except for the letter n. If we could devise a scheme whereby only the transition for n is stored, a dramatic reduction in table size requirements could be realized.

This can be put into effect by adding a default array in parallel with the base and tokval arrays (one default entry per state). The interpretation scheme is now modified to read like

```
if (check (base(s) + ichar(c)) = s) then
    s = s2
else if (default(s) <> 0) then
    backup one character
    s = default(s)
else
    return token value
end if
```

It is necessary to retract the input character and examine it again from the default state because information is lost in replacing valid transitions with a single

"default" value. For example, if we have just seen the and the next character is
=, we cannot just blindly accept it and jump to the accepting state for identifiers;
the proper action is to first make the jump and then look at the character again,
in which case we would correctly recognize the identifier the.

As an estimate of how much table space is eliminated by this approach, assume
that 60% of the tokens are keywords. Instead of 36 entries in next for each letter
of each keyword (26 letters and 10 digits), we now have just one. The reduction
is 35/36, or 97%, per state in keyword recognizing states. If 60% of the states
are due to keywords, then the overall reduction is by 58%.

The expression of this data organization in Fortran is as follows:

```
! lexscan.cmn  -  common block declaration for lexscan

      integer   MAXSTATE, MAXENTRY
      parameter (MAXSTATE = 500)
      parameter (MAXENTRY = 4000)

      integer   base(MAXSTATE), tokval(MAXSTATE), default(MAXSTATE)
      integer   next(0:MAXENTRY), check(0:MAXENTRY)

      common /lextable/ base, tokval, default, next, check
      save   /lextable/
```

This is the final form that will be used for our lexical scanner, so we have dispensed with all of the odd terminology and called the transition array next.

The implementation of indirect, overlapping state storage is quite straightforward; selecting and encoding default states is more tricky. On careful exami-
nation it is apparent that the requirements for replacing transitions by a default
state entry are:

- If i and j are DFA states, state i can be the default for state j only if the
  set of characters for which i and j have valid transitions is identical.

- If the first condition is met, i should be chosen as the default for j only if
  the number of different target states for i is less than the number of target
  states for j; if j has fewer target states than i, j should be the default state
  for i.

- If the first two criteria are met and j is a possible default state for i, transitions on character c should be removed from the table only if dfanext(c,i)
  is the same state as dfanext(c,j), that is, only if both transitions are to
  the same state.

As an illustration of these criteria, suppose again that we have just seen the
and there is a keyword then. The current state must have transitions on all
characters allowed in identifiers, since the is a valid identifier as well as a prefix
of then; thus the first criterion is met if i is the current state and j is the closure
state for identifiers. State i will therefore have a transition to the closure state

for all identifier characters except n, which causes a transition to the recognizing state for then. Since state j has nonzero transitions to only one state (itself), and i has transitions to two different states, then j is chosen as the default state for i.

For speed considerations, some additional criteria are considered to reduce the number of states that are ever considered for defaults. If a state has transitions only to itself then it will not be defaulted, since it is generally the state that should become the default for other states. As an example, the accepting state for identifiers generally has transitions only to itself, on all characters valid in identifiers. If this state is defaulted, it will be to another state that also has transitions to it on all identifier characters; this would have the effect of requiring every character in an identifier to be examined twice, once in the identifier state and once in the default state. In addition, defaults are not attempted if there are MINTRANS or fewer transitions for state i (MINTRANS is set to 4). In other words, we are willing to pay a penalty of up to three extra transitions in the next array in order to save the time associated with testing a character a second time in the default state.

It is fairly easy to test the criteria with the DFA in matrix form. mkdflt performs the necessary checks, makes entries in the default array, and then removes all of the defaulted transitions from the DFA by setting them to zero. This makes the routine for producing the indirect addressing table oblivious to the existence of default states.

```
! mkdflt   -  choose default states for DFA states

      subroutine mkdflt ()
      include   'global.def'
      include   'dfa.cmn'
      include   'lexscan.cmn'
      integer   MINTRANS          !min # transitions to consider defaults
      parameter (MINTRANS = 4)
      logical   used (MAXDFA)      !true if state has been used as a default
      logical   changed (MAXDFA) !true if state has been defaulted
      integer   i, j, k, trcount
      integer   ilist(MAXCHAR+1), ii, jlist(MAXCHAR+1), jj
      logical   same(0:MAXCHAR), sameset, closure, is_element

! initialize
      do i = 1, d
        default(i) = 0
        used(i) = .false.
        changed(i) = .false.
      end do

      do i = 1, d               !state under consideration
        closure = .true.
        trcount = 0
        do k = 0, MAXCHAR
          if (dfanext(k,i) .ne. 0) then
```

```
            trcount = trcount + 1
            if (dfanext(k,i) .ne. i) closure = .false.
          end if
        end do
        if (closure .or. trcount .le. MINTRANS) then
          used(i) = .true.
          goto 1   !cycle to next i
        end if
        do j = 1, d              !compare i with all other states
          if ((i.ne.j) .and. (.not.used(i)) .and. (.not.changed(j))) then
            sameset = .true.   !true only if set of characters with nonzero
                               !transitions is the same for states i and j
            k = 0
            do while (k .le. MAXCHAR .and. sameset)
              same(k) = ((dfanext(k,i).eq.0 .and. dfanext(k,j).eq.0) .or.
    &                    (dfanext(k,i).ne.0 .and. dfanext(k,j).ne.0))
              if (.not. same(k)) sameset = .false.
              k = k + 1
            end do
            if (sameset) then
              ii = 1
              jj = 1
              do k = 0, MAXCHAR
                same(k) = (dfanext(k,i) .eq. dfanext(k,j))
                !count # of states reachable from states i and j
                if (.not. is_element(dfanext(k,i), ilist, 1)) then
                  ilist(ii) = dfanext(k,i)
                  ii = ii + 1
                end if
                if (.not. is_element(dfanext(k,j), jlist, 1)) then
                  jlist(jj) = dfanext(k,j)
                  jj = jj + 1
                end if
              end do
              ilist(ii) = ENDLIST
              jlist(jj) = ENDLIST
              if (ii .ge. jj) then   !make j the default state for i
                default(i) = j
                changed(i) = .true.
                used(j) = .true.
                do k = 0, MAXCHAR       !remove all defaulted transitions
                  if (same(k)) dfanext(k,i) = 0
                end do
                goto 1                 !done with state i
              !else i is a suitable default for j
              end if
            !else transitions not on same character set
            end if
          !else i = j
          end if
        end do                     !j
1       continue
      end do
```

```
      return
      end
```

The tests performed on state i before considering default states reduce the run-
time of mkdflt by at least a factor of two (and more like an order of magnitude).
For a reasonable sized lexical analyzer (d=300), the statements

```
do i = 1, d
  do j = 1, d
    do k = 0, 255
      . . .
    end do
    . . .
  end do
  . . .
end do
```

imply that the code inside the inner loop will be executed 30 million times, which
can take a while, even on a VAX. The inner loops are short-circuited in mkdflt
by goto statements, which are used to cycle the outer loop. Since Fortran has no
cycle statement or equivalent to cause the next iteration of a looping construct
to begin, goto is the only way to simulate it.

The mklex routine builds the base, next and check arrays from the matrix
DFA form. The initial state of the compacted table has entries for all possible
input characters, even though some may not produce any defined token. This
prevents any other state from having a negative base address, so illegal array
subscripts cannot happen.

```
! mklex  -  make compressed lex table from DFA matrix form

      subroutine mklex (nstates, nentries)
      integer           nstates, nentries  !return values
      include           'global.def'
      include           'dfa.cmn'
      include           'lexscan.cmn'
      integer           freep, p, s, i, offset
      logical           conflict, done
      character*(MAXSTR) itoa

! initialize tables
      do i = 1, MAXSTATE
        base(i) = 0
        tokval(i) = 0
      end do
      do i = 0, MAXENTRY
        next(i) = 0
        check(i) = 0
      end do

! set token values
```

```
        do i = 1, d
           tokval(i) = dfatoken(i)
        end do

! set up initial state
        base(1) = 0
        default(1) = 0
        do i = 0, MAXCHAR
           next(i) = dfanext (i, 1)
           if (dfanext(i, 1) .eq. 0) then
              check(i) = 0
           else
              check(i) = 1
           end if
        end do

        freep = MAXCHAR + 1
        do s = 2, d
           do while (check(freep) .ne. 0)
              freep = freep + 1
           end do
           p = freep      !candidate position for 1st used character in s
           done = .false.
           do while (.not. done)          !find 1st available base address
              offset = 0
              do while (dfanext(offset, s) .eq. 0 .and. !find 1st transition
     &                     offset .le. MAXCHAR)          !from this state
                 offset = offset + 1
              end do
              base(s) = p - offset
              conflict = .false.
              do i = offset, MAXCHAR
                 if (dfanext(i,s) .ne. 0) then
                    if (check(base(s)+i) .ne. 0) conflict = .true.
                 end if
              end do
              if (conflict) then    !advance to next candidate position
                 p = p + 1
                 do while (check(p) .ne. 0)
                    p = p + 1
                 end do
              else
                 done = .true.
              end if
           end do
           do i = offset, MAXCHAR      !install transitions in next/check
              if (dfanext(i,s) .ne. 0) then
                 next(base(s)+i) = dfanext(i,s)
                 check(base(s)+i) = s
              end if
           end do
        end do
```

```
nstates = d
nentries = base(d) + MAXCHAR
call fputstr (STDOUT, 'lexscan table size = '//itoa(nentries))
call fputc (STDOUT, NEWLINE)
i = 0
do s = 1, nentries
    if (check(s) .eq. 0) i = i + 1
end do
call fputstr (STDOUT, 'lexscan unused entries = '//itoa(i))
call fputc (STDOUT, NEWLINE)

return
end
```

mklex can be expected to find the most compact table possible, since it begins searching for a usable location for each state at the lowest unused subscript in next/check. Naturally, its dumbo approach to finding a suitable location is also slow, but we have a few seconds to spare.

We now have a completely optimized table in memory, and the only job left is to write it out for future use. lexdump writes a file of data statements to be included into a scanner driver routine. The driver can load the data into saved local variables, since no other routines need access to the table. lexdump uses the same routine for making data statements as the one introduced in Chapter 5 for making hash tables.

```
! lexdump  -  dump lexscan tables as Fortran DATA statements

      subroutine lexdump (uout, nstates, nentries)
      integer   uout, nstates, nentries
      include   'global.def'
      include   'lexscan.cmn'
      integer   p

      p = 1
      do while (p .le. nstates)
          if (p + 10 .le. nstates) then
              call mk_idata (uout, 10, 'base'//NULL, base(p), p)
              call mk_idata (uout, 10, 'default'//NULL, default(p), p)
              call mk_idata (uout, 10, 'tokval'//NULL, tokval(p), p)
              p = p + 10
          else
              call mk_idata (uout, nstates-p+1, 'base'//NULL, base(p), p)
              call mk_idata (uout, nstates-p+1, 'default'//NULL, default(p), p)
              call mk_idata (uout, nstates-p+1, 'tokval'//NULL, tokval(p), p)
              p = nstates + 1
          end if
      end do
      p = 0
      do while (p .le. nentries)
          if (p + 10 .le. nentries) then
              call mk_idata (uout, 10, 'next'//NULL, next(p), p)
```

```
          call mk_idata (uout, 10, 'check'//NULL, check(p), p)
          p = p + 10
       else
          call mk_idata (uout, nentries-p+1, 'next'//NULL, next(p), p)
          call mk_idata (uout, nentries-p+1, 'check'//NULL, check(p), p)
          p = nentries + 1
       end if
    end do

    return
    end
```

All of the pieces are now in place for the lexical analyzer generator. The main routine is called lexgen, and it just calls the routines one after another. All of the real work takes place in the subroutines, and the data interface to most of the routines is the DFA common block, so the subroutines don't even have arguments. lexgen prints out informative messages on the terminal to give some idea where all those milliseconds are going.

```
! lexgen  -  lexical analyzer table generator

       program lexgen
       include           'global.def'
       include           'nfa.cmn'
       include           'dfa.cmn'
       integer           argc, uin, uout
       character*(MAXSTR) argv(MAXARGS), line, itoa, upper
       integer           startstate(256)
       integer           i, j, lp, ival, s, olds, nstates, nentries
       logical           ppline, is_ival, caseflag, errflag

       call ioinit ()
       call getargs (argc, argv)
       call stdargs (argc, argv, uin, uout)
       if (uin .eq. IOERROR .or. uout .eq. IOERROR) stop ' '
       caseflag = .false.
       do i = 1, argc
          if (argv(i)(1:1) .eq. QUALIFIER) then
             argv(i) = upper(argv(i))
             j = index(argv(i),NULL)
             if (index(argv(i)(1:j), 'U') .gt. 0) caseflag = .true.
          end if
       end do
       call ppinit (uin)

! initialize NFA
       do i = 1, MAXNFA
          chrset(i) = NONE
          cval1(i) = 0
          cval2(i) = 0
          nfatoken(i) = 0
       end do
```

```
! process all input  -  reserve initial state of NFA
    call fputstr (STDOUT, 'constructing NFA...'//EOL)
    i = 1
    s = 2
    epstabp = 1
    errflag = .false.
    do while (ppline (line))
       lp = 1
       do while (line(lp:lp) .eq. BLANK)
          lp = lp + 1
       end do
       if (line(lp:lp) .eq. NEWLINE .or. line(lp:lp) .eq. COMMENT) then
          continue
       else if (is_ival (ival, line, lp)) then
          do while (line(lp:lp) .eq. BLANK)
             lp = lp + 1
          end do
          if (line(lp:lp) .ne. '=') then
             call fputstr (STDERR, 'missing assignment operator'//EOL)
             call fputstr (STDERR, line)
          else
             lp = lp + 1
             startstate(i) = s
             i = i + 1
             olds = s
             call mknfa (s, line, lp)
             if (s .eq. olds) then
                call fputstr (STDERR,
   &            'no NFA states generated for token '//itoa(ival))
                call fputc (STDERR, NEWLINE)
                errflag = .true.
             else
                nfatoken(s) = ival
             end if
             s = s + 1
          end if
       else
          call fputstr (STDERR, 'invalid token value'//EOL)
          call fputstr (STDERR, line)
       end if
    end do
    s = s - 1
    call fputstr (STDOUT, '# NFA states = '//itoa(s))
    call fputc (STDOUT, NEWLINE)
    if (errflag) stop 'lexgen aborted due to NFA errors.'

! link startstates together with epsset(1)
    startstate(i) = ENDLIST
    epsset(1) = epstabp
    call ascopy (startstate, epstabp, epstab)

! convert NFA to upper case if casefeflag set
```

```
      if (caseflag) then
        call fputstr (STDOUT, 'converting NFA to upper case...'//EOL)
        do i = 1, s
          if (cval1(i) .ge. ichar('a') .and.
   &            cval1(i) .le. ichar('z')) then
            cval1(i) = cval1(i) - ichar('a') + ichar('A')
          end if
          if (cval2(i) .ge. ichar('a') .and.
   &            cval2(i) .le. ichar('z')) then
            cval2(i) = cval2(i) - ichar('a') + ichar('A')
          end if
        end do
      end if

! convert NFA to DFA
      call fputstr (STDOUT, 'converting NFA to DFA...'//EOL)
      call mkdfa ()
      call fputstr (STDOUT, 'number of DFA states = '//itoa(d))
      call fputc (STDOUT, NEWLINE)
      if (dfatoken(1) .ne. 0) then
        call fputstr (STDERR, 'token value '//itoa(dfatoken(1)))
        call fputstr (STDERR, ' requires no input'//EOL)
        stop 'lexgen aborted due to DFA error.'
      end if

! optimize DFA
      call fputstr (STDOUT, 'optimizing DFA...'//EOL)
      call mkrfa ()
      call fputstr (STDOUT, 'number of DFA states = '//itoa(d))
      call fputc (STDOUT, NEWLINE)

! choose default states
      call fputstr (STDOUT, 'choosing default states...'//EOL)
      call mkdflt ()

! construct compacted table
      call fputstr (STDOUT, 'creating compacted table...'//EOL)
      call mklex (nstates, nentries)

! write output
      call fputstr (STDOUT, 'writing output...'//EOL)
      call lexdump (uout, nstates, nentries)

      end
```

Like match, lexgen has an optional argument -u, which causes all alphabetic characters in the NFA to be converted to uppercase. Finally, here is the Big Picture for lexgen:

```
! lexgen.fil  -  files list for lexical analyzer generator

! common blocks
```

```
# nfa.cmn        !NFA data structure
# dfa.cmn        !DFA data structure
# lexscan.cmn    !compressed DFA data structure


lexgen
   mknfa
   mkdfa
      eps_union
         eps_closure
   mkrfa
      eqvarray
   mkdflt
   mklex
   lexdump
      mk_idata

! set manipulation tools
   bubblesort
   sacopy
   ascopy
   is_element
   eqvset
   union
   intersection

# lexscan.for     !driver for output table
```

The routine that actually uses these tables on real input is a prewritten routine
called lexscan, which only needs to be modified to include the appropriate data
statements or perhaps change the routine name. It keeps on scanning the input
buffer until it can go no further (no transitions exist for the current character) and
then returns the token value and token text corresponding to the last accepting
state visited; thus it finds the longest possible input string that matches a token.

```
! lexscan  -  table-driven lexical scanner
! returns string matched as token, integer code as function value

      integer function lexscan (token, line, lp)
      character*(*)    token, line
      integer          lp
      include          'global.def'
      include          'lexscan.cmn'
      integer          sp, startp, tokp, s, scancode, addr
      logical          done

      integer          LEXERROR
      parameter        (LEXERROR = -1)  !reserved lexical token

      do while (line(lp:lp) .eq. BLANK)
         lp = lp + 1
      end do
```

```
startp = lp
tokp = lp
scancode = LEXERROR

s = 1
done = .false.
do while (.not. done)
   addr = base(s) + ichar(line(lp:lp))
   if (check(addr) .eq. s) then
      s = next(addr)
      if (tokval(s) .ne. 0) then
         scancode = tokval(s)
         tokp = lp
      end if
      lp = lp + 1
   else if (default(s) .ne. 0) then
      s = default(s)
   else
      done = .true.
   end if
end do

token = line(startp:tokp)//NULL
lexscan = scancode
if (scancode .eq. LEXERROR) lp = startp + 1

return
end
```

Note that `lexscan` does not do any input reading on its own—the input buffer must be filled and supplied by the caller of `lexscan`. Generally, lexical analyzers do other things besides finding tokens in the input text. For example, management of tables for identifiers and constants is often performed in the lexical analysis phase of compilers. The caller of `lexscan` may also need to do operations like uppercase conversion, deletion of insignificant blanks, or other things that depend on the specifics of how it is to be used. `lexscan` does the least it can do but does it efficiently and without any application specific actions; it can thus be used almost as is by many programs.

As a rather comprehensive example, the following is a complete specification of the lexical analyzer tokens for the spl interpreter developed in Chapter 8. The symbolic names for all of the tokens (which by our convention all start with $ to distinguish them from valid Fortran identifiers) are defined in the file spl.mac.

```
!  spl.lex  -  lexical analyzer input for spl
      #include spl.mac

! keywords
      $int      = integer
      $real     = real
```

```
$log        = logical
$char       = character
$if         = if
$elseif     = else {\b} if
$else       = else
$endif      = end {\b} if
$while      = while
$endwhile   = end {\b} while
$repeat     = repeat
$until      = until
$read       = read
$print      = print
```

```
! arithmetic and logical operators
$add        = +
$sub        = -
$mult       = *
$div        = /
$pwr        = **
$eq         = ==
$ne         = <>
$gt         = >
$ge         = >=
$lt         = <
$le         = <=
$and        = and
$or         = or
$not        = not
$assign     = =
```

```
! identifiers and constants
$intnum     = [0-9] { [0-9] }
#define dec_num  ([0-9]{[0-9]}.{[0-9]} | {[0-9]}.[0-9]{[0-9]})
$realnum    = (dec_num | dec_num (e|E) (+|-|) [0-9]{[0-9]})
$true       = true
$false      = false
$id         = ( [a-z] | [A-Z] ) { ( [a-z] | [A-Z] | [0-9] | $ | _ ) }
! all printable characters except quote
#define pnq   ([\\h20-\\h26]|[\\h28-\\h7E])
$string     = ' {pnq} ' { '{pnq}' }
```

```
! punctuation
$lparen     = \(
$rparen     = \)
$comma      = ,
$eol        = \n
```

By convention we use the file name extension .lex for input files to lexgen. The NFA generated for spl.lex has 262 states, which is converted to a DFA with 137 states (117 states after optimization). In the matrix form the optimized DFA requires 29,952 integer storage units of memory (120K bytes for 4-byte integers). The compacted table used by lexscan uses a total of 779 integers in memory for the each of the next and check arrays, and 117 integers each for base and default. Thus the total space required for the compacted state table is 1792 integers (not counting the token values), a total space savings of 28,160 integers or 94% of the matrix table size.

The spl input tokens are case-sensitive, so that an identifier ABC is considered different from abc. The file spl.mac contains all of the declarations for the integer token codes with statements of the form

```
#define  $int   1
```

spl.mac also contains global parameters for use in the source code of the spl program. The use of the preprocessor in both the lexical analyzer input file and program source code provides a single global declaration file for all of the token codes. The token code symbolic names in spl.mac all begin with "$", which can never conflict with a legal Fortran identifier.

The master lexical analyzer routine for spl is simply called lex; it returns the token value and token text to its caller, and manages getting logical lines of input and updating the line pointer for the next scan internally. The preprocessor is built in to lex through the use of getlogline.

```
! lex  -  lexical analyzer for spl

        integer function lex (t,token)
        integer          t
        character*(*)    token
        #include         global.def
        #include         options.cmn
        #include         perror.cmn
        #include         spl.mac
        integer          splscan, tp, i
        logical          getlogline, first, is_sval, junk
        character*(MAXSTR) itoa, doescape
        data   first  /.true./

        if (first) then     !first call to lex
           first = .false.
           llp = 0
           lc = 0
        end if

        t = 0
        if (llp .eq. 0) then
           if (getlogline(line)) then
              llp = 1
              lc = lc + 1
              if (listflag) then
                 call fputstr (STDOUT, itoa(lc))
                 call fputc (STDOUT, BLANK)
                 call fputstr (STDOUT, line)
              end if
```

```
            else
                t = $eof
                lex = $eof
                return
            end if
        end if
        tp = llp
        t = splscan (token, line, llp)
        if (t .eq. LEXERROR) then
            if (line(llp:llp) .eq. QUOTE) then  !probably missing quote
                call perror ('missing quote'//NULL)
                do while (line(llp:llp) .ne. NEWLINE)
                    llp = llp + 1
                end do
                t = $string
                token = NULL
            else                                !probably bad character
                call perror ('unrecognized token'//NULL)
                do while (t .eq. LEXERROR)
                    !eat input until something makes sense
                    t = splscan (token, line, llp)
                end do
            end if
        else if (t .eq. $string) then           !convert to internal form
            junk = is_sval (token, line, tp)
            token = doescape (token)
        end if
        if (line(llp:llp) .eq. NULL) llp = 0

        lex = t
        return
        end
```

The scanner routine `splscan` is identical to `lexscan` except that it includes data statements from a different file, and of course it has a different name. The logical line and line pointer are kept in a common block so that the error-handling routines can have access to the input line for diagnostic messages. The common block file `perror.cmn` stores the line and also an error count.

```
! perror.cmn  -  common block for lex variables

        integer            llp, lc, errcount
        character*(MAXSTR) line
        common /lexval/    llp, lc, errcount
        common /lexstr/    line
        save               /lexval/, /lexstr/
```

When a parser error occurs in `spl`, an error handler routine `perror` is called. `perror` prints an informative message and then prints the current input line and the current location within the line to STDERR.

```
! perror  -  report error and input location
```

```
subroutine perror (message)
character*(*)      message
include            'global.def'
include            'perror.cmn'
character*(MAXSTR) itoa

errcount = errcount + 1
call fputstr (STDERR, 'line '//itoa(lc))
call fputc (STDERR, ':')
call fputstr (STDERR, message)
call fputc (STDERR, NEWLINE)
call errloc ()

return
end
```

The routine errloc does the printing of the input line based on the current value of llp stored in perror.cmn; it prints a caret pointing to the spot just underneath the last character read, which is kind of nice:

```
! errloc  -  display lex location in input line

      subroutine errloc ()
#include  global.def
#include  perror.cmn
      integer   cp, ep, i

      if (llp .lt. 80) then
         cp = llp - 1
         if (index(line, NULL) .gt. 80) then
            call fputstr (STDERR, line(1:79)//EOL)
         else
            call fputstr (STDERR, line)
         end if
      else if (index(line, NULL) .lt. llp + 79) then
         ep = index(line, NULL)
         cp = 80 - (ep - llp)
         call fputstr (STDERR, line(ep-79:ep))
      else
         cp = 39
         call fputstr (STDERR, line(llp-39:llp+40)//EOL)
      end if
      do i = 1, cp - 1
         call fputc (STDERR, BLANK)
      end do
      call fputstr (STDERR, '^'//EOL)

      return
      end
```

This forms a complete lexical analyzer for use in a simple compiler (spl), and is suitable for use as a template with just about any other program that processes statements of some kind, with hardly any changes at all.

`lexgen` is the most conceptually difficult program in this book because the algorithms used to construct the compacted state table from a sequence of high-level regular expressions are rather involved and abstract. It was a lot of work to get `lexgen` debugged and running because after the first pass over the input the regular expressions are reduced to matrices of numbers, dumps of which are not exactly user-friendly.

However, the use of `lexgen` is conceptually simple. Using it just requires a list of the tokens to be recognized and their corresponding regular expressions, along with a prewritten driver routine. `lexgen` is worth the effort, because it reduces the labor in constructing an efficient lexical analyzer from days to an hour or two. Since the need for a lexical analyzer crops up in all sorts of situations, `lexgen` is an investment in the future.

Exercises

1. Write a regular expression for identifiers with at most six characters.

2. Write a `lexgen` input regular expression for unsigned integers that accepts decimal, hexadecimal, octal, and binary notation.

3. Modify `lexgen` to accept an option -b that causes blanks to be ignored. What changes must be made to the table structures and the driver routine?

4. Modify `lexgen` and its input language to allow positive closure of regular expression r (one or more occurrences of r) to be specified.

5. Modify `lexgen` and its input language to allow specification of identifiers with at most six characters.

6. Modify `lexgen` and its input language to allow specification of a negated range; that is, the negated range a-z matches all characters except lower-case letters.

7. Construct a lexical analyzer to recognize Fortran 77 tokens.

8. Construct a lexical analyzer to recognize Fortran 77 edit descriptors used in `format` statements.

9. Develop a driver routine that can scan text using the NFA representation of a token directly, rather than converting it to a DFA. For what applications is such a routine well-suited?

10. In the match program, would it be worthwhile to optimize the DFA?

11. Correct recognition of tokens in some languages requires multiple characters of "lookahead." For example, because keywords are not reserved and blanks are insignificant in Fortran 77, a lookahead capability is needed to distinguish the looping statement do 10 i = 1, 10 from the assignment statement do10i = 1, and the text fragment if(i could potentially be an array reference instead of an if statement. How would you go about implementing a lexical analyzer with lookahead?

Further Reading

The classic text *Compilers: Principles, Techniques and Tools* by Aho, Sethi, and Ullman (Addison-Wesley, 1986) provides a thorough and rigorous treatment of lexical analysis. The algorithms used in lexgen are based on those given in their discussion. A more intense mathematical presentation of the theory of regular grammars is givem in Hopcroft and Ullman, *Formal Languages and their Relation to Automata* (Addison Wesley, 1979).

A well-known lexical analyzer generator for C programs, LEX, is available on UNIX systems. The program was originally described by Lesk in "LEX–A Lexical Analyzer Generator," Computing Science Technical Report 39 at Bell Laboratories. A generator program called ALEX for Modula-2 is described by Mossenbock in "ALEX—A Simple and Efficient Scanner Generator," *SIGPLAN Notices* Vol. 21 #5 (1986). ALEX uses a less restrictive grammar as input as compared to the usual regular expression syntax. The fastest lexical analyzers are hand coded with transition functions implemented as directly executable code. V. P. Heuring describes a generator program to produce directly executable code in "The Automatic Generation of Fast Lexical Analyzers," *Software Practice and Experience* Vol. 16 #9 (1986).

CHAPTER 8

Simple Programming Language

This chapter is going to pull together everything we have done so far into a powerful tool. We will develop a compiler for a simple programming language (spl) that is a useful program on its own and that can be adapted to many special applications easily. We will use the lexical analyzer of Chapter 7 and preprocessor from Chapter 6 as the "front end" of the compiler, as well as the hash table tools from Chapter 5 to manage symbol tables, to make the task of writing a compiler more manageable.

8.1   Syntax Analysis

We have been doing "parsing" throughout this book for simple jobs without much discussion. In writing a compiler, an overall parsing strategy is required to keep the problem manageable. It helps to put the problem in perspective and to examine the alternatives available, so we will first study the problem of parsing generally and present an overview of commonly used parsing techniques. The theories of grammars and parsing are very well developed and formalized. A formal, mathematical treatment of the subject has been given by many authors and is recommended (if not required) reading material for getting into the subject. However, in keeping with the practical bent of this book, we will keep the discussion somewhat informal, and get the ideas across without a lot of hoopla.

In order to understand the mechanics of parsing, we need first to understand the concept of a *grammar*. A grammar is nothing more or less than a formal, mathematical description of a language. A *parser* is nothing more or less than a program that determines whether an input string conforms to a grammar.

Grammars are expressed formally by a set of pseudoequations called *productions*. For example, the productions for statements in a simple programming language might read

```
stmt ::= assign_stmt | "while" (expr) stmt | "if" (expr) stmt
```

The syntax used for writing the production is called *Backus-Naur Form* or BNF for short. The items in quotes are literal character sequences that our lexical analyzer can recognize as tokens; in grammar lingo, they are called *terminal symbols*. The other entities are called *nonterminal symbols* because they are defined in terms of other grammar symbols (terminal or nonterminal). Ultimately, each nonterminal symbol corresponds to some sequence of terminals (tokens) in the input. As an example of a complete grammar, here is one for the input language of `lexgen`:

```
stmt            ::=   token_value  "=" reg_expr  \n          (1)
token_value     ::=   $int                                  (2)
reg_expr        ::=   reg_construct rest                     (3)
rest            ::=   ~ | reg_expr                           (4)
reg_construct   ::=   alt | closure | range | $char          (5)
alt             ::=   "(" alt_list ")"                       (6)
alt_list        ::=   reg_expr list                          (7)
list            ::=   ~ | "|" alt_list                       (8)
closure         ::=   "{" reg_expr "}"                       (9)
range           ::=   "[" $char "-" $char "]"                (10)
```

We have adopted the convention of representing tokens other than literal character sequences as identifiers beginning with $, such as $int to represent any integer or $char to represent any character. The $ convention is used for all of the tokens in the `lexgen` input file and in the compiler source code since we have a preprocessor to convert the symbolic names to integers in both places. This strategy effectively makes `lexgen` into a specialized extension of Fortran, and would not be possible without the preprocessor. The tildes represent transitions on the empty string, like the ε-transitions in the NFA's constructed by `lexgen`. Here the empty string represents an empty production, which means in effect that the nonterminal on the left side is optional.

In the formal notation used by convention in grammar theory, lowercase letters denote terminal symbols, uppercase letters denote nonterminal symbols, and greek letters represent strings of terminal and/or nonterminal symbols. The production

$$A ::= \alpha$$

is read "*A derives* α," and the process of applying productions of the grammar is called a *derivation*. A parse of a sentence in some language starting from the start symbol of the grammar and producing a sequence of terminals is called a *top-down* parse. For example, here is a top-down parse of the sentence

```
42 = [a-z]
```

using the grammar for lexgen:

```
input token     production
------------------------------------------------------------
42              token_value "=" reg_expr \n
                ^

42              $int
                ^

=               token_value "=" reg_expr \n
                          ^

[a-z]           token_value "=" reg_expr \n
                              ^

[a-z]           reg_construct rest
                ^

[a-z]           alt | closure | range | $char
                                        ^

[a-z]           "[" $char "-" $char "]"
                ^

a-z]            "[" $char "-" $char "]"
                     ^

-z]             "[" $char "-" $char "]"
                          ^

z]              "[" $char "-" $char "]"
                              ^

]               "[" $char "-" $char "]"
                                    ^

\n              token_value "=" reg_expr \n
                                         ^

(empty)         (end of statement)
```

Alternatively, a *bottom-up* parser starts with terminal symbols of a grammar and derives the start symbol.

In this example, the parsing process is represented as a pointer moving through a sequence of grammar symbols and matching them to the actual input string. At each point during the parse, the pointer is pointing to a terminal or nonterminal symbol from the right side of some production in the grammar. If the pointer is at a terminal value and it matches the input token, the token is "accepted" and the next input token is fetched. If the grammar pointer points to a nonterminal, then the right-hand side of one of its productions becomes the current production with the pointer at its beginning. When the entire production has been recognized, the previous production is resumed, and the parsing process continues until all input tokens have been accepted and the pointer is at the end of the production for the grammar start symbol. If at some point during the process there is no way to match an input token to some terminal symbol, an error is detected.

The productions used in parsing a sentence or phrase of a grammar can be represented as a *parse tree*, with each node representing a nonterminal and each leaf representing a terminal symbol. The child branches of a node are the right-hand sides of productions for the nonterminals involved in the parse. For example, the parse tree for the preceding example is shown in Figure 8.1.

In our example, the input string was scanned from left to right, and the corresponding parse is called a left-to-right parse; it is equally possible (but not too practical) to write a parser for right-to-left parsing. If the grammar is unambiguous, then each sentence in the language recognized by the grammar produces a unique syntax tree. An ambiguous grammar is one that can have more than one valid syntax tree for any sentence, that is, one in which there is more than one combination of productions which can derive the same sentence.

Even though the syntax tree for a sentence is unique for an unambiguous grammar, the order in which the productions are applied is not. The derivation produced by the parsing steps in the [a-z] example is called a *leftmost derivation* because the leftmost nonterminal at each step is expanded. The sequence of productions applied can be stated as

```
stmt ::= token_value "=" reg_expr \n
stmt ::= $int "=" reg_expr \n
```

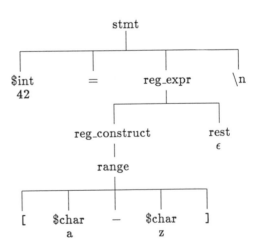

Figure 8.1: Parse tree for the lexgen sentence "42 = [a-z]".

```
stmt ::= $int "=" reg_construct rest \n
stmt ::= $int "=" range rest \n
stmt ::= $int "=" "[" $char "-" $char "]" rest \n
stmt ::= $int "=" "[" $char "-" $char "]" ~ \n
```

or more succinctly as the sequence 1, 2, 3, 5, 10, 4. In a rightmost derivation
the rightmost nonterminal is expanded first; a rightmost derivation of the same
sentence is

```
stmt ::= token_value "=" reg_expr \n
stmt ::= token_value "=" reg_construct rest \n
stmt ::= token_value "=" reg_construct ~ \n
stmt ::= token_value "=" range ~ \n
stmt ::= token_value "=" "[" $char "-" $char "]" ~ \n
stmt ::= $int "=" "[" $char "-" $char "]" ~ \n
```

or the sequence 1, 3, 4, 5, 10, 2. The productions used in both cases are the
same, but the order is different. The type of derivation performed is an important
characteristic of a parsing algorithm.

Mathematicians have classified grammars according to their complexity. One
such classification is known as the *Chomsky heirarchy*, and divides grammars into
four types according to restrictions in the type of productions the grammar may
contain.

Type 0: Type 0 grammars are unrestricted, and encompass natural human languages. There are no known algorithms for parsing type 0 grammars with
a mere computer.

Type 1: A *context-sensitive* grammar, formally, is a grammar whose only pro-
ductions are of the form $\alpha = \beta$ with $|\alpha| \leq |\beta|$, that is, the length of α
is no longer than the length of β. It isn't obvious, but this implies that
productions can have the form $\alpha_1 A \alpha_2 = \beta$ or that the meaning of nonterminal A depends on its appearance in the context of α_1 and α_2, hence
the term context-sensitive. Although most programming languages have
some context sensitivity (e.g. the requirement that variables be declared
before they are used is a context-sensitive requirement), general methods
of parsing context-sensitive grammars are not very efficient. The context-
sensitive aspects of programming languages can generally be dealt with by
compiler actions rather than by the grammar itself.

Type 2: A grammar with the same requirements as context-sensitive grammars,
but with the additional restriction that the left-hand side of any production
is a single nonterminal is a *context-free* grammar. There are a number of
efficient parsing algorithms for context-free grammars, and such grammars
are capable of representing the syntax of almost all computer language
constructs.

Type 3: A grammar with all productions of the form $A = aB$ or $A = a$ is a
regular grammar. This form is also called a left linear grammar; a grammar

with all productions of the form $A = Ba$ or $A = a$ is called right linear, and is also regular. Regular grammars correspond exactly to the regular expressions discussed in Chapter 7. For example, the productions

$$IDENT ::= letter \mid letter\, Z$$
$$Z ::= letter \mid digit \mid letter\, Z \mid digit\, Z$$

are equivalent to the regular expression $IDENT ::= letter\{(letter|digit)\}$.

Note that the hierarchy is inclusive in that all regular grammars also meet the requirements for context-free grammars, all context-free grammars meet the requirements for context-sensitive grammars, and types 1, 2, and 3 are all subsets of type 0 grammars.

Since context-free grammars can be parsed efficiently and can also express computer language syntax, it should be no surprise that these are the grammars we are most interested in. It should be noted that the grammar used in our example syntax tree had a production of the form $A = \epsilon$, where ϵ is the empty string. Strictly speaking, this violates the rule given for the length of the left and right sides of a production in a context-free grammar. However, it has been shown that for any grammar with $A = \epsilon$ as a production, an equivalent context-free grammar exists that does not contain ϵ-rules. Therefore we shall regard grammars with ϵ rules as context-free grammars.

There are various restrictions that can be placed on context-free grammars that do not limit too seriously the languages that can be described, but that result in simple parsers. The following are most widely used:

Operator precedence grammars have all productions of the form

$$A = B \operatorname{op} C,$$

and each operator op has an associated precedence. Operator precedence parsers are easy to write by hand, with parse actions determined by consulting precedence tables. As the name suggests, they are well-suited to parsing arithmetic expressions. The operator precedence method can be extended to handle assignment statements, and if statements and looping constructs, but its ability to describe all syntax of a programming language is limited. However, it is efficient, and some commercial compilers use operator precedence for arithmetic expressions, and another more powerful method for the remainder of the grammar.

LL(1) grammars and parsers are widely used for compiler construction. The "1" in LL(1) means one token of lookahead; the L's denote that the parse is from left to right, and that a leftmost derivation is obtained. LL(1) parsing is a form of *predictive parsing*; it requires the use of a restricted form of context-free grammar called an *LL(1) grammar*. The parsing method starts from the sentence symbol and attempts to derive a string matching the input string from the grammar rules and requires a grammar restricted in a way such that no more than one token of lookahead is ever required in order to determine which production to apply. An LL(1) parser can be implemented as a table-driven parser or as a set of handwritten recursive functions (in languages that allow recursive procedures). The handwritten form of LL(1) parsing is called *recursive descent* parsing.

LL(1) parsers are bottom-up parsers and can handle just about any context-free grammar. An LR parser essentially keeps track of all possible derivations that could produce the input read so far. Unlike LL(1) parsers, LR parsers are impractical for hand implementation, and the principal drawback is the size of the parsing tables. However, as lexgen illustrates, it is possible to build large tables efficiently. LR parsing is the method most widely used for professional compiler development environments and for commercial compilers.

A big problem for us with both LL and LR table-driven parsers is that it is impractical to implement the parsing tables by hand. A parser generator is necessary to use the table-driven methods, and although writing a parser generator is not out of the question, it is a lot of work. Table-driven parsers are elegant and can greatly enhance the ease of maintaining a program. However, we decided to stick with handwritten parsing in spl, because of the lack of availability of a good parser generator for Fortran, and because with careful program design the disadvantages of ad hoc parsing can be minimized.

The spl compiler uses a combination of operator precedence and indirect recursive descent in spl. As noted previously, the operator precedence method is well-suited to parsing arithmetic expressions and assignments, and that's how it's used in spl. Recursive descent parsers cannot be implemented directly in Fortran because recursive functions or subroutines are not allowed. However, the same principle can be used indirectly by saving the necessary information on a stack explicitly.

8.2 spl

The name "spl" stands for "simple programming language," and it is indeed simple, much simpler than Fortran or C or Pascal or even BASIC. However, it is not so simple as to be useless. It provides the essential features of real programming languages such as arrays, looping constructs, a block if construct, a reasonably complete capability for evaluating arithmetic expressions, input and output, and a modest set of intrinsic mathematics and string-handling functions. It provides Fortran programmers with a couple of other features of interest as well: it is portable and can be integrated with an application program without too much work.

The getlogline function is built into the lexical analyzer of spl, so all of the preprocessor statements like #include and #define are part of the spl language, and the same rules for statement continuation, multiple statements on a single line, and comments are in effect. The escape mechanism is also built-in for all character string operations. Tokens in spl are case-sensitive just like macro names in prep (i.e., abc is not the same identifier as ABC). There is no predefined limit on the number of characters in an identifier, and all characters are significant. The following keywords are reserved (may not be used as identifiers):

```
integer     real       logical    if
else        while      repeat     until
read        print      end        and
or          not        true       false
```

In addition, any place the syntax requires two of these keywords together, the combined keywords form a single reserved word. For example, endwhile and elseif may not be used as identifiers.

An spl program is a sequence of statements. Statements are either executable statements or variable declarations, in any order. The visibility of variable names is chronological, meaning that names in a declaration statement are undefined for executable statements before the declaration and defined for all statements after it.

There are just four data types in spl: integer, real, logical, and character. One-dimensional arrays of any type are also supported. There is no default typing, so every identifier used must be declared except for the names of intrinsic functions, which are predeclared. The syntax of declarations is similar to that of Fortran; for example,

```
integer    i, j, k(20)
character  c, s(255)
```

declares i and j to be scalar integer variables and k to be an array of 20 integers; c is a single character and s is a character string. Character strings are null-terminated by the compiler, so for uniformity c is actually allocated two character storage units (one for the NULL).

Executable statements consist of assignment statements, read and write statements, and multiline constructs. There is no restriction on the order of declarations and executable statements within a program unit, but executable statements may not occur outside the scope of a program unit. Expressions are like those in any other programming language. Here are the operators allowed in arithmetic expressions:

```
arithmetic:    +    -    *    /    **
relational:    ==   <>   >    >=   <    <=
logical:       and  or   not
assignment:    =
```

There are no character operators; string manipulation may only be accomplished through intrinsic and user-written functions. Note that assignments are considered to be arithmetic expressions; this allows use of expressions like

```
while ((k = array(i)) > 0)
```

which assigns k to be the ith element of array before comparing it with zero, and

```
a = b = c = 0
```

which assigns all of the variables to zero. Assignments leave a result on the stack for use in an expression, so an assignment statement results in a single value left on the stack that is discarded.

Like any other programming language, spl statements are executed sequentially unless the order of execution is changed by control statements. The spl language has two types of looping constructs, a while construct

```
while (condition)
    statements
end while
```

that tests the condition before executing the body of the loop, and a repeat until construct that tests the condition at the end of the loop:

```
repeat
    statements
until (condition)
```

spl also has a block-structured if construct modeled after that of Fortran:

```
if (condition_1)
    statements
else if (condition_2)
    statements
    .
    .
    .
else
    statements
end if
```

As in Fortran, the else if and else clauses are optional; unlike Fortran, no then keyword is used, and there is no single-statement form of if. In all of these control constructs, the parentheses surrounding the conditional expression are not required but are allowed by the syntax.

spl has a simple I/O capability that allows the user to read and write from STDIN and STDOUT. There is an intrinsic logical function readln that reads the next line from the input, returning true if the read was successful and false otherwise. The data in the input record can then be accessed with one or more read statements. For example, if the next input record contains three integer fields that are to be read into variables i, j, and k, it can be accomplished with

```
if readln()
    read i, j, k
end if
```

or the fields can each be read with separate statements:

```
if readln()
    read i
    read j
    read k
end if
```

A quoted string is expected for input to a character variable. If an attempt is made to read more fields from a record than are present, an error is reported. A call to the readln function is always required to get a new input line, a behavior quite different from Fortran, in which the read statement always implies record advance. The Fortran statement

```
read i, j, k
```

is roughly equivalent to the spl statements

```
readln(); read i, j, k
```

If a function is called as a procedure, its result value is ignored.

The list items in a read statement must be names of variables or array elements. In the print statement, the list items may be any valid expression of any data type. There is no implied record advance on the print statement, and lines must be terminated with NEWLINE. The variables in the preceding examples could be printed on one output line with the statement

```
print i, ' ', j, ' ', k, '\n'
```

or with

```
print i, ' '
print j, ' '
print k, '\n'
```

There is also no implied spacing or field width for output fields in the print statement, so spacing must be provided explicitly. In read statements, there is no implied field width, and any number of blanks can separate fields.

spl has a predeclared identifier input$ which is a character string holding the current input line. Thus the input can be copied to the output with the statements

```
while readln()
    print input$
end while
```

The individual characters of input$ can also be accessed using the substr intrinsic function. If spl is used with the shell presented in the next chapter, the standard input and output can be conveniently redirected to files.

readln and substr are intrinsic or predeclared functions. spl has a healthy selection of them, listed in Table 8.1. An r as an argument or result type in Table 8.1 denotes real type; i, L, and s denote integer, logical and string types respectively. Since spl does not support any string operations directly in syntax, all string manipulation must be accomplished with the intrinsic functions.

spl is a one-shot or "compile and go" system with no facility for separate compilation, so the input file must contain all of the source code of the program (although the source can be organized into separate files by using #include statements). The command

```
$ spl prog
```

compiles and links the program and then executes it. There are four compiler options:

Table 8.1: spl intrinsic functions

function(arguments)	result	description
sin(r)	r	sine of angle in radians
cos(r)	r	cosine of angle in radians
tan(r)	r	tangent of angle in radians
arcsin(r)	r	inverse sine
arccos(r)	r	inverse cosine
arctan(r)	r	inverse tangent
exp(r)	r	e^x
ln(r)	r	natural logarithm
float(i)	r	real conversion
int(r)	i	integer conversion
abs(r)	r	absolute value
iabs(i)	i	absolute value
index(s,s)	i	location of substring
ord(s)	i	integer conversion of first character
len(s)	i	dynamic string length
chr(i)	s	character conversion
cat(s,s)	s	concatenation
substr(s,i,i)	s	substring
eqs(s,s)	L	string comparison for equality
readln()	L	line input

    -c   Run in calculator (interactive) mode
    -l   List input lines and symbol tables to STDOUT
    -m   List assembly code generated
    -t   Trace machine state during execution

The options can be combined; -lm produces a listing file with each source line
followed by the code generated for it. The "calculator" mode works just like
the normal "batch" mode of spl, except that each statement is executed as it is
typed in.

    The following is an attempt at writing a formal grammar for spl as a guide
for implementation; however, as noted earlier, with ad hoc methods there is no
guarantee that the grammar and parser correspond exactly.

```
spl_prog        ::= stmt_sequence | ~

stmt_sequence   ::= stmt \n stmt_sequence | ~
stmt            ::= declaration |
                    while_stmt |
                    until_stmt |
                    if_stmt |
                    return_stmt |
                    read_stmt |
                    write_stmt |
                    assign_expr

declaration     ::= type_keyword declist
type_keyword    ::= "integer" | "real" | "logical" | "character"
declist         ::= $id dlist | $id ( $intnum ) dlist
dlist           ::= , declist | ~

while_stmt      ::= "while" logical_expr \n
                    stmt_sequence
                    "end while"
until_stmt      ::= "repeat" \n
                    stmt_sequence
                    "until" logical_expr
if_stmt         ::= "if" logical_expr \n
                    stmt_sequence
                    else_if_part
                    else_part
                    "end if"
else_if_part    ::= "else if" logical_expr \n stmt_sequence | ~
else_part       ::= "else" \n stmt_sequence | ~

read_stmt       ::= "read" mem_ref ilist
ilist           ::= , mem_ref | , ilist | ~
mem_ref         ::= $id | array_ref
constraint: The external record must contain at least as many fields as
            there are instances of mem_ref, and the tokens in each field
            must agree with the type of mem_ref.

print_stmt      ::= "print" expr olist
```

```
olist            ::= , expr | , olist | ~

expr             ::= logical_expr |
                     relational_expr |
                     arith_expr |
                     string_expr |
                     assign_expr

logical_expr     ::= "true" |
                     "false" |
                     $id |
                     array_ref |
                     function_ref |
                     assign_expr |
                     relational_expr |
                     logical_expr "and" logical_expr |
                     logical_expr "or" logical_expr |
                     "not" logical_expr |
                     ( logical_expr )
constraint: The $id, array_ref, function_ref or assign_expr must have a
            type of logical.

relational_expr ::= arith_expr relational_op arith_expr |
                    ( relational_expr )

relational_op    ::= == | <> | > | >= | < | <=

arith_expr       ::= term | term + term | term - term
term             ::= factor | factor * factor | factor / factor
factor           ::= base | base ** power
power            ::= base
base             ::= $intnum |
                     $realnum |
                     $id |
                     array_ref |
                     function_ref |
                     ( arith_expr ) |
                     ( assign_expr )
constraint: The $id, array_ref, function_ref or assign_expr must have a
            type of real or integer.

string_expr      ::= $id | function_ref | assign_expr
constraint: The $id, function_ref or assign_expr must have a type of string.

assign_expr      ::= mem_ref = expr
constraint: The data types of mem_ref and expr must be conformable:
            type of mem_ref      permissible types of expr
            ---------------      -------------------------

            real                 real or integer
            integer              real or integer
            logical              logical
            string               string
            The result type of an assign_expr is the same as the type of the
```

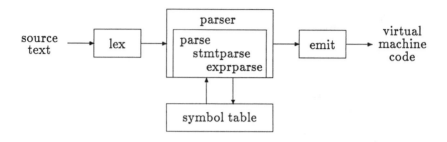

Figure 8.2: Top-level organization of spl.

```
        mem_ref.

array_ref       ::= $id ( arith_expr )
constraint: The arith_expr must be of type integer.

function_ref    ::= $id ( exprlist )

exprlist        ::= expr | expr , exprlist | ~
```

The formal grammar is worth a little study since it is a description of the spl language that is both precise and concise.

8.3   Compiler Organization

We have already said a lot in this chapter without even beginning to discuss the code, but hopefully all of the preceding discussion will help to make understanding easier. Conceptually, the compiler's transformation of source text into output code can be viewed as three stages, as depicted in Figure 8.2. The program doesn't actually work this way since all of the translation happens in one pass, but from the point of view of a line of source code it is an accurate picture.

To further aid in grasping the Big Picture, the compiler will be presented with the main routines first to show the overall organization of the program. Here is the files list for spl:

```
! spl.fil  -  files list for spl interpreter

! generator programs and associated files
        # splgen.com    !regenerate spl from scratch
        # exprgen.for   !generator for class.def and exprparse.def
        # exprgen.in    !input file for exprgen: classes and allowed pairs
```

```
! documentation files
    # vinstr.doc    !virtual machine instruction set reference
    # vmem.doc       !virtual machine memory map

! declaration and data definition
    # options.cmn    !command line options

    # spl.mac        !global macro definitions for spl:
                     !lexical analyzer codes
                     !symbol table codes
                     !token class codes
    # spl.lex        !lexgen input for splscan
    # splscan.def    !data statements for splscan table
    # perror.cmn     !error count, logical line, lp

    # symbol.cmn     !symbol table for global variables

    # parse.cmn      !common block for all parser stacks
    # exprparse.def  !data definitions for operator precedence parser
    # class.def      !operator/operand class definitions

    # vm.mac         !opcode symbolic codes for virtual machine
    # mnemonic.def   !virtual machine instruction mnemonics
    # vstate.cmn     !common block for virtual machine memory and registers

! program organization

    spl              !main program
      initfunc       !initialize intrinsic functions
      parse          !parse statement sequence
      calc           !parse statement sequence in calculator mode
        stmtparse    !parse statement
          exprparse  !parse arithmetic and logical expressions
            class    !classify token for arithmetic expressions
            operand  !generate code for arithmetic operands
            operator !generate code for arithmetic operators
              emit1  !emit 1-word instruction
              emit2  !emit 2-word instruction
          declist    !parse variable declarations
          printstmt  !expression list for print stmt
          readstmt   !generate code for read stmt
        vexec        !execute program for virtual machine

! lex/perror organization
    lex              !main lexical analyzer routine
      splscan        !table driven scanner
    perror           !parse error handler
      errloc         !print input line and location

! symbol table organization
    syminit          !initialize symbol table
    symdef           !install name and attributes in table
    symref           !return attributes of name if defined
```

```
symsize          !get storage allocated to variables
symchr           !get storage allocated to strings
symalloc         !allocate space for temporary storage
```

Some of the program has already been covered in previous chapters, and some
other parts are straightforward applications of other tools such as the hash table
management routines.
The main program is short and sweet:

```
! spl  -  simple programming language

        program spl
        #include          global.def
        #include          options.cmn
        #include          spl.mac
        integer           argc, fopen, u, i, j, basefp, basebp, lex, t
        character*(MAXSTR) argv (MAXARGS), infile, upper, token
        logical           parse, calc, fnflag

        call ioinit ()
        call getargs (argc, argv)
        fnflag = .false.
        calcflag = .false.
        listflag = .false.
        codeflag = .false.
        traceflag = .false.
        do i = 1, argc
           j = index (argv(i), NULL)
           if (argv(i)(1:1) .eq. QUALIFIER) then
              argv(i) = upper(argv(i))
              if (index(argv(i)(2:j),'C') .gt. 0) calcflag = .true.
              if (index(argv(i)(2:j),'L') .gt. 0) listflag = .true.
              if (index(argv(i)(2:j),'M') .gt. 0) codeflag = .true.
              if (index(argv(i)(2:j),'T') .gt. 0) traceflag = .true.
           else
              if (fnflag) then
                 call fputstr (STDERR,'syntax: spl [infile] [-options]'//EOL)
                 call fputstr (STDERR,'options: -L   produce listing'//EOL)
                 call fputstr (STDERR,'         -M   list machine code'//EOL)
                 call fputstr (STDERR,'         -T   trace execution'//EOL)
                 call fputstr (STDERR,'         -C   calculator mode'//EOL)
                 stop ' '
              else
                 fnflag = .true.
                 if (index(argv(i)(1:j), '.') .gt. 0) then
                    infile = argv(i)
                 else
                    infile = argv(i)(1:j-1) // '.SPL' // NULL
                 end if
              end if
           end if
        end do
```

```
      if (fnflag) then
         if (fopen (u, infile, IOREAD) .eq. IOERROR) then
            call fputstr (STDERR, 'cannot open '//infile)
            call fputstr (STDERR, ' for input'//EOL)
            stop 'aborted.'
         end if
      else
         u = STDIN
      end if
      call ppinit (u)
      call syminit ()
      call initfunc ()


      if (calcflag) then
         do while (lex(t,token) .ne. $eof)
            if (calc (t, token, basefp, basebp)) then
               call vexec (basefp, basebp)
            else
               call fputstr (STDERR, 'statement ignored'//EOL)
            end if
         end do
      else
         if (parse (basefp, basebp)) then
            call vexec (basefp, basebp)
         else
            stop 'aborted.'
         end if
      end if

      end
```

Like most of our programs, the main routine of spl is mostly code for processing
of command line arguments. The real guts of the compiler are in the include
files and the parsing routines. Throughout the code, file inclusion is performed
with our own preprocessor rather than with the Fortran include statement,
so that the same files can be used for the Fortran source code and the lexical
analyzer. An additional advantage of using the preprocessor is that we don't
have to restrict the length of names of symbolic constants, so more verbose but
descriptive names can be used. The file spl.mac contains macros needed just
about everywhere throughout the compiler:

```
!  spl.mac  -  macro definitions for spl

!  token names
      #define   MAXTOKEN   40
      #define   LEXERROR   -1

!  keywords
      #define   $int       1
```

```
        #define   $real       2
        #define   $log        3
        #define   $char       4
        #define   $if         5
        #define   $elseif     6
        #define   $else       7
        #define   $endif      8
        #define   $while      9
        #define   $endwhile   10
        #define   $repeat     11
        #define   $until      12
        #define   $read       13
        #define   $print      14
! arithmetic and logical operators
        #define   $add        15
        #define   $sub        16
        #define   $mult       17
        #define   $div        18
        #define   $pwr        19
        #define   $eq         20
        #define   $ne         21
        #define   $gt         22
        #define   $ge         23
        #define   $lt         24
        #define   $le         25
        #define   $and        26
        #define   $or         27
        #define   $not        28
        #define   $assign     29
! identifiers and constants
        #define   $intnum     30
        #define   $realnum    31
        #define   $true       32
        #define   $false      33
        #define   $id         34
        #define   $string     35
! punctuation
        #define   $lparen     36
        #define   $rparen     37
        #define   $comma      38
        #define   $eol        39

! special token for end of file
        #define   $eof        40

! symbol table definitions

! number of symbol attributes
        #define   NATTR   5
! attribute definition
        #define   IDCLASS 1
        #define   IDTYPE  2
        #define   IDADDR  3
```

```
        #define  IDSIZE   4
        #define  IDORG    5
! type codes
        #define  INTTYPE    1
        #define  REALTYPE   2
        #define  LOGTYPE    3
        #define  STRTYPE    4
        #define  BOGUSTYPE -1

! token class definitions
        #define  MAXCLASS    15

        #define  OTHER                   1
        #define  UNARY_SIGN              2
        #define  IDENTIFIER              3
        #define  FUNCTION_ID             4
        #define  ARRAY_ID                5
        #define  STRING_ID               6
        #define  CONSTANT                7
        #define  BINARY_ARITHMETIC_OP    8
        #define  BINARY_RELATIONAL_OP    9
        #define  UNARY_LOGICAL_OP       10
        #define  BINARY_LOGICAL_OP      11
        #define  ASSIGN_OP              12
        #define  COMMA_SEPARATOR        13
        #define  OPEN_PAREN             14
        #define  CLOSE_PAREN            15

! evaluation stack aorv codes
        #define  VALUE    1
        #define  ADDRESS  2
```

In addition to assigning integer values for all of the lexical analyzer tokens, spl.mac defines codes for the symbol table interface and for data types of items on the stack during parsing. In addition, codes for token classes are defined for use in expression parsing.

Because the command line options are needed in several places and sometimes several levels down from the main program, a common block is provided to hold them:

```
! options.cmn  -  common block for spl command line options

        logical          calcflag, listflag, codeflag, traceflag
        common /options/ calcflag, listflag, codeflag, traceflag
        save   /options/
```

An options common block is advisable for any large program or any program that has lots of options.

8.4   The Virtual Machine

Underlying the spl compiler is a *virtual machine*, a simulated computer designed just for the compiler. The compiler generates code for this simulated machine and then interprets the output code. The concept of a virtual machine is a very powerful one and is useful in many diverse kinds of software systems, from compilers to spreadsheets and graphics packages. A virtual machine has an instruction set that it "understands" and a memory and some registers collectively referred to as the "machine state." The instruction set is simple, so that an efficient interpreter can be written for it. The machine is called virtual because its instructions are interpreted rather than being directly executed by the hardware of the real computer underneath. The distinction between compilers and interpreters is generally based on whether the output code is in the native instruction set of the machine; however, even the instruction set of a real computer is interpreted at a lower level.

The virtual machine for spl is a stack-oriented computer. It has registers for management of the stack, and most of its instructions have no operands because the operands are on the stack. It is designed specifically as the target machine for a high-level language and has special facilities for high-level constructs. Although spl has no support for modular program units or local variables, its underlying virtual machine provides full support for procedures, so that an enhanced version of spl could be constructed without modifying the underlying machine.

The virtual machine supports four data types: integer, real, logical, and character. The machine registers are

```
pc      program counter
sp      stack pointer
fp      frame pointer
lp      local pointer
bp      buffer pointer
lbp     local buffer pointer
```

The program counter points to the current instruction and is incremented when the instruction is fetched. The stack pointer points to the top of the run-time stack, which holds all variables and function call information such as return addresses, argument addresses, and so on. The virtual machine is designed for storage allocation on the stack and uses the local pointer to access local variables. The registers bp and lbp are analogous to sp and lp, respectively, but are only used to access character data. Figure 8.3 is a memory map of the virtual machine, showing how the registers are used for stack management. The memory map shows the configuration of memory when the main program has called one function; stack frames are created when a function is called and destroyed when a function exits. The storage for character data is completely separated from the rest of memory; the reasons for this separation will be made clear later. The character memory layout mimics that of main memory, as indicated by figure 8.4; the map assumes the same conditions as in the map of main memory (i.e., a main program and one function).

The virtual machine has a special machine stack for managing function calls and special instructions to manipulate the call stack. The stack arrangement allows functions to be called recursively maintaining a completely separate "activation record" for each invocation of the function. The arguments to a called routine are passed by reference, meaning that the address of the argument rather than its value is placed on the stack.

When a function is called, a *stack frame* is created, consisting of stack space for the program counter following the call instruction, the old values of lp, lbp, and fp, and the function arguments. The call to a function requires two instructions to set up the frame: mark to allocate storage for the registers and move the stack pointer past them, and call to store the register values and jump to the start address of the called routine. Any number of instructions can occur between mark and call, and mark leaves sp in the right spot for the first argument to the function; code can therefore be executed to evaluate the arguments and put them on the stack prior to the call. The following is an example of the procedure call protocol:

```
      . . .
mark  result
pushl a
pushf b
call  fcn
      . . .
```

result is the address where the function result will be stored; the function fcn receives two arguments when the call instruction passes control to it. The pushl instruction pushes the address of a local variable onto the stack; its operand is an offset from lp, so if, for instance, a=2 and lp=120, then the absolute address 122 is placed on the stack. The pushf instruction pushes an argument for fcn which is itself an argument of the calling routine. pushf actually does indirect addressing; the address pushed is the value in memory at address fp+b. The purpose of using two instructions for implementing function calls is to allocate the necessary stack locations for the stack frame via mark, without actually changing any of the registers except sp. Then code can be included to evaluate expressions involving local variables or arguments of the caller before the caller's values for lp and fp are modified by the call instruction. There is a markl instruction that differs from mark only in that markl op pushes lp+op, rather than op, as the function address.

Once inside the called routine, additional stack space may be allocated for the called routine's local variables. The alloc instruction does this by simply bumping sp by the specified amount (i.e., alloc 5 allocates five stack addresses for local variables). The calloc instruction does the same thing, but for local character variables.

There are two instructions rtn and rtns for returning control to a calling routine by resetting the machine registers to the values in the current stack frame.

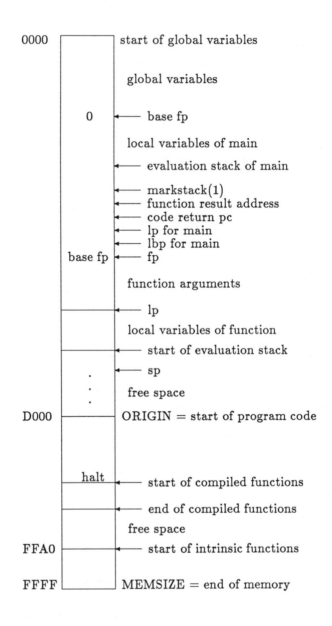

Figure 8.3: Virtual machine main memory map.

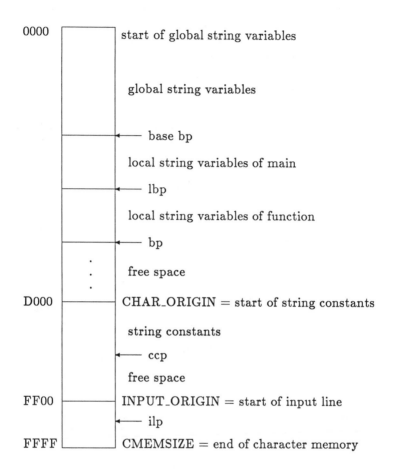

Figure 8.4: Virtual machine character memory map.

The rtn instruction copies the value on top of the stack to the result address stored in the stack frame. The rtns instruction is for character functions and uses the value on the stack (as well as the function result address) as an address in character memory.

The rest of the virtual machine instructions are very straightforward; all have either one operand or none. Most have none because the operands are implied, both the operands and the result destination being the top of the stack. Many instructions operate on one of the four primitive data types, and the data type must be indicated in the instruction mnemonic. Data types are indicated by appending a one-letter code, in brackets, to the end of the instruction name (with no intervening spaces). For instance, print[r] prints the top of the stack

as a real number, print[l] prints it as a logical value, and print[s] prints the
character string pointed to by the top of the stack. All instructions involving
character strings expect strings to be null-terminated.

For all of the typed instructions, integer data is the default and no type code is
used. Other instructions have the type implied; for instance, the sin instruction
only operates on real data. A complete reference table for the virtual machine
instruction set is given in Table 8.2.

The virtual machine and its assembler are implemented in Fortran, with no
machine-dependent code. It is thus portable to any computer with a Fortran
compiler. The machine registers and memory are defined in vstate.cmn:

```
! vstate.cmn  -  state variables of virtual machine

! virtual machine initial origin
      #define   ORIGIN       53248
      #define   CHAR_ORIGIN  53248
      #define   INPUT_ORIGIN 65280

      integer             MEMSIZE           !virtual machine address space
      parameter           (MEMSIZE = 65535)
      integer             CMEMSIZE          !character address space
      parameter           (CMEMSIZE = 65535)
      integer             mem (MEMSIZE)
      real                rmem (MEMSIZE)
      logical             lmem (MEMSIZE)
      equivalence         (mem(1), rmem(1))
      equivalence         (mem(1), lmem(1))
      character*(CMEMSIZE) cmem
      integer             sp, fp, lp, pc     !virtual machine registers
      integer             lbp, bp            !character pointer registers
      common   /vstate/   sp, fp, lp, pc, lbp, bp, mem
      common   /cstate/   cmem
      save                /vstate/, /cstate/
```

Standard Fortran forbids character and noncharacter entities to be in the same
common block and forces an important choice. Given that portability is desired,
either characters must be represented as integers or character memory must be
segregated from the other memory. The latter option was chosen primarily for
efficiency in character storage. The underlying Fortran restriction on character association is reflected directly in the virtual machine architecture, with its
separate character memory and special instructions and registers for character
data.

The choice of location for ORIGIN deserves some explanation. It would be
more efficient with memory to start the code at the bottom of memory, and let
the data begin immediately after the code. But spl is designed to be easy to
customize, and one of the easiest ways to do this is to map the user input variables
of a model or simulator into the virtual machine's memory via an equivalence
statement. As an unrealistically simple example, suppose we have a program with

Table 8.2: Virtual Machine Instruction Set Summary.

Legend: I, R, L = integer, real, logical
x = integer or real
a = address
v = value (integer or real or logical)

vm opcode	mnemonic, format	stack(sp,sp-1) before	after	operation
1	add	i,i	i	integer add
2	add[r]	r,r	r	real add
3	sub	i,i	i	integer subtract (mem(sp-1)-mem(sp))
4	sub[r]	r,r	r	real subtract (rmem(sp-1)-rmem(sp))
5	mult	i,i	i	integer multiply
6	mult[r]	r,r	r	real multiply
7	div	i,i	i	integer divide (mem(sp-1)/mem(sp))
8	div[r]	r,r	r	real divide (rmem(sp-1)/rmem(sp))
9	pwr	i,i	i	integer power (mem(sp-1)**mem(sp))
10	pwr[r]	r,r	r	real power (rmem(sp-1)**rmem(sp))
11	neg	i	i	integer negate
12	neg[r]	r	r	real negate
13	eq	i,i	L	true if equal
14	eq[r]	r,r	L	true if equal
15	ne	i,i	L	true if not equal
16	ne[r]	r,r	L	true if not equal
17	gt	i,i	L	true if (mem(sp-1) > mem(sp))
18	gt[r]	r,r	L	true if (rmem(sp-1) > rmem(sp))
19	ge	i,i	L	true if (mem(sp-1) >= mem(sp))
20	ge[r]	r,r	L	true if (rmem(sp-1) >= rmem(sp))
21	lt	i,i	L	true if (mem(sp-1) < mem(sp))
22	lt[r]	r,r	L	true if (rmem(sp-1) < rmem(sp))
23	le	i,i	L	true if (mem(sp-1) <= mem(sp))
24	le[r]	r,r	L	true if (rmem(sp-1) <= rmem(sp))
25	and	L,L	L	true if (lmem(sp-1) and lmem(sp))
26	or	L,L	L	true if (lmem(sp-1) or lmem(sp))
27	not	L	L	logical negate
28	mark op			mark stack frame with global address (advance sp to sp+5 and set result address = op)

```
stack effect: +5  <--sp
              +4  <--lbp
              +3  <--lp
              +2  <--pc+1
              +1  <--result address = op
markstack(msp)-->  <--initial sp
```

Virtual Machine Instruction Set Summary, continued

vm opcode	mnemonic, format	stack(sp,sp-1) before after	operation
29	markl op		mark stack frame with local address (advance sp to sp+5 and set result address = lp + op)
	stack effect:	+5 <--sp	
		+4 <--lbp	
		+3 <--lp	
		+2 <--pc+1	
		+1 <--result address = lp + op	
	markstack(msp)-->	<--initial sp	
30	call op		call function (fill in values in stack frame and transfer control to pc = op) mem(markstack(msp)+2) = pc + 1 mem(markstack(msp)+3) = lp mem(markstack(msp)+4) = lbp mem(markstack(msp)+5) = fp fp = markstack(msp) + 5 lbp = bp pc = mem(pc) msp = msp - 1
31	rtn		return from function and assign result (integer, real and logical functions) mem(mem(fp-4)) = mem(sp) sp = fp-4 pc = mem(fp-3) lp = mem(fp-2) bp = lbp lbp = mem(fp-1) fp = mem(fp)
32	rtns		return from function and assign result (character functions) string at cmem(mem(fp-4)) = string at cmem(mem(sp)) sp = fp-4 pc = mem(fp-3) lp = mem(fp-2) bp = lbp lbp = mem(fp-1) fp = mem(fp)
33	alloc op	i	allocate main memory for local variables (op storage units)

Virtual Machine Instruction Set Summary, continued

vm opcode	mnemonic, format	stack(sp,sp-1) before	after	operation
34	calloc op		i	allocate character memory for local variables (op character units)
35	halt			stop execution
36	push op		i	push integer
37	push[r] op		r	push real
38	push[l] op		L	push logical
39	pushl op		i	push local address lp + op
40	pushlc op		i	push local char address lbp + op
41	pushf op		i	push argument address fp + mem(op)
42	pop	v		pop stack
43	asnv	a,v	v	assign value
44	asna	v,a	a	assign address
45	asns	a1,a2	a1	assign string
46	val	a	v	replace address at sp with value
47	val2	a,v	v,v	replace address at sp-1 with value
48	ixa	a,i	a	compute indexed address a = a + i
49	readln		L	read line and test for EOF (lmem(sp) = true if not EOF)
50	read	a		read integer
51	read[r]	a		read real
52	read[l]	a		read logical
53	read[s]	a		read character
54	print	i		print integer
55	print[r]	r		print real
56	print[l]	l		print logical
57	print[s]	a		print character
58	jt op	L		branch to op if (lmem(sp) = true)
59	jf op	L		branch to op if (lmem(sp) = false)
60	jmp op			branch to op
61	flt	i	r	real conversion of mem(sp)
62	flt2	i,v	r,v	real conversion of mem(sp-1)
63	int	r	i	integer conversion of rmem(sp)
64	int2	r,v	i,v	integer conversion of rmem(sp-1)
65	sin	r	r	function sin
66	cos	r	r	function cos
67	tan	r	r	function tan
68	asin	r	r	function arcsin
69	acos	r	r	function arccos
70	atan	r	r	function arctan

Virtual Machine Instruction Set Summary, continued

vm opcode	mnemonic, format	stack(sp,sp-1) before after		operation
71	exp	r	r	function power of e
72	log	r	r	function natural logarithm (ln)
73	abs	i	i	integer absolute value
74	abs[r]	r	r	real absolute value
75	cat	a1,a2	a1	character concatenation
				string at a1 =
				string at a1 // string at a2
76	indx	a1,a2	i	substring index
				i = index(string at a1, string at a2)
77	chr	a,i	a	character conversion
				string at a = char(i)//NULL
78	ord	a	i	i = ichar(1st character of string at a)
79	eqs	a1,a2	L	compare strings for equality
80	substr	a1,a2,i,i	a1	character substring
				j = mem(sp), i = mem(sp-1)
				string at a1 = cmem(a2+i-1:cmem(a2+j-1)
81	len	a	i	length of character string
				i = index(cmem(a:),NULL) - 1

four user input variables a, b, c, and d. If they are all in a common block, then the common block can be equivalenced to the start of memory and manipulated by virtual machine instructions. Adding the statements

```
real        a, b, c, d
common /user/ a, b, c, d
equivalence  (a, mem(1))
```

would do the trick. Then the value of b could be added to a with the following code:

```
push 2
val
push 1
val
add[r]
```

Of course, these variables look no different from any others in the assembly code; the beauty of this idea is that the names in the user common block are known to the Fortran program,which the virtual machine is presumably part of, and can be used in scientific or numerical analysis routines within the program. This is a little-known trick in Fortran programming. It allows the programmer to write scientific code in terms that are familiar and appropriate to the problem at hand rather than as just locations in mem, while also allowing the generalization that is possible with all of the storage in one array.

The virtual machine instruction mnemonics all have corresponding symbolic codes, which are formed by putting an underscore before the mnemonic name; in the case of instructions with several data type variants, an underscore followed by a letter denoting the type is appended to the name.

```
! vm.mac  -  macro definitions for virtual machine

        #define  MAXINSTRUCTIONS  81

! opcodes
        #define  _add_i   1
        #define  _add_r   2
        #define  _sub_i   3
        #define  _sub_r   4
        #define  _mult_i  5
        #define  _mult_r  6
        #define  _div_i   7
        #define  _div_r   8
        #define  _pwr_i   9
        #define  _pwr_r   10
        #define  _neg_i   11
        #define  _neg_r   12
        #define  _eq_i    13
        #define  _eq_r    14
        #define  _ne_i    15
        #define  _ne_r    16
        #define  _gt_i    17
        #define  _gt_r    18
        #define  _ge_i    19
        #define  _ge_r    20
        #define  _lt_i    21
        #define  _lt_r    22
        #define  _le_i    23
        #define  _le_r    24
        #define  _and     25
        #define  _or      26
        #define  _not     27
        #define  _mark    28
        #define  _markl   29
        #define  _call    30
        #define  _rtn     31
        #define  _rtns    32
        #define  _alloc   33
        #define  _calloc  34
        #define  _halt    35
        #define  _push    36
        #define  _push_r  37
        #define  _push_l  38
        #define  _pushl   39
        #define  _pushlc  40
        #define  _pushf   41
        #define  _pop     42
        #define  _asnv    43
```

```
#define _asna    44
#define _asns    45
#define _val     46
#define _val2    47
#define _ixa     48
#define _readln  49
#define _read_i  50
#define _read_r  51
#define _read_l  52
#define _read_s  53
#define _print_i 54
#define _print_r 55
#define _print_l 56
#define _print_s 57
#define _jt      58
#define _jf      59
#define _jmp     60
#define _flt     61
#define _flt2    62
#define _int     63
#define _int2    64
#define _sin     65
#define _cos     66
#define _tan     67
#define _asin    68
#define _acos    69
#define _atan    70
#define _exp     71
#define _log     72
#define _abs_i   73
#define _abs_r   74
#define _cat     75
#define _indx    76
#define _chr     77
#define _ord     78
#define _eqs     79
#define _substr  80
#define _len     81
```

Once the program has been compiled in memory, it is ready to be executed. All it needs is an address to start executing and a place to initialize data storage. The program always starts at ORIGIN as defined in vstate.cmn.

The execution of a program is performed by vexec. It is an infinite loop of fetching an instruction and then executing it, mimicking the way real machines execute instructions, at least to some extent. In real machines, instructions are bit-encoded and there is generally an instruction decoding step between fetching and execution. For a Fortran implementation, however, the most direct possible implementation uses the computed goto construct, and no decoding is necessary to dispatch each instruction to its corresponding code. vexec illustrates use of macros for things Fortran can't do, in this case by providing symbolic statement labels. Using symbolic names in place of line numbers makes the code much easier to read, and simplifies maintaining the code by eliminating any need for changing statement labels when the instruction set is modified. It doesn't solve all of the problems of the computed goto, however; the list of labels in the goto statement still must correspond exactly to the integer codes for the instructions, and this statement must be updated each time the instruction set is modified.

```
! vexec  -  execute program for virtual machine

        subroutine vexec (basefp,basebp)
        integer         basefp, basebp
        #include        global.def
        #include        vm.mac
        #include        vstate.cmn
        #include        options.cmn
        integer         CALLSTKSIZE  !max number of nested function calls
        parameter       (CALLSTKSIZE = 8)
        integer         markstack(CALLSTKSIZE), msp
        integer         opcode, i, j, k, addr
        integer         statio, ip
        logical         fgetline, equal, is_ival, is_rval, is_sval
        character*(MAXSTR) itoa, ftoa, doescape, buffer, tracebuf
        character*1     c

        pc = ORIGIN
        fp = basefp
        lbp = basebp
        mem(fp) = 0
        sp = fp + 1
        statio = .true.

        if (traceflag) then
            call fputstr (STDOUT,
        &' --------- registers ------------    -------- values --------'//EOL)
            call fputstr (STDOUT,
        &' pc      fp      lp      lbp     sp      pc      sp-1      sp'//EOL)
        end if

! fetch instruction
        #define _fetch 999

_fetch  continue
        if (traceflag) then
            write (tracebuf, '(6(I5,2x),2(I11),A2)')
        &           pc, fp, lp, lbp, sp, mem(pc), mem(sp-1), mem(sp), EOL
            call fputstr (STDOUT, tracebuf)
        end if
        opcode = mem(pc)
        pc = pc + 1

! execute instruction
        goto (
        & _add_i,   _add_r,   _sub_i,   _sub_r,   _mult_i,   _mult_r,
```

```
        &  _div_i,   _div_r,   _pwr_i,   _pwr_r,   _neg_i,   _neg_r,
        &  _eq_i,    _eq_r,    _ne_i,    _ne_r,    _gt_i,    _gt_r,
        &  _ge_i,    _ge_r,    _lt_i,    _lt_r,    _le_i,    _le_r,
        &  _and,     _or,      _not,     _mark,    _markl,   _call,
        &  _rtn,     _rtns,    _alloc,   _calloc,  _halt,    _push,
        &  _push_r,  _push_l,  _pushl,   _pushlc,  _pushf,   _pop,
        &  _asnv,    _asna,    _asns,    _val,     _val2,    _ixa,
        &  _readln,  _read_i,  _read_r,  _read_l,  _read_s,  _print_i,
        &  _print_r, _print_l, _print_s, _jt,      _jf,      _jmp,
        &  _flt,     _flt2,    _int,     _int2,    _sin,     _cos,
        &  _tan,     _asin,    _acos,    _atan,    _exp,     _log,
        &  _abs_i,   _abs_r,   _cat,     _indx,    _chr,     _ord,
        &  _eqs,     _substr,  _len
        &  ), opcode

           call fputstr (STDERR, 'unknown opcode, pc = '//itoa(pc-1))
           call fputc   (STDERR, NEWLINE)
           return

_add_i          continue
      mem(sp-1) = mem(sp-1) + mem(sp)
      sp = sp - 1
      goto _fetch


_add_r          continue
      rmem(sp-1) = rmem(sp-1) + rmem(sp)
      sp = sp - 1
      goto _fetch


_sub_i          continue
      mem(sp-1) = mem(sp-1) - mem(sp)
      sp = sp - 1
      goto _fetch


_sub_r          continue
      rmem(sp-1) = rmem(sp-1) - rmem(sp)
      sp = sp - 1
      goto _fetch


_mult_i         continue
      mem(sp-1) = mem(sp-1) * mem(sp)
      sp = sp - 1
      goto _fetch


_mult_r         continue
      rmem(sp-1) = rmem(sp-1) * rmem(sp)
      sp = sp - 1
      goto _fetch


_div_i          continue
      if (mem(sp) .eq. 0) then
          call fputstr (STDERR, 'division by zero at pc = '//itoa(pc))
          return
```

```
      else
         mem(sp-1) = mem(sp-1) / mem(sp)
      end if
      sp = sp - 1
      goto _fetch


_div_r       continue
      if (mem(sp) .eq. 0) then
         call fputstr (STDERR, 'division by zero at pc = '//itoa(pc))
         return
      else
         rmem(sp-1) = rmem(sp-1) / rmem(sp)
      end if
      sp = sp - 1
      goto _fetch


_pwr_i       continue
      mem(sp-1) = mem(sp-1) ** mem(sp)
      sp = sp - 1
      goto _fetch


_pwr_r       continue
      rmem(sp-1) = rmem(sp-1) ** rmem(sp)
      sp = sp - 1
      goto _fetch


_neg_i       continue
      mem(sp) = -1 * mem(sp)
      goto _fetch


_neg_r       continue
      rmem(sp) = -1.0 * rmem(sp)
      goto _fetch


_eq_i        continue
      lmem(sp-1) = (mem(sp-1) .eq. mem(sp))
      sp = sp - 1
      goto _fetch


_eq_r        continue
      lmem(sp-1) = (rmem(sp-1) .eq. rmem(sp))
      sp = sp - 1
      goto _fetch


_ne_i        continue
      lmem(sp-1) = (mem(sp-1) .ne. mem(sp))
      sp = sp - 1
      goto _fetch


_ne_r        continue
      lmem(sp-1) = (rmem(sp-1) .ne. rmem(sp))
      sp = sp - 1
      goto _fetch
```

```
_gt_i        continue
    lmem(sp-1) = (mem(sp-1) .gt. mem(sp))
    sp = sp - 1
    goto _fetch

_gt_r        continue
    lmem(sp-1) = (rmem(sp-1) .gt. rmem(sp))
    sp = sp - 1
    goto _fetch

_ge_i        continue
    lmem(sp-1) = (mem(sp-1) .ge. mem(sp))
    sp = sp - 1
    goto _fetch

_ge_r        continue
    lmem(sp-1) = (rmem(sp-1) .ge. rmem(sp))
    sp = sp - 1
    goto _fetch

_lt_i        continue
    lmem(sp-1) = (mem(sp-1) .lt. mem(sp))
    sp = sp - 1
    goto _fetch

_lt_r        continue
    lmem(sp-1) = (rmem(sp-1) .lt. rmem(sp))
    sp = sp - 1
    goto _fetch

_le_i        continue
    lmem(sp-1) = (mem(sp-1) .le. mem(sp))
    sp = sp - 1
    goto _fetch

_le_r        continue
    lmem(sp-1) = (rmem(sp-1) .le. rmem(sp))
    sp = sp - 1
    goto _fetch

_and         continue
    lmem(sp-1) = (lmem(sp-1) .and. lmem(sp))
    goto _fetch

_or          continue
    lmem(sp-1) = (lmem(sp-1) .or. lmem(sp))
    goto _fetch

_not         continue
    lmem(sp) = (.not. lmem(sp))
    goto _fetch
```

```
_mark          continue
    if (msp .eq. CALLSTKSIZE) then
        call fputstr (STDERR, 'call stack overflow at pc = '//itoa(pc))
        return
    end if
    msp = msp + 1
    markstack(msp) = sp
    mem(sp+1) = mem(pc)
    sp = sp + 5
    pc = pc + 1
    goto _fetch

_markl         continue
    if (msp .eq. CALLSTKSIZE) then
        call fputstr (STDERR, 'call stack overflow at pc = '//itoa(pc))
        return
    end if
    msp = msp + 1
    markstack(msp) = sp
    mem(sp+1) = lp + mem(pc)
    sp = sp + 5
    pc = pc + 1
    goto _fetch

_call          continue
    mem(markstack(msp)+2) = pc + 1
    mem(markstack(msp)+3) = lp
    mem(markstack(msp)+4) = lbp
    mem(markstack(msp)+5) = fp
    fp = markstack(msp) + 5
    lbp = bp
    pc = mem(pc)
    msp = msp - 1
    goto _fetch

_rtn           continue
    mem(mem(fp-4)) = mem(sp)    !assign function result
    sp = fp-4
    pc = mem(fp-3)
    lp = mem(fp-2)
    bp = lbp
    lbp = mem(fp-1)
    fp = mem(fp)
    goto _fetch

_rtns          continue
    i = mem(fp-4)               !result address in caller
    j = mem(sp)                 !result address in function
    do while (cmem(j:j) .ne. NULL)
        cmem(i:i) = cmem(j:j)
        i = i + 1
        j = j + 1
    end do
```

```
        cmem(i:i) = NULL
        sp = fp-4
        pc = mem(fp-3)
        lp = mem(fp-2)
        bp = lbp
        lbp = mem(fp-1)
        fp = mem(fp)
        goto _fetch

_alloc        continue
        lp = sp + 1
        sp = lp + mem(pc)
        pc = pc + 1
        goto _fetch

_calloc       continue
        bp = lbp + mem(pc)
        pc = pc + 1
        goto _fetch

_halt         continue
        call fflush (STDOUT)   !flush output buffer
        return
        !goto _fetch

_push         continue
        sp = sp + 1
        mem(sp) = mem(pc)
        pc = pc + 1
        goto _fetch

_push_r       continue
        sp = sp + 1
        rmem(sp) = rmem(pc)
        pc = pc + 1
        goto _fetch

_push_l       continue
        sp = sp + 1
        lmem(sp) = lmem(pc)
        pc = pc + 1
        goto _fetch

_pushl        continue
        sp = sp + 1
        mem(sp) = lp + mem(pc)
        pc = pc + 1
        goto _fetch

_pushlc       continue
        sp = sp + 1
        mem(sp) = lbp + mem(pc)
        pc = pc + 1
```

```
        goto _fetch

_pushf      continue
    sp = sp + 1
    mem(sp) = mem(fp+mem(pc))
    pc = pc + 1
    goto _fetch

_pop        continue
    sp = sp - 1
    goto _fetch

_asnv       continue
    mem(mem(sp-1)) = mem(sp)
    mem(sp-1) = mem(sp)
    sp = sp - 1
    goto _fetch

_asna       continue
    mem(mem(sp)) = mem(sp-1)
    mem(sp-1) = mem(sp)
    sp = sp - 1
    goto _fetch

_asns       continue
    i = mem(sp-1)
    j = mem(sp)
    do while (cmem(j:j) .ne. NULL)
        cmem(i:i) = cmem(j:j)
        i = i + 1
        j = j + 1
    end do
    cmem(i:i) = NULL
    sp = sp - 1
    goto _fetch

_val        continue
    mem(sp) = mem(mem(sp))
    goto _fetch

_val2       continue
    mem(sp-1) = mem(mem(sp-1))
    goto _fetch

_ixa        continue
    mem(sp-1) = mem(sp-1) + mem(sp)
    sp = sp - 1
    goto _fetch

_readln     continue
    statio = fgetline (STDIN, cmem(INPUT_ORIGIN:))
    sp = sp + 1
    lmem(sp) = statio
```

```
      ip = INPUT_ORIGIN
      goto _fetch

_read_i      continue
      if (statio) then
         if (.not. is_ival (mem(mem(sp)), cmem, ip)) then
            call fputstr (STDERR,
   &         'integer input error at pc = '//itoa(pc-1))
         end if
      else
         call fputstr (STDERR,
   &      'integer read past eof at pc = '//itoa(pc-1))
      end if
      goto _fetch

_read_r      continue
      if (statio) then
         if (.not. is_rval (rmem(mem(sp)), cmem, ip)) then
            call fputstr (STDERR,
   &         'real input error at pc = '//itoa(pc-1))
         end if
      else
         call fputstr (STDERR,
   &      'real read past eof at pc = '//itoa(pc-1))
      end if
      goto _fetch

_read_l      continue
      if (statio) then
         do while (cmem(ip:ip) .eq. BLANK)
            ip = ip + 1
         end do
         c = cmem(ip:ip)
         if (c .eq. 't' .or. c .eq. 'T' .or. c .eq. '1') then
            lmem(mem(sp)) = .true.
         else if (c .eq. 'f' .or. c .eq. 'F' .or. c .eq. '0') then
            lmem(mem(sp)) = .false.
         else
            call fputstr (STDERR,
   &         'logical input error at pc = '//itoa(pc-1))
         end if
      else
         call fputstr (STDERR,
   &      'logical read past eof at pc = '//itoa(pc-1))
      end if
      goto _fetch

_read_s      continue
      if (statio) then
         if (is_sval (buffer, cmem, ip)) then
            buffer = doescape (buffer)
            i = 1
            j = mem(sp)
```

```
            do while (buffer(i:i) .ne. NULL)
               cmem(j:j) = buffer(i:i)
               i = i + 1
               j = j + 1
            end do
         else
            call fputstr (STDERR,
    &         'character input error at pc = '//itoa(pc-1))
         end if
      else
         call fputstr (STDERR,
    &      'character read past eof at pc = '//itoa(pc-1))
      end if
      goto _fetch

_print_i     continue
      call fputstr (STDOUT, itoa(mem(sp)))
      sp = sp - 1
      goto _fetch

_print_r     continue
      call fputstr (STDOUT, ftoa(rmem(sp)))
      sp = sp - 1
      goto _fetch

_print_l     continue
      if (lmem(sp)) then
         call fputstr (STDOUT, 'true'//NULL)
      else
         call fputstr (STDOUT, 'false'//NULL)
      end if
      sp = sp - 1
      goto _fetch

_print_s     continue
      call fputstr (STDOUT, cmem(mem(sp):))
      sp = sp - 1
      goto _fetch

_jt          continue
      if (lmem(sp)) then
         pc = mem(pc)
      else
         pc = pc + 1
      end if
      sp = sp - 1
      goto _fetch

_jf          continue
      if (.not. lmem(sp)) then
         pc = mem(pc)
      else
         pc = pc + 1
```

```
          end if
          sp = sp - 1
          goto _fetch

_jmp              continue
          pc = mem(pc)
          goto _fetch

_flt              continue
          rmem(sp) = real(mem(sp))
          goto _fetch

_flt2             continue
          rmem(sp-1) = real(mem(sp-1))
          goto _fetch

_int              continue
          mem(sp) = int(rmem(sp))
          goto _fetch

_int2             continue
          mem(sp-1) = int(rmem(sp-1))
          goto _fetch

_sin              continue
          rmem(sp) = sin(rmem(sp))
          goto _fetch

_cos              continue
          rmem(sp) = cos(rmem(sp))
          goto _fetch

_tan              continue
          rmem(sp) = tan(rmem(sp))
          goto _fetch

_asin             continue
          rmem(sp) = asin(rmem(sp))
          goto _fetch

_acos             continue
          rmem(sp) = acos(rmem(sp))
          goto _fetch

_atan             continue
          rmem(sp) = atan(rmem(sp))
          goto _fetch

_exp              continue
          rmem(sp) = exp(rmem(sp))
          goto _fetch

_log              continue
```

```
          rmem(sp) = log(rmem(sp))
          goto _fetch

_abs_i        continue
          mem(sp) = iabs(mem(sp))
          goto _fetch

_abs_r        continue
          rmem(sp) = abs(rmem(sp))
          goto _fetch

_cat          continue
          i = mem(sp-1)
          do while (cmem(i:i) .ne. NULL)
            i = i + 1
          end do
          j = mem(sp)
          do while (cmem(j:j) .ne. NULL)
            cmem(i:i) = cmem(j:j)
            i = i + 1
            j = j + 1
          end do
          cmem(i:i) = NULL
          sp = sp - 1
          goto _fetch

_indx         continue
          i = mem(sp)
          do while (cmem(i:i) .ne. NULL)
            i = i + 1
          end do
          j = mem(sp-1)
          do while (cmem(j:j) .ne. NULL)
            j = j + 1
          end do
          mem(sp-1) = index(cmem(mem(sp-1):j-1),cmem(mem(sp):i-1))
          sp = sp - 1
          goto _fetch

_chr          continue
          cmem(mem(sp-1):mem(sp-1)+1) = char(mem(sp))//NULL
          sp = sp - 1
          goto _fetch

_ord          continue
          mem(sp) = ichar(cmem(mem(sp):mem(sp)))
          goto _fetch

_eqs          continue
          lmem(sp-1) = equal(cmem(mem(sp):),cmem(mem(sp-1):))
          sp = sp - 1
          goto _fetch
```

```
_substr       continue
    j = mem(sp)                        !position 2
    i = mem(sp-1)                      !position 1
    if (j .lt. i) then
        call fputstr (STDERR, 'substring range error at pc = '//itoa(pc))
        call fputc (STDERR, NEWLINE)
    end if
    k = mem(sp-2)                      !address of string argument
    addr = mem(sp-3)                   !address of result
    cmem(addr:addr+j-i+1) = cmem(k+i-1:k+j-1)//NULL
    sp = sp - 3
    goto _fetch


_len          continue
    i = mem(sp)
    j = 0
    do while (cmem(i:i) .ne. NULL)
        i = i + 1
        j = j + 1
    end do
    mem(sp) = j
    goto _fetch

    end
```

The halt instruction, which should occur as the last instruction in a program, flushes the character output buffer and returns to the calling routine. In addition, any error detection in math operations or an errant program counter or unrecognized instruction signals an emergency exit.

The virtual machine is an example of an important technique for constructing many kinds of programs. Using a virtual machine as the executive for a program makes the overall program into something like a compiler, and the approach can be applied to all sorts of applications besides compilers. The machine described here sets the stage for the spl compiler and is probably not very useful for anything else; however, the concept behind it is very powerful and should be a part of your mental toolbox. Machines for other applications are easy to design, and a good abstract machine in combination with our lexical scanner generator can simplify considerably the writing of programs of significant size and complexity.

The use of a virtual machine separates the job of figuring out what to do from the logic of how to do it. A virtual machine permits a kind of abstraction in problem solving that goes a long way toward the goals of concealing complexity, since all of the details of execution are hidden from programs that generate code for a virtual machine, and of minimizing connection between routines, since a virtual machine is pretty much self-contained. The logical separation of execution from interpreting input aids maintenence and eases understanding of a large program.

8.5   The Symbol Table

The symbol tables were developed before any of the parsing routines since the symbol table interface needed to be well-defined to write parser code. After initial development, there was some feedback in the design as requirements became clearer. The symbol table was also the first part of the compiler to be tested and debugged; source files were written to test just the symbol table and parsing of declarations to ensure that everything was working right before spending any time on the parsing of executable statements. The symbol table offers few difficulties since it is based on the hash table management routines of Chapter 5.

All of the symbol table routines access the symbol.cmn common block:

```
! symbol.cmn  -  declarations for symbol table

      integer   HASHSIZE
      parameter (HASHSIZE = 53)      !number of linked lists
      integer   BUFSIZE
      parameter (BUFSIZE = 1024)     !total space for names
      integer   MAXSYMBOL
      parameter (MAXSYMBOL = 128)    !max # symbols

      character*(BUFSIZE) buffer
      integer             htable(HASHSIZE) !table of pointers to lists
      integer             nextfree
      integer             nextsymbol
      integer             nextaddr          !next available address
      integer             nextchr           !next character address
      integer             namepos(MAXSYMBOL) !ptr to name
      integer             nextptr(MAXSYMBOL) !ptr to next list element
      integer             attr(NATTR, MAXSYMBOL) !symbol attributes

      common /symtab/   htable, nextfree, nextsymbol, nextaddr, nextchr,
     &                  namepos, nextptr, attr
      common /symbuf/   buffer
      save    /symtab/, /symbuf/
```

The attr array for each table entry specifies everything the compiler needs to know about a name, such as its address, its class (scalar or array or function name), and (for arrays) its size. Codes for these entries are defined in spl.mac. To define a name, the caller loads up the attr array with the proper codes and calls symdef:

```
! symdef  -  install symbol in table

      subroutine symdef (name, attributes)
      character*(*) name
      integer       attributes (*)
      #include      spl.mac
```

```
#include      global.def
#include      symbol.cmn
integer       hash1, i
logical       status
external      hash1

status = ((nextfree + index(name,NULL) .le. BUFSIZE) .and.
&          (nextsymbol .le. MAXSYMBOL))
if (status) then
   call hinstall (name, buffer, nextfree,
&                 namepos, nextptr, nextsymbol,
&                 htable, hash1, HASHSIZE)
   nextfree = nextfree + index(name,NULL)
   attr(IDCLASS,nextsymbol) = attributes(IDCLASS)
   attr(IDTYPE,nextsymbol) = attributes(IDTYPE)
   if (attributes(IDTYPE) .eq. STRTYPE) then
      attr(IDADDR,nextsymbol) = nextchr
      nextchr = nextchr + attributes(IDSIZE)
   else
      attr(IDADDR,nextsymbol) = nextaddr
      nextaddr = nextaddr + attributes(IDSIZE)
   end if
   attr(IDSIZE,nextsymbol) = attributes(IDSIZE)
   attr(IDORG,nextsymbol) = attributes(IDORG)
   nextsymbol = nextsymbol + 1
else
   call perror ('symbol table overflow'//NULL)
end if

return
end
```

The symbol table has an internal counter nextaddr to determine where the next address to be allocated is and fills in the value accordingly. nextchr is analogous to nextaddr for character string addresses. The process is just the opposite for referencing a symbol: given a name, symref returns its attributes.

```
! symref  -  return attributes of name if defined

      logical function symref (name, attributes)
      character*(*) name
      integer       attributes (*)
#include      spl.mac
#include      symbol.cmn
      integer       hlookup, hash1, p, i
      external      hash1

      p = hlookup(name,buffer,namepos,nextptr,htable,hash1,HASHSIZE)
      if (p .gt. 0) then
         symref = .true.
         do i = 1, NATTR
            attributes(i) = attr(i,p)
```

```
      end do
   else
      symref = .false.
   end if

   return
   end
```

The function symalloc supports the parser by allocating a single address with no name associated with it and returning the address to the caller:

```
! symalloc  -  allocate temporary storage for intermediate result

      integer function symalloc ()
#include   spl.mac
#include   symbol.cmn

      symalloc = nextaddr
      nextaddr = nextaddr + 1
      return
      end
```

After parsing has been completed, the compiler needs to know how much storage has been allocated for variables to initialize the frame pointer. The symsize function returns this information to the caller, and since it always must be called and is called only at the end of parsing a complete program, it is a convenient place to provide the symbol table listing:

```
! symsize  -  return storage allocated for variables

      integer function symsize ()
#include   global.def
#include   spl.mac
#include   symbol.cmn
#include   options.cmn
      character*80 id, outbuf
      integer    i

      symsize = nextaddr
      if (listflag) then
         call fputstr (STDOUT, NEWLINE//'symbol table:'//EOL)
         outbuf = ' '
         outbuf(1:) = 'identifier'
         outbuf(22:) = 'class'
         outbuf(34:) = 'type'
         outbuf(44:) = 'address'
         outbuf(53:) = 'size'
         outbuf(78:) = EOL
         call fputstr (STDOUT, outbuf)
         do i = 1, nextsymbol-1
```

```
         outbuf = ' '
         id(1:) = buffer(namepos(i):)
         outbuf(1:20) = id(1:index(id,NULL)-1)
         if (attr(IDCLASS,i) .eq. IDENTIFIER) outbuf(22:32) = 'scalar'
         if (attr(IDCLASS,i) .eq. ARRAY_ID) outbuf(22:32) = 'array'
         if (attr(IDCLASS,i) .eq. STRING_ID) outbuf(22:32) = 'string'
         if (attr(IDCLASS,i) .eq. FUNCTION_ID) outbuf(22:32) = 'function'
         if (attr(IDTYPE,i) .eq. INTTYPE) outbuf(34:42) = 'integer'
         if (attr(IDTYPE,i) .eq. REALTYPE) outbuf(34:42) = 'real'
         if (attr(IDTYPE,i) .eq. LOGTYPE) outbuf(34:42) = 'logical'
         if (attr(IDTYPE,i) .eq. STRTYPE) outbuf(34:42) = 'character'
         write (outbuf(44:56), '(I5,2x,I5)')
   &           attr(IDADDR,i), attr(IDSIZE,i)
         outbuf(78:79) = EOL
         call fputstr (STDOUT, outbuf)
       end do
       call fputc (STDOUT, NEWLINE)
     end if

     return
     end
```

The symchr routine performs the analogous operation for character memory allocation, and is much shorter because it does not print a table listing.

```
! symchr  -  return storage allocated for string variables

       integer function symchr ()
#include     global.def
#include     spl.mac
#include     options.cmn
#include     symbol.cmn

       symchr = nextchr

       return
       end
```

The symbol table is cleared at the start of compilation, by simply resetting all of the table pointers and address counters:

```
! syminit  -  clear symbol table

       subroutine syminit ()
#include  global.def
#include  spl.mac
#include  symbol.cmn
#include  vstate.cmn
       integer  hash1, i
       external  hash1
```

```
      do i = 1, HASHSIZE
         htable(i) = 0
      end do
      nextfree = 1
      nextsymbol = 1
      nextaddr = 1
      nextchr = 1

! install "input$" identifier
      call hinstall ('input$'//NULL, buffer, nextfree,
     &                namepos, nextptr, nextsymbol,
     &                htable, hash1, HASHSIZE)
      nextfree = nextfree + 7
      attr(IDCLASS,nextsymbol) = STRING_ID
      attr(IDTYPE,nextsymbol) = STRTYPE
      attr(IDSIZE,nextsymbol) = 255
      attr(IDADDR,nextsymbol) = INPUT_ORIGIN
      nextsymbol = nextsymbol + 1

      return
      end
```

The initialization of the global symbol table provides the definition of the pre-declared identifier input$. It is necessary to initialize input$ inside one of the symbol table routines rather than to install it with a call to defglobal because its address must be set to INPUT_ORIGIN and is outside the normal sequence of addresses allocated.

8.6 Code Generation

All code in spl is generated in memory. Since all virtual machine instructions have either no operands or one operand, there are two code generation routines. emit1 generates a 1-word instruction (i.e., an instruction with no operand):

```
! emit1  -  assemble a 1-word instruction

      subroutine emit1 (opcode)
      integer     opcode
#include     global.def
#include     vm.mac
#include     options.cmn
#include     vstate.cmn
      character*80  buffer

#include mnemonic.def

      if (codeflag) then
         write (buffer,'(2i12)') pc, opcode
         buffer(40:) = mnemonic(opcode)//EOL
```

```
        call fputstr (STDOUT, buffer)
      end if
      mem(pc) = opcode
      pc = pc + 1

      return
      end
```

emit2 generates code for 2-word instructions:

```
! emit2  -  assemble a 2-word instruction

      subroutine emit2 (opcode, op, optype)
      integer      opcode, op, optype
      #include     global.def
      #include     vm.mac
      #include     spl.mac
      #include     options.cmn
      #include     vstate.cmn
      character*80 buffer, itoa, ftoa
      integer      iop
      real         rop
      logical      lop
      equivalence  (iop, rop)
      equivalence  (iop, lop)

      #include mnemonic.def

      if (codeflag) then
          iop = op
          write (buffer,'(3i12)') pc, opcode, iop
          if (optype .eq. INTTYPE) then
              buffer(40:) = mnemonic(opcode)//itoa(iop)
          else if (optype .eq. REALTYPE) then
              buffer(40:) = mnemonic(opcode)//ftoa(rop)
          else if (optype .eq. LOGTYPE) then
              if (lop) then
                  buffer(40:) = mnemonic(opcode)//'true'//NULL
              else
                  buffer(40:) = mnemonic(opcode)//'false'//NULL
              end if
          else
              call fputstr (STDERR, 'bad instruction at pc = '//itoa(pc))
              call fputc (STDERR, NEWLINE)
          end if
          call fputstr (STDOUT, buffer)
          call fputc (STDOUT, NEWLINE)
      end if
      mem(pc) = opcode
      mem(pc+1) = op
      pc = pc + 2
```

```
      return
      end
```

Both routines make use of the include file mnemonic.def, which contains the
instruction mnemonics as character strings so that pretty machine code listings
can be printed.

```
! mnemonic.def  -  virtual machine opcode mnemonics

      character*10 mnemonic (MAXINSTRUCTIONS)

      data mnemonic(_add_i)    / 'add[i]' /
      data mnemonic(_add_r)    / 'add[r]' /
      data mnemonic(_sub_i)    / 'sub[i]' /
      data mnemonic(_sub_r)    / 'sub[r]' /
      data mnemonic(_mult_i)   / 'mult[i]' /
      data mnemonic(_mult_r)   / 'mult[r]' /
      data mnemonic(_div_i)    / 'div[i]' /
      data mnemonic(_div_r)    / 'div[r]' /
      data mnemonic(_pwr_i)    / 'pwr[i]' /
      data mnemonic(_pwr_r)    / 'pwr[r]' /
      data mnemonic(_neg_i)    / 'neg[i]' /
      data mnemonic(_neg_r)    / 'neg[r]' /
      data mnemonic(_eq_i)     / 'eq[i]' /
      data mnemonic(_eq_r)     / 'eq[r]' /
      data mnemonic(_ne_i)     / 'ne[i]' /
      data mnemonic(_ne_r)     / 'ne[r]' /
      data mnemonic(_gt_i)     / 'gt[i]' /
      data mnemonic(_gt_r)     / 'gt[r]' /
      data mnemonic(_ge_i)     / 'ge[i]' /
      data mnemonic(_ge_r)     / 'ge[r]' /
      data mnemonic(_lt_i)     / 'lt[i]' /
      data mnemonic(_lt_r)     / 'lt[r]' /
      data mnemonic(_le_i)     / 'le[i]' /
      data mnemonic(_le_r)     / 'le[r]' /
      data mnemonic(_and)      / 'and' /
      data mnemonic(_or)       / 'or' /
      data mnemonic(_not)      / 'not' /
      data mnemonic(_mark)     / 'mark' /
      data mnemonic(_markl)    / 'markl' /
      data mnemonic(_call)     / 'call' /
      data mnemonic(_rtn)      / 'rtn' /
      data mnemonic(_rtns)     / 'rtns' /
      data mnemonic(_alloc)    / 'alloc' /
      data mnemonic(_calloc)   / 'calloc' /
      data mnemonic(_halt)     / 'halt' /
      data mnemonic(_push)     / 'push' /
      data mnemonic(_push_r)   / 'push[r]' /
      data mnemonic(_push_l)   / 'push[l]' /
      data mnemonic(_pushl)    / 'pushl' /
      data mnemonic(_pushlc)   / 'pushlc' /
      data mnemonic(_pushf)    / 'pushf' /
```

```
data mnemonic(_pop)     / 'pop' /
data mnemonic(_asnv)    / 'asnv' /
data mnemonic(_asna)    / 'asna' /
data mnemonic(_asns)    / 'asns' /
data mnemonic(_val)     / 'val' /
data mnemonic(_val2)    / 'val2' /
data mnemonic(_ixa)     / 'ixa' /
data mnemonic(_readln)  / 'readln' /
data mnemonic(_read_i)  / 'read[i]' /
data mnemonic(_read_r)  / 'read[r]' /
data mnemonic(_read_l)  / 'read[l]' /
data mnemonic(_read_s)  / 'read[s]' /
data mnemonic(_print_i) / 'print[i]' /
data mnemonic(_print_r) / 'print[r]' /
data mnemonic(_print_l) / 'print[l]' /
data mnemonic(_print_s) / 'print[s]' /
data mnemonic(_jt)      / 'jt' /
data mnemonic(_jf)      / 'jf' /
data mnemonic(_jmp)     / 'jmp' /
data mnemonic(_flt)     / 'flt' /
data mnemonic(_flt2)    / 'flt2' /
data mnemonic(_int)     / 'int' /
data mnemonic(_int2)    / 'int2' /
data mnemonic(_sin)     / 'sin' /
data mnemonic(_cos)     / 'cos' /
data mnemonic(_tan)     / 'tan' /
data mnemonic(_asin)    / 'asin' /
data mnemonic(_acos)    / 'acos' /
data mnemonic(_atan)    / 'atan' /
data mnemonic(_exp)     / 'exp' /
data mnemonic(_log)     / 'log' /
data mnemonic(_abs_i)   / 'abs[i]' /
data mnemonic(_abs_r)   / 'abs[r]' /
data mnemonic(_cat)     / 'cat' /
data mnemonic(_indx)    / 'indx' /
data mnemonic(_chr)     / 'chr' /
data mnemonic(_ord)     / 'ord' /
data mnemonic(_eqs)     / 'eqs' /
data mnemonic(_substr)  / 'substr' /
data mnemonic(_len)     / 'len' /
```

The symbol table attribute attr(IDORG) is only used for intrinsic functions, to store the start address in the code. Function calls can be nested, and the need to recover the function name later during the parse arises because the call instruction is generated only after the arguments have been collected. To illustrate, the nested function call

```
sin (cos (2. * z))
```

must generate the virtual machine code:

```
mark sin        !storage address for result of sin
mark cos        !storage address for result of cos
push[r] 2.0
push z          !address of local variable z
mult[r]
push tmp        !temporary address of result
asna            !store value in temporary address
call cos        !transfer address for cos function
call sin        !transfer address for sin function
```

When the function name is encountered the mark instruction is generated. In the preceding example, the argument to cos is an expression rather than a simple variable or array element reference. Since all arguments are passed by reference, the parser allocates a temporary local address for the result.

8.7 Parsing

Everything is now in place to tackle the most difficult part of the compiler. The parsing routines are really the heart of the compiler since they call the lexical analyzer whenever tokens are needed, put information into and get information from the symbol table, and generate all of the code. Fortunately, they are not too difficult to understand, even though they collectively have many lines of code, because they are organized methodically into a well-defined hierarchy.

The parsing routines form a hierarchy from the highest level (parse) to the lowest (exprparse). Each level passes control to the next lower level when the rules of the grammar indicate it should. The decision of what to do next is always based on what has been seen so far (which is reflected in the current location in the parsing code) and the next token. This organization of control from the highest levels to the lowest is a top-down parsing strategy, like the LL(1) grammars discussed previously, and the parsing method is akin to the recursive descent method. However, since recursion is not allowed in Fortran 77, the parsing problem must be carefully partitioned to avoid any need for recursive procedure calls while implementing all of the recursion in the grammar rules.

parse handles the highest level of the grammar, that is, the statement sequence that comprises the program.

```
! parse  -  main parsing routine

        logical function parse (basefp, basebp)
        integer         basefp, basebp
        #include        global.def
        #include        spl.mac
        #include        vm.mac
        #include        perror.cmn
        #include        vstate.cmn
        #include        parse.cmn
        character*(MAXSTR) token, cat, itoa
        integer         t, lex, symsize, symchr
```

```
pc = ORIGIN
ccp = CHAR_ORIGIN

do while (lex(t,token) .ne. $eof)
    call stmtparse (t,token)
end do

call emit1 (_halt)
do while (nsp .gt. 0)
    if (nest(nsp) .eq. $if) then
        call perror ('unclosed if block'//NULL)
    else if (nest(nsp) .eq. $while) then
        call perror ('unclosed while loop'//NULL)
    else if (nest(nsp) .eq. $until) then
        call perror ('unclosed repeat loop'//NULL)
    end if
    nsp = nsp - 1
end do

basefp = symsize ()              !initial frame pointer
basebp = symchr ()               !initial buffer pointer
if (errcount .gt. 0) then
    call fputstr (STDERR, cat(itoa(errcount), ' parse errors'//EOL))
    parse = .false.
else
    parse = .true.
end if

return
end
```

parse has control of advancing through the input. Each pass through the main
loop should process exactly one logical line, so the next token at the top of the
loop is the token that begins a statement. When the -c option is in effect, spl
calls calc instead of parse, and handles getting input lines itself.

```
! calc  -  parsing routine for spl calculator mode

      logical function calc (t, token, basefp, basebp)
      integer          t, basefp, basebp
      character*(*)    token
#include          global.def
#include          spl.mac
#include          vm.mac
#include          perror.cmn
#include          vstate.cmn
#include          parse.cmn
      character*(MAXSTR) cat, itoa
      integer          lex, symsize, symchr

      pc = ORIGIN
```

```
ccp = CHAR_ORIGIN

call stmtparse (t, token)
if (errcount .eq. 0) then
   if (nsp .gt. 0) then
      do while (nsp .gt. 0 .and. lex(t,token) .ne. $eof)
         call stmtparse (t,token)
      end do
      if (t .eq. $eof) call perror ('unclosed block on eof'//EOL)
   end if
end if

call emit1 (_halt)
basefp = symsize ()          !initial frame pointer
basebp = symchr ()           !initial buffer pointer
if (errcount .gt. 0) then
   call fputstr (STDERR, cat(itoa(errcount), ' parse errors'//EOL))
   errcount = 0
   calc = .false.
else
   calc = .true.
end if

return
end
```

stmtparse processes individual statements. Rather than define special codes
for each of the multiline statements, the lexical codes themselves are used since
the routine must be recompiled whenever they are changed anyway. In parallel
with the stack holding the token codes, two stacks for code locations are used
as necessary to backpatch the code in virtual machine branching instructions.
For this reason, if a machine language listing is produced, these addresses always
show up as zero since they are printed before the backpatching occurs.

```
! stmtparse  -  parse statements within program units

      subroutine stmtparse (t, token)
      integer      t
      character*(*)  token
      #include     global.def
      #include     spl.mac
      #include     vm.mac
      #include     vstate.cmn
      #include     parse.cmn
      integer      lex, av, exprtype
      logical      exprparse, done

      if (t .eq. $id) then                    !assignment or function call
         if (exprparse (t, token, av, exprtype)) call emit1 (_pop)
      else if (t .eq. $int .or. t .eq. $real .or.
     &           t .eq. $log .or. t .eq. $char) then
         call declist (t)
```

```
else if (t .eq. $while) then           !while lexpr
   nsp = nsp + 1
   nest(nsp) = $while
   pc1(nsp) = pc
   if (exprparse (t, token, av, exprtype)) then
      if (exprtype .ne. LOGTYPE) then
         call perror ('logical valued expression required'//NULL)
      end if
   end if
   if (av .eq. ADDRESS) call emit1 (_val)
   call emit2 (_jf, 0, INTTYPE)
   pc2(nsp) = pc - 1
else if (t .eq. $endwhile) then        !end while
   if (nest(nsp) .eq. $while) then
      call emit2 (_jmp, pc1(nsp), INTTYPE)
      mem(pc2(nsp)) = pc
   else
      call perror ('improper nesting of while statement'//NULL)
   end if
   nsp = nsp - 1
   t = lex(t,token)
else if (t .eq. $repeat) then          !repeat
   nsp = nsp + 1
   nest(nsp) = $until
   pc1(nsp) = pc
   t = lex(t,token)
else if (t .eq. $until) then           !until lexpr
   if (nest(nsp) .ne. $until) then
      call perror ('improper nesting of UNTIL statement'//NULL)
   end if
   if (exprparse (t, token, av, exprtype)) then
      if (exprtype .ne. LOGTYPE) then
         call perror ('logical valued expression required'//NULL)
      end if
   end if
   if (av .eq. ADDRESS) call emit1 (_val)
   call emit2 (_jf, pc1(nsp), INTTYPE)
   nsp = nsp - 1
else if (t .eq. $if) then              !if lexpr
   nsp = nsp + 1
   nest(nsp) = $if
   if (exprparse (t, token, av, exprtype)) then
      if (exprtype .ne. LOGTYPE) then
         call perror ('logical valued expression required'//NULL)
      end if
   end if
   if (av .eq. ADDRESS) call emit1 (_val)
   call emit2 (_jf, 0, INTTYPE)
   pc2(nsp) = pc - 1
   pc1(nsp) = pc2(nsp)        !in case of no else or elseif
else if (t .eq. $elseif) then          !else if lexpr
   if (nest(nsp) .ne. $if .and. nest(nsp) .ne. $elseif) then
      call perror ('else if without if'//NULL)
```

```
            end if
         call emit2 (_jmp, 0, INTTYPE)
         pc1(nsp) = pc - 1
         mem(pc2(nsp)) = pc
         nsp = nsp + 1
         nest(nsp) = $elseif
         if (exprparse (t, token, av, exprtype)) then
            if (exprtype .ne. LOGTYPE) then
               call perror ('logical valued expression required'//NULL)
            end if
         end if
         if (av .eq. ADDRESS) call emit1 (_val)
         call emit2 (_jf, 0, INTTYPE)
         pc2(nsp) = pc - 1
      else if (t .eq. $else) then             !else
         if (nest(nsp) .ne. $if .and. nest(nsp) .ne. $elseif) then
            call perror ('else without matching if'//NULL)
         end if
         call emit2 (_jmp, 0, INTTYPE)
         pc1(nsp) = pc - 1
         mem(pc2(nsp)) = pc
         t = lex(t,token)
      else if (t .eq. $endif) then         !end if
         done = .false.
         do while (.not. done)
            if (nest(nsp) .eq. $if) then
               mem(pc1(nsp)) = pc
               nsp = nsp - 1
               done = .true.
            else if (nest(nsp) .eq. $elseif) then
               mem(pc1(nsp)) = pc
               nsp = nsp - 1
            else
               call perror ('end if without matching if'//NULL)
               done = .true.
            end if
         end do
         t = lex(t,token)
      else if (t .eq. $read) then              !read idlist
         call readstmt (t)
      else if (t .eq. $print) then             !print exprlist
         call printstmt (t)
      else
         call perror ('unrecognized statement'//NULL)
         do while (t .ne. $eol)
            t = lex(t,token)
         end do
      end if

      if (t .ne. $eol) then
         call perror ('unexpected tokens after valid statement'//NULL)
         do while (t .ne. $eol)
            t = lex(t,token)
```

```
    end do
  end if

  return
end
```

If the first token of a statement is an identifier, exprparse is called and is equipped to handle assignments and procedure calls. exprparse always leaves a single value on the machine stack, so stmtparse generates code to discard this value. This mechanism allows functions, which always return a result, to be called as procedures and also allows assignments to be used within expressions, since they also always leave a value on the stack. It also allows do-nothing statements such as an identifier on a line by itself; any valid expression beginning with $id is acceptable to both stmtparse and exprparse even though it may not do anything except to generate useless code.

exprparse uses a simple, well-known operator precedence parsing algorithm which converts an arithmetic expression written in normal algebraic notation (also called "infix" notation) into reverse Polish notation (known as RPN for short). The reverse Polish form is familiar to HP calculator fans; in it the operators occur after the operands, and evaluation is most conveniently performed on a stack. Thus the expression 2 + 2 in infix notation becomes 2 2 + in RPN. To evaluate the expression, the two numbers are pushed onto a stack, and the + operator pops the top two elements from the stack, adds them, and pushes the result back onto the stack. RPN has the nice property that parentheses are never required; the order of operators determines the order of evaluation. Thus the expression 132 - (5+6)*7**2 can be represented in RPN as 132 5 6 + 7 2 ** * -. The advantage of the reverse Polish form as far as the computer is concerned is the ease of evaluation.

The parsing algorithm uses two stacks, one for operands and one for operators. The operands are simply pushed onto the operand stack as they are read; the precedences of the operator on top of the stack and the operator in the input are compared to determine whether the input operator should be stacked or the stacked operator should be executed. The following is a pseudocode description of the algorithm:

```
do while (not at end)
   get next token
   if (token is operand) then
      push token onto operand stack
   else if (token is operator) then
      if (precedence > precedence of operator on top of stack) then
         push token onto operator stack
      else
         pop operator on top of stack and execute
         push token onto operator stack
      end if
   else if (token is opening parenthesis) then
      push token onto operator stack
```

```
        else if (token is closing parenthesis) then
            unstack and execute operators until opening parenthesis found
            unstack opening parenthesis
        end if
    end do
    unstack all remaining operators and execute
```

To illustrate the algorithm, Figure 8.5 is an example of the conversion of an infix string to RPN, showing the remaining input, operand stack, operator stack, and output string at each step.

Addition of relational operators and logical conjunctive and disjunctive operators (.and. and .or.) is easily accomplished by assigning appropriate precedence values. The precedence should be lower than the precedence of any arithmetic operator, so that an expression like 2+2 == 8/2 or 3*7 <= 21 .or. 7*7 == 50 is evaluated in the correct order without extra parentheses. It is also possible to keep track of the type of an expression result by keeping a code denoting type with each entry on the operand stack.

The preceding algorithm does what is required for syntactically correct infix expressions, but has no provision for dealing with errors. This is entirely unsuitable behavior; a program that crashes on simple errors without some message alerting the user, or worse yet, successfully completes without any error messages on a syntactically incorrect input and returns a bogus result, is unacceptable. To incorporate error checking some description of the syntax restrictions is necessary. One appropriate representation to use with this algorithm is as a matrix of allowed token combinations. Note that in all valid infix expressions, a binary operator never follows an opening parenthesis, a number never follows a closing

input string	stack	opstack	output string
7+5*(6-8)/2**3			
+5*(6-8)/2**3	7		
5*(6-8)/2**3	7	+	
*(6-8)/2**3	7 5	+	
(6-8)/2**3	7 5	+ *	
6-8)/2**3	7 5	+ * (	
-8)/2**3	7 5 6	+ * (	
8)/2**3	7 5 6	+ * (-	
)/2**3	7 5 6 8	+ * (-	
/2**3	7 5	+ *	6 8 -
2**3	7	+ /	6 8 - 5 *
**3	7 2	+ /	6 8 - 5 *
3	7 2	+ / **	6 8 - 5 *
	7 2 3	+ / **	6 8 - 5 *
	7	+	6 8 - 5 * 2 3 ** /
			6 8 - 5 * 2 3 ** / 7 +

Figure 8.5: Conversion of infix expression to reverse Polish notation.

parenthesis, and two operators or two numbers back-to-back are not allowed. These restrictions are embodied in a matrix allowed, which contains true or false for every possible combination of two successive tokens. To simplify the coding and reduce the size of the allowed array, the tokens are first organized into token classes, so that, for instance, all binary logical operators are in the same class.

The simple algorithm described here also has just one precedence associated with each operator, and the algorithm described produces left associativity for all binary operators. Left associativity means that when two operators of equal precedence are compared, the first one occurring in the expression is the first one executed, so that $3-4-1$ is evaluated as $(3-4)-1 = -2$ rather than $3-(4-1) = 0$. However, in mathematics exponentiation is considered to be right associative, so that a**b**c is evaluated as a**(b**c). Associativity of operators can be incorporated into the algorithm by assigning two kinds of precedence to each operator: one precedence for when it is seen in the input and another for when it is on the operator stack. For example, to obtain left associativity for an operator we will make its stack precedence higher than its input precedence, so that the one on the stack will be output before the one in the input is stacked. For right associativity we do just the opposite, assigning the input precedence to be higher than the stack precedence.

The assignment of tokens to arithmetic expression token classes and the assignment of precedence values and allowed matrix entries for the tokens is done by data statements in the routines which need them. Since we expected to need to revise the data statements several times during development, we wrote a little generator program to simply make data statements from a more easily revised input file. The generator can be easily recreated so we will present only its input file:

```
! exprgen.in - input tables for spl expression evaluator
#include spl.mac


tokens 40
! token       class          iprecedence          sprecedence
!-----------------------------------------------------------------
$int          OTHER               0                    0
$real         OTHER               0                    0
$log          OTHER               0                    0
$char         OTHER               0                    0
$if           OTHER               0                    0
$elseif       OTHER               0                    0
$else         OTHER               0                    0
$endif        OTHER               0                    0
$while        OTHER               0                    0
$endwhile     OTHER               0                    0
$repeat       OTHER               0                    0
$until        OTHER               0                    0
$read         OTHER               0                    0
$print        OTHER               0                    0
```

```
$intnum      CONSTANT                 16              17
$realnum     CONSTANT                 16              17
$true        CONSTANT                 16              17
$false       CONSTANT                 16              17
$string      CONSTANT                 16              17
$id          IDENTIFIER               16              17
$add         BINARY_ARITHMETIC_OP     10              11
$sub         BINARY_ARITHMETIC_OP     10              11
$mult        BINARY_ARITHMETIC_OP     12              13
$div         BINARY_ARITHMETIC_OP     12              13
$pwr         BINARY_ARITHMETIC_OP     15              14
$eq          BINARY_RELATIONAL_OP      6               7
$ne          BINARY_RELATIONAL_OP      6               7
$gt          BINARY_RELATIONAL_OP      6               7
$ge          BINARY_RELATIONAL_OP      6               7
$lt          BINARY_RELATIONAL_OP      6               7
$le          BINARY_RELATIONAL_OP      6               7
$and         BINARY_LOGICAL_OP         4               5
$or          BINARY_LOGICAL_OP         4               5
$not         UNARY_LOGICAL_OP          8               9
$assign      ASSIGN_OP                 3               2
$lparen      OPEN_PAREN               20               1
$rparen      CLOSE_PAREN               1              -1
$comma       COMMA_SEPARATOR           1               1
$eol         OTHER                     0               0
$eof         OTHER                     0               0

classes 15
!                   right token
!    OTHER
!    | UNARY_SIGN
!    | | IDENTIFIER
!    | | | FUNCTION_ID
!    | | | | ARRAY_ID
!    | | | | | STRING_ID
!    | | | | | | CONSTANT
!    | | | | | | | BINARY_ARITHMETIC_OP
!    | | | | | | | | BINARY_RELATIONAL_OP
!    | | | | | | | | | UNARY_LOGICAL_OP
!    | | | | | | | | | | BINARY_LOGICAL_OP
!    | | | | | | | | | | | ASSIGN_OP
!    | | | | | | | | | | | | COMMA_SEPARATOR
!    | | | | | | | | | | | | | OPEN_PAREN
!    | | | | | | | | | | | | | | CLOSE_PAREN    left token
!    -------------------------------------------------------
     f t t t t t t f f t f f f t f    |  OTHER
     f f t t t f t f f f f f f t f    |  UNARY_SIGN
     t f f f f f f t t f t t t f t    |  IDENTIFIER
     f f f f f f f f f f f f f t f    |  FUNCTION_ID
     f f f f f f f f f f f f t t f    |  ARRAY_ID
     t f f f f f f f f f f t t f t    |  STRING_ID
     t f f f f f f t t f t f t f t    |  CONSTANT
     f t t t t f t f f f f f f t f    |  BINARY_ARITHMETIC_OP
```

```
f t t t t f t f f t f f f t f        |  BINARY_RELATIONAL_OP
f f t t t f t f f f f f f t f        |  UNARY_LOGICAL_OP
f t t t t f t f f f f f f t f        |  BINARY_LOGICAL_OP
f t t t t t t f f t f f f t f        |  ASSIGN_OP
f t t t t t t f f t f f f t f        |  COMMA_SEPARATOR
f t t t t t t f f t f f f t t        |  OPEN_PAREN
t f f f f f f t t f t t t f t        |  CLOSE_PAREN
```

The precedence values assigned to operands are never used by exprparse. In a generalized operator precedence parser all tokens would be treated as operators, and the operands would need the highest precedence so that they would be output immediately. The precedence values are assigned as if this were the case; however, exprparse is not a formalized operator precedence parser and explicitly handles operands separately from operators. The important thing is that among the operators the numerical relationships between precedence values must be correct.

The classification of tokens cannot be handled entirely by data statements, since, for example, a minus sign can be either a subtraction operator or unary sign operator. In addition, all the lexical analyzer determines about an identifier is that it is one, and the symbol table must be consulted to find out if it is an ARRAY_ID or other special identifier class. The routine class does these special checks on identifiers and unary operators and just consults the xclass array on everything else.

```
! class  -  return token class of t

        integer function class (ptok, t, token, attr)
        integer       ptok, t, attr (*)
        character*(*) token
        #include      global.def
        #include      spl.mac
        logical       symref
        integer       xclass (MAXTOKEN), i
        #include      class.def

        if (t .eq. $id) then
           if (symref(token, attr)) then
              class = attr(IDCLASS)
           else
              call perror ('reference to undeclared identifier'//NULL)
              class = IDENTIFIER
           end if
        else if (t .eq. $sub .or. t .eq. $add) then
           if (ptok .eq. IDENTIFIER .or.
        &        ptok .eq. CONSTANT .or.
        &        ptok .eq. CLOSE_PAREN) then
              class = BINARY_ARITHMETIC_OP
           else
              class = UNARY_SIGN
           end if
```

```
      else
         class = xclass(t)
      end if

      return
      end
```

All of the stacks for all of the parsing are declared in one common file:

```
! parse.cmn  -  common block for parser stacks

! character constant pointer
      integer     ccp
      common /charconst/ ccp

! statement nesting stack
      integer     MAXNEST
      parameter   (MAXNEST = 32)      !max nesting level
      integer     nest (MAXNEST)      !type of multiline statement
      integer     pc1 (MAXNEST)       !associated code loc
      integer     pc2 (MAXNEST)
      integer     nsp                 !nesting stack pointer
      common /neststack/ nest, pc1, pc2, nsp

! expression parser stacks
      integer     MAXSTACK
      parameter   (MAXSTACK = 32)

! evaluation stack
      integer     aorv (MAXSTACK)     !address or value
      integer     type (MAXSTACK)     !data type
      integer     esp                 !evaluation stack pointer
      common /evalstack/ aorv, type, esp

! operator stack
      integer  opclass (MAXSTACK)  !operator arithmetic class
      integer  optoken (MAXSTACK)  !operator token value
      integer  org (MAXSTACK)      !function code start address
      integer  osp                 !operator stack pointer
      common /opstack/ opclass, optoken, org, osp

! parentheses stack
      integer  depth (MAXSTACK)     !eval stack depth at open_paren
      integer  prevdepth (MAXSTACK) !depth at last comma or open_paren
      integer  psp                  !parentheses stack pointer
      common /parenstack/ depth, psp

      save  /charconst/, /neststack/, /evalstack/, /opstack/, /parenstack/
```

exprparse maintains three stacks. The evaluation stack with stack pointer esp mimics the real machine stack during execution, holding operand values or addresses. The aorv array has a code for each stack entry indicating whether it is a value or the address of a value, and the type array indicates the data types of items on the stack. In general, addresses rather than values are placed on the stack, since arguments to procedures must be passed by address.

The operator stack with stack pointer osp stores the operators stacked by the precedence algorithm, along with several associated values; for each operator, both the specific token value and its class are stored. Function and array names are treated as both operands and operators. The operator stack entry made for an array is used when the closing parenthesis of the subscript expression comes along to generate an ixa (compute indexed address) instruction. When the name of a function is read as input, a location on the stack is immediately reserved for the function result as if it were any other kind of operand, and a mark instruction is generated to begin a stack frame. When the closing parenthesis of a function argument list is found, the call to the function is generated.

The parentheses stack is used to determine how many expressions have occurred between parentheses. For parentheses used to specify precedence in expressions, the evaluation stack depth must grow by exactly one between the opening and closing parentheses; in other words, a valid expression must leave exactly one value on the stack. This is also true for spl arrays since multidimensional arrays are not allowed. For functions, however, there can be zero or more arguments between parentheses, with multiple arguments separated by commas. The parentheses following a function name are required even if there are no arguments.

The first thing exprparse does is get a handle on the expression to figure out where it starts. It can be called either before or after the first token of the expression has been read and, in fact, is called both ways by stmtparse. For if statements and others with conditional expressions, the keyword is the last token scanned before exprparse is called, so exprparse gets the first token before entering the main loop to get things started. For assignment statements or procedure calls, the first token (an identifier) is in hand when exprparse is called.

```
! exprparse  -  parse arithmetic and logical expressions

        logical function exprparse (t, token, av, exprtype)
        integer         t, av, exprtype
        character*(*)   token
        #include        global.def
        #include        spl.mac
        #include        vm.mac
        #include        vstate.cmn
        integer         class, c, ptok, lex, symalloc, i
        logical         symref
        integer         attr (NATTR)
        #include        parse.cmn
```

```
! parse tables
    integer  iprecedence (MAXTOKEN), sprecedence (MAXTOKEN)
    logical  allowed (MAXCLASS, MAXCLASS)
    #include exprparse.def

! initialize and get initial token
    esp = 0
    psp = 0
    ptok = OTHER
    osp = 1
    opclass(1) = OTHER
    optoken(1) = $eol
    c = class(ptok, t, token, attr)
    if (c .eq. OTHER) then
        t = lex(t, token)
    end if
    c = class (ptok, t, token, attr)
    if (c .eq. OTHER) then
        call perror ('invalid expression'//NULL)
        do while (t .ne. $eol)
            t = lex(t,token)
        end do
        exprparse = .false.
        return
    end if

! read and parse expression
    #define endcondition &
    c .eq. OTHER .or. (c .eq. COMMA_SEPARATOR .and. psp .eq. 0)

    do while (.not.(endcondition))
        !check for errors
        if (.not. allowed(c, ptok)) then
            call perror ('invalid expression syntax'//NULL)
            do while (t .ne. $eol)
                t = lex(t,token)
            end do
            return
        else if (esp .eq. MAXSTACK .or.
    &            osp .eq. MAXSTACK .or.
    &            psp .eq. MAXSTACK) then
            call perror ('expression stack overflow'//NULL)
            do while (t .ne. $eol)
                t = lex(t,token)
            end do
            return
        end if

        ! process current token
        if (c .eq. CONSTANT .or. c .eq. IDENTIFIER .or.
    &       c .eq. ARRAY_ID .or. c .eq. STRING_ID .or.
    &       c .eq. FUNCTION_ID) then
            call operand (c, t, token, attr)
```

```
    if (c .eq. ARRAY_ID .or. c .eq. FUNCTION_ID) then
      osp = osp + 1
      optoken(osp) = t
      opclass(osp) = c
      org(osp) = attr(IDORG)
    end if
  else if (c .eq. OPEN_PAREN) then
    psp = psp + 1
    depth(psp) = esp
    prevdepth(psp) = esp
    osp = osp + 1
    opclass(osp) = OPEN_PAREN
    optoken(osp) = t
  else if (c .eq. COMMA_SEPARATOR) then
    do while (opclass(osp) .ne. OPEN_PAREN .and. osp .gt. 1)
      call operator (optoken(osp), opclass(osp))
      osp = osp - 1
    end do
    if (opclass(osp) .ne. OPEN_PAREN) then
      call perror ('missing parentheses in argument list'//NULL)
    else if (opclass(osp-1) .ne. FUNCTION_ID) then
      call perror ('allowed only in function argument list'//NULL)
    else if (esp - prevdepth(psp) .ne. 1) then
      call perror ('invalid argument expression'//NULL)
    else
      prevdepth(psp) = esp
    end if
    if (aorv(esp) .eq. VALUE) then  !allocate temporary address
      call emit2 (_push, symalloc(), INTTYPE)
      call emit1 (_asna)
    end if
  else if (c .eq. CLOSE_PAREN) then
    do while (opclass(osp) .ne. OPEN_PAREN .and. osp .gt. 1)
      call operator (optoken(osp),opclass(osp))
      osp = osp - 1
    end do
    if (opclass(osp) .eq. OPEN_PAREN) then
      osp = osp - 1            !discard opening parentheses
      if (opclass(osp) .eq. ARRAY_ID) then
        if (esp - depth(psp) .ne. 1) then
          call perror ('invalid subscript expression'//NULL)
        else
          if (type(esp) .eq. INTTYPE) then
            if (aorv(esp) .eq. ADDRESS) call emit1 (_val)
            call emit1 (_ixa)
            esp = esp - 1
            aorv(esp) = ADDRESS
          else
            call perror ('array index must be integer'//NULL)
          end if
        end if
        osp = osp - 1      !discard ARRAY_ID
      else if (opclass(osp) .eq. FUNCTION_ID) then
```

```
            if (esp .ne. depth(psp)) then   !arguments on stack
                if (esp - prevdepth(psp) .ne. 1) then
                    call perror ('invalid argument expression'//NULL)
                end if
                if (aorv(esp) .eq. VALUE) then
                    call emit2 (_push, symalloc(), INTTYPE)
                    call emit1 (_asna)
                end if
                esp = depth(psp)
            end if
            call emit2 (_call, org(osp), INTTYPE)
        else              ! (expression)
            if (esp - depth(psp) .ne. 1) then
                call perror ('invalid expression'//NULL)
                if (esp - depth(psp) .eq. 0) then
                    esp = esp + 1      !fake it for operator
                    type(esp) = INTTYPE
                    aorv(esp) = VALUE
                end if
            end if
        end if
        psp = psp - 1
    else
        call perror ('missing left parentheses'//NULL)
    end if
else if (iprecedence(t) .gt. sprecedence(optoken(osp))) then
    if (osp .eq. MAXSTACK) then
        call perror ('operator stack overflow'//EOL)
        do while (t .ne. $eol)
            t = lex(t,token)
        end do
    else
        osp = osp + 1
        opclass(osp) = c
        optoken(osp) = t
    end if
else
    do while (iprecedence(t) .le. sprecedence(optoken(osp)))
        call operator (optoken(osp),opclass(osp))
        osp = osp - 1
    end do
    osp = osp + 1
    opclass(osp) = c
    optoken(osp) = t
end if
ptok = c
t = lex(t,token)
c = class(ptok,t,token,attr)
end do

do while (osp .gt. 1)            !unstack any remaining operators
    if (opclass(osp) .eq. OPEN_PAREN) then
        call perror ('missing right parentheses'//NULL)
```

```
    else
        call operator (optoken(osp), opclass(osp))
    end if
    osp = osp - 1
end do

exprparse = (esp .eq. 1)
exprtype = type(1)
av = aorv(1)

return
end
```

The code generated by exprparse is simply the reverse Polish equivalent of
the expression, in virtual machine assembly code. The code generated for any
expression can be studied easily once spl is running by using the -lm compiler
options.

The translation of ordinary algebraic expressions to virtual machine code is
straightforward, but the actions of exprparse in dealing with array references
and function calls deserve special attention. Array references and function calls
are treated as both operands and operators. For array references, a place in
the operand stack is reserved for the base address of the array; an entry in the
operator stack is also made so that an ixa instruction can be generated after
the code for evaluation of the subscript has been evaluated. A similar treatment
is given to functions since the mark instruction is generated when the function
name is encountered and the call instruction is generated after the code to
evaluate the arguments. When gathering the arguments for a function, each
comma results in the unstacking of any operators that appeared after the opening
parenthesis of the argument list or the previous comma. The prevdepth stack
entry is compared with esp to make sure that each argument produces exactly
one value on the stack. If an argument is a constant or an arithmetic expression,
it will produce a value rather than an address on the stack. Therefore in such
cases exprparse calls symalloc to allocate a temporary address. Note that this
means an spl function can modify the value of an argument that was a constant
or expression in the caller with no ill effect.

exprparse is a rather long routine, even though it has two slaves to dispatch
menial work to. Most of the code deals with the entry and exit interface requirements and with the actions needed for opening and closing parentheses. The
operand and operator routines have lots more lines of code but don't do any
parsing and are entirely straightforward. The operand routine takes care of code
generation for pushing operands onto the machine stack and sets the evaluation
stack entries for operands:

```
! operand  -  generate code for arithmetic expression operands

        subroutine operand (c, t, token, attr)
        integer         c, t, attr (*)
```

```
character*(*)   token
#include        global.def
#include        spl.mac
#include        vm.mac
#include        parse.cmn
#include        vstate.cmn
integer         atoi
real            atof
logical         equal


esp = esp + 1
if (c .eq. CONSTANT) then
   if (t .eq. $string) then
      aorv(esp) = ADDRESS
      type(esp) = STRTYPE
      cmem(ccp:ccp+index(token,NULL)-1) = token(1:index(token,NULL))
      call emit2 (_push, ccp, INTTYPE)
      ccp = ccp + index(token,NULL)
   else
      aorv(esp) = VALUE
      if (t .eq. $intnum) then
         type(esp) = INTTYPE
         call emit2 (_push, atoi(token), INTTYPE)
      else if (t .eq. $realnum) then
         type(esp) = REALTYPE
         call emit2 (_push_r, atof(token), REALTYPE)
      else if (t .eq. $true .or. t .eq. $false) then
         type(esp) = LOGTYPE
         if (equal (token, 'true'//NULL)) then
            call emit2 (_push_l, .true., LOGTYPE)
         else
            call emit2 (_push_l, .false., LOGTYPE)
         end if
      end if
   end if
else if (c.eq.IDENTIFIER .or. c.eq.ARRAY_ID .or. c.eq.STRING_ID) then
   aorv(esp) = ADDRESS
   type(esp) = attr(IDTYPE)
   call emit2 (_push, attr(IDADDR), INTTYPE)
else if (c .eq. FUNCTION_ID) then
   aorv(esp) = ADDRESS
   type(esp) = attr(IDTYPE)
   call emit2 (_mark, attr(IDADDR), INTTYPE)
end if

return
end
```

The operator routine is called whenever the precedence algorithm has decided it is finished with an operator. The code is lengthy but is mostly just
concerned with type checking and emitting instructions to perform arithmetic
operations based on the entries in the evaluation stack. For arithmetic opera-

tors, mixed-mode expressions (those with both real and integer operands) are handled automatically by converting the integers to reals before emitting an instruction. When an operand is an address rather than a value, val and/or val2 instructions are issued just prior to performing the operation. For other operators such as the logical operators, type conversion is not performed, and the operand types are simply checked and incompatible types reported. After an operator has been processed, the evaluation stack contents are modified accordingly.

```
! operator   -   generate code for arithmetic expression operators

       subroutine operator (t, c)
       integer     t, c
       #include    global.def
       #include    spl.mac
       #include    vm.mac
       #include    parse.cmn

       if (c .eq. UNARY_SIGN) then
           if (type(esp) .eq. REALTYPE .or. type(esp) .eq. INTTYPE) then
               if (aorv(esp) .eq. ADDRESS) then
                   call emit1 (_val)
                   aorv(esp) = VALUE
               end if
           else
               call perror ('type mismatch'//NULL)
           end if
           if (t .eq. $sub) then
               if (type(esp) .eq. INTTYPE) call emit1 (_neg_i)
               if (type(esp) .eq. REALTYPE) call emit1 (_neg_r)
           end if
       else if
     & (c .eq. BINARY_ARITHMETIC_OP .or. c .eq. BINARY_RELATIONAL_OP) then
           if (aorv(esp) .eq. ADDRESS) then
               call emit1 (_val)
               aorv(esp) = VALUE
           end if
           if (aorv(esp-1) .eq. ADDRESS) then
               call emit1 (_val2)
               aorv(esp-1) = VALUE
           end if
           if (type(esp) .eq. REALTYPE .or. type(esp-1) .eq. REALTYPE) then
               if (type(esp) .eq. INTTYPE) call emit1 (_flt)
               if (type(esp-1) .eq. INTTYPE) call emit1 (_flt2)
               if (type(esp) .eq. LOGTYPE .or. type(esp-1) .eq. LOGTYPE) then
                   call perror ('type conversion error'//NULL)
               end if
               if (t .eq. $add)   call emit1 (_add_r)
               if (t .eq. $sub)   call emit1 (_sub_r)
               if (t .eq. $mult)  call emit1 (_mult_r)
               if (t .eq. $div)   call emit1 (_div_r)
               if (t .eq. $pwr)   call emit1 (_pwr_r)
```

```
      if (t .eq. $eq)    call emit1 (_eq_r)
      if (t .eq. $ne)    call emit1 (_ne_r)
      if (t .eq. $gt)    call emit1 (_gt_r)
      if (t .eq. $ge)    call emit1 (_ge_r)
      if (t .eq. $lt)    call emit1 (_lt_r)
      if (t .eq. $le)    call emit1 (_le_r)
      esp = esp - 1
      if (c .eq. BINARY_ARITHMETIC_OP) then
         type(esp) = REALTYPE
      else
         type(esp) = LOGTYPE
      end if
   else if (type(esp).eq.INTTYPE .and. type(esp-1).eq.INTTYPE) then
      if (t .eq. $add)   call emit1 (_add_i)
      if (t .eq. $sub)   call emit1 (_sub_i)
      if (t .eq. $mult)  call emit1 (_mult_i)
      if (t .eq. $div)   call emit1 (_div_i)
      if (t .eq. $pwr)   call emit1 (_pwr_i)
      if (t .eq. $eq)    call emit1 (_eq_i)
      if (t .eq. $ne)    call emit1 (_ne_i)
      if (t .eq. $gt)    call emit1 (_gt_i)
      if (t .eq. $ge)    call emit1 (_ge_i)
      if (t .eq. $lt)    call emit1 (_lt_i)
      if (t .eq. $le)    call emit1 (_le_i)
      esp = esp - 1
      if (c .eq. BINARY_ARITHMETIC_OP) then
         type(esp) = INTTYPE
      else
         type(esp) = LOGTYPE
      end if
   else
      call perror ('operator not allowed on operand data type'//NULL)
   end if
else if (c .eq. UNARY_LOGICAL_OP) then
   if (aorv(esp) .eq. ADDRESS) then
      call emit1 (_val)
      aorv(esp) = VALUE
   end if
   if (type(esp) .eq. LOGTYPE) then
      call emit1 (_not)
   else
      call perror ('logical operand type required'//NULL)
   end if
else if (c .eq. BINARY_LOGICAL_OP) then
   if (aorv(esp) .eq. ADDRESS) then
      call emit1 (_val)
      aorv(esp) = VALUE
   end if
   if (aorv(esp-1) .eq. ADDRESS) then
      call emit1 (_val2)
      aorv(esp-1) = VALUE
   end if
   if (type(esp) .eq. LOGTYPE .and. type(esp-1) .eq. LOGTYPE) then
```

```
            if (t .eq. $and) call emit1 (_and)
            if (t .eq. $or) call emit1 (_or)
            esp = esp - 1
      else
            call perror ('logical operand types required'//NULL)
      end if
else if (c .eq. ASSIGN_OP) then
      if (aorv(esp-1) .ne. ADDRESS) then
            call perror ('object of assign must be an address'//NULL)
      end if
      if (type(esp-1) .eq. STRTYPE) then
            if (type(esp) .eq. STRTYPE) then
                  call emit1 (_asns)
            else
                  call perror ('string assignment type mismatch'//NULL)
            end if
            esp = esp - 1
      else
            if (aorv(esp) .eq. ADDRESS) then
                  call emit1 (_val)
                  aorv(esp) = VALUE
            end if
            if (type(esp-1) .eq. INTTYPE) then
                  if (type(esp) .eq. INTTYPE) then
                        call emit1 (_asnv)
                  else if (type(esp) .eq. REALTYPE) then
                        call emit1 (_flt)
                        call emit1 (_asnv)
                  else
                        call perror ('integer assignment type mismatch'//NULL)
                  end if
            else if (type(esp-1) .eq. REALTYPE) then
                  if (type(esp) .eq. INTTYPE) then
                        call emit1 (_flt)
                        call emit1 (_asnv)
                  else if (type(esp) .eq. REALTYPE) then
                        call emit1 (_asnv)
                  else
                        call perror ('real assignment type mismatch'//NULL)
                  end if
            else if (type(esp-1) .eq. LOGTYPE) then
                  if (type(esp) .eq. LOGTYPE) then
                        call emit1 (_asnv)
                  else
                        call perror ('logical assignment type mismatch'//NULL)
                  end if
            else
                  call perror ('compiler error on assign'//NULL)
            end if
            esp = esp - 1
            aorv(esp) = VALUE
      end if
end if
```

```
     return
     end
```

That concludes the parsing and code generation routines of spl, except for the parsing of declarations and of read and print statements that follow. In all, there are eight routines involved in parsing, but the three main ones—parse, stmtparse, and exprparse—really define the overall structure. The others, declist, operator, operand, readstmt and printstmt, are supporting routines to the main ones. declist processes declaration statements. It has a loop designed to process one scalar or array name declaration per iteration, until end of line is encountered.

```
! declist  -  parse declaration statements and define symbols
! <def> := id | id ( intnum )
! <declist> ::= <def> | <def> , <declist> eol

     subroutine declist (t)
     integer            t
     #include           global.def
     #include           spl.mac
     integer            lex, type, asize, atoi
     integer            attr (NATTR), dummyattr (NATTR)
     logical            symref
     character*(MAXSTR) id, token

     type = t
     if (type .eq. $int) then
        attr(IDTYPE) = INTTYPE
     else if (type .eq. $real) then
        attr(IDTYPE) = REALTYPE
     else if (type .eq. $log) then
        attr(IDTYPE) = LOGTYPE
     else if (type .eq. $char) then
        attr(IDTYPE) = STRTYPE
     else
        call perror ('unknown data type'//NULL)
     end if

     do while (t .ne. $eol)
        t = lex (t,token)
        if (t .ne. $id) then
           call perror ('declaration error: id expected'//NULL)
        else
           id = token
           if (symref(id,dummyattr)) then
              call perror ('multiple name declaration'//NULL)
           end if
           if (lex(t,token) .eq. $lparen) then    !array declaration
              if (lex(t,token) .eq. $intnum) then
                 asize = atoi(token)
```

```
            if (lex(t,token) .eq. $rparen) then
                t = lex (t,token)
                if (t .ne. $comma .and. t .ne. $eol) then
                    call perror ('comma or end of line expected'//NULL)
                end if
            else
                call perror ('missing parentheses'//NULL)
            end if
        else
            call perror ('integer constant expected'//NULL)
        end if
        if (type .eq. $char) then
            attr(IDCLASS) = STRING_ID
            attr(IDSIZE) = asize + 1
        else
            attr(IDCLASS) = ARRAY_ID
            attr(IDSIZE) = asize
        end if
    else if (t .eq. $comma .or. t .eq. $eol) then !scalar declaration
        if (type .eq. $char) then
            attr(IDCLASS) = STRING_ID
            attr(IDSIZE) = 2
        else
            attr(IDCLASS) = IDENTIFIER
            attr(IDSIZE) = 1
        end if
    end if
    call symdef (id, attr)                    ! install in table
    end if
end do

return
end
```

8.8   spl I/O Statements

The readstmt and printstmt subroutines process spl I/O statements. Both
expect a list of items separated by commas following the keyword, and both are
called by stmtparse after the keyword has already been scanned. In the case
of read statements, each item in the list must resolve to an address to transfer
data into. For print statements each item must resolve to a single value to be
written to the output.

```
! readstmt   -  generate code for read statements

        subroutine readstmt (t)
        integer         t
        #include        global.def
        #include        spl.mac
```

```
#include          vm.mac
integer           lex, av, exprtype
logical           done, exprparse
character*(MAXSTR) token

done = .false.
do while (.not. done)
    t = lex (t,token)
    if (exprparse (t, token, av, exprtype)) then
        if (av .eq. ADDRESS) then
            if (exprtype .eq. INTTYPE) call emit1 (_read_i)
            if (exprtype .eq. REALTYPE) call emit1 (_read_r)
            if (exprtype .eq. LOGTYPE) call emit1 (_read_l)
            if (exprtype .eq. STRTYPE) call emit1 (_read_s)
        else
            call perror ('read must refer to an address'//NULL)
        end if
        if (t .ne. $comma .and. t .ne. $eol) then
            call perror ('missing comma in read statement'//NULL)
            do while (t .ne. $eol)
                t = lex(t,token)
            end do
            done = .true.
        else
            if (t .eq. $eol) done = .true.
        end if
    else
        call perror ('invalid expression in read statement'//NULL)
        do while (t .ne. $eol)
            t = lex(t,token)
        end do
        done = .true.
    end if
end do

return
end
```

readstmt and printstmt are identical routines except that readstmt requires
av=ADDRESS and printstmt requires av=VALUE.

```
! printstmt  -  generate code for print statements

        subroutine printstmt (t)
        integer           t
        #include          global.def
        #include          spl.mac
        #include          vm.mac
        integer           lex, av, exprtype
        logical           done, exprparse
        character*(MAXSTR) token
```

```
        done = .false.
        do while (.not. done)
            t = lex(t,token)
            if (exprparse (t, token, av, exprtype)) then
                if (exprtype .eq. STRTYPE) then
                    call emit1 (_print_s)
                else
                    if (av .eq. ADDRESS) call emit1 (_val)
                    if (exprtype .eq. INTTYPE) call emit1 (_print_i)
                    if (exprtype .eq. REALTYPE) call emit1 (_print_r)
                    if (exprtype .eq. LOGTYPE) call emit1 (_print_l)
                end if
                if (t .ne. $comma .and. t .ne. $eol) then
                    call perror ('missing comma in print statement'//NULL)
                    do while (t .ne. $eol)
                        t = lex(t,token)
                    end do
                    done = .true.
                else
                    if (t .eq. $eol) done = .true.
                end if
            else
                call perror ('invalid expression in print statement'//NULL)
                do while (t .ne. $eol)
                    t = lex(t,token)
                end do
                done = .true.
            end if
        end do

        return
        end
```

8.9   Intrinsic Functions

The final missing piece of spl is the implementation of intrinsic functions. spl
has a healthy selection of them, all of which are set up in the initfunc routine.
There are two things needed to initialize the functions: they must be stored in
the symbol table so they can be referenced by name, with their start addresses
stored as attr(IDLOC), and their code must be loaded into memory.

```
    ! initfunc - initialize intrinsic functions

        subroutine initfunc ()
#include  global.def
#include  spl.mac
#include  vm.mac
#include  vstate.cmn
        integer   attr(NATTR)
```

```
! start address for intrinsic function code (MEMSIZE-127)
      #define   START   65408

! define symbol table entries
      attr(IDCLASS) = FUNCTION_ID

! real functions
      attr(IDTYPE) = REALTYPE
      attr(IDSIZE) = 1

      attr(IDORG) = START+0
      call symdef ('sin'//NULL, attr)
      attr(IDORG) = START+3
      call symdef ('cos'//NULL, attr)
      attr(IDORG) = START+6
      call symdef ('tan'//NULL, attr)
      attr(IDORG) = START+9
      call symdef ('arcsin'//NULL, attr)
      attr(IDORG) = START+12
      call symdef ('arccos'//NULL, attr)
      attr(IDORG) = START+15
      call symdef ('arctan'//NULL, attr)
      attr(IDORG) = START+18
      call symdef ('exp'//NULL, attr)
      attr(IDORG) = START+21
      call symdef ('ln'//NULL, attr)
      attr(IDORG) = START+24
      call symdef ('abs'//NULL, attr)
      attr(IDORG) = START+27
      call symdef ('float'//NULL, attr)

! integer functions
      attr(IDTYPE) = INTTYPE

      attr(IDORG) = START+30
      call symdef ('int'//NULL, attr)
      attr(IDORG) = START+33
      call symdef ('iabs'//NULL, attr)
      attr(IDORG) = START+36
      call symdef ('index'//NULL, attr)
      attr(IDORG) = START+38
      call symdef ('ord'//NULL, attr)
      attr(IDORG) = START+72
      call symdef ('len'//NULL, attr)

! logical functions
      attr(IDTYPE) = LOGTYPE

      attr(IDORG) = START+40
      call symdef ('eqs'//NULL, attr)
      attr(IDORG) = START+42
      call symdef ('readln'//NULL, attr)
```

```
! string functions
      attr(IDTYPE) = STRTYPE
      attr(IDSIZE) = 2

      attr(IDORG) = START+44
      call symdef ('chr'//NULL, attr)

      attr(IDSIZE) = 256

      attr(IDORG) = START+51
      call symdef ('cat'//NULL, attr)
      attr(IDORG) = START+60
      call symdef ('substr'//NULL, attr)

! initialize code for functions
! sin
      mem(START+0) = _val
      mem(START+1) = _sin
      mem(START+2) = _rtn
! cos
      mem(START+3) = _val
      mem(START+4) = _cos
      mem(START+5) = _rtn
! tan
      mem(START+6) = _val
      mem(START+7) = _tan
      mem(START+8) = _rtn
! arcsin
      mem(START+9) = _val
      mem(START+10) = _asin
      mem(START+11) = _rtn
! arccos
      mem(START+12) = _val
      mem(START+13) = _acos
      mem(START+14) = _rtn
! arctan
      mem(START+15) = _val
      mem(START+16) = _atan
      mem(START+17) = _rtn
! exp
      mem(START+18) = _val
      mem(START+19) = _exp
      mem(START+20) = _rtn
! ln
      mem(START+21) = _val
      mem(START+22) = _log
      mem(START+23) = _rtn
! abs
      mem(START+24) = _val
      mem(START+25) = _abs_r
      mem(START+26) = _rtn
! float
```

```
        mem(START+27) = _val
        mem(START+28) = _flt
        mem(START+29) = _rtn
! int
        mem(START+30) = _val
        mem(START+31) = _int
        mem(START+32) = _rtn
! iabs
        mem(START+33) = _val
        mem(START+34) = _abs_i
        mem(START+35) = _rtn
! index
        mem(START+36) = _indx
        mem(START+37) = _rtn
! ord
        mem(START+38) = _ord
        mem(START+39) = _rtn
! eqs
        mem(START+40) = _eqs
        mem(START+41) = _rtn
! readln
        mem(START+42) = _readln
        mem(START+43) = _rtn
! chr
        mem(START+44) = _pushf
        mem(START+45) = -4        !loc of result address
        mem(START+46) = _pushf
        mem(START+47) = 1
        mem(START+48) = _val
        mem(START+49) = _chr
        mem(START+50) = _rtns
! cat
        mem(START+51) = _pushf
        mem(START+52) = -4        !loc of result address
        mem(START+53) = _pushf
        mem(START+54) = 1         !1st arg
        mem(START+55) = _asns
        mem(START+56) = _pushf
        mem(START+57) = 2         !2nd arg
        mem(START+58) = _cat
        mem(START+59) = _rtns
! substr
        mem(START+60) = _pushf
        mem(START+61) = -4
        mem(START+62) = _pushf
        mem(START+63) = 1
        mem(START+64) = _pushf
        mem(START+65) = 2
        mem(START+66) = _pushf
        mem(START+67) = 3
        mem(START+68) = _val
        mem(START+69) = _val2
        mem(START+70) = _substr
```

```
      mem(START+71) = _rtns
! len
      mem(START+72) = _len
      mem(START+73) = _rtn

      return
      end
```

The code for the intrinsics is so straightforward that it is easily assembled by hand since there is an underlying virtual machine instruction for every intrinsic function.

8.10   Customizing spl

spl is not the best or most efficient of compilers, but it is methodically organized, easy to understand, and therefore easy to modify. Certain types of application programs can be easily adapted to spl with hardly any modifications to the compiler. This adaptability is the main reason spl is useful and the main reason for writing a compiler in Fortran in the first place.

A standard garden-variety Fortran application program can be adapted to use spl (or spl can be adapted to use the application program, depending on how you look at it) by doing just a few things. A characteristic of most Fortran programs is that they usually have a common block to store all of the user inputs, which are read from an input data file as one of the first actions of the program (if this isn't the case, some programs can at least be modified without too much fuss to make it so). Such a program can be converted into a powerful interpreter based on spl by the following actions:

- Equivalence the start of the "user inputs" common block to the start of memory in vstate.cmn. The effect of doing so is to make all of the user input variables addressable in the virtual machine memory. In addition, the variable names as previously used in the application program can be referenced in analysis routines as if nothing happened.

- Use hashgen to generate a hash table for names of user input variables, along with addresses, data types and array dimensions. The address to be supplied for each variable is the offset from the start of the common block in Fortran storage units (usually 4 bytes each, the size of integers and reals).

- Use the output from hashgen to make a block data routine that initializes the spl symbol table. This predeclares all of the user inputs as variables and allows user inputs to be set using spl assignment statements (with the capability of using an expression rather than a constant as the right hand side). syminit should be modified to set the global symbol table pointers to just beyond the data initialized by hashgen so that the user can still declare his own variables.

- Add a keyword that runs the application program by defining a token code in spl.mac, adding a regular expression definition in spl.lex, and adding code to detect the keyword in stmtparse. This can be something as simple as "go," or anything else appropriate to the problem.

- Add a virtual machine instruction to invoke the program, which is generated when the new keyword is encountered. To add a virtual machine instruction, simply define its numerical code in vm.mac, its opcode mnemonic in mnemonic.def, and a new target label in the computed goto in vexec. One virtual machine instruction is all that is needed to run a complete application program, even if it has a million lines of code.

- If default values for user inputs are needed, initialize them with a block data routine for vstate.cmn. As already pointed out, the variables can be initialized by name rather than as anonymous locations in mem.

- Recompile all of the spl routines and link them with the application program.

There are a few cautions that should be added to this list. One is that since a block data routine is never actually called, no references to it are ever made in the code and most linkers must be told to include them. On the VAX, the use of a block data program can be ensured by referencing it as external in the declarations of at least one executable routine. For example,

```
external   usersym_data
```

might be placed in syminit or some other routine so that the VAX linker will include the hash table block data without being told to do so in the link command.

Beware of the requirement for keywords occurring before the regular expression for identifiers in the lexgen input files; lexgen returns the first token specified in its input file when a token can match two different regular expressions, and identifiers have the same lexical form as keywords. If the user input has character variables, they must be in a separate common block in the application program even if the host compiler (such as VAX Fortran) doesn't require it because the memory architecture of spl's virtual machine conforms to the requirements of Fortran 77 and stores characters differently from noncharacter data.

The steps outlined are a minimal set of changes needed to map spl into an application-specific program, but other interesting possibilities exist. One obvious one that happens to be both easy and highly worthwhile is the addition of new intrinsic functions appropriate to the problem at hand. For example, an application program for analyzing infrared sensors might provide Planck's blackbody laws as intrinsic functions.

spl is a big program—it encompasses just about everything we have done so far. It is organized to use the file management system at the very beginning of this book and requires the use of the file I/O system. It uses several routines from our string-handling library and the hash table and hashgen for symbol table management. The preprocessor is used not only as a built-in feature of the spl lexical analyzer but also in all of the source code of the spl program itself. The preprocessor is the interface that allows lexgen input files to be treated like Fortran source files, with token codes specified in a common file. But for all its complexity, the development of spl was relatively painless because its components were developed independently and were written as reusable tools for program development, with clean interfaces and well-encapsulated data structures. The major components of spl—the lexical analyzer, symbol table, parser, and virtual machine—each have well-defined interfaces and hide their underpinnings from each other, yet are controlled together from a few common definition files.

spl is a different kind of tool from the others we have developed. The others have been self-contained subroutine structures for doing things like preprocessing or file I/O, in which all that is needed to use them is perhaps to call an initialization routine, or else the tools have been generators like hashgen and lexgen to automate development of new programs. In contrast, spl is not self-contained but rather is designed to be modified. Indeed, it is not even very useful in its plain vanilla form. It becomes much more useful when it is used as a platform for other programs, which is what makes it a tool. Given the power of an interpreter/compiler, many ordinary programs can become much more useful by turning the program into something more than just a program. A real language understanding allows a program to be used in ways the programmer never dreamed of, allowing users to apply their imagination and resourcefulness to solving a wider variety of problems.

Exercises

1. Write a grammar that describes Backus-Naur syntax.

2. Real machines have a more complicated instruction format than our machine has; they have fields for addressing modes for internal registers that perform arithmetic. In the PDP-11, for instance, frequently used instructions have 4 bit opcodes and a source field and destination field to indicate operand addresses or registers. Branch instructions have the offset from the current PC stored in the same machine word as the opcode. Less frequently used instructions have more opcode bits and perhaps one operand address field.

   (a) How could you design addressing modes for the virtual machine?

(b) Would a bit-encoded instruction format make the virtual machine more efficient?

3. Discuss the merits (and drawbacks) of incorporating a data type field into the virtual machine instruction format. For instance, the **add** instruction could have a field indicating real, integer, or logical mode, or it might even have separate codes for the top two elements on the stack and perform automatic type conversion. From your results in this and the previous problem, define an instruction format for your new machine.

4. The virtual machine allocates one integer storage unit (32 bits) for each instruction, even though 7 bits would be enough to identify every instruction. Discuss the merits of packed instructions in which each 4-byte entry in the program memory can contain up to four instructions. Indicate how you would modify **asm** and **vexec** to implement packed instructions.

5. Add new instructions **tron** and **troff** to provide a selective execution trace; that is, **tron** would cause the contents of the registers and the top of the stack to be printed on every instruction until the next **troff** instruction.

6. Add a **mon** instruction that allows interactive debugging, with the ability to examine and change registers or memory.

7. Add a symbolic traceback mechanism to the virtual machine, so that if an error is detected at run-time the symbolic name and pc of every active routine (every routine with an active stack frame) is printed.

8. Modify **spl** to support user-defined functions.

9. Write a routine to generate Fortran data statements from a section of assembled code. Add a -d command line option to **spl** to write a section of program memory as data statements; that is, the option -dff00:ffff would write the last 256 words of memory as data.

10. Implement multidimensional arrays in **spl**.

11. Design a syntax for and implement array assignment statements in **spl**, so that all the elements of an array can be assigned in just one statement.

12. Compilers for most programming languages produce special code to avoid evaluation of unnecessary parts of expressions involving and and or. Specifically, given the expression

```
(expr1 and expr2)
```

expr2 is evaluated only if expr1 is true, and in

```
(expr1 or expr2)
```

expr2 is evaluated only if expr1 is `false`. Implement this behavior in `spl`.

13. Identify all compile-time and run-time errors that `spl` could check for but doesn't. Which ones need fixing the most? Which ones are the easiest?

Further Reading

There are many good references for digging further into the subjects covered in this chapter. More substantial compilers for real programming languages can be found in source code form. A good example of this is the Small-C compiler, which was originally published by Ron Cain in a magazine article (*Dr. Dobb's Journal*, #45, May and September, 1980). The original articles contained a self-compiler for a subset of the C language and a run-time library written in assembly language for the CP/M operating system. The compiler was developed further by James Hendrix, who wrote *The Small-C Handbook* and ported the compiler to MS–DOS (but as far as we know he does not play electric guitar). Another example is *Pascal Implementation* by Pemberton and Daniels (Ellis Horwood, 1982), which contains a p-code compiler for a subset of the Pascal programming language and has a p-code machine similar in design to our virtual machine. It is written as a two-volume set, with one volume containing the source code for the compiler and p-code interpreter and the other a detailed set of implementation notes. Kernighan and Pike in *The UNIX Programming Environment* (Prentice-Hall, 1984) describe the development and refinement of a simple calculator language using UNIX compiler development and software maintenence tools, and *Compiler Construction with UNIX* by Schreiner and Friedman (Prentice-Hall, 1985) uses the same tools to construct yet another C compiler.

Pascal Implementation by Pemberton and Daniels describes a virtual machine for a Pascal compiler that is quite similar to the one presented here. A classic example of the idea is Knuth's MIX language, in Volume 1 of *The Art of Computer Programming*. One of the best ways to get ideas for the architecture of a virtual computer is to model the architecture after that of a real machine. *Structured Computer Organization* by Andrew Tanenbaum describes the architecture of computers at various levels, from digital logic through operating systems, and contains brief descriptions of several popular processors including the PDP-11. The use of virtual machines is common in other types of software, but information is often hard to come by because of its proprietary nature. A description of a novel instruction set, for Lotus 1-2-3 spreadsheets, is given in *File Formats for Popular PC Software* by Jeffrey Walden (Wiley, 1986).

A good source of ideas for writing good simulation languages in Fortran can be found in the documentation of the SPICE circuit analysis program. The documentation and the program itself can be obtained from the University of

California; the main book that describes the SPICE software is *SPICE2: A Program for Computer Circuit Simulation* by Ellis Cohen. For anyone seriously interested in compiler writing, several good advanced textbooks are available. *Compilers: Their Design and Construction using Pascal* by Robin Hunter (Wiley, 1985) contains a good discussion of grammars and particularly of LL(1) parsing, and Hopcroft and Ullman give a thorough formal mathematical treatment of languages and grammars in *Formal Languages and their Relation to Automata* (Addison-Wesley, 1969). Both *Compilers: Principles, Techniques and Tools* by Aho, Sethi and Ullman (Addison-Wesley, 1986) and *The Theory and Practice of Compiler Writing* by Tremblay and Sorenson (McGraw-Hill, 1985) are complete general references for all aspects of compiler writing.

CHAPTER 9

VAX System Tools

We have squeezed a lot of mileage from the I/O primitives of Chapter 3 and a few string manipulation routines. Many useful programs have been developed using only these few simple tools. We now return to the very beginning, in a sense, to develop some additional primitive routines. These new primitives are "system" primitives, since their primary function is as a standardized set of interface routines for the services provided by the operating system.

The getargs routine in chapter 2 is actually a system primitive; it calls upon the VMS Command Line Interpreter (CLI) routine cli$get_value to gain access to the command line that invoked the program. We have a selection of other routines to provide similar interfaces for other services of the operating system; these system primitives are the basic tools from which we will develop a command shell for the VMS system. The serious VMS programmer can study the routines in this chapter, comparing our code for calling each system service to the corresponding official VMS documentation, and thereby learn VMS system programming in general. Less ambitious readers can just use the interfaces provided as a toolbox for performing VMS operations conveniently.

9.1 System Programming

VMS is a multitasking, time-sharing, virtual memory operating system. *Multitasking* means that a user can have more than one *process* active simultaneously. A process is a logically distinct entity that runs more or less independently of all the other processes in the system. A *time-sharing* system is necessarily a multitasking system, and each user logged in has a separate *job* consisting of the "parent" process and all of its "child" subprocesses.

Virtual memory means that the machine remaps virtual memory addresses into physical addresses to simulate a machine with much more memory than is actually present. The "virtual address space" of the VAX is 4 gigabytes, but typical installations have only 8–32 megabytes of physical RAM memory. When the virtual demand for memory is greater than the physical supply, the overflow is stored in a disk file called the *paging file*. Data is swapped in and out of memory in 512-byte chunks called *pages*. When a program references a virtual memory address that has been shuffled off to the disk, it is called a *page fault*; the referenced page must be copied back into memory in place of some other page that hasn't been referenced for a while. Virtual memory works because of the property exhibited by almost all computer programs that memory addresses used tend to be close together most of the time, a property known as *locality of reference*.

VMS is a pleasant environment for Fortran programming because from a program's point of view, the computer isn't shared with anybody and has essentially limitless memory. Fortran's static memory allocation makes it necessary to always declare arrays to be big enough to handle the largest expected data set, which is inefficient and poses a real problem for computers with limited memory like IBM-PCs. Virtual memory is a distinct advantage for Fortran programming because arrays can be huge without running out of virtual memory; the operating system automatically takes care of dynamic memory allocation. However, the memory really isn't limitless, even if it looks that way, and a failure to understand the basic mechanics of virtual memory can lead to serious inefficiencies. For example, assume a program has a huge multidimensional array

```
integer array (64, 128, 16)
```

that needs to be looped through to perform some operation (for purposes of illustration it will just be zeroed). This array is $64 \times 128 \times 16 \times 4$ or 524K bytes, not too big by virtual memory standards. If the loop is written in the form

```
do i = 1, 64
  do j = 1, 128
    do k = 1, 16
      array(i,j,k) = 0
```

```
      end do
    end do
  end do
```

then each successive element reference is separated by $64 \times 128 \times 4$ or 32768 addresses in memory since Fortran stores arrays with the first subscript varying fastest and the last varying slowest. Because of the large separation between addresses, a page fault is likely on every array reference (524K page faults). If the nested loops are rewritten as

```
  do k = 1, 16
    do j = 1, 128
      do i = 1, 64
        array(i,j,k) = 0
      end do
    end do
  end do
```

then the referenced elements are adjacent in memory, and there should be no more page faults than the number of pages occupied by the array (1024 pages). Since a virtual page must be loaded from disk when a page fault occurs and disk drives are comparatively slow, the second form of the loop can be expected to execute a thousand times faster than the first form. The morale of this story is that to do good programming on a VAX you need to know something about the operating system, even if you are not writing system programs.

VAX system routines are system-supplied subprograms that can be called from VAX MACRO (the VAX assembly language) or from high-level languages. The system routines are divided into several groups:

CLI	Command language interpreter (DCL interface)
DCX	Data compression
EDT	EDT editor interface
FDL	File definition language
LIB	VAX run-time library
LBR	Librarian interface
MTH	Math
SMG	Screen management
SOR	Sort and merge
STR	String manipulation
SYS	System services

The ones we find use for most often are the CLI, LIB, and SYS facilities, although some of the others are often useful. We have never found a burning need for DCX or FDL routines, and the MTH routines are unnecessary in a language like Fortran.

Once the mechanics of calling system routines are understood, it is tempting to make heavy use of the system services in programs since they provide such sophisticated capabilities. However, the previous chapters of this book hopefully have shown that it is possible to write capable software on your own, and that the do-it-yourself approach has distinct advantages.

We shouldn't get too carried away with writing programs that depend on system-supplied routines since each one is a primitive, and it is a good practice to keep the number of primitives to a bare minimum for programs to have any hope of portability. Several of the facilities provide services that are not inherently system-dependent. For instance, SMG routines provide extensive screen management capabilities, but there is no fundamental reason why a system-supplied routine must be used for screen management; if you write your own screen management routines, you can avoid tying your program forever to a specific environment. A program that calls system routines willy-nilly throughout the code is a program that will never run anywhere except on a VAX.

On the other hand, having a few such routines can open a lot of new possibilities, and system routines can often be used without seriously limiting portability. For example, the VMS sorting facility provides fast and reliable subroutines for all types of sorting applications, and writing your own sorting routines would be a time-consuming chore. If you write your programs to call the VMS sorting routines directly, then the code will have to be modified everywhere when the day comes that you must get it running on an IBM. If, however, you write a special routine to do sorting that simply calls the VMS sort facility, then only that routine will need to be changed. Good sorting routines have been published, and the VMS call can be replaced at a later date if the interface is properly designed. System services can be used to postpone work.

The trick is to be able to recognize when a program is inherently system dependent and when it isn't, and to write the code accordingly. If it is really necessary to write special library management routines, then using LBR routines is the only practical choice. Both kinds of software are in this chapter.

VAX/VMS has a well-defined calling standard that specifies how the run-time stack is structured in a subroutine call, and almost all compilers written for VAX/VMS adhere to the standard, making it possible to mix code written in different languages without any special assembly language interface routines. However, even with such a well-defined standard there are still differences in the assumptions about how individual arguments are passed to a function or subroutine. For instance, some languages expect the value of an argument to be passed on the stack, while others expect its address. System routines have specific requirements for the way arguments are passed, and the requirements vary from one service to the next. By default, Fortran passes all variables by reference (meaning that the address of the variable is passed and used indirectly in the invoked routine) except for character strings, which are passed by descriptor. A descriptor is a pair of numbers indicating the start address and length of a string. VAX Fortran has built-in functions that make it possible to pass arguments by any one of the three methods:

Function Passing Mechanism
%ref   by reference
%val   by value
%descr   by descriptor

These functions are allowed only in procedure call argument lists. An additional function %loc produces the longword (4-byte) address of its argument. Its function is thus identical to %ref, except that %loc is not allowed in procedure calls and %ref is not allowed anywhere except in procedure calls. These routines can be used to call system routines as well as routines written in other high-level languages with different argument passing conventions. For instance, if a procedure abc is written in some language that wants integers to be passed by value and strings to be passed by reference, it can be called from Fortran with a statement like

```
call abc (%val(i), %ref(string))
```

Most of the system routines expect information to be passed via an information block containing function codes, character buffer lengths and addresses, and so on. The structure statement in VAX Fortran defines a named data entity consisting of multiple data items and is especially well-suited to setting up the information blocks required for calling system routines.

```
structure /itemlist/
  union
    map
      integer*2 buflen
      integer*2 itemcode
      integer*4 bufaddr
      integer*4 rtnlen_addr
    end map
    map
      integer*4 end_list
    end map
  end union
end structure
```

is an example of the structure construct that declares a typical VMS system service data structure. The components of a structure are stored consecutively in memory, and the union statement does a sort of equivalence on each map within it. In this structure each record has a length of 12 bytes; if maps are not all the same length, the longest is the record length and unused bytes in shorter maps are ignored. Structures can also be nested, and previously defined structures can be used as components of new structure declarations.

A structure declaration does not allocate any storage, but merely defines a derived type. Storage is allocated by the record statement:

```
record /itemlist/ namelist (10)
```

declares an array of 10 objects with the itemlist derived type. Records can be assigned all at once to another record of the same type:

```
namelist(2) = namelist(1)
```

or the components of a record can be referenced by the record name and structure
component name:

```
namelist(1).itemcode = LNM$_STRING
namelist(1).buflen   = index(name,NULL)-1
namelist(1).bufaddr  = %loc(name)
namelist(2).end_list = 0
```

Up to this point, we have avoided use of the VAX Fortran structure derived
data type, even in places where it would be a real improvement, to preserve
portability. It isn't strictly necessary since the following produces the same arrangement in memory:

```
integer*2 buflen, itemcode
integer*4 bufaddr, rtnlen_addr, end_list
common /itemlist/ buflen, itemcode, bufaddr, rtnlen_addr, end_list
```

However, these routines are VAX primitives and are not expected to be portable,
and the record construct is easier to understand.

As an example of what is usually involved in making a system call, the following is a routine that enables the VAX EDT editor to be called from within a
Fortran program:

```
! edt  -  invoke edt to edit file

      subroutine    edt (infile)
      character*(*) infile
      include       'global.def'
      include       '($ssdef)'
      integer*4     edt$fileio, edt$workio, edt$xlate, edt$edit
      external      edt$fileio, edt$workio, edt$xlate, edt$edit
      integer       ok, fio(2), wio(2), xlt(2)

! define locations of utility routines to be used by edt$edit
      fio(1) = %loc(edt$fileio) !edt file I/O
      fio(2) = 0
      wio(1) = %loc(edt$workio) !edt work I/O
      wio(2) = 0
      xlt(1) = %loc(edt$xlate)  !target of XLATE command
      xlt(2) = 0

! call edt
      ok =  edt$edit (infile(1:index(infile,NULL)-1),
     &                ,
     &                'SYS$LOGIN:EDTINI.EDT',
     &                ,
     &                0,
     &                %ref(fio),%ref(wio),%ref(xlt))

      if (.not. ok) call lib$signal (%val (ok))
```

```
return
end
```

The system documentation for calling EDT says that the workspace addresses must be supplied as quadwords (8 bytes). The VAX instruction set directly supports data types with any of the following sizes:

Data Type	Size
Byte	8 bits
Word	2 bytes
Longword	4 bytes
Quadword	8 bytes

VAX Fortran can access bytes, words and longwords with the data types byte, integer*2, and integer*4, respectively. There is no integer*8 Fortran data type, so an integer array of length 2 is used to simulate it.

The statement

```
include '($ssdef)'
```

causes inclusion of a module from a special library supplied with the Fortran compiler called forsysdef.tlb; the library is located in the system-defined directory sys$library. The library contains over 100 include modules for defining interface parameters to the various system facilities. The somewhat verbose command

```
$ lib/extract=($ssdef)/output=ss.def sys$library:forsysdef.tlb
```

extracts the module $ssdef from the library and puts it into the file ss.def.

All of the VAX system routines are integer functions, and the return code on an unsuccessful call gives specific information about the cause of failure. The routine lib$signal stops the program with a traceback if an error occurs.

With all this happening, in most cases isolation of system calls in special routines of their own is advisable even if portability isn't a concern, just to keep the real program uncluttered.

Logical Names

Access to the system logical name facility is a useful capability for VMS programming. Logical names are often used when developing programs intended to be ported to many different VAX systems or to be run from any specified location on the system. They are important for system programmers because they provide a high degree of flexibility in managing the VMS file system. A brief outline of how logical names are used in VMS will help to show how.

A logical name is a symbolic representation of some object in the system. If this sounds similar to the usual definition of a variable or symbol, it's because they are essentially the same beasts. Logical name operations are performed by a set of operating system kernel routines loosely grouped into a facility called *logical name services*. Logical names are organized into related groups referred to as *tables*, which may be created and maintained via routines from the logical name facility. A process under VMS has four standard logical name tables associated with it: the *process, job, group*, and *system* tables. Each table provides VMS an area for storing information pertinent to a process or a set of related processes.

The process table contains information regarding the current process, such as its home directory sys$login and its standard input, output, and error devices sys$input, sys$output, and sys$error. This table is used by VMS to store process-specific information. An example is the logical name TT, which translates to the name of the primary physical device associated with the process (the terminal in most cases). The process table may be accessed only by the owning process and the operating system.

The job table is common to all processes belonging to the same job; its use is to provide a communication medium between processes associated with a single job. A new VMS job is initiated with the creation of a new independent process on the system (such as someone logging in). Every dependent process descended from this root process is classified as part of the same job, and access is provided to the common job logical name table. In all other respects the job table operates in the same manner as the process table.

The group table is common to all processes that are members of the same UIC (user identification code) group. The UIC identifies the process owner to the operating system for purposes such as protection and resource accounting. The UIC is an ordered pair of octal numbers, the first number denoting the group association and the second the specific group member. The UIC is usually displayed in the format [group,member], where group and member are octal constants. Access to the group table is limited to read-only for processes that do not possess the grpnam privilege.

The system table is accessible for reading by all processes on the system. The system table is the main method used by the system for communicating information to all users. The system table may be altered only by processes which possess the sysnam privilege.

These logical name tables are the standard ones provided by the operating system, and are the only ones needed in day-to-day use of VMS. However, it is possible to define additional logical name tables. The name of a logical name table is itself a logical name resident in a table of (you guessed it) logical name table names. The table name is often specified as a search list indicating a sequence of logical name tables to be searched. It's all quite logical, isn't it?

Logical name search lists are specified by means of an attribute called the *equivalence index*. A logical name may be defined with a number of parallel translations, each assuming an equivalence index one larger than that of the previous translation in the search list. These parallel translations may themselves be logical names, so that translations can be controlled by the specification of alternate equivalence indices. A logical name can have numerous translations, each with a different combination of table name, equivalence index, and access mode.

There are four access modes for which translations may be requested: *kernel*, *executive*, *supervisor*, and *user*. Kernel mode is rarely used directly; its chief use is by the kernel routines responsible for logical name table management. Accessing tables in kernel mode requires the process to possess the privilege chgkrnl. Most executive mode logical name definitions are made during process initiation and remain unchanged for the duration of the process. The executive mode definitions are copied to the supervisor mode definitions during process creation and when the supervisor mode definition of an non-record-oriented process-permanent file (usually a terminal or mailbox device) is deassigned. The DCL command interpreter, for example, reads its input from the executive mode definition of sys$command, which is usually the initial sys$input of the process. The supervisor mode access level is most commonly used and is the default access mode for the DCL commands assign, define, deassign and show logical. Supervisor level is used by the DCL command interpreter when translating logical names encountered while parsing user commands. The last access mode is the user mode. User mode definitions are deleted during the next image rundown performed by the process; put another way, user mode definitions exist only until completion of the next program executed by the process.

DCL defaults to supervisor mode access and the lowest equivalence index. The table to be searched for the translation is usually specified as the logical name lnm$filedev; this logical name is a table search path that translates to an ordered sequence of logical name table names, each of which is to be searched for the logical name with the specified access mode. The search ends when either a valid translation is found or all tables in the search list have been checked. The default search path assigned to lnm$filedev causes the search to occur in the process, job, group, and system logical name tables in order. A set of translation attributes is returned with a translation; when the translation attribute terminal is returned, it indicates that no further translation of the name is available.

To put it in a nutshell, VAX logical name translation is downright complicated. Now for the good news: although we need to know quite a bit to call VAX logical name services, we can make simple assumptions that make logical names easy to understand and use in Fortran programs. The three operations most commonly performed on logical names are definition, translation, and deletion; the VMS system services that provide these functions are the basis of three system primitives. These routines have simple interfaces because of simplifying assumptions about how they will be used, and are thus easier to use than the underlying system services, albeit less general as well.

For most purposes it suffices to define logical names using supervisor access mode and the process logical name table. set_logical defines a logical name in the process logical name table at the next highest equivalence index. The routine calls upon the VMS $setlnm system service to perform the actual installation of the name and its equivalence string into the process table. Using the process logical name table assures that any names defined by this routine will override any other preexisting definitions since the process table is searched first on lookups.

```
! set_logical - set VAX logical name

        subroutine    set_logical (logname, trans)
        character*(*) logname, trans
        include       '($lnmdef)'
        include       'global.def'
        integer       status, sys$crelnm

        structure /itemlist/
         union
           map
             integer*2 buflen
             integer*2 itemcode
             integer*4 buf_addr
             integer*4 rtnlen_addr
           end map
           map
             integer*4 end_list
           end map
         end union
        end structure

        record /itemlist/ namelist(2)

        namelist(1).itemcode    = LNM$_STRING
        namelist(1).buflen      = index (trans, NULL) - 1
        namelist(1).buf_addr    = %loc (trans)
        namelist(1).rtnlen_addr = 0
        namelist(2).end_list    = 0

        status = sys$crelnm (,'LNM$FILE_DEV',
     &                       logname(1:index (logname, NULL) - 1),,
     &                       namelist)

        if (.not. status) call lib$signal (%val (status))

        return
        end
```

Likewise, for most applications to look up a name it is sufficient to search only the standard VMS tables and to iteratively translate names to the lowest equivalence index available. get_logical returns the translation of a logical name, returning the lowest equivalence from the first table in which it is found. The routine is implemented as a logical function that returns the search status as its value; a null string is returned for the translation in an unsuccessful search.

```
! get_logical  -  translate VAX logical name to maximum equivalence index

      logical function get_logical (logname, trans)
      character*(*) logname, trans
      include       '($lnmdef)'            !logical name attribute codes
      include       '($syssrvnam)'         !system service names
      include       '($ssdef)'             !system service status codes
      include       'global.def'           !symbolic constants
      integer       status, attr, eq_ind, ret_len, ret_attr
      logical       found_trans, done

      structure /itemlist/
       union
        map
         integer*2 buflen
         integer*2 itemcode
         integer*4 bufaddr
         integer*4 rtnlen_addr
        end map
        map
         integer*4 end_list
        end map
       end union
      end structure

      record /itemlist/ translist(4)       !sys$trnlnm item list

      translist(1).itemcode    = LNM$_INDEX
      translist(1).buflen      = 4
      translist(1).bufaddr     = %loc (eq_ind)
      translist(1).rtnlen_addr = 0
      translist(2).itemcode    = LNM$_STRING
      translist(2).buflen      = len  (trans)
      translist(2).bufaddr     = %loc (trans)
      translist(2).rtnlen_addr = %loc (ret_len)
      translist(3).itemcode    = LNM$_ATTRIBUTES
      translist(3).buflen      = 4
      translist(3).bufaddr     = %loc (ret_attr)
      translist(3).rtnlen_addr = 0
      translist(4).end_list    = 0

      attr     = LNM$M_CASE_BLIND           !ignore case of logname
      ret_len  = index (logname, NULL) - 1  !length of logname
      eq_ind   = 0                          !initialize equivalence index
      trans = logname(1:ret_len)            !initialize work buffer

      done  = .false.
      found_trans = .false.
      get_logical = .false.

      do while (.not. done)
         status = sys$trnlnm (attr,
     &                        'LNM$FILE_DEV',
```

```
&                          trans(1:ret_len),,
&                          translist)
   if (status .eq. SS$_NOLOGNAM) then
      done = .true.
   else if (iand (ret_attr, LNM$M_EXISTS) .ne. 0) then
      found_trans = .true.
      if (iand (ret_attr, LNM$M_TERMINAL) .ne. 0) done = .true.
   end if
end do

get_logical = found_trans
trans     = trans(1:ret_len)//NULL
if (trans(1:2) .eq. ESC//NULL) trans = trans(5:)

return
end
```

get_logical specifies the search path lnm$filedev as the table name to cause all of the standard VMS name tables to be searched, with the process table first.

The final routine in this set is del_logical, which deletes logical name definitions from the process logical name table. del_logical provides a means for removing definitions made via set_logical.

```
! del_logical - delete VAX logical name (largest equivalence index)

   subroutine    del_logical (logname)
   character*(*) logname
   include       'global.def'
   integer       status, sys$dellnm

   status = sys$dellnm ('LNM$PROCESS', logname(1:index(logname,NULL)-1),)

   if (.not. status) call lib$signal (%val (status))

   return
   end
```

Command Interpreter Symbols

Another useful set of system primitives provides access to the DCL command interpreter's global symbol table. The operations performed on symbols are the same as those for logical names, a fact reflected by similar names for the routines. Symbols definitions are stored in a table local to the copy of the DCL command interpreter for the process; information in this table is available only to the current process. Logical names can be stored in tables that are defined on a system-wide basis, hence many processes may share a single logical name table (assuming the table name is known and the required privileges are possessed).

Command interpreter symbols come in two flavors: local and global. Local symbols are known only by the current DCL command level. In other words, if a local symbol is defined in a command procedure, it is not defined in other command procedures. Global symbols, in contrast, remain defined at all levels after their definition; a global symbol assignment in a command procedure remains in effect after control is returned to the terminal. Local symbol assignments are made with the operator :=, while global assignments use :==.

The command interpreter substitutes symbols with their definition during the parsing of the command line, much like a macro expansion. We often use symbols to provide short command synonyms for long command strings. We define many symbols in our login procedures; a few examples are

```
$ ssy    :== show symbol/global
$ snoop  :== dir/owner/prot/size
$ pound  :== $toolscmd:pound.exe
```

The use of symbols as command synonyms can drastically reduce the amount of typing necessary to use DCL. Another major use for symbols is the definition of *foreign commands*, illustrated by the last example. A VMS foreign command is simply a symbol whose definition begins with a $ character. Foreign commands are interpreted by DCL as a request to execute the image indicated by the string following the $. The full path (disk, directory, and file name) for the image must be included in the command definition; a file type of .exe is assumed if not specified. The programs we have developed from our tools are all installed as foreign commands by our login procedures; this is a requirement for the getargs routine to work. getargs uses the command line interpreter facility routine cli$get_value to access the command line; cli$get_value is a "hook" into the current copy of the command processor and hence has access to the line that has just been processed. DCL makes a distinction between programs run as foriegn commands and those run with the DCL run command. A foreign command is invoked by the command processor directly, while "running" the program causes the DCL run routine to execute the program; in the latter case the command line that caused the program to be executed is not available.

set_symbol defines (or redefines) a global symbol. The definition is made via the VMS lib$set_symbol run-time library routine.

```
! set_symbol - set VAX global symbol value

        subroutine   set_symbol (symbol, value)
        character*(*) symbol, value
        include      'global.def'
        integer      global, status, lib$set_symbol

        global = 2

        status = lib$set_symbol (symbol(1:index(symbol,NULL)-1),
     &                           value(1:index(value,NULL)-1),
     &                           global)
```

```
if (.not. status) call lib$signal (%val (status))

return
end
```

The VAX run-time library is a common library used by compilers for high-level languages like Fortran, and its routines are thus easier to call from Fortran in general.

get_symbol returns the equivalence string (if found) from the global symbol table. As with get_logical, the routine is a logical function whose value is used to indicate the result of the search, and a null string is returned for unsuccessful searches.

```
! get_symbol - get VAX symbol value

        logical function get_symbol (symbol, value)
        character*(*)      symbol, value
        include           '($ssdef)'
        include           'global.def'
        integer            status, length, table, lib$get_symbol

        length = index (symbol, NULL) - 1

        status = lib$get_symbol (symbol(1:length), value, length, table)

        if (status .eq. SS$_NORMAL) then
           get_symbol = .true.
           value(length+1:length+1) = NULL
        else
           get_symbol = .false.
           value(1:1) = NULL
        end if

        return
        end
```

The del_symbol routine deletes definitions from the global symbol table:

```
! del_symbol - delete VAX global symbol

        subroutine     del_symbol (symbol)
        character*(*)  symbol
        include        'global.def'
        integer        status, table, lib$delete_symbol

        table = 2  !global symbol table
        status = lib$delete_symbol (symbol(1:index(symbol,NULL)-1), table)
        if (.not. status) call lib$signal (%val (status))

        return
        end
```

File and Directory Names

One of the major differences between VMS logical names and CLI symbols is that a logical name can be used directly to open a file, with the translation handled automatically by the system. However, there are some situations where it is desirable to explicitly handle the translation of a logical name to a file name, for instance to get the directory of the input file so that output can be written to the same place. A complete VMS file name looks like

```
vax1::dua1:[tools.source]fnexpand.for;1
```

The name of the computer itself is vax1, one among many such names accessible via DECNet; dua1 is a typical name for a disk drive. [tools.source] is a directory name, fnexpand a file name, .for is the file extension, and 1 is the file version number. All of these components are secretly present whenever a file name is used in VMS; behind the scenes the operating system fills in any information missing in a file specification with default values.

Performing the translation of a partial file name into a full file specification is not a simple problem. Consider these examples, all valid file specifications on VMS:

```
myfile.txt
[tools.source]fnexpand.for
myfile
userdir:infile
```

The problem becomes more complicated by the fact that myfile could be a logical name which translates to a disk, directory, and file name, or to a directory and file name, or to just a file name in the default directory. userdir must be a logical name for a directory, but it may or may not include a disk drive in its translation. Even without the complication of logical names, names can be supplied with or without the disk and directory, in which case the defaults should be provided.

The fnexpand function is a tool that takes a valid, possibly incomplete file name and expands it to its full specification. The bad news is that there are no SYS or LIB facility routines that do the job adequately, and the RMS sys$parse service must be used directly (oddly enough, this routine as well as the sys$setddir routine is documented in the RMS manual even though both have the SYS facility prefix). RMS routines seem to be written for use at the assembly language level and are more difficult to use from Fortran than are the system services.

The main reason for the difficulty of RMS is that it has complex record structures, and this complexity makes it necessary to do more preparatory work before calling an RMS routine. RMS has three commonly used data structures for accessing the VMS file system: *file attribute blocks (FAB)*, *name blocks (NAM)*, and *record attribute blocks (RAB)*. The record attribute block contains information of the structure of records in a file, but isn't necessary for file name expansion. We do need the other two, however, and fortunately the forsys-def library has include modules that declare the data structures for each.

```
! fnexpand  -  expand file name

    character*(*) function fnexpand (filespec,dev,dir,name,type,vers)
    character*(*) filespec, dev, dir, name, type, vers
    include      'global.def'
    include      '($fabdef)'     !file attribute block (FAB) definitions
    include      '($namdef)'     !NAM block definitions
    integer      sys$parse, status, i

    record /fabdef/ filefab      !FAB structure from $fabdef
    record /namdef/ filenam      !NAM block structure from $namdef

    filefab.FAB$B_BID = FAB$C_BID                !FAB block ID code
    filefab.FAB$B_BLN = FAB$C_BLN                !FAB block length
    filefab.FAB$L_FNA = %loc (filespec)          !file name buffer address
    filefab.FAB$B_FNS = index (filespec,NULL)-1  !file name buffer length
    filefab.FAB$W_IFI = 0                         !required (init ?)
    filefab.FAB$L_NAM = %loc (filenam)           !NAM block address

    filenam.NAM$B_BID = NAM$C_BID                !NAM block ID code
    filenam.NAM$B_BLN = NAM$C_BLN                !NAM block length
    filenam.NAM$L_ESA = %loc (fnexpand)          !equivalence buffer addr
    filenam.NAM$B_ESS = NAM$C_MAXRSS             !equivalence buffer length
    filenam.NAM$L_RSA = %loc (fnexpand)          !resultant buffer address
    filenam.NAM$B_RSS = NAM$C_MAXRSS             !resultant buffer length
    filenam.NAM$B_NOP = NAM$V_SYNCHK             !perform syntax check
    filenam.NAM$L_RLF = 0                         !related file buffer addr

    status = sys$parse (filefab)

    if (status) then
       fnexpand(filenam.NAM$B_ESL+1:filenam.NAM$B_ESL+1) = NULL
       i = filenam.NAM$L_DEV - %loc (fnexpand) + 1
       dev = fnexpand(i:i+filenam.NAM$B_DEV-1)//NULL
       i = filenam.NAM$L_DIR - %loc (fnexpand) + 1
       dir = fnexpand(i:i+filenam.NAM$B_DIR-1)//NULL
       i = filenam.NAM$L_NAME - %loc (fnexpand) + 1
       name = fnexpand(i:i+filenam.NAM$B_NAME-1)//NULL
       i = filenam.NAM$L_TYPE - %loc (fnexpand) + 1
       type = fnexpand(i:i+filenam.NAM$B_TYPE-1)//NULL
       i = filenam.NAM$L_VER - %loc (fnexpand) + 1
       vers = fnexpand(i:i+filenam.NAM$B_VER-1)//NULL
    else
       call fputstr (STDERR, 'fnexpand: invalid file specification'//EOL)
       fnexpand = NULL
       dev  = NULL
       dir  = NULL
       name = NULL
       type = NULL
```

```
        vers = NULL
    end if

    return
    end
```

sys$parse returns the address in memory for the start of a requested file specification component as well as the component length; the %loc routine is needed to get the start address of the input string itself, so that the offset of the component can be calculated. It is not really important to know much about RMS for this application, which is good because we don't. RMS is the realm of serious VAX hackers, system wizards, and computer nerds.

A primary application of fnexpand is to supply default file types to input files. For example, later in this chapter we will need to add the default extension .sh to input files for the shell if it is missing. The code fragment

```
if (fnexpand(filename, dev, dir, name, type, vers)) then
    if (type(2:2) .eq. NULL) then     !not supplied
        filename = cat(cat(cat(dev,dir), cat(name,'.SH'//NULL)), vers)
    end if
end if
```

would do the job.

To get the current default directory, fnexpand can be called with a file name containing no directory; RMS will fill the directory field in with the current default. We have another tool that does the same job with a more appropriate name, called getdir:

```
! getdir  -  get default directory specification

    character*(*) function getdir (dir)
    character*(*) dir
    include       'global.def'
    integer       status, sys$setddir
    integer*2     dirlen

    status = sys$setddir (%val(0), %ref(dirlen), dir)
    if (.not. status) call lib$signal (%val (status))
    dir(dirlen+1:dirlen+1) = NULL
    getdir = dir

    return
    end
```

The sys$setddir routine can be used to get the current default directory or to change it, depending on the arguments supplied in the call. The converse routine is also useful, and can't be accomplished with fnexpand.

```
! setdir  -  set default directory specification
```

```
subroutine setdir (dir)
character*(*)   dir
include         'global.def'
integer         status, sys$setddir

status = sys$setddir (dir(1:index(dir,NULL)-1),%val(0),%val(0))
if (.not. status) then
   call fputstr (STDERR, 'setdir: invalid directory'//EOL)
end if

return
end
```

VMS supports wildcards in file names directly at the RMS level, and providing the means to process wildcard file specifications gives programs a flexibility and slickness that can impress your friends. The getfile routine makes use of two run-time library routines to search through a directory or tree of directories for all files matching a file specification pattern that may contain wildcards:

```
! getfile  -  search for files matching pattern

      logical function getfile (pattern, filename)
      character*(*)      pattern, filename
      include           'global.def'
      character*(MAXSTR) prevpat, nullstr
      integer            context, status, lib$find_file, lib$find_file_end
      logical            equal
      save               prevpat, context
      data prevpat(1:1)  /NULL/
      data context       /0/

      if (.not. equal (prevpat, pattern)) then    !new search
         prevpat = pattern
         filename(1:2) = EOL
         status = lib$find_file_end (context)
         context = 0
      end if
      status = lib$find_file (pattern(1:index(pattern,NULL)-1),
     &                        filename,
     &                        context,,,,
     &                        %ref(0))
      filename = nullstr(filename)
      getfile = status

      return
      end
```

The LIB routines used are just wrappers for the user-unfriendly RMS routines underneath. getfile keeps returning names matching the pattern and true as the function result until no more files exist that match. The next time it is called, it should have a new pattern argument (otherwise it is being used incorrectly) and the lib$file_find_end routine is called to clean up RMS context information left over from the previous search.

It is easy to convert programs using getargs to process one input file at a time into programs that process any number of files specified with wildcards. The following code fragment shows in principle how it could be done.

```
call ioinit ()
call getargs (argc, argv)
do while (getfile(argv(1), infile)
    . . .
    {code for each input file}
    . . .
end do
```

Here argv(1) is assumed to be the input file argument; with each successive call to getfile, the infile argument is returned containing the complete file specification of the next matching file. When all files matching the pattern have been returned, getfile returns false. The same program can still be used for individual files, since a command line argument with no wildcards can only match the file name given.

Terminal I/O

Up to this point, all I/O in our programs has been performed through the I/O primitives of Chapter 3. The I/O primitives use record-oriented Fortran read and write operations and are suitable for almost any file-oriented input and output. For interactive programs, however, something a little better is often needed. With the record-oriented operations, nothing happens until the return key is pressed, and some vague entity called the *terminal driver* takes care of editing the input. With direct terminal I/O, a keypress can be acted on immediately without waiting for the carriage return key to be pressed, so that programs like screen editors can be written, and characters can be output immediately instead of waiting until a NEWLINE comes along, so things like prompts can be written out.

We only use the direct terminal I/O routines when they are really needed, namely for programs designed to be interactive. As we shall see very soon, reading from STDIN and writing to STDOUT with the standard file I/O routines allows input and output to be redirected to files by the shell. In contrast, the terminal I/O routines presented here access the terminal directly even if STDIN and STDOUT have been redirected. Thus they should be avoided if a program really doesn't need to be interactive. However, they are a real improvement for interactive programs, because of their immediate response to keypresses and because they provide command line recall.

Since the terminal I/O routines are not used in many programs, they have their own initialization routine rather than being initialized by ioinit. Direct communication with the terminal is performed on VAXes through the sys$qio or sys$qiow system services (the difference is that sys$qiow waits for the I/O operation to complete before returning to the calling routine, and is the one used in our terminal I/O primitives). ttinit sets up for use of sys$qiow by assigning a channel to the terminal (via the sys$assign service), and defines the codes to be used in the read and write I/O operations. It also checks to see if the logical name TERMINAL is defined, and if not, defines it in the job logical name table so that subprocesses can use it. If the name is already defined, its translation is used as the terminal name; otherwise the terminal name is obtained by translating sys$command.

```
! ttinit  -  initialize terminal I/O system

        subroutine ttinit ()
        include   '($iodef)'
        include   'global.def'
        include   'ttio.cmn'
        integer   status, sys$assign, lib$set_logical
        logical   get_logical

        ttread  = IO$_READVBLK.or.IO$M_NOECHO.or.IO$M_NOFILTR.or.IO$M_ESCAPE
        ttwrite = IO$_WRITEVBLK

! install job table terminal name if not already there
        if (.not. get_logical ('TERMINAL'//NULL, ttname)) then
           status = get_logical ('sys$command'//NULL, ttname)
           status = lib$set_logical ('TERMINAL',
     &                               ttname(1:index(ttname,NULL)-1),
     &                               'LNM$JOB')
        end if

! assign a unique channel to the terminal
        if (.not. sys$assign (ttname(1:index(ttname,NULL)-1),ttchan,,)) then
           stop  'unable to assign terminal channel - aborted'
        end if

        call setprompt ('$ '//NULL)    !default terminal prompt

        return
        end
```

The variables ttread and ttwrite are qio function codes used to tell sys$qiow what operation is to be performed. The qio function modifier IO$M_NOFILTER is required to prevent the terminal driver from filtering editing keys like the delete key. The prompt variable is used to initialize the terminal prompt to the standard VMS $.

The ttio common block has storage for the terminal channel and name and the sys$qio read and write function codes:

```
! ttio.cmn  -  common block for terminal I/O

      integer*2          ttchan
      integer            ttread, ttwrite
      common  /ttio/     ttchan, ttread, ttwrite

      character*(MAXSTR)  ttname, prompt
      common  /ttbuffer/  ttname, prompt
```

The keys are mapped to their scan codes in the file keyboard.def, which allows the same symbolic names to be included in any program that needs access to special keys.

```
! keyboard.def  -  keyboard/keypad definition file

! keys on keypad, plus arrow keys, valid for vt100 and vt200 terminals
      character*1 K$DEL
      parameter (K$DEL = char(127))
! keypad
      character*1 K$KP0, K$KP1, K$KP2, K$KP3, K$KP4, K$KP5, K$KP6,
     &           K$KP7, K$KP8, K$KP9, K$MINUS, K$COMMA, K$PERIOD, K$ENTER
      parameter (K$KP0 = char(128))
      parameter (K$KP1 = char(129))
      parameter (K$KP2 = char(130))
      parameter (K$KP3 = char(131))
      parameter (K$KP4 = char(132))
      parameter (K$KP5 = char(133))
      parameter (K$KP6 = char(134))
      parameter (K$KP7 = char(135))
      parameter (K$KP8 = char(136))
      parameter (K$KP9 = char(137))
      parameter (K$MINUS = char(138))
      parameter (K$COMMA = char(139))
      parameter (K$PERIOD = char(140))
      parameter (K$ENTER = char(141))
! edt pf keys
      character*1 K$PF1, K$PF2, K$PF3, K$PF4
      parameter (K$PF1 = char(142))
      parameter (K$PF2 = char(143))
      parameter (K$PF3 = char(144))
      parameter (K$PF4 = char(145))
! cursor keys
      character*1 K$UP, K$DOWN, K$RIGHT, K$LEFT
      parameter (K$UP = char(146))
      parameter (K$DOWN = char(147))
      parameter (K$RIGHT = char(148))
      parameter (K$LEFT = char(149))
! keys valid only on LK201 keyboards (vt200 series)
      character*1 K$FIND, K$INSERT, K$REMOVE, K$SELECT,
     &            K$PREVSCR, K$NEXTSCR
      parameter (K$FIND = char(150))
      parameter (K$INSERT = char(151))
```

```
parameter (K$REMOVE = char(152))
parameter (K$SELECT = char(153))
parameter (K$PREVSCR = char(154))
parameter (K$NEXTSCR = char(155))
character*1 K$F6, K$F7, K$F8, K$F9, K$F10, K$F11, K$F12, K$F13, K$F14
parameter (K$F6 = char(156))
parameter (K$F7 = char(157))
parameter (K$F8 = char(158))
parameter (K$F9 = char(159))
parameter (K$F10 = char(160))
parameter (K$F11 = char(161))
parameter (K$F12 = char(162))
parameter (K$F13 = char(163))
parameter (K$F14 = char(164))
character*1 K$HELP, K$DO
parameter (K$HELP = char(165))
parameter (K$DO = char(166))
character*1 K$F17, K$F18, K$F19, K$F20
parameter (K$F17 = char(167))
parameter (K$F18 = char(168))
parameter (K$F19 = char(169))
parameter (K$F20 = char(170))
```

getc either returns the character code of a key pressed directly or, in the case of function keys, recognizes the corresponding escape code and returns a single character code with a value greater than 128. It is written the old-fashioned way, with handwritten code to recognize all of the different escape sequences. The escape sequences recognized are those that can be generated by LK201-style DEC keyboards (used by VT200 series terminals).

```
! getc  -  get character from terminal (vt100 or vt200 series)

      character*1 function getc (c)
      character*1 c, d
      include   'global.def'
      include   'keyboard.def'

      call qiowget (d)

      if (d .eq. ESC) then              !interpret escape sequence
        call qiowget (d)
        if (d .eq. ESC) then            !literal escape
          c = ESC
        else if (d .eq. '[') then       !CSI escape sequence
          call qiowget (d)
          if (d .eq. 'A') then
            c = K$UP
          else if (d .eq. 'B') then
            c = K$DOWN
          else if (d .eq. 'C') then
            c = K$RIGHT
          else if (d .eq. 'D') then
```

```
            c = K$LEFT
       else if (d .eq. '1') then
          call qiowget (d)
          if (d .eq. '~') then
             c = K$FIND
          else
             if (d .eq. '7') then
                c = K$F6
             else if (d .eq. '8') then
                c = K$F7
             else if (d .eq. '9') then
                c = K$F8
             end if
             call qiowget (d)    !remove tilda (terminator) from buffer
          end if
       else if (d .eq. '2') then
          call qiowget (d)
          if (d .eq. '~') then
             c = K$INSERT
          else
             if (d .eq. '0') then
                c = K$F9
             else if (d .eq. '1') then
                c = K$F10
             else if (d .eq. '3') then
                c = K$F11
             else if (d .eq. '4') then
                c = K$F12
             else if (d .eq. '5') then
                c = K$F13
             else if (d .eq. '6') then
                c = K$F14
             else if (d .eq. '8') then
                c = K$HELP
             else if (d .eq. '9') then
                c = K$DO
             end if
             call qiowget (d)
          end if
       else if (d .eq. '3') then
          call qiowget (d)
          if (d .eq. '~') then
             c = K$REMOVE
          else
             if (d .eq. '1') then
                c = K$F17
             else if (d .eq. '2') then
                c = K$F18
             else if (d .eq. '3') then
                c = K$F19
             else if (d .eq. '4') then
                c = K$F20
             end if
```

```
          call qiowget (d)
        end if
      else if (d .eq. '4') then
        c = K$SELECT
        call qiowget (d)
      else if (d .eq. '5') then
        c = K$PREVSCR
        call qiowget (d)
      else if (d .eq. '6') then
        c = K$NEXTSCR
        call qiowget (d)
      end if
    else if (d .eq. 'O') then         !SS3 escape sequence
      call qiowget (d)
      if (d .eq. 'p') then
        c = K$KP0
      else if (d .eq. 'q') then
        c = K$KP1
      else if (d .eq. 'r') then
        c = K$KP2
      else if (d .eq. 's') then
        c = K$KP3
      else if (d .eq. 't') then
        c = K$KP4
      else if (d .eq. 'u') then
        c = K$KP5
      else if (d .eq. 'v') then
        c = K$KP6
      else if (d .eq. 'w') then
        c = K$KP7
      else if (d .eq. 'x') then
        c = K$KP8
      else if (d .eq. 'y') then
        c = K$KP9
      else if (d .eq. 'm') then
        c = K$MINUS
      else if (d .eq. 'l') then
        c = K$COMMA
      else if (d .eq. 'n') then
        c = K$PERIOD
      else if (d .eq. 'M') then
        c = K$ENTER
      else if (d .eq. 'P') then
        c = K$PF1
      else if (d .eq. 'Q') then
        c = K$PF2
      else if (d .eq. 'R') then
        c = K$PF3
      else if (d .eq. 'S') then
        c = K$PF4
      end if
    end if
  else if (d .eq. CR) then
```

```
      c = NEWLINE
    else
      c = d
    end if

    getc = c

    return
    end
```

qiowget is the underlying interface to the sys$qiow function:

```
! qiowget  -  get character from terminal

    subroutine  qiowget (c)
    character*1 c
    include     'global.def'
    include     'ttio.cmn'
    integer     status, sys$qiow

    status = sys$qiow (,%val(ttchan),%val(ttread),,,,%ref(c),%val(1),,,,,)
    if (.not. status) call lib$signal (%val (status))

    return
    end
```

putc is considerably less complicated than getc, as it has no need to know anything about keyboards:

```
! putc  -  put characters to terminal

    subroutine  putc (c)
    character*1 c
    include     'global.def'
    include     'ttio.cmn'
    integer     status, sys$qiow

    status = sys$qiow (,%val(ttchan),%val(ttwrite),,,,%ref(c),%val(1),,,,,)
    if (.not. status) call lib$signal (%val (status))

    return
    end
```

The DCL command interpreter provides a nifty feature called *command line recall*. When the up arrow is pressed, the present command line is cleared and replaced with the last command entered, retrieved from an internal buffer containing the 20 most recently entered commands. Subsequent presses of the up arrow replace the current command line with the contents of the next oldest command in the buffer. The down arrow moves through the buffer in the opposite direction, retrieving progressively more recent commands until the last one entered is displayed, after which it clears the current command line. At any time the displayed command line may be edited and then re-entered for execution. This is a very nice (and addictive) feature, but it unfortunately isn't available while executing a program. Inside an executing program only one line of recall is available, provided by the VAX terminal driver. Having come to the conclusion that this capability is not a feature, but rather a requirement for any suitable programming environment (we are thoroughly addicted), we wish to develop a similar capability that will work inside our own programs. The relative complexity of getline is the direct consequence of this need, even though our version is considerably simpler than DCL recall.

Before plunging into getline, we need to know how to perform screen updating on the terminal. Fortunately, there are ANSI (American National Standards Institute) standards for such things, and ANSI control sequences are honored in more places than American Express. The ones we need are defined in ansi.def:

```
! ansi.def  -  define standard ANSI sequences for terminal screen control

       character*15 CLRSCREEN
       parameter    (CLRSCREEN = esc//'[1;24r'//esc//'[2J'//esc//'[H'//null)
       character*3  NEXTLINE
       parameter    (NEXTLINE = esc//'E' //null)
       character*5  BOLD
       parameter    (BOLD = esc//'[1m' //null)
       character*5  UNDERLINE
       parameter    (UNDERLINE = esc//'[4m' //null)
       character*5  BLINK
       parameter    (BLINK = esc//'[5m' //null)
       character*5  RVSVIDEO
       parameter    (RVSVIDEO = esc//'[7m' //null)
       character*5  CLRLINE
       parameter    (CLRLINE = ESC//'[2K'//NULL)
       character*5  CLREND
       parameter    (CLREND = ESC//'[0K'//NULL)
       character*5  CLRCHAR
       parameter    (CLRCHAR = ESC//'[1X'//NULL)
       character*5  INSCHAR
       parameter    (INSCHAR = ESC//'[1@'//NULL)
       character*5  CRSLEFT
       parameter    (CRSLEFT = ESC//'[1D'//NULL)
       character*5  CRSRIGHT
       parameter    (CRSRIGHT = ESC//'[1C'//NULL)
```

We only have the ones we need here, but there are lots more that could be added. getline allows a maximum line length of 79 characters, so that the complexity of cursor movement with line wrapping is avoided. This is a great simplification for the programming task with little or no penalty in usefulness. The recall buffer is organized as a circular list, unlike DCL recall; pressing the down or up key forever just loops around the buffer endlessly. This means that if the recall buffer is full, once the buffer has been entered there is no way to get

back to a blank line. Therefore, a special check for CONTROL/X is performed
to clear the current line. Since it gets all of its input through getc, getline is
almost portable—the only special keys needed are DELETE and the cursor keys.

```
! getline  -  get input line from terminal (with recall)

        logical function getline (line)
        character*(*)      line
        include           'global.def'
        include           'keyboard.def'
        include           'ansi.def'
        include           'ttio.cmn'
        integer           MAXRECALL
        parameter         (MAXRECALL = 20)
        integer           MAXCMD
        parameter         (MAXCMD = 79)
        character*1       CTRLX
        parameter         (CTRLX = char(21))
        integer           rbp, nbp, ebp, ebl, i, j
        character*1       getc, c
        character*(MAXSTR)    itoa, cb
        character*(MAXCMD+1)  rbuf(MAXRECALL), ebuf
        save  rbuf, nbp
        data  nbp  /0/

        nbp = mod (nbp, MAXRECALL) + 1
        rbp = nbp
        ebp = 1
        ebl = 0
        rbuf(nbp)(1:1) = NULL
        ebuf(1:1) = NULL

        call putstr (CR//LINEFEED//prompt)

        do while (getc(c) .ne. NEWLINE)
           if (c .eq. EOF) then
              getline = .false.
              line(1:2) = EOF//NULL
              return
           else if (c .eq. K$UP) then
              rbp = rbp - 1
              if (rbp .lt. 1) rbp = MAXRECALL    !previous line
              ebuf = rbuf(rbp)                   !wrap to bottom
              ebp  = index (ebuf, NULL)          !fill edit buffer
              ebl  = ebp - 1                     !cursor at end of line
              call putstr (CLRLINE)              !refresh screen
              call putstr (CR//prompt)
              call putstr (ebuf)
           else if (c .eq. K$DOWN) then
              rbp = rbp + 1
              if (rbp .gt. MAXRECALL) rbp = 1    !next line
              ebuf = rbuf(rbp)                   !wrap to top
                                                 !fill edit buffer
```

```
         ebp  = index (ebuf, NULL)            !cursor at end of line
         ebl  = ebp - 1
         call putstr (CLRLINE)                !refresh screen
         call putstr (CR//prompt)
         call putstr (ebuf)
       else if (c .eq. K$LEFT) then
         if (ebp .gt. 1) then
             ebp = ebp - 1
             call putstr (CRSLEFT)
         end if
       else if (c .eq. K$RIGHT) then
         if (ebp .le. ebl) then
             ebp = ebp + 1
             call putstr (CRSRIGHT)
         end if
       else if (c .eq. K$DEL) then
         if (ebp .gt. 1) then
             ebuf(ebp-1:) = ebuf(ebp:)        !delete character
             ebp = ebp - 1                    !update pointers
             ebl = ebl - 1
             cb  = itoa (ebl-ebp+1)           !build escape sequence
             call putstr (CRSLEFT)            !refresh screen
             call putstr (CLREND)
             call putstr (ebuf(ebp:))
             if (ebl-ebp+1 .ne. 0)
  &              call putstr (ESC//'['//cb(1:index(cb,NULL)-1)//'D'//NULL)
         end if
       else if (c .eq. CTRLX) then            !clear line
         ebl = 0
         ebp = 1
         ebuf(1:1) = NULL
         call putstr (CLRLINE)
         call putstr (CR//prompt)
       else                                   !insert character
         if (ebl .eq. 0) then
             ebuf = c//NULL
             ebl = 1
             ebp = 2
         else if (ebl .ge. MAXCMD) then
             if (ebp .eq. 1) then
                 ebuf = c//ebuf(1:MAXCMD-1)//NULL
                 ebp = ebp + 1
             else if (ebp .ge. MAXCMD) then
                 ebuf(MAXCMD:MAXCMD) = c
             else
                 ebuf = ebuf(1:ebp-1)//c//ebuf(ebp:MAXCMD-1)//NULL
                 ebp = ebp + 1
             end if
         else
             if (ebp .eq. 1) then
                 ebuf = c//ebuf(1:ebl)//NULL
             else
                 ebuf = ebuf(1:ebp-1)//c//ebuf(ebp:)
```

```
            end if
            ebp = ebp + 1
            ebl = ebl + 1
        end if
        call putstr (INSCHAR)
        call putc   (c)
    end if
end do
call putstr (CR//NULL)

rbuf(nbp) = ebuf                    !copy edit buffer to recall buffer
if (ebl .eq. 0) then
    line = EOL
else
    line = ebuf(1:ebl)//EOL
end if

getline = .true.

return
end
```

The putstr routine is simpler than its input counterpart getline because it
doesn't need to know anything about command line recall. getline must get its
input by characters via getc so that it can implement the recall buffering feature;
writing terminal output is by comparison an extremely simple operation. putstr
is a simple derivative of putc, with the only difference being that an arbitrary
number of characters are output:

```
! putstr  -  output string to terminal

        subroutine putstr (string)
        character*(*) string
        include     'global.def'
        include     'ttio.cmn'
        integer     status, sys$qiow, l

        l = index (string, NULL) - 1

        status = sys$qiow (,%val(ttchan),%val(ttwrite),,,,
    &                      %ref(string),%val(l),,,,,)
        if (.not. status) call lib$signal (%val (status))

        return
        end
```

The putstr routine is useful for doing things like putting out prompts to the
terminal because it is unbuffered and outputs its argument on each call. fputstr
can't do this and waits for a NEWLINE before it ever outputs anything.

9.2   A Shell for DCL

Throughout the book we have remarked on how useful a shell that provides
I/O redirection at the DCL command level would be, and at last we are ready
to quit complaining and do something about it. The shell presented here is a
very simple one, which doesn't do anything except perform I/O redirection and
pipeline operations.

The command

    $ shell

invokes the shell interactively, and the terminal I/O routines in the previous
section are used to provide command line recall and prompting. The shell can
also be run in a "batch" mode, with a script file as input by saying

    $ shell filename

A shell script file is like a DCL command procedure, except that it can contain
commands with I/O redirection and pipelines. Script files can contain any of the
preprocessor commands of prep. If no file name extension is given, it is assumed
to be .sh.

The shell provides the following I/O redirection operations on DCL command
lines:

<file	Redirect standard input to file
>file	Redirect standard output to file
>>file	Append standard output to file
prog1 | prog2	Direct standard output of prog1 to
	standard input of prog2

The shell can be used with just about any DCL command; the commands not
supported by the shell are those that aren't allowed interactively in DCL, such
as the goto command.

The shell has a few internal commands, that is, commands that are processed
by the shell program itself rather than by DCL. The DCL set prompt command
produces no errors but has no effect since we use getline to process input and
output prompts; therefore the shell has a prompt command:

    $ prompt prompt_str

sets the shell prompt to the specified string. The prompt_str may contain escape
sequences. The default prompt is $. The shell also has a shell command that
processes shell script files, with exactly the same behavior as if the shell were
invoked from DCL with a file name argument.

The shell is terminated by typing CONTROL/Z or by the exit or lo commands, which are also internal commands. I/O redirection is prohibited on internal commands. Typing CONTROL/C interrupts the program currently executing

the shell without stopping the shell; typing CONTROL/Y terminates the shell and returns the user to DCL.

Anything other than an internal command is just passed to the DCL interpreter, with the redirection characters and file names stripped. The executing program never knows that I/O redirection has taken place. Thus pound receives three arguments with the command line

```
$ pound "$ type #" shell.fil shell.txt
```

but only one argument with the command line

```
$ pound "$ type #" <shell.fil >shell.txt
```

In the second case the shell removes the file names and pound is unaware of the redirection, so it reads from STDIN and writes to STDOUT.

The ability to redirect I/O often gives programs capabilities they wouldn't have otherwise. For instance, our lexgen program writes messages about the status of the program and statistics of the generated tables to STDOUT; these messages can be captured in a file by saying

```
$ lexgen spl.lex splscan.def >report.txt
```

The spl compiler was written with the shell in mind—the I/O statements of spl operate only on STDIN and STDOUT, so there is no way to use files in spl programs without I/O redirection. With it, an spl program to copy input to output can be used to copy files:

```
$ spl copy <infile >outfile
```

The ability to pipeline the output of one program into the input of another makes it possible to use combinations of simple programs to perform complex tasks. For instance, we never built the preprocessor into v77, and the f77name Fortran identifier was never incorporated either. Instead of building those features in, we can get them when needed in one succinct command line:

```
$ prep <prog.for | f77name | v77 -i >prog.f77
```

Pipelines provide a sort of dynamic linking, and let programs be treaded like subroutines. A user can, in effect, construct a one-shot custom program to do anything for which he or she has the components. The programs in this book have been written to be useful in pipelines, by making STDIN and STDOUT the default I/O units when file name arguments are not present.

Most DCL commands that expect file names as arguments can be used with sys$input or sys$output as the file name, so DCL commands can be used with the shell. In fact, even the DCL command procedure executive can be used in pipelines, as in the following command:

```
$ pound "$ update tools #" <spl.fil | @sys$input
```

However, the shell does not process commands within command procedures.
The shell can be wedged into the normal DCL login by putting the following
statement at the end of the DCL login procedure:

```
$ if "''f$mode()'" .eqs. "INTERACTIVE" then shell
```

On startup, the shell inherits all of the logical names and symbols of the current process. It does not inherit commands defined via the DCL set command facility. On startup the shell also executes the shell commands in the file sys$login:login.sh if it exists. login.sh could contain commands to set the shell prompt or to initialize custom DCL commands via set command.

Other shells have been written for VMS, but most have attempted to do too much. Digital Equipment Corporation, for example, sells a product called DEC/Shell that is an implementation, of sorts, of the UNIX Bourne shell. The problem with DEC/Shell, aside from its price, is that it requires the use of UNIX syntax for commands, for defining them, and for logging in. UNIX syntax is just fine, but doesn't make a lot of sense on a VMS machine. In addition, some programs that work fine without the shell don't work with it, such as any commands that rely on the DCL command language interpreter (CLI). DEC apparently thinks that I/O redirection isn't useful except for people who aren't used to DCL, so they have never given DCL an I/O redirection facility of its own. Our shell has the advantage of being practically transparent to the user. It appears to be the ordinary DCL environment, complete with command line recall; the I/O redirection is a feature added to DCL rather than an alternate environment. We are not trying to reinvent UNIX, but rather, to make one of its best qualities available in VMS.

The basic idea behind the shell is the use of a subordinate "child" process to execute DCL commands, while the main program merely supervises the work by changing the input and output of the child process as appropriate. It took some experimentation to come up with an adequate design. Our first attempt at a shell used the lib$spawn run-time library procedure to do essentially the same job as the DCL spawn command, creating a subprocess for each command to be executed:

```
! spawn  -  spawn a subprocess

       subroutine spawn (cmdstr)
       character*(*) cmdstr
       include     'global.def'
       include     '($clidef)'
       integer     status, lib$spawn, flags, end

       flags = CLI$M_NOKEYPAD
       end   = index(cmdstr, NULL)

       if (end .eq. 0) then
```

```
        status = lib$spawn (cmdstr,,,flags)
    else if (end .ne. 1) then
        status = lib$spawn (cmdstr(1:end-1),,,flags)
    end if

    if (.not. status) call lib$signal(%val(status))

    return
    end
```

If the command string passed to spawn is empty, the call results in the creation of an interactive subprocess attached to the standard input and output devices of the calling process. The parent process is placed into a hibernating state until the subprocess logs out, at which time the subprocess is deleted and control is returned to the parent. If the command string is not empty, it is passed to the newly created process for execution as a DCL command. After the command is processed, the subprocess is deleted and control returns to the parent. The spawn routine provides an interface to a very powerful and extensive set of programming tools: the DCL command processor and the VMS system utilities.

The spawn routine is one of the most often used system primitives because it provides a means of executing DCL commands from within a program. However, it isn't suitable for the shell, and an example will show why. Here's how it would work:

- The shell process would gather command lines and parse them into separate pipelines and I/O redirection files;

- The shell would call spawn with the command as an argument and redirected file names for sys$input and sys$output;

- The call to spawn would create a new process, execute the command, terminate the process, and return control to the shell.

This sounds ok on paper, but consider what happens when the user types

```
$ set def [joeuser]
```

The command would be passed as is to the spawn routine. A subprocess would be created, the command executed, and then the process would be terminated, leaving the user right where she started. The problem is that the set def command is executed in the subprocess, not the parent, and then the subprocess is deleted.

When a subprocess is spawned, it inherits the context (default directory, command symbols, and logical names) of the parent; when the child process is terminated, there is no way to copy the information back. The solution to this problem is either to intercept set default commands (and all other commands that modify the process environment in any way) or to keep the child process around after commands are executed—that is, create a single process to execute all commands. The latter is preferred because the former approach is full of special cases. Another problem with this failed approach is that process creation in VMS is time-consuming, so creating a new process for every command is unbearably slow. If the subprocess can be kept alive and able to read new commands, both problems are solved.

A variation of the spawn routine can create a subprocess without putting the parent into hibernation, by using the flag CLI$M_NOWAIT modifier (as described in the documentation for lib$spawn). Then, given a working child process eager to do something, the only problem the shell has is giving it work to do. In order to control its child, the shell must provide a means of communicating with it; communication is achieved by using a VMS mailbox as the sys$command of the child. It is important to note that DCL always reads commands from sys$command, which often is equated to sys$input. The big difference is that sys$command is the primary input channel associated with the process; it is defined to be the sys$input at the time the process is created. While the subprocess sys$input can be changed at will, the sys$command is not directly specified to the subprocess, but rather, DCL sets it automatically to the initial sys$input. The subprocess therefore cannot disconnect itself from its command channel accidentally.

A mailbox in a VMS system is a virtual device used to pass information between cooperating processes. Mailboxes are areas in memory that function sort of like files. The creation of a mailbox causes a logical name for the mailbox to be inserted into the job logical name table of the creating process, where it may be accessed by any other process in the same job. The mailbox is used as a single record device to pass information between two processes in the same job. VAX Fortran works nicely with mailboxes, and VMS automatically synchronizes the parent and child when Fortran I/O is used with a mailbox as the I/O unit. The statement

```
call fputstr (umbx, command)
```

causes command to be written to the mailbox unit umbx once the mailbox has been set up (just how to do it will be shown soon); the program cannot proceed from this statement until the cooperating child process has read the message. If we need to be sure the previous command has completely finished executing before performing some action, we can use any do-nothing command such as a DCL comment

```
call fputstr (umbx, '!wait for previous command to complete'//EOL)
```

since a command is never read until the previous one has finished.

So far we have a means of creating a child process running DCL and a means of sending commands to it. Now we need to figure out a way to redirect sys$input and sys$output for the subprocess, from the parent shell. The easiest way is to simply send a sequence of DCL define commands before each user command and deassign commands afterwards. This method works ok, and early versions

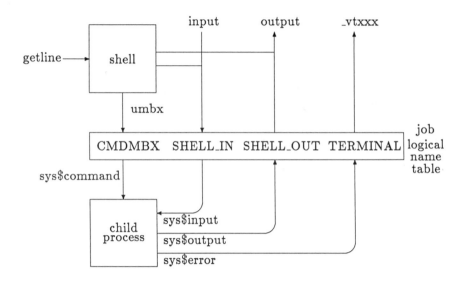

Figure 9.1: Shell parent and child process communication.

of the shell used it. However, each **define** and **deassign** command is an added overhead requiring an image to be loaded and executed, and if the shell is too slow nobody will want to use it. It is therefore desirable to keep the overhead for each user command low and to avoid executing separate images if possible.

The overhead of defining the child input and output is partially avoided by use of logical names in the job table. The job logical name table is common to both parent and child and thus provides a convenient way of communication between them. The scheme is that the subprocess **sys$input** is defined just once to be the logical name **SHELL_IN** in the job table, and **SHELL_IN** is translated whenever input from **sys$input** happens in the subprocess. The parent shell just changes the definition of **SHELL_IN** via system service calls, avoiding the overhead of image execution for DCL **define** commands. Figure 9.1 is a picture of the relationship between the shell and its child process, showing the job logical name table as an intermediary between the parent and the child. The logical name **TERMINAL** is defined by the terminal I/O system.

There are a couple of hitches in this basic design. The use of the job table logical names would never require any images other than those invoked by user commands if it weren't for command procedures. Command procedures redirect **sys$input** to the procedure file, and when it is finished, DCL *always* reopens **sys$input** to the *executive* mode definition, that is, to the value of **sys$input** at process creation. Since there is no way to prevent full logical name translation to a file or device when the process is created (at least no way we could find), the execution of a command procedure causes the subprocess to get disconnected from the job table names on which we are depending. The only way we can circumvent the problem is by reconnecting the names after every command; doing so only after command procedures is not practical since the symbol translation of the DCL parser would have to be duplicated in the shell to make sure no synonyms equated to command procedures slipped by. It would be as much work to figure out when reconnection is necessary as to just do it every time.

Another problem concerns the processing of script files. When a `shell` command is entered, the shell just changes the input source from the terminal to the named file, and therefore the shell needs to track the default directory of the subprocess so that script file names get the right defaults applied when the shell tries to open them. Once again, a logical name in the job table is used to communicate between processes, and once again the only way to ensure that both processes are always at the same place is to set the default directory of the shell after every command. The logical name used is SHELL_DIR, and the subprocess sets it to its default directory after every command; the shell then uses the `setdir` routine to follow the subprocess.

Pipelines are implemented by use of temporary files. It may appear inefficient at first glance to handle pipes this way, as opposed to creation of a separate process for each command in a pipe. The latter method could be accomplished by setting up a mailbox between each pair of processes, with the mailbox serving as `sys$output` for one and `sys$input` for the other, and VMS would automatically synchronize the processes so that the the second process would never attempt to read input that the first hasn't yet generated as output. However, consider these drawbacks:

- It takes time to create processes in VMS, much longer than in some other operating systems such as UNIX.

- Foreign commands are made known to DCL with symbol definitions, usually defined at login, as opposed to other operating systems in which commands are made known by putting them on the directory search path. Each process must therefore be created with all required symbols defined for it, by executing the login, since otherwise some programs that depend on a DCL interface (like getting DCL symbols) could fail.

- Some means of error handling must be provided to clean up everything in case one of the commands in the pipeline fails; this is much simpler to do when only two processes are involved.

- By default, user accounts on VMS systems are allowed only two subprocesses, and to use more the system manager has to increase the subprocess quota in the user's authorization file entry.

It appears that the simpler approach is also the better one.

This is starting to look like a complete plan, and the design to this point covers everything necessary when things are going right. When something goes wrong, we need to handle it properly. A means must be provided to stop a program running in the subprocess if it is in an infinite loop or the like, and we don't want to kill the shell or the subprocess. On the other hand, a guaranteed method of killing the shell completely and returning the user to DCL must be provided in case things get really screwed up. This is pointing to the need to handle interrupts, also known as asynchronous traps (ASTs) in VAX lingo. ASTs are used to allow a program to respond to events as they occur; when the AST is delivered (i.e., when the event happens), the task currently being performed is interrupted, and control is passed to a routine specified when the AST handler is set up. The shell needs to handle CONTROL/C, CONTROL/Y, and CONTROL/T interrupts; CONTROL/C is used to halt whatever is happening in the subprocess and CONTROL/Y is the emergency exit. CONTROL/T needs to indicate what's going on in the subprocess as well as the main process.

Whether an error has occurred or not, when the shell is terminated several things need to be done to clean up, namely:

- Remove the shell I/O logical names from the job table,

- Delete the subprocess, and

- Re-enable normal DCL handling of interrupts.

The best way to ensure that all of this happens no matter what is to use an exit handler. An exit handler is a routine wedged into the VMS image run-down sequence by calling the sys$dclexh (declare exit handler) system service routine.

It is daunting to think that all of these strategies must be implemented to get the shell to work, and that the result must be fast and very reliable for the shell to be really useful. As it turns out, the code to do all of this is surprisingly brief (although each line of code embodies an unusual amount of blood, sweat, and tears). The shell, using VMS system services, packs a lot of punch in each line of code. Here is a files list that spells out what is involved:

```
! shell.fil - files list for I/O redirection shell

        # shell.cmn       !shell common block
        # ttio.cmn        !terminal I/O system common block
        # shell.mac       !token codes for scanner
        # shell.lex       !lexgen input for scanner
        # shellscan.def   !data statements for scanner

        shell             !main program
          shellinit       !initialize mailbox, AST's, and AST handlers
            setccast      !declare control/c AST handler
            subinit       !create DCL subprocess
          shellexec       !parse and execute commands
            shellscan     !lexical analyzer
```

```
cntlcast        !control/c AST handler
cntlyast        !control/y AST handler
shellfinit      !exit handler

shelldef        !image to set subprocess i/o logical names
```

The first thing to get out of the way is the error and interrupt handling since they are the underpinnings of the program. The exit handler `shellfinit` cleans up everything:

```
! shellfinit  -  shell exit handler

        subroutine shellfinit (exstat)
        integer   exstat
        include   '($libclidef)'
        include   'global.def'
        include   'shell.cmn'
        integer   status, sys$delprc
        integer   lib$enable_ctrl, lib$delete_logical

! remove subprocess input and output logical names from job table
        status = lib$delete_logical ('SHELL_IN', 'LNM$JOB')
        status = lib$delete_logical ('SHELL_OUT','LNM$JOB')
        status = lib$delete_logical ('SHELL_DIR','LNM$JOB')

! delete subprocess
        status = sys$delprc (spid, %val(1))

! enable DCL control_y handling
        status = lib$enable_ctrl (LIB$M_CLI_CTRLY)

        end
```

Execution of `shellfinit` is guaranteed when the shell is terminated, no matter what causes termination. Thus we can exit gracefully at any time by using a Fortran `stop` statement. Thus the code to handle a CONTROL/Y interrupt is not too involved:

```
! cntlyast  -  control/y AST handler

        subroutine cntlyast ()
        stop ' '
        end
```

The CONTROL/Y AST is enabled just once since, if it is ever invoked, it halts the shell. Likewise, the exit handler is enabled only once; both are set up in the `shellinit` routine. CONTROL/C interrupts are a little different, since they can occur many times during the life of the shell. The strategy for handling CONTROL/C interrupts is to stop whatever is executing in the subprocess and have the AST rearm itself. In order for the AST to rearm itself after it has been

delivered, a separate routine must be used to set and handle the AST since a
routine may not reference itself recursively. The routine that queues the AST is
setccast:

```
! setccast  -  enable control/c AST handler

        subroutine setccast ()
        include    'global.def'
        include    'ttio.cmn'
        include    'shell.cmn'
        integer    status, sys$qiow
        external   cntlcast

        status = sys$qiow (,%val(ttchan),%val(ccast),,,,cntlcast,,,,,)

        return
        end
```

The argument ccast is a flag to the sys$qiow service to indicate the purpose
of the call; it is initialized in shellinit. The routine cntlcast handles the
CONTROL/C AST. It uses the system service sys$forcex to force the program
executing in the subprocess to exit.

```
! cntlcast  -  control/c AST handler

        subroutine cntlcast ()
        include  'shell.cmn'
        integer  status, sys$forcex

! force subprocess to exit current image or command
        status = sys$forcex (spid,,%val(1))

! reset control_c handler
        call setccast ()

        return
        end
```

Most of the hard part of the shell is in shellinit and subinit. shellinit
is responsible for enabling the AST handlers and the exit handler, and creating
the communication mailbox before creating the subprocess:

```
! shellinit  -  initialize shell mailbox, subprocess, and communications

        subroutine shellinit (inprep)
        logical    inprep
        include    '($iodef)'
        include    '($libclidef)'
        include    'global.def'
        include    'shell.cmn'
        include    'ttio.cmn'
```

```
      integer   lib$disable_ctrl
      integer   sys$qiow, sys$crembx, sys$dclexh
      integer   status, exstat, fopen
      external  cntlyast, shellfinit

! exit handler data block
      structure /exitblock/
        integer forward_link
        integer handler_addr
        integer args
        integer condvalue_addr
      end structure
      record /exitblock/ exblock

! declare exit handler
      exblock.args = 1
      exblock.handler_addr = %loc (shellfinit)
      exblock.condvalue_addr = %loc (exstat)
      status = sys$dclexh (exblock)

      ccast = IO$_SETMODE .or. IO$M_CTRLCAST    !ctrl/c qio code
      cyast = IO$_SETMODE .or. IO$M_CTRLYAST    !ctrl/y qio code

! disable DCL control_y handling
      status = lib$disable_ctrl (LIB$M_CLI_CTRLY)

! enable shell control_y handler
      status = sys$qiow (,%val(ttchan),%val(cyast),,,,cntlyast,,,,,)

! establish cntrl/c handler
      call setccast ()

! create mailbox
      status = sys$crembx (,mbxchan,,,,,'CMDMBX')

! open unit to mailbox
      if (fopen (umbx,'CMDMBX'//NULL,IOWRITE) .eq. IOERROR) then
        stop 'error opening subprocess command mailbox'
      end if

! create the subprocess
      call subinit (inprep)

      return
      end
```

The VMS system service routine sys$crembx is used by shellinit to create the mailbox and install the logical name in the job table. The shell accesses the mailbox by opening a unit umbx via a call to fopen with the file specified as the mailbox CMDBOX. The subprocess is created with its initial sys$input device specified as the mailbox, and its initial sys$output is not specified in the call. The creation and initialization of the subprocess is handled by subinit:

```
! subinit  -  create and initialize DCL subprocess and job table entries

        subroutine subinit (inprep)
        logical             inprep
        include             '($clidef)'
        include             '($lnmdef)'
        include             'global.def'
        include             'ttio.cmn'
        include             'shell.cmn'
        integer             status, lib$spawn, lib$set_logical, fopen, u
        logical             getfile
        character*(MAXSTR)  line, logfile

! spawn the subprocess
        status = lib$spawn ('@CMDMBX',,,CLI$M_NOWAIT,,spid,,,,,,)
        if (.not. status) call lib$signal (%val(status))

        call fputstr (umbx, 'set noon'//EOL)
        call fputstr (umbx, 'define/nolog/notrans sys$input  SHELL_IN'//EOL)
        call fputstr (umbx, 'define/nolog/notrans sys$output SHELL_OUT'//EOL)

! process shell login file if found
        if (getfile ('sys$login:login.sh'//NULL, logfile)) then
            if (fopen(u,'sys$login:login.sh'//NULL,IOREAD).ne.IOERROR) then
                if (inprep) then
                    call pushincl (u)
                else
                    call ppinit (u)
                end if
                inprep = .true.
            else
                call fputstr (STDERR, 'error opening login.sh - ignored'//EOL)
            end if
        end if

        return
        end
```

After the process is created, the input and output of the subprocess are initialized to point to the job table intermediate names. The notrans qualifier is used to make sure the names do not get translated by the subprocess when I/O occurs. Since sys$error is set to sys$output for processes created with lib$spawn, and the sys$output argument was omitted in the call, sys$error ends up pointing to the terminal as desired.

The shell has one small common block for holding the I/O channel identifier and fopen unit number assigned to the command mailbox, the subprocess ID, and the CONTROL/C and CONTROL/Y flags for sys$qiow:

```
! shell.cmn  -  common block for VMS operating shell

      integer*2  mbxchan
      integer    umbx, spid, ccast, cyast

      common     /shellcmn/
     &           mbxchan,
     &           umbx, spid, ccast, cyast
```

That takes care of all of the setup for the shell processing. The rest of the code deals with reading command lines, processing script files, tokenizing and parsing command lines, and dispatching the result to the child process for execution. The main program parses the initial command line arguments, and thereafter just gets lines of input and dispatches them to shellexec. A flag called inprep is used to keep track of whether input is presently being obtained from a script file or the terminal, so that the appropriate routine (ppline or getline) can be called to get the next line.

```
! shell  -  VMS operating system shell with io redirection and pipelines

      program shell
      include           'global.def'
      include           'shell.cmn'
      integer           argc, uin, fopen, i
      logical           ppline, getline, inprep, get_logical
      character*(MAXSTR) argv(MAXARGS), line
      character*(MAXSTR) fnexpand, dev, dir, name, type, vers

      call ioinit ()
      call getargs (argc, argv)
      if (argc .ge. 1) then
         argv(1) = fnexpand (argv(1), dev, dir, name, type, vers)
         if (type(1:1) .eq. NULL) then
            argv(1) = dev(1:index(dev,NULL)-1)//dir(1:index(dir,NULL)-1)//
     &                name(1:index(name,NULL)-1)//'.sh'//NULL
         end if
         if (fopen (uin,argv(1),IOREAD) .eq. IOERROR) then
            call fputstr (STDERR, 'shell: unable to open file '//argv(1))
            call fputstr (STDERR, EOL)
            stop ' '
         else
            call ppinit (uin)
            inprep = .true.
         end if
      else
         inprep = .false.
      end if
      call ttinit ()
      call shellinit (inprep)

      do while (.true.)
```

```
      if (inprep) then
         if (.not. ppline (line)) then
            inprep = .false.
            if (argc .eq. 0) then
               if (.not. getline(line)) stop ' '
            else
               stop ' '
            end if
         end if
      else
         if (.not. getline(line)) stop ' '
      end if
      call shellexec (inprep, line)
   end do

end
```

The shell knows whether it is interactive or not initially by the value of argc; thus if argc is zero the shell is interactive, and when the end of a script file is reached interactive input is resumed.

The command scanning and parsing of the shell is the easy part, since the logic is pretty similar to the logic of other parsing programs we have written. The scanner is one produced by lexgen since it can be expected to be both fast and reliable, both of which are key requirements for the shell. The scanner recognizes just a few tokens:

```
! shell.mac  -  tokens for shell command lines

      #define  LEXERROR   -1
      #define  $in         1
      #define  $out        2
      #define  $append     3
      #define  $pipe       4
      #define  $exit       5
      #define  $prompt     6
      #define  $shell      7
      #define  $quote      8
      #define  $dquote     9
      #define  $token     10
      #define  $newline   11
```

The regular expressions for the tokens are specified in shell.lex:

```
! shell.lex  -  tokens for shell command line

#include shell.mac

! shell metacharacters

$in     = <
$out    = >
```

```
$append  = >>
$pipe    = \|

! internal commands

$exit    = ( (e|E)(x|X)(i|I)(t|T) | (1|L)(o|O) )
$prompt  = (p|P)(r|R)(o|O)(m|M)(p|P)(t|T)
$shell   = (s|S)(h|H)(e|E)(1|L)(1|L)

! other tokens

! all printable nonblank characters except shell metacharacters and quotes
#define pnm &
   (\\h21|[\\h23-\\h26]|[\\h28-\\h3B]|\\h3D|[\\h3F-\\h7B]|\\h7D|\\h7E)
! all printable characters except quote
#define    pnq   ( [\\h20-\\h26] | [\\h28-\\h7E] )
! all printable characters except DQUOTE
#define    pnd   ( [\\h20-\\h21] | [\\h23-\\h7E] )

#quote

$quote   = ' {pnq} ' { '{pnq}' }
$dquote  = " {pnd} " { "{pnd}" }
$token   = pnm {pnm}
$newline = \n
```

Rather than convert the tables to uppercase, the keyword expressions themselves
are written to accept upper or lowercase, since otherwise the the input line would
need to be converted to uppercase before scanning. As it is, no case conversion is
necessary and the table scanner is a standard adaptation of the generic **lexscan**
routine. The shell's scanner is called **shellscan**.

Each line of input is tokenized and interpreted by **shellexec**. In **shellexec**,
the variable **pc** holds the number of pipe sections found so far in the input line and
is used to generate the names for temporary files used in pipelines. The temporary
files used by the shell are called **vmspipe.tmp1** and **vmspipe.tmp2**, and are used
alternately as the input and output for each successive pipe section (no more than
two temporary files are needed since only one program at a time is running in the
subprocess). The variables **input** and **output** hold the input and output file or
device to be used for each pipe section. **append** contains the name of the file to
which the output has been directed for append access (if one exists). **shellexec**
also executes all internal commands and dispatches the others to the subprocess.
When a **shell** command is encountered while running the shell, the script file is
simply opened and pushed onto the **finclude** stack so that it will be the next file
processed, and **inprep** is set true to tell the main routine where to get the next
line.

```
! shellexec  -  execute shell command

      subroutine shellexec (inprep, line)
      logical            inprep
      character*(*)      line
      include            'global.def'
      #include           shell.mac
      include            'shell.cmn'
      include            'ttio.cmn'
      integer            u, fopen
      integer            lp, i, cp, pc, t, shellscan
      character*1        escchar
      character*(MAXSTR) pstring, token, itoa
      character*(MAXSTR) fnexpand, dev, dir, name, type, vers
      character*(MAXSTR) input, output, append, command
      integer            status,lib$set_logical,lib$delete_file,sys$setddir

      lp = 1
      cp = 1
      pc = 0
      append(1:1) = NULL
      t = LEXERROR
      input  = ttname
      output = ttname
      do while (t .ne. $newline)
         t = shellscan (token,line,lp)
         if (t .eq. $in) then
            if (shellscan (token,line,lp) .eq. $token) then
               input = token
            else
               call fputstr (STDERR, 'invalid filespec: '//token)
               call fputstr (STDERR, EOL)
               return
            end if
         else if (t .eq. $out) then
            if (shellscan (token,line,lp) .eq. $token) then
               output = token
            else
               call fputstr (STDERR, 'invalid filespec: '//token)
               call fputstr (STDERR, EOL)
               return
            end if
         else if (t .eq. $append) then
            if (shellscan (token,line,lp) .eq. $token) then
               append = token
               output = 'append.tmp'//NULL
            else
               call fputstr (STDERR, 'invalid filespec: '//token)
               call fputstr (STDERR, EOL)
               return
            end if
         else if (t .eq. $exit) then
            stop ' '
```

```
      else if (t .eq. $prompt) then
         do while (line(lp:lp).eq.' ' .or. line(lp:lp).eq.'=')
            lp = lp + 1
         end do
         i = 1
         do while (line(lp:lp) .ne. NEWLINE)
            if (line(lp:lp) .eq. ESCAPE) then
               pstring(i:i) = escchar(line,lp)
            else
               pstring(i:i) = line(lp:lp)
               lp = lp + 1
            end if
            i = i + 1
         end do
         pstring(i:i) = NULL
         call setprompt (pstring)
         return
      else if (t .eq. $shell) then
         t = shellscan (token,line,lp)
         if (t .eq. $token) then
            token = fnexpand (token, dev, dir, name, type, vers)
            if (type(2:2) .eq. NULL) then
               token =
&              dev(1:index(dev,NULL)-1)//dir(1:index(dir,NULL)-1)//
&              name(1:index(name,NULL)-1)//'.sh'//vers
            end if
            if (fopen (u,token,IOREAD) .ne. IOERROR) then
               if (inprep) then
                  call pushincl (u)
               else
                  call ppinit (u)
               end if
               inprep = .true.
            else
               call fputstr (STDERR, 'shell command ignored'//EOL)
            end if
         else
            call fputstr (STDERR, 'invalid file specification'//EOL)
         end if
         return
      else if (t .eq. $quote) then
         command(cp:) = ' '//token(1:)
         cp = cp + index(token,NULL)
      else if (t .eq. $dquote) then
         command(cp:) = ' '//token(1:)
         cp = cp + index(token,NULL)
      else if (t .eq. $token) then
         command(cp:) = ' '//token(1:)
         cp = cp + index(token,NULL)
      else if (t .eq. $pipe .or. t .eq. $newline) then
         command(cp:cp+1) = EOL
         cp = 1
         if (t .eq. $pipe) then
```

```
              pc = pc + 1
              if (pc .eq. 1) then
                 output = 'vmspipe.tmp1'//NULL
              else
                 input  = 'vmspipe.tmp' // itoa (mod(pc,2)+1)
                 output = 'vmspipe.tmp' // itoa (mod(pc+1,2)+1)
              end if
           else
              if (pc .eq. 1) then
                 input = 'vmspipe.tmp1'//NULL
              else if (pc .ne. 0) then
                 input = 'vmspipe.tmp' // itoa (mod(pc,2)+1)
              end if
           end if
           status = lib$set_logical ('SHELL_IN',
  &                                  input(1:index(input,NULL)-1),
  &                                  'LNM$JOB')
           status = lib$set_logical ('SHELL_OUT',
  &                                  output(1:index(output,NULL)-1),
  &                                  'LNM$JOB')
           call fputstr (umbx, 'shelldef'//EOL)
           call fputstr (umbx, '! wait for shelldef to complete'//EOL)
           status = sys$setddir ('SHELL_DIR',%val(0),%val(0))
           call fputstr (umbx, command)
           call fputstr (umbx, '! wait for command to complete'//EOL)
           if (t .eq. $pipe) then
              input  = ttname
              output = ttname
           else
              if (pc .gt. 0) status = lib$delete_file ('vmspipe.tmp*;*')
              if (append(1:1) .ne. NULL) then
                 call fputstr (umbx, 'append/new append.tmp '//append)
                 call fputstr (umbx, EOL)
                 call fputstr (umbx, '! wait for append to complete'//EOL)
                 status = lib$delete_file ('append.tmp;')
              end if
           end if
        else
           call fputstr (STDERR, 'unrecognized token'//EOL)
        end if
     end do

     return
     end
```

If append access was specified with the shell's **>>** operator, the DCL **append** command is used to tack the output onto the end of the named file.

When **shellexec** has a command line to send to the child process, it first sets the job table entries for SHELL_IN and SHELL_OUT to whatever was indicated in the command line. Then the image **shelldef** is executed in the child process before executing the command to make sure the subprocess input and output are still directed through the job table entries and to set SHELL_DIR to the default directory. When **shelldef** completes, the parent shell sets its default directory to the same place.

The last piece of the puzzle is **shelldef**, a separate image required to run the shell. It must be defined as a DCL symbol when the shell is invoked.

```
! shelldef  -  define shell process default logical names

        program shelldef
        include         'global.def'
        integer         status, lib$set_logical, length
        character*(MAXSTR) getdir, dir, out, err
        logical         equal, get_logical

        !process-permanent output file (terminal) name header
        character*4     OUTPPF
        parameter       (OUTPPF = ESC//NULL//char(2)//char(129))

        dir = getdir (dir)

        ! set supervisor mode logical names
        status = lib$set_logical('SHELL_DIR',dir(1:index(dir,NULL)-1),'LNM$JOB')
        status = lib$set_logical('SYS$INPUT', 'SHELL_IN', 'LNM$PROCESS')
        if (.not. get_logical('SHELL_OUT'//NULL,out)) stop 'error in SHELL_OUT'
        if (.not. get_logical('TERMINAL'//NULL, err)) stop 'error in TERMINAL'
        if (equal (out, err)) then
           length = index(err,NULL) + 3
           err = OUTPPF//err
           status = lib$set_logical ('SYS$OUTPUT',err(1:length),'LNM$PROCESS')
        else
           status = lib$set_logical ('SYS$OUTPUT','SHELL_OUT','LNM$PROCESS')
        end if

        end
```

The **shelldef** routine contains some odd-looking code that solves an odd problem. DCL commands, using the **sys$putmsg** system service, detect whether **sys$error** and **sys$output** are directed to the same place, and if they are not, error messages are written to both **sys$error** and **sys$output**. The problem is that DCL doesn't seem to be very good at figuring out that both are directed to the terminal when one (**sys$output**) is aimed there indirectly. As a result, error messages get written to the terminal twice most of the time. While this behavior is not a real problem, it is annoying, and the only way we have found to prevent it is by assigning **sys$output** to the terminal directly when **SHELL_OUT** says that's where it should go. The device name for a VMS terminal (in the DECese language, a process-permanent file) contains an invisible escape code that is optional for RMS services but must be included in the name to get DCL to recognize that **sys$output** and **sys$error** are the same.

Throughout the book, our programs have used getargs to get file name arguments from the command line, and in many cases we used stdargs to apply the
standard default conventions—if no output file is named, the output is to STDOUT,
and if no input file is provided, it is obtained from STDIN. The same functionality
can be obtained using the shell and I/O redirection, with the program reading
and writing to STDIN and STDOUT. The file name arguments of programs can be
dispensed with entirely and I/O performed to STDIN and STDOUT unconditionally;
such programs would be cumbersome with only DCL but are made easy to use
by the shell.

Learning to use pipelines effectively takes some getting used to and a healthy
selection of software components for use in pipe sections. There are many incred-
ibly simple programs that can be written to do useful work in pipelines with the
shell. For example, here is tee, which copies STDIN to both STDOUT and another
file:

```
! tee  -  put T-section in a pipeline

      program tee
      include        'global.def'
      integer        argc, uout, fopen
      character*(MAXSTR) argv (MAXARGS), cat, line
      logical        ok, fgetline

      call ioinit ()
      call getargs (argc, argv)
      ok = .true.
      if (argc .eq. 1) then
          if (fopen (uout, argv(1), IOWRITE) .eq. IOERROR) then
              call fputstr (STDERR, cat(argv(1), 'in tee'//EOL)
              ok = .false.
          end if
      else
          call fputstr (STDERR, 'syntax: tee filename'//EOL)
          ok = .false.
      end if

      do while (fgetline (STDIN, line))
          call fputstr (STDOUT, line)
          if (ok) call fputstr (uout, line)
      end do

      call iofinit ()
      end
```

tee is used to view intermediate results when programs are strung together in a
pipeline. For example,

```
$ pound "$ update tools #" <shell.fil | tee aaa.com | @sys$input
```

would write the update commands generated by pound to aaa.com before executing them as a command procedure.

As another example, here is another seemingly useless program called more, which copies STDIN to STDOUT, pausing after each screenful of output:

```
! more  -  copy STDIN to STDOUT one screenful at a time

      program more
      include           'global.def'
      character*(MAXSTR) line
      logical            fgetline
      integer            i

      call ioinit ()
      do while (.true.)
         do i = 1, 24
            if (.not. fgetline (STDIN, line)) then
               call iofinit ()
               stop ' '
            end if
            call fputstr (STDOUT, line)
         end do
         call fputstr (STDOUT, '---more---'//EOL)
      end do

      end
```

Although this program wouldn't be much use with plain DCL, it can be used to advantage with the shell. The command

```
$ dir | more
```

illustrates one application. The important thing to note is that more can be used with any program that outputs to STDOUT.

We have come full circle. We started out in this book with a set of basic I/O routines, and eventually wound up working on exotic things like captive subprocesses, asynchronous traps, and mailboxes. Now that we have I/O redirection and pipelines, the door is opened for many new tools constructed from the simple components in the early part of this book.

Exercises

1. Write a program wc that writes to STDOUT a count of the lines, words and characters in its input. The arguments -l, -w, and -c should enable output of lines, words, and characters, respectively.

2. Write an interpreter for the shell with block if, while, and until statements.

3. Add path to the shell as an internal command. The shell should examine the directories on the path for a file with the command name and a type of .exe or .com.

4. Modify getline to handle lines up to 255 characters in length.

5. Rewrite getc to use a table generated by lexgen to recognize escape sequences.

6. Write ttlogline, the equivalent of getlogline for direct terminal I/O.

7. Write a routine input that switches between file input and direct terminal input automatically by detecting whether or not the input source is a terminal.

8. Write a routine to get system privilege on any VMS system (and be sure to send us your results).

Further Reading

The VAX/VMS manuals and help libraries provide excellent documentation of just about everything one would want to know about programming in the VMS environment, even if it is sometimes hard to find the right information. The Master Index manual for VMS is a big help in finding stuff. Perhaps the most important manual for Fortran programmers is *Guide to Programming on VAX/VMS (Fortran Edition)*. Structure statements are discussed in Section 6 of *Programming in VAX Fortran*, which defines the VAX Fortran language. The start of each volume of the *System Services* manual contains comprehensive descriptions of the major services in the manual, such as processes, mailboxes, logical names, and so on. Unfortunately, DEC manuals are often difficult to understand, and one can never find a place where a whole topic is discussed at once. Some good places to look in the manuals for background information related to the programs in this chapter are

- *VMS I/O User's Guide*: the section describing the terminal driver explains the qio codes used for getc and putstr and for handling AST's.

- *System Services Manual*, Section 10: "Condition Handling Services" and *Run-time Library Manual*, Section 9: "Image Initialization and Termination": explanations of exit handlers and how they fit into image run-down.

- *DCL Dictionary*: describes how DCL uses the sys$input, sys$output, and sys$error logical names as well as the special considerations for using sys$command.

Many UNIX-like shells have been written; some well-written books about MS-DOS and its I/O redirection are available, and other shells that are more like UNIX have been written for the PCs. One example, by Alan Holub, can be found in *Dr. Dobb's Journal* in the December 1985–March 1986 issues. *The UNIX Programming Environment*, by Kernighan and Pike (Prentice-Hall, 1984), provides a very thorough explanation of how to use the UNIX shell programming language and could be a source of many good ideas for additional work on our shell.

Epilog

At the time of this writing, Fortran is undergoing a big change. The venerable Fortran 77 standard is being revised to create what is in many respects a new language, presently called "Fortran 8X." The proposed standard is presently mired in controversy and may not be released in its present form. Several essential improvements are virtually assured, however, such as the addition of derived types and recursive procedures, and standardization of `implicit none` statements, ! comments, and the `do...end do` loop construct. The syntax of source lines and statement continuation is the same as the convention used by our `getlogline` routine. Although `do while` has not been standardized, an unconditional "do forever" loop has, and the `exit` statement can be used to break out of such a loop. All of the `do while` loops in the tools can be recast into the new form easily, for example,

```
do while (ppline(line))
   . . .
end do
```

can be written as

```
do; if (.not. ppline(line)) exit
   . . .
end do
```

If the tools are properly converted, then many routines will be simplified. Most of the occurrences of the logical variable `done` in statements like `do while (.not. done)` will be unnecessary.

The new standard is not without its drawbacks, however, not the least of which is its sheer size and complexity. All of Fortran 77 is included in the "revision," even obsolete and unhealthy features, since there is a large and vocal crowd that wails and moans at the thought of having to fix ancient code. While lots of new features are being added, some deficiencies in the old standard have been ignored. There are no significant changes in the interface to the file system, so a set of primitives for file I/O is still needed. It will be interesting to see what happens to Fortran now and after the new standard is eventually released. In any case, the tools in this book will still be useful and can be made standard conforming with little effort.

Now it is time to summarize what we have done. We began with a set of primitive routines for file I/O, which perform well-defined functions and conceal the peculiarities of the system interface. They are the first thing needed to get the tools running. Here's a list:

```
fgetc       fgetline
fputc       fputstr
ioinit      iofinit
falloc      fdealloc
fopen       fclose
fflush
```

With these routines we proceeded to develop almost all of the programs in the book. We avoided using VAX Fortran extensions beyond those we could easily translate into standard form, and as a result the programs are portable to any computer with a Fortran 77 compiler. We found out that tools come in several flavors: they can be routines that encapsulate a useful capability with a clean interface for use in other programs, like the preprocessor and `getlogline`; they can be generators like `hashgen` and `lexgen` that build still more tools; or they can be tools to relieve us from some of the drudgery of programming, like `pound` or `change`. The programs we wrote grew gradually from simple to complex, as the number of tools available grew to make it easier to write big programs. Finally, we returned to the task of writing primitives for other interfaces to the system and developed a selection complete enough to write an I/O redirection shell for DCL.

Don't feel bad or mad if you did not find the programs crystal clear on the first reading. It takes real mental effort to understand any program, whether written by you or by someone else. But it's worth the effort, because more can be learned from studying one real working program and understanding it than from reading whole books of generalities. Programming is best learned by example.

Nevertheless, there are some general rules we follow that we think make it easier to write reliable and readable Fortran programs. Most rules for programming style are matters of opinion, and there are as many rules as there are programmers. Here are some of our opinions on the subject, illustrated by the code in this book:

- Use `implicit none` if it is available, so that errors are detected by the compiler rather than by the user at run time.

- Choose some conventions for source code format and stick with them everywhere. Don't restrict yourself to Fortran 77 form since it looks horrible and is hard to understand. Instead, write a simple preprocessor to convert your programs to Fortran 77 if necessary.

- Use parameter statements to define names with mnemonic value for internal codes. Parameters take no space in the compiled program; their only purpose in life is to make programs more readable.

- Put enough comments in the code so that a reader can easily identify what the purpose of a routine is, and what major sections of code are doing. If you find that it takes a lot of comments to explain what you're doing, there is probably a better way to do it. Routines with too many comments are more difficult to understand than routines with only a few if the code itself is well-written.

- Use short but descriptive names for variables. Very long names lead to excessive statement continuation, and in almost all cases a name like bp is just as descriptive as buffer_pointer. However, don't make names short at the expense of their mnemonic value.

- Concealing complexity is the name of the game in programming, and there are a few important techniques for Fortran programming that help:

  - In defining the interface between two routines, try to find the line between them where the number of things that must cross it is minimized. This means that you should try to keep the number of arguments for a routine small, so that they can be easily remembered, and avoid communication through common blocks wherever possible.

  - Routines can maintain significant data structures on their own without communicating the data to the caller by use of the save statement.

  - When coupling between cooperating routines requires the use of a common block, the visibility of the common block can be concealed from the rest of the program by using the save statement.

- Code defensively. Always assume that the program will receive the worst possible input since it almost certainly will, and write code that can handle it. Always check for errors when the opportunity arises.

- Don't worry too much about efficiency when writing a program. Use common sense to avoid doing things that are ridiculously inefficient, but don't put a lot of extra effort into efficiency when writing the first draft. If efficiency is a real concern, then get the program running first and use a profiling tool to find out where the bottlenecks are. Then you can concentrate your effort on the parts of the code that will provide the greatest benefit from improved efficiency.

- Figure out what to do before writing any code. The worst way to code is to start writing without a well-conceived algorithm, adding code little by little and inserting goto statements until the program seems to be working. The problem with this approach is that the resulting code looks awful, is difficult even for the programmer to understand, and probably will never work again if it is ever modified.

- Define an appropriate representation for the data needed by a program and then write the code around it. Code seems to fall into place easily when it is viewed as a well-defined operation on well-defined data.

- Design programs from the top down, but code them from the bottom up. Get some idea of the top-level organization of the program and what the major pieces must do, and then write the underlying support routines that are needed for the major pieces to come together. Use existing tools wherever possible to simplify a job.

- Don't be afraid to rewrite a program. Programs rarely come out right the first time, much less elegant. Just about every routine in this book has been rewritten at least once, and some of them have been through an embarrassing number of iterations. But a program can often be simplified once all of the problems have been worked out the first time, and a rewrite to make it simpler also makes it more readable, understandable, and maintainable.

The purpose of developing software tools is to solve problems, solve them in a general way, and use them to simplify development of still more tools. We hope that the tools in this book solve problems for you and that you can use them to advantage in your own programs. But the process does not stop here. The size and quality of a programmer's toolbox is in some sense an indicator of experience and productivity since having tools and knowing how to use them means large parts of just about any program are already written. We suspect that most readers have some sort of toolbox already for the particular kinds of problems that interest them, whether for numerical analysis, simulation programs, graphics, or even games. Whatever your interests, we hope that you will have a tools approach.

APPENDIX A

global.def

```
! global.def  -  global symbolic constants for tools


    ! maximum character string lengths and string termination
        character*1   NULL
        parameter     (NULL = char(0))
        integer       MAXLINE
        parameter     (MAXLINE = 132)
        integer       MAXSTR
        parameter     (MAXSTR = 255)

    ! file i/o parameters
        integer       MAXOPEN
        parameter     (MAXOPEN = 30)
        character*1   NEWLINE
        parameter     (NEWLINE = char(10))
        character*1   EOF
        parameter     (EOF = char(26))
        character*2   EOL
        parameter     (EOL = NEWLINE//NULL)
    ! standard units
        integer       STDIN
        parameter     (STDIN = 5)
        integer       STDOUT
        parameter     (STDOUT = 6)
        integer       STDERR
        parameter     (STDERR = 7)
    ! i/o unit access codes
        integer       IOERROR
        parameter     (IOERROR = -1)
        integer       IOREAD
        parameter     (IOREAD = -2)
        integer       IOWRITE
        parameter     (IOWRITE = -3)
        integer       IOAPPEND
        parameter     (IOAPPEND = -4)
        integer       IOFORTRAN
```

```
        parameter    (IOFORTRAN = -5)

!  command line arguments
        integer      MAXARGS
        parameter    (MAXARGS = 10)
        character*1  QUALIFIER
        parameter    (QUALIFIER = '-')

!  preprocessor buffer size
        integer      PPLINESIZE
        parameter    (PPLINESIZE = 2048)
!  other standard definitions
        character*1  COMMENT
        parameter    (COMMENT = '!')
        character*1  ESCAPE
        parameter    (ESCAPE = '\')
        character*1  WILDCARD
        parameter    (WILDCARD = '*')
        character*1  SKIPCARD
        parameter    (SKIPCARD = '~')
        integer      ENDLIST
        parameter    (ENDLIST = -2147483647)   ! -(2**31)

!  ascii characters
        character*1  BELL
        parameter    (BELL = char(7))
        character*1  BACKSPACE
        parameter    (BACKSPACE = char(8))
        character*1  TAB
        parameter    (TAB = char(9))
        character*1  LINEFEED
        parameter    (LINEFEED = char(10))
        character*1  FORMFEED
        parameter    (FORMFEED = char(12))
        character*1  CR
        parameter    (CR = char(13))
        character*1  ESC
        parameter    (ESC = char(27))
        character*1  BLANK
        parameter    (BLANK = char(32))
        character*1  APOSTROPHE
        parameter    (APOSTROPHE = char(39))  !' '
        character*1  DQUOTE
        parameter    (DQUOTE = char(34))      !" "
        character*1  QUOTE
        parameter    (QUOTE = APOSTROPHE)
```

APPENDIX B

Tools for MS–DOS

This appendix describes implementations of our I/O primitives on systems running MS–DOS with Lahey Fortran. The primitives for MS–DOS may also serve as a guide in porting them to other operating environments.

Some of the tools presented in the book were initially developed under MS–DOS and subsequently ported to the VMS system. The computers used were IBM XTs and ATs, equipped with hard disk drives, 640K of memory, EGA-compatible graphics adapter boards, and the "enhanced" keyboards. The XT setup has proven to be a marginal software development system, lacking in raw speed of the CPU and disk drives. However, the AT is tolerably slow, and the speed of MS–DOS-compatible systems is increasing rapidly; any of the 80386-based machines is plenty fast enough. The software presented here does not depend on a particular hardware configuration.

All of the software in this book will run without change on a PC once the primitives and v77 are working, with the exception of lexgen and spl. The size of the cmem array in spl exceeds the implementation limit of Lahey Fortran character variables, which is 32K. If the cmem array size is reduced to 32K and INPUT_ORIGIN and CHAR_ORIGIN are redefined accordingly, spl works just fine on the PC. The executable image size for spl is 480K bytes. The lexgen program is more of a problem—as presently implemented, it requires 1.3MB of memory. The dfa array alone is 512K bytes in the VAX version; its size can be cut in half by declaring it to be integer*2, and can be halved again by allowing only ASCII character codes with values up to 127 (by changing the declaration of MAXCHAR). The size can be reduced further only by reducing the maximum number of states, but reasonable sized lexical analyzers can be generated with only about half as many states. The changes in combination will reduce the size of the dfa array to 64K bytes, a quite reasonable size. Other possibilities for making lexgen fit into 640K of memory are removal of the preprocessor as a built-in feature and using prep, or splitting the program in half, with communication via a temporary file. If a compiler supporting extended memory (such as Lahey F77L/EM) is available, lexgen can be run without change.

B.1   The MS–DOS Programming Environment

A brief outline of the MS–DOS programming environment is the first order of business in discussing the IBM-PC primitives. A thorough understanding of the programming environment is essential to the design of the operating system interface. Throughout this discussion the Lahey Fortran compiler is assumed, although the situation is nearly the same with any other compiler.

MS–DOS is structured in three distinct levels: the manufacturer supplied basic input/output system (BIOS), the DOS kernel, and the command shell. The BIOS completely insulates the DOS kernel routines from the hardware through the use of standard names and interfaces for primitive I/O functions. The DOS kernel provides a standardized set of system services in a hardware independent manner. The command shell is responsible for prompting the user for commands, interpreting the user's request, and executing the command. The I/O primitives routines presented here use the MS–DOS kernel routines only.

The MS–DOS operating shell is provided with the operating system in a file named command.com. The shell is comprised of an initialization routine, memory resident error handlers, and the command processor. When the system boots, the error-handling routines are loaded into memory just above the MS–DOS kernel, followed immediately by the initialization routine. Control is then transferred to the initialization routine, which redefines the interupt vectors to use the MS–DOS handlers, processes the autoexec.bat file, initializes the I/O system, and loads the command processor into high memory. The initialization routine then exits, leaving the condition handlers resident, and control is passed to the command processor.

The command processor maintains an internal buffer called the *environment block*. The environment block is organized as a series of null-terminated strings called *environment variables* with a null string as the terminator of the block. The strings are used to equate a symbolic name to a literal translation string in a manner analogous to symbols in the DCL command processor. Each of the strings in the enviroment block is of the form symbol=value, where symbol is the symbolic name being assigned and value is a string of ASCII characters, terminated by a NULL. The command processor uses the environment block to store information such as the current command path PATH, the form of the user prompt PROMPT, and the full file specification of the command processor executable image COMSPEC. Certain applications also make use of the environment block, such as the Microsoft object linker; it uses the variable lib as a search path for default libraries. A copy of the environment block is made for each child process when it is created. This copying of the environment is strictly a one-way operation and may not be used to pass information from a child process back to the originating process.

The command processor classifies the user's input as either an internal or external command. Internal commands are implemented by code that is present in the command processor itself. An external command is any program placed on the command path. The command processor is also responsible for the implementation of I/O redirection. This is easily accomplished via the **exec** service, which creates and passes control to a child process. By default, **exec** passes the environment block and the handles associated with any open files to the child process. I/O redirection is accomplished by scanning the command line for the input redirection symbol <; if found, the standard input (handle 0) is closed and reopened to the new file or device. Output redirection (>) is implemented in a similar manner. When the **exec** service is then invoked, the child inherits the new standard input and output handles. After the child process exits, the standard input and output handles are closed and reopened to the console device.

Our PC operating system setup is different from the usual installation of DOS. The command.com program is in a directory \bin along with the DOS external commands and other "system" software. The config.sys file contains the line

```
shell=c:\bin\command.com /p /e:640
```

to tell DOS where to find command.com (otherwise it must be in the root directory). The option /e sets the number of bytes of memory allocated to environment strings in all versions of DOS after DOS 3.1; in DOS 3.1 the parameter is the number of paragraphs allocated (16 bytes per paragraph), so /e:640 would be replaced by /e:20 in DOS 3.1. The /p option tells DOS to execute autoexec.bat, which must be in the root directory. The files= command in config.sys should also be set to agree with the value of MAXOPEN in global.def. Our autoexec file just finishes the DOS setup by setting comspec to the correct path name, setting a default path and prompt, and passing control to the real login:

```
set comspec=c:\bin\command.com
path=c:\usr\bin;c:\bin
prompt=$$
login
```

There is a directory tree for all our home-brewed software called \usr. The file \usr\bin\login.bat contains all of the other things one likes to do at login, such as set environment variables for software packages, initialize the print queue, run a clock program, and so on. It defines two environment variables to support the tools system:

```
set toolslib=c:\usr\lib\tools.lib
set f77lib=c:\usr\lib\f77lib.lib
```

B.2 MS–DOS Program Development Tools

There are several Fortran compilers available for the IBM-PC, the most popular of which are Ryan-McFarland, Microsoft, and Lahey Fortran. All of these are full Fortran 77 compilers with a few extensions. Lahey Fortran is probably the best of the three because it has several desirable features in addition to the standard: implicit none declarations, several system service routines, access to registers,

and stack allocation of local variables. The stack allocation of variables allows
for recursive functions and, more importantly, preserves memory by freeing space
when not in use. Lahey Fortran also allows source lines up to column 80 and
long identifier names.

The Lahey system supplies a set of extended intrinsic functions that are tailored for the MS–DOS environment. The command line may be accessed via a
call to the routine getcl, which retrieves it from the program segment prefix
(PSP) of the executing program. The getcl routine operates in a manner similar to that of the lib$get_foriegn routine used on the VAX, with the notable
exception that only the command tail is returned. The intrup routine provides
the means to generate 8086 software interrupts. The interrupt number and a set
of 8086 register masks are used to pass MS–DOS the information required by the
routine that handles the interrupt. The routines segment and offset provide
the segment and offset addresses of their arguments; these greatly simplify the
use of many of the DOS kernel routines. Another routine worthy of mention here
is the system routine, which provides a service similar to the VMS lib$spawn
routine. The system routine loads a copy of command.com via the MS–DOS exec
routine, then passes its argument to be executed by the new copy of the command
interpreter. This provides a program with easy access to the services available
from the MS–DOS external commands.

Lahey Fortran (F77L) is not without drawbacks, however. It doesn't support
the end do statement or do while loops, and versions we have used don't deal
properly with ! as a comment delimiter. One version of the compiler produced
incorrect code for character*(*) arguments, and another went into an infinite
loop on include statements (both of these bugs were fixed promptly by Lahey).
Even with these problems we still think Lahey Fortran is the best Fortran compiler for MS–DOS. The moral of this story is that a PC ain't a VAX, even if it
is just as fast, so beware.

We therefore have v77 built in to the f command. As with the VAX, we use
the compiler switches for the implicit none and extended source line features,
and the -l option generates a listing file by appending the switches /h/x to the
f77l command.

```
rem f  -  compile Fortran source

if 0%1==0    goto help
if 0%2==0-n  goto nov77

if exist lf77.for  delete lf77.for
if exist lf77.obj  delete lf77.obj
if exist %1.for    v77 %1.for lf77.for
if 0%2==0-l        f77l lf77.for /0/a/f/b/l/p/w/ns/ni/no/nt/h/x
if not 0%2==0-l    f77l lf77.for /0/a/f/b/l/p/w/ns/ni/no/nt
if exist lf77.obj  rename lf77.obj %1.obj
if exist lf77.for  del lf77.for
goto done
```

```
:nov77
f771 %1.for /O/a/f/b/l/p/w/ns/ni/no/nt
goto done

:help
echo    syntax: f source [-l][-n]
echo            [-l]   produce list file
echo            [-n]   no v77 processing

:done
```

Ordinarily, MS–DOS chains batch file execution and never returns to the calling file; the command/c before the f command invokes a "secondary command processor," so that execution returns to update when f is finished.

We use Microsoft lib to manage the tools library. lib is similar in function, but not in syntax or performance, to the VAX librarian. Its commands take the form

```
$ lib [op]module library;
```

where the operators perform these library operations:

op	operation
+	Append module to library
−	Delete module from library
*	Extract module into object file
−*	Extract module into object file and delete from library

lib will allow only one main program unit in each object library. This difference forces us to implement update and image for MS–DOS in a slightly different manner. Here is the version of update we use with MS–DOS:

```
rem update  -  compile Fortran source and update object library

command/c  f %2 %3
if exist %2.obj   lib %1-+%2,%1.lis;
if exist %2.obj   del %2.obj
```

The Microsoft linker utility binds object modules together into relocatable images. The only command line option we have found necessary is the /seg switch, which overrides the default maximum of 128 segments for an executable image. It should be set to at least 512 (the maximum is 1024). Since the lib utility does not allow multiple main programs to be stored in the same object library, image was written to assume that the object module for the main program exists prior to its invocation.

```
rem image  -  create executable image from library

if not exist %2.obj   goto err
```

```
link/seg:512  %2,%2,NUL,%1
goto done
:err
   echo object module not found - aborted
:done
```

The name of an environment string enclosed in % in a batch file causes substitution with the replacement string, providing a simple logical name facility in
DOS. The linker is painfully S L O W on XTs with standard disk drives but is
tolerable on ATs.

B.3   Lahey Fortran I/O Primitives

The Lahey compiler has a combination of extensions that make implementation
of the primitives a piece of cake. For instance, it supplies a routine getcl to get
the command line, in a format almost identical to the VAX cli$get_value so
getargs is almost unchanged. It also has a carriagecontrol='LIST' qualifier
for the open statement, and it can be used to override the Fortran carriage control
default for output to STDOUT. Here is ioinit:

```
*  ioinit  -  initialize file system and connect standard units

        subroutine ioinit()
        integer   i, ios
        include   'global.def'
        include   'iox.cmn'

        do 1 i = 1, MAXOPEN     !initalize i/o buffers
           call freset(i)
           alloc(i) = .false.
           access(i) = 0
1       continue

        do 2 i = 5, 7
           alloc(i) = .true.
2       continue

        access(5) = IOREAD
        access(6) = IOWRITE
        access(7) = IOWRITE
        open (unit = *, status = 'OLD', iostat = ios,
    &        carriagecontrol = 'LIST',
    &        err = 10)
        open (unit = 7, file = 'CON', status = 'OLD', iostat = ios,
    &        carriagecontrol = 'LIST',
    &        err = 10)

        return

10 call ioerr (ios)
```

```
    return
    end
```

Opening a file to the DOS device CON results in a console connection that cannot
be redirected, which is just what is desired for STDERR. Lahey provides precon-
nection of units 5 and 6 to STDIN and STDOUT, and the open statement for unit
* changes the carriage control on STDOUT without any other effect.

Lahey provides a message facility for I/O errors, and ioerr uses it for all
error reporting:

```
*  ioerr  -  writes appropriate I/O error message to STDERR

    subroutine ioerr(ios)
    integer    ios
    include    'global.def'
    character*80 message

    call iostat_msg (ios, message)
    call fputstr (STDERR, message(1:64)//EOL)

    return
    end
```

There is no Q edit descriptor in Lahey Fortran, so the buffer length in iox
must be determined by searching backwards through the input line for the first
nonblank character:

```
*  fgetc  -  get character from file

    character*1 function fgetc (u, c)
    integer    u, i
    character*1 c
    include    'global.def'
    include    'iox.cmn'

    bp(u) = bp(u) + 1
    if (bp(u) .eq. 1) then
        read (u, ' (A) ',end=10) buffer(u)
        i = MAXLINE
   1 if (buffer(u)(i:i) .eq. BLANK .and. i .gt. 0) then
        i = i - 1
        goto 1
      end if
      length(u) = i
      if (i .eq. 0) then
        c = NEWLINE
        bp(u) = 0
      else
        c = buffer(u)(bp(u):bp(u))
      end if
    else if (bp(u) .eq. i+1) then
```

```
              c = NEWLINE
              bp(u) = 0
          else
              c = buffer(u)(bp(u):bp(u))
          end if
          fgetc = c
          return

      10  c = EOF
          fgetc = c
          return
          end
```

`fgetline` is similar. Since there is no "run-time format" for F77L, the actual
integer value of `MAXLINE` must be used in the format statement in `fputc`:

```
*  fputc  -  output character to file

        subroutine fputc (u, c)
        integer     u, i
        character*1 c
        include     'global.def'
        include     'iox.cmn'

        bp(u) = bp(u) + 1
        if (c .eq. NEWLINE) then
            write (u,'(132 A1:)') (buffer(u)(i:i),i= 1,bp(u)-1)
            bp(u) = 0
        else if (bp(u) .eq. MAXLINE) then
            buffer(u)(MAXLINE:MAXLINE) = c
            write (u,'(132 A1:)') (buffer(u)(i:i),i= 1,MAXLINE)
            bp(u) = 0
        else
            buffer(u)(bp(u):bp(u)) = c
        end if

        return
        end
```

Again, `fputstr` is similar. All of the other primitives are the same as the VAX
versions, except that some mechanical translation of `while` loops is necessary.

B.4   Generic MS–DOS I/O primitives

Although the implementation of the primitives using Lahey Fortran I/O is easy,
it is also somewhat slow and relies on extensions to do the job. This section
describes a generic set of primitives that bypass Fortran I/O altogether and
call DOS directly. The only extensions used are nonstandard intrinsic routines
that can be easily duplicated for other compilers. The use of MS–DOS kernel

routines to provide primitive system services results in a set of tools that are applicable to any MS–DOS system, since the MS–DOS kernel is designed to be independent of the particular hardware on which it runs. The MS–DOS I/O primitives strictly adhere to the documented standard DOS entry points to preserve portability among PC-compatible computers. The MS–DOS primitives maintain the standards and functionality established by the VMS versions and provide an efficient and fast I/O capability.

The MS–DOS tools use the same global.def file for relaying standard symbol definitions to the Fortran compiler. An additional file msdos.cmn, used only by the I/O primitives, provides further symbolic constants for use with the MS–DOS service routines and declares a common block for the 8088 register array used by the Lahey intrup routine.

```
* msdos.cmn  -  MS-DOS interface definitions

* character io
        integer*2  DOS$GETC
        parameter  (DOS$GETC    = 1 * 256)
        integer*2  DOS$PUTC
        parameter  (DOS$PUTC    = 2 * 256)
        integer*2  DOS$PUTSTR
        parameter  (DOS$PUTSTR  = 9 * 256)
        integer*2  DOS$GETKBUF
        parameter  (DOS$GETKBUF = 10 * 256)

* disk operations
        integer*2  DOS$SETDISK
        parameter  (DOS$SETDISK  = 14 * 256)
        integer*2  DOS$GETDISK
        parameter  (DOS$GETDISK  = 25 * 256)
        integer*2  DOS$SETDTA
        parameter  (DOS$SETDTA   = 26 * 256)
        integer*2  DOS$GETDTA
        parameter  (DOS$GETDTA   = 47 * 256)

* system functions
        integer*2  DOS$GETERROR
        parameter  (DOS$GETERROR = 89 * 256)

* directory operations
        integer*2  DOS$SETDIR
        parameter  (DOS$SETDIR  = 59 * 256)
        integer*2  DOS$GETDIR
        parameter  (DOS$GETDIR  = 71 * 256)
        integer*2  DOS$GETFILE
        parameter  (DOS$GETFILE  = 79 * 256)
        integer*2  DOS$GETFILE1
        parameter  (DOS$GETFILE1 = 78 * 256)

* file operations
        integer*2  DOS$CREATE
```

```
      parameter  (DOS$CREATE     = 60 * 256)
      integer*2  DOS$OPEN
      parameter  (DOS$OPEN       = 61 * 256)
      integer*2  DOS$CLOSE
      parameter  (DOS$CLOSE      = 62 * 256)
      integer*2  DOS$READ
      parameter  (DOS$READ       = 63 * 256)
      integer*2  DOS$WRITE
      parameter  (DOS$WRITE      = 64 * 256)
      integer*2  DOS$DELETE
      parameter  (DOS$DELETE     = 65 * 256)
      integer*2  DOS$FSETPTR
      parameter  (DOS$FSETPTR    = 66 * 256)
      integer*2  DOS$RENAME
      parameter  (DOS$RENAME     = 86 * 256)


*  8086 microprocessor interface
      integer*2   registers(9)
      integer*2   reg$ax, reg$bx, reg$cx, reg$dx
      integer*2   reg$ds, reg$es, reg$di, reg$si, reg$flags
      equivalence (registers(1), reg$ax)
      equivalence (registers(2), reg$bx)
      equivalence (registers(3), reg$cx)
      equivalence (registers(4), reg$dx)
      equivalence (registers(5), reg$ds)
      equivalence (registers(6), reg$es)
      equivalence (registers(7), reg$di)
      equivalence (registers(8), reg$si)
      equivalence (registers(9), reg$flags)

      common /int8086/ registers
      save   /int8086/
```

The equivalence statements for the registers allows them to be referred to by name individually or as a set.

The I/O primitives for MS–DOS, like their VMS counterparts, are organized around the iox common block. In the MS–DOS version an additional array is needed to associate file unit numbers with DOS file handles.

```
*  iox  -  common block for I/O primitives (MS-DOS file system)

      integer    MAXOPEN
      parameter  (MAXOPEN = 20)
      integer    MAXBUFFER
      parameter  (MAXBUFFER = 512)

      logical*1  alloc(MAXOPEN)                    !allocation flag array
      integer*2  access(MAXOPEN)                   !access mode array
      integer*2  handle(MAXOPEN)                   !unit-handle conversion array

      character*(MAXBUFFER)  buffer(MAXOPEN)       !i/o line buffer array
      integer*2  bp(MAXOPEN)                       !buffer pointer array
```

```
      integer*2  bl(MAXOPEN)                    !buffer length array

      common  /iox/     alloc, access, handle
      common  /iof/     buffer
      common  /iofptr/  bp, bl
      save    /iox/, /iof/, /iofptr/
```

The MS–DOS file open service allocates a handle for use in any further addressing of the newly opened file. MS–DOS file handles are analogous to the file units of Fortran, with the exception that MS–DOS controls which handle is allocated when a file open is requested. The standard input, output, and error devices (stdin, stdout, and stderr) are allocated and connected to the handles 0, 1, and 2, respectively, by MS–DOS before a program begins execution (DOS also allocates handles 3 and 4 to stdprn and stdaux, respectively). The handle array is used to store the handle returned from MS–DOS for a file which has been successfully opened. MS–DOS's automatic connection of the standard input and output devices to the standard file handles greatly simplifies the required I/O system initialization, as reflected by the MS–DOS version of ioinit:

```
* ioinit  -  initialize I/O system for MS-DOS tools

      subroutine ioinit ()
      include  'global.def'
      include  'msdos.cmn'
      include  'iox.cmn'
      integer  i

      do 1 i = 1, MAXOPEN
         handle(i) = 0
         alloc(i)  = .false.
         access(i) = 0
         bp(i) = 1
         bl(i) = 0
         buffer(i)(1:1) = NULL
    1 continue

! allocate and define standard units
      alloc(STDIN)  = .true.
      handle(STDIN) = 0
      access(STDIN) = IOREAD

      alloc(STDOUT)  = .true.
      handle(STDOUT) = 1
      access(STDOUT) = IOWRITE

      alloc(STDERR)  = .true.
      handle(STDERR) = 2
      access(STDERR) = IOWRITE

      return
```

```
        end
```

The MS–DOS file close service performs a flush of the buffer associated with a given file handle (if open with write access) before the file is closed. However, the fflush routine is still required for flushing the buffers internal to the I/O primitives.

```
* iofinit  -  cleanup io system: flush, close, and deallocate open units

        subroutine iofinit ()
        include  'global.def'
        include  'iox.cmn'
        integer  u

        do 1 u = 1, MAXOPEN
           if (alloc(u)) then
              if (access(u) .ne. IOREAD) call fflush(u)
              call fclose (u)
              alloc(u) = .false.
              access(u) = 0
           end if
      1 continue

        return
        end
```

The error tracing and reporting facilities of the VMS operating system are more complete than their MS–DOS counterparts. An extended error reporting mechanism was introduced in DOS 3.0 that greatly augmented the error handling of previous versions. Errors occurring during MS–DOS service calls are signaled by the carry flag being set, and an error code is returned in the low byte of the accumulator (reg$ax). The extended error information is obtained by passing the error code to another MS–DOS service routine, which then returns the extended error code, class, locus, and recommended action.

```
* ioerr  -  error reporting routine (MS-DOS system)

        subroutine ioerr (caller)
        character*(*)  caller
        include        'global.def'
        include        'msdos.cmn'
        character*(60) message(83), class(12), action(7), locus(5)
        save           message, class, action, locus
        integer        errmsg, erract
        include        'ioerr.def'

        reg$ax = DOS$GETERROR
        reg$bx = 0
        call intrup (registers, 33)
```

```
if (reg$ax .ne. 0) then
  errmsg = reg$ax
  erract = mod (reg$bx, 256)
  call fputstr (STDERR, caller)
  call fputstr (STDERR, message(errmsg))
  call fputstr (STDERR, EOL)
  if (erract.eq.5 .or. erract.eq.6) then
      call fputstr (STDERR, 'Program aborted, io status unknown'//NULL)
      call iofinit ()
  end if
end if

return
end
```

The interface to `ioerr` is a little different than that of the VMS version. `ioerr` has as its only argument the name of the calling routine (the registers are available through the common block `msdos.cmn`); it is called only by primitive routines, and only if the carry flag is set after performing an MS–DOS service call. The error messages are declared in `ioerr.def`:

```
* ioerr.def  -  MS-DOS extended error messages

      character*40  MESSAGE1
      parameter     (MESSAGE1 = ' invalid function number'//NULL)
      character*40  MESSAGE2
      parameter     (MESSAGE2 = ' file not found'//NULL)
      character*40  MESSAGE3
      parameter     (MESSAGE3 = ' path not found'//NULL)
      character*40  MESSAGE4
      parameter     (MESSAGE4 = ' too many open files'//NULL)
      character*40  MESSAGE5
      parameter     (MESSAGE5 = ' access denied'//NULL)
      character*40  MESSAGE6
      parameter     (MESSAGE6 = ' invalid handle'//NULL)
      character*40  MESSAGE7
      parameter     (MESSAGE7 = ' memory control blocks destroyed'//NULL)
      character*40  MESSAGE8
      parameter     (MESSAGE8 = ' insufficient memory'//NULL)
      character*40  MESSAGE9
      parameter     (MESSAGE9 = ' invalid memory block address'//NULL)
      character*40  MESSAGE10
      parameter     (MESSAGE10 = ' invalid environment'//NULL)
      character*40  MESSAGE11
      parameter     (MESSAGE11 = ' invalid format'//NULL)
      character*40  MESSAGE12
      parameter     (MESSAGE12 = ' invalid access code'//NULL)
      character*40  MESSAGE13
      parameter     (MESSAGE13 = ' invalid data'//NULL)
      character*40  MESSAGE14
      parameter     (MESSAGE14 = ' reserved'//NULL)
      character*40  MESSAGE15
```

```
parameter    (MESSAGE15 = ' invalid drive specified'//NULL)
character*40  MESSAGE16
parameter    (MESSAGE16 = ' cannot remove current directory'//NULL)
character*40  MESSAGE17
parameter    (MESSAGE17 = ' not same device'//NULL)
character*40  MESSAGE18
parameter    (MESSAGE18 = ' no more files'//NULL)
character*40  MESSAGE19
parameter    (MESSAGE19 = ' write protected diskette'//NULL)
character*40  MESSAGE20
parameter    (MESSAGE20 = ' unknown unit'//NULL)
character*40  MESSAGE21
parameter    (MESSAGE21 = ' drive not ready'//NULL)
character*40  MESSAGE22
parameter    (MESSAGE22 = ' unknown command'//NULL)
character*40  MESSAGE23
parameter    (MESSAGE23 = ' error (crc)'//NULL)
character*40  MESSAGE24
parameter    (MESSAGE24 = ' bad request structure length'//NULL)
character*40  MESSAGE25
parameter    (MESSAGE25 = ' seek error'//NULL)
character*40  MESSAGE26
parameter    (MESSAGE26 = ' unknown media type'//NULL)
character*40  MESSAGE27
parameter    (MESSAGE27 = ' sector not found'//NULL)
character*40  MESSAGE28
parameter    (MESSAGE28 = ' printer out of paper'//NULL)
character*40  MESSAGE29
parameter    (MESSAGE29 = ' write fault'//NULL)
character*40  MESSAGE30
parameter    (MESSAGE30 = ' read fault'//NULL)
character*40  MESSAGE31
parameter    (MESSAGE31 = ' general failure'//NULL)
character*40  MESSAGE32
parameter    (MESSAGE32 = ' sharing violation'//NULL)
character*40  MESSAGE33
parameter    (MESSAGE33 = ' lock violation'//NULL)
character*40  MESSAGE34
parameter    (MESSAGE34 = ' invalid disk change'//NULL)
character*40  MESSAGE35
parameter    (MESSAGE35 = ' fcb unavailable'//NULL)
character*40  MESSAGE36
parameter    (MESSAGE36 = ' reserved'//NULL)
character*40  MESSAGE37
parameter    (MESSAGE37 = ' reserved'//NULL)
character*40  MESSAGE38
parameter    (MESSAGE38 = ' reserved'//NULL)
character*40  MESSAGE39
parameter    (MESSAGE39 = ' reserved'//NULL)
character*40  MESSAGE40
parameter    (MESSAGE40 = ' reserved'//NULL)
character*40  MESSAGE41
parameter    (MESSAGE41 = ' reserved'//NULL)
```

```
character*40  MESSAGE42
parameter     (MESSAGE42 = ' reserved'//NULL)
character*40  MESSAGE43
parameter     (MESSAGE43 = ' reserved'//NULL)
character*40  MESSAGE44
parameter     (MESSAGE44 = ' reserved'//NULL)
character*40  MESSAGE45
parameter     (MESSAGE45 = ' reserved'//NULL)
character*40  MESSAGE46
parameter     (MESSAGE46 = ' reserved'//NULL)
character*40  MESSAGE47
parameter     (MESSAGE47 = ' reserved'//NULL)
character*40  MESSAGE48
parameter     (MESSAGE48 = ' reserved'//NULL)
character*40  MESSAGE49
parameter     (MESSAGE49 = ' reserved'//NULL)
character*40  MESSAGE50
parameter     (MESSAGE50 = ' reserved'//NULL)
character*40  MESSAGE51
parameter     (MESSAGE51 = ' reserved'//NULL)
character*40  MESSAGE52
parameter     (MESSAGE52 = ' reserved'//NULL)
character*40  MESSAGE53
parameter     (MESSAGE53 = ' reserved'//NULL)
character*40  MESSAGE54
parameter     (MESSAGE54 = ' reserved'//NULL)
character*40  MESSAGE55
parameter     (MESSAGE55 = ' reserved'//NULL)
character*40  MESSAGE56
parameter     (MESSAGE56 = ' reserved'//NULL)
character*40  MESSAGE57
parameter     (MESSAGE57 = ' reserved'//NULL)
character*40  MESSAGE58
parameter     (MESSAGE58 = ' reserved'//NULL)
character*40  MESSAGE59
parameter     (MESSAGE59 = ' reserved'//NULL)
character*40  MESSAGE60
parameter     (MESSAGE60 = ' reserved'//NULL)
character*40  MESSAGE61
parameter     (MESSAGE61 = ' reserved'//NULL)
character*40  MESSAGE62
parameter     (MESSAGE62 = ' reserved'//NULL)
character*40  MESSAGE63
parameter     (MESSAGE63 = ' reserved'//NULL)
character*40  MESSAGE64
parameter     (MESSAGE64 = ' reserved'//NULL)
character*40  MESSAGE65
parameter     (MESSAGE65 = ' reserved'//NULL)
character*40  MESSAGE66
parameter     (MESSAGE66 = ' reserved'//NULL)
character*40  MESSAGE67
parameter     (MESSAGE67 = ' reserved'//NULL)
character*40  MESSAGE68
```

```
parameter   (MESSAGE68 = ' reserved'//NULL)
character*40 MESSAGE69
parameter   (MESSAGE69 = ' reserved'//NULL)
character*40 MESSAGE70
parameter   (MESSAGE70 = ' reserved'//NULL)
character*40 MESSAGE71
parameter   (MESSAGE71 = ' reserved'//NULL)
character*40 MESSAGE72
parameter   (MESSAGE72 = ' reserved'//NULL)
character*40 MESSAGE73
parameter   (MESSAGE73 = ' reserved'//NULL)
character*40 MESSAGE74
parameter   (MESSAGE74 = ' reserved'//NULL)
character*40 MESSAGE75
parameter   (MESSAGE75 = ' reserved'//NULL)
character*40 MESSAGE76
parameter   (MESSAGE76 = ' reserved'//NULL)
character*40 MESSAGE77
parameter   (MESSAGE77 = ' reserved'//NULL)
character*40 MESSAGE78
parameter   (MESSAGE78 = ' reserved'//NULL)
character*40 MESSAGE79
parameter   (MESSAGE79 = ' reserved'//NULL)
character*40 MESSAGE80
parameter   (MESSAGE80 = ' file exists'//NULL)
character*40 MESSAGE81
parameter   (MESSAGE81 = ' reserved '//NULL)
character*40 MESSAGE82
parameter   (MESSAGE82 = ' cannot make'//NULL)
character*40 MESSAGE83
parameter   (MESSAGE83 = ' fail on interupt 24'//NULL)

character*40 CLASS1
parameter   (CLASS1 = 'Error class: out of resource'//NULL)
character*40 CLASS2
parameter   (CLASS2 = 'Error class: temporary situation'//NULL)
character*40 CLASS3
parameter   (CLASS3 = 'Error class: authorization'//NULL)
character*40 CLASS4
parameter   (CLASS4 = 'Error class: internal'//NULL)
character*40 CLASS5
parameter   (CLASS5 = 'Error class: hardware failure'//NULL)
character*40 CLASS6
parameter   (CLASS6 = 'Error class: system failure'//NULL)
character*40 CLASS7
parameter   (CLASS7 = 'Error class: application program error'//NULL)
character*40 CLASS8
parameter   (CLASS8 = 'Error class: not found'//NULL)
character*40 CLASS9
parameter   (CLASS9 = 'Error class: bad format'//NULL)
character*40 CLASS10
parameter   (CLASS10 = 'Error class: locked'//NULL)
character*40 CLASS11
```

```
parameter    (CLASS11 = 'Error class: media'//NULL)
character*40  CLASS12
parameter    (CLASS12 = 'Error class: unknown'//NULL)


character*40  ACTION1
parameter    (ACTION1 = 'Suggested action: retry'//NULL)
character*40  ACTION2
parameter    (ACTION2 = 'Suggested action: delay retry'//NULL)
character*40  ACTION3
parameter    (ACTION3 = 'Suggested action: user'//NULL)
character*40  ACTION4
parameter    (ACTION4 = 'Suggested action: abort'//NULL)
character*40  ACTION5
parameter    (ACTION5 = 'Suggested action: immediate exit'//NULL)
character*40  ACTION6
parameter    (ACTION6 = 'Suggested action: ignore'//NULL)
character*40  ACTION7
parameter    (ACTION7 =
&             'Suggested action: retry after user intervention'//NULL)

character*40  LOCUS1
parameter    (LOCUS1 = 'Error locus: unknown'//NULL)
character*40  LOCUS2
parameter    (LOCUS2 = 'Error locus: block device'//NULL)
character*40  LOCUS3
parameter    (LOCUS3 = 'Error locus: reserved'//NULL)
character*40  LOCUS4
parameter    (LOCUS4 = 'Error locus: serial device'//NULL)
character*40  LOCUS5
parameter    (LOCUS5 = 'Error locus: memory'//NULL)

data message(1)   /MESSAGE1/
data message(2)   /MESSAGE2/
data message(3)   /MESSAGE3/
data message(4)   /MESSAGE4/
data message(5)   /MESSAGE5/
data message(6)   /MESSAGE6/
data message(7)   /MESSAGE7/
data message(8)   /MESSAGE8/
data message(9)   /MESSAGE9/
data message(10)  /MESSAGE10/
data message(11)  /MESSAGE11/
data message(12)  /MESSAGE12/
data message(13)  /MESSAGE13/
data message(14)  /MESSAGE14/
data message(15)  /MESSAGE15/
data message(16)  /MESSAGE16/
data message(17)  /MESSAGE17/
data message(18)  /MESSAGE18/
data message(19)  /MESSAGE19/
data message(20)  /MESSAGE20/
data message(21)  /MESSAGE21/
data message(22)  /MESSAGE22/
```

```
data message(23)  /MESSAGE23/
data message(24)  /MESSAGE24/
data message(25)  /MESSAGE25/
data message(26)  /MESSAGE26/
data message(27)  /MESSAGE27/
data message(28)  /MESSAGE28/
data message(29)  /MESSAGE29/
data message(30)  /MESSAGE30/
data message(31)  /MESSAGE31/
data message(32)  /MESSAGE32/
data message(33)  /MESSAGE33/
data message(34)  /MESSAGE34/
data message(35)  /MESSAGE35/
data message(36)  /MESSAGE36/
data message(37)  /MESSAGE37/
data message(38)  /MESSAGE38/
data message(39)  /MESSAGE39/
data message(40)  /MESSAGE40/
data message(41)  /MESSAGE41/
data message(42)  /MESSAGE42/
data message(43)  /MESSAGE43/
data message(44)  /MESSAGE44/
data message(45)  /MESSAGE45/
data message(46)  /MESSAGE46/
data message(47)  /MESSAGE47/
data message(48)  /MESSAGE48/
data message(49)  /MESSAGE49/
data message(50)  /MESSAGE50/
data message(51)  /MESSAGE51/
data message(52)  /MESSAGE52/
data message(53)  /MESSAGE53/
data message(54)  /MESSAGE54/
data message(55)  /MESSAGE55/
data message(56)  /MESSAGE56/
data message(57)  /MESSAGE57/
data message(58)  /MESSAGE58/
data message(59)  /MESSAGE59/
data message(60)  /MESSAGE60/
data message(61)  /MESSAGE61/
data message(62)  /MESSAGE62/
data message(63)  /MESSAGE63/
data message(64)  /MESSAGE64/
data message(65)  /MESSAGE65/
data message(66)  /MESSAGE66/
data message(67)  /MESSAGE67/
data message(68)  /MESSAGE68/
data message(69)  /MESSAGE69/
data message(70)  /MESSAGE70/
data message(71)  /MESSAGE71/
data message(72)  /MESSAGE72/
data message(73)  /MESSAGE73/
data message(74)  /MESSAGE74/
data message(75)  /MESSAGE75/
```

```
data message(76)  /MESSAGE76/
data message(77)  /MESSAGE77/
data message(78)  /MESSAGE78/
data message(79)  /MESSAGE79/
data message(80)  /MESSAGE80/
data message(81)  /MESSAGE81/
data message(82)  /MESSAGE82/
data message(83)  /MESSAGE83/

data class(1)   /CLASS1/
data class(2)   /CLASS2/
data class(3)   /CLASS3/
data class(4)   /CLASS4/
data class(5)   /CLASS5/
data class(6)   /CLASS6/
data class(7)   /CLASS7/
data class(8)   /CLASS8/
data class(9)   /CLASS9/
data class(10)  /CLASS10/
data class(11)  /CLASS11/
data class(12)  /CLASS12/

data action(1)  /ACTION1/
data action(2)  /ACTION2/
data action(3)  /ACTION3/
data action(4)  /ACTION4/
data action(5)  /ACTION5/
data action(6)  /ACTION6/
data action(7)  /ACTION7/

data locus(1)   /LOCUS1/
data locus(2)   /LOCUS2/
data locus(3)   /LOCUS3/
data locus(4)   /LOCUS4/
data locus(5)   /LOCUS5/
```

The iox line buffers in the MS–DOS primitives are larger than their VMS counterparts so that a file can be completely read in a smaller number of operations, increasing the efficiency of the routines. If the handle of the file being read is associated with a record-oriented device (a file), the number of characters requested (if available) is transferred from the file to the buffer without any interpretation of carriage control. If the handle is associated with a character device (i.e., the keyboard), the read operation is completed upon reception of a carriage return.

The fgetc routine returns the next character in the buffer and increments the buffer pointer, unless the buffer is empty or the next character is a carriage return. If the buffer is empty, the MS–DOS read-by-handle routine is called to fill the buffer. When a carriage return is seen, it is returned as NEWLINE and the buffer pointer is incremented past the linefeed character following it.

```
* fgetc  -  get character from file I/O buffer

      character*1 function fgetc (u, c)
      integer    u
      character*1 c
      include    'global.def'
      include    'msdos.cmn'
      include    'iox.cmn'

      if (bp(u).le.0 .or. bp(u).gt.bl(u)) then
         reg$ax = DOS$READ
         reg$bx = handle(u)
         reg$ds = segment (buffer(u))
         reg$dx = offset (buffer(u))
         reg$cx = MAXBUFFER
         call intrup (registers, 33)
         if (mod (reg$flags,2) .eq. 1) then
            c = NULL
            bp(u) = 0
            bl(u) = 0
            call ioerr ('fgetc: '//NULL)
         else if (reg$ax .eq. 0) then
            c = EOF
            bp(u) = 0
            bl(u) = 0
         else
            c = buffer(u)(1:1)
            bp(u) = 2
            bl(u) = reg$ax
         end if
      else
         c = buffer(u)(bp(u):bp(u))
         if (c .eq. CR) then
            c = NEWLINE
            bp(u) = bp(u) + 2
         else
            bp(u) = bp(u) + 1
         end if
      end if

      fgetc = c

      return
      end
```

The relationship between fgetline and fgetc is the same as the relationship
between their VAX counterparts. fgetline returns the contents of the buffer
from the current buffer pointer to the first carraige return character that follows,
converting the carriage return to a NEWLINE and adding a NULL terminator.

```
* fgetline  -  get line via MS-DOS file handle
```

```
logical function fgetline (u, line)
character*(*) line
integer     u
include     'global.def'
include     'msdos.cmn'
include     'iox.cmn'
integer     lp
save        lp

if (bp(u).gt.0 .and. bp(u).le.bl(u)) then
   lp = index (buffer(u)(bp(u):bl(u)), CR)
   if (lp .eq. 0) then
      fgetline = .false.
      lp = bl(u) - bp(u) + 1
      line(1:lp) = buffer(u)(bp(u):bl(u))
      bp(u) = 0
      bl(u) = 0
      lp = lp + 1
   else if (lp .eq. 1) then
      fgetline = .true.
      line(1:2) = EOL
      bp(u) = bp(u) + 2
      lp = 1
   else
      fgetline = .true.
      line(1:lp+1) = buffer(u)(bp(u):bp(u)+lp-2)//EOL
      bp(u) = bp(u) + lp
      if (buffer(u)(bp(u):bp(u)) .eq. LINEFEED) bp(u) = bp(u) + 1
      lp = 1
   end if
else
   bp(u) = 0
   lp = 1
end if

if (bp(u). eq. 0) then
   reg$ax = DOS$READ
   reg$bx = handle(u)
   reg$ds = segment (buffer(u))
   reg$dx = offset  (buffer(u))
   reg$cx = MAXBUFFER
   call intrup (registers, 33)
   if (mod (reg$flags,2) .eq. 1) then
      fgetline = .false.
      line(lp:lp) = NULL
      bl(u) = 0
      bp(u) = 0
      call ioerr ('fgetline: '//NULL)
   else if (reg$ax .eq. 0) then
      fgetline = .false.
      line(1:2) = EOF//NULL
      bp(u) = 0
```

```
            bl(u) = 0
         else
            fgetline = .true.
            bl(u) = reg$ax
            bp(u) = index (buffer(u)(1:bl(u)), CR)
            line(lp:lp+bp(u)) = buffer(u)(1:bp(u)-1)//EOL
            if (buffer(u)(bp(u)+1:bp(u)+1) .eq. LINEFEED) then
               bp(u) = bp(u) + 2
            else
               bp(u) = bp(u) + 1
            end if
         end if
      end if

      return
      end
```

The fputc and fputstr routines place output characters into the buffer until
a NEWLINE character is received, in which case a carriage return/linefeed pair
is put in the buffer and the MS–DOS write-by-handle routine is invoked.

```
* fputc  -  output character to I/O buffer

      subroutine   fputc (u, c)
      integer      u
      character*1  c
      include      'global.def'
      include      'msdos.cmn'
      include      'iox.cmn'

      if (c .eq. NEWLINE) then
         reg$ax = DOS$WRITE
         reg$bx = handle (u)
         reg$ds = segment (buffer(u))
         reg$dx = offset  (buffer(u))
         buffer(u)(bp(u):bp(u)+1) = CR//LINEFEED
         reg$cx = bp(u) + 1
         call intrup (registers, 33)
         if (mod (reg$flags,2) .eq. 1) call ioerr ('fputc: '//NULL)
         bp(u) = 1
      else
         buffer(u)(bp(u):bp(u)) = c
         bp(u) = bp(u) + 1
      end if

      return
      end
```

```
* fputstr  -  output string to I/O buffer

      subroutine fputstr (u, string)
      integer        u
      character*(*)  string
      include        'global.def'
      include        'msdos.cmn'
      include        'iox.cmn'
      integer        se, sp

      se = index (string, NULL) - 1

      if (se .ne. 0) then
          sp = index (string(1:se), NEWLINE) - 1
          if (sp .lt. 0) then
              buffer(u)(bp(u):bp(u)+se-1) = string(1:se)
              bp(u) = bp(u) + se
          else
              if (sp .eq. 0) then
                  buffer(u)(bp(u):bp(u)+1) = CR//LINEFEED
                  bp(u) = bp(u) + 1
              else
                  buffer(u)(bp(u):bp(u)+sp+1) = string(1:sp)//CR//LINEFEED
                  bp(u) = bp(u) + sp + 1
              end if
              reg$ax = DOS$WRITE
              reg$bx = handle(u)
              reg$ds = segment (buffer(u))
              reg$dx = offset  (buffer(u))
              reg$cx = bp(u)
              call intrup (registers, 33)
              if (mod (reg$flags,2) .eq. 1) call ioerr ('fputstr: '//NULL)
              bp(u) = 1
              bl(u) = 0
          end if
      end if

      return
      end
```

The iof part of the primitives—the part that handles opening and closing
files—is considerably more complicated than the VMS version. The main reason
for the added complexity is the addition of the nice feature of automatic backup
file creation when a file is opened for output. The Fortran I/O version simply
writes over an existing file on output; the generic DOS version renames an existing
file with the extension of .bak before creating an output file with the original
name. Several new routines are needed to implement this feature, but they are
useful in their own right as MS–DOS system primitives.

The MS–DOS fopen has to do more work than its VMS counterpart since it
controls the file renaming and since the file open attempt will fail if the file does
not exist. If a new file is to be created (i.e., if it is opened for write access), the

file must first be created. If the file exists and a new version is desired, the old
version must be renamed before creating the new version.

```
* fopen  -  open file, assign unit, store handle

      integer function fopen (unit, filename, mode)
      integer      unit, mode
      character*(*)  filename
      include       'global.def'
      include       'msdos.cmn'
      include       'iox.cmn'
      integer       fcreate, falloc

      if (falloc (unit) .ne. IOERROR) then
         if (mode .eq. IOREAD) then
            reg$ax = DOS$OPEN
         else if (mode.eq.IOWRITE .or. mode.eq.IOAPPEND) then
            reg$ax = DOS$OPEN + 1
         else
            alloc(unit) = .false.
            unit = IOERROR
            fopen = IOERROR
            call ioerr ('fopen: '//NULL)
            return
         end if
         reg$ds = segment (filename)
         reg$dx = offset  (filename)
         call intrup (registers, 33)
         if (mod (reg$flags,2) .eq. 1) then
            if (mode.eq.IOREAD .or. fcreate(unit,filename).eq.IOERROR) then
               alloc(unit) = .false.
               unit = IOERROR
               call ioerr ('fopen: '//NULL)
            else
               bp(unit) = 1
            end if
         else
            handle(unit) = reg$ax
            access(unit) = mode
            call fsetptr (unit, 2)
            if (mode .eq. IOWRITE) then
               call fclose (unit)
               call fbackup (filename)
               if (falloc (unit) .ne. IOERROR) then
                  if (fcreate (unit, filename) .eq. IOERROR) then
                     alloc(unit) = .false.
                     unit = IOERROR
                     call ioerr ('fopen: '//EOL)
                  else
                     bp(unit) = 1
                  end if
               end if
            end if
         end if
```

```
          end if
       end if

       fopen = unit

       return
       end
```

The creation of a new file is performed by fcreate via the MS–DOS create function; fcreate opens the file and returns its handle to fopen.

```
* fcreate  -  create and open file, store handle

       integer function fcreate (unit, filename)
       character*(*)  filename
       integer  unit
       include  'global.def'
       include  'msdos.cmn'
       include  'iox.cmn'

       reg$ax = DOS$CREATE
       reg$ds = segment (filename)
       reg$dx = offset (filename)
       reg$cx = 0

       call intrup (registers, 33)

       if (mod (reg$flags,2) .eq. 1) then
          alloc(unit) = .false.
          unit = IOERROR
          call ioerr ('fcreate: '//NULL)
       else
          handle(unit) = reg$ax
          access(unit) = IOWRITE
       end if

       fcreate = unit

       return
       end
```

If a file open is requested and the file already exists, MS–DOS responds by opening the file with the file pointer set to the beginning of the file. If write access was requested, fbackup is called to delete any previously existing backup file and rename the current version to have the extension .bak. fopen sets the file pointer of the old file to the end of the file and closes it before calling fbackup, since the file length is defined by the position of the pointer when the file is closed. fsetptr sets the file pointer to the end:

```
* fsetptr  -  set file read/write pointer
```

```
subroutine fsetptr (unit, mode)
integer  unit, mode
include  'msdos.cmn'
include  'iox.cmn'

reg$ax = DOS$FSETPTR + mode
reg$bx = handle(unit)
reg$cx = 0
reg$bx = 0

call intrup (registers, 33)

return
end
```

The routine fbackup is used by fopen when write access to a pre-existing
file is requested and performs all of the operations necessary to implement the
backup feature. As an overview of what it does, here is a files list of just the
fbackup portion of the primitives:

```
fbackup            !backup an output file
  fnexpand         !expand file name to full pathname
    getdisk        !get default disk
    getdir         !get default directory
  getfile          !search for file name matching input string
    getdta         !get disk transfer address
    setdta         !set disk transfer address
  fdelete          !delete file
  frename          !rename file
```

```
* fbackup  -  back up previous version of file

      subroutine fbackup (filename)
      character*(*)      filename
      include           'global.def'
      logical           getfile
      character*(MAXSTR) fullspec, backup, dummy
      character*(MAXSTR) fnexpand, disk, dir, name, type

      fullspec = fnexpand (filename, disk, dir, name, type)
      backup   = fullspec(1:index (fullspec, '.')) // 'bak' // NULL

      if (getfile (backup, dummy)) call fdelete (backup)

      call frename (fullspec, backup)

      return
      end
```

The renaming of files is accomplished by frename, using the MS–DOS service call supplied for this function. This routine requires the full path to and name of the old and new files and may be used to move files from one directory to another, an operation not allowed by the MS–DOS shell rename command.

```
* frename  -  rename file

        subroutine frename (oldname, newname)
        character*(*)  oldname, newname
        include        'global.def'
        include        'msdos.cmn'

        reg$ax = DOS$RENAME
        reg$ds = segment (oldname)
        reg$dx = offset  (oldname)
        reg$es = segment (newname)
        reg$di = offset  (newname)
        call intrup (registers, 33)

        if (mod (reg$flags,2) .eq. 1) call ioerr ('frename: '//NULL)

        return
        end
```

File deletion is performed by the routine fdelete, using the MS–DOS delete file service.

```
* fdelete  -  delete file

        subroutine fdelete (filename)
        character*(*)  filename
        include        'global.def'
        include        'msdos.cmn'
        character*(MAXSTR) fnexpand, fname, disk, dir, name, type

        fname = fnexpand (filename, disk, dir, name, type)

        reg$ax = DOS$DELETE
        reg$ds = segment (fname)
        reg$dx = offset  (fname)
        call intrup (registers, 33)

        if (mod (reg$flags,2) .eq. 1) call ioerr ('fdelete: '//NULL)

        return
        end
```

Both the rename and delete functions (as well as most other MS–DOS file service routines) require a complete file path name, including the device, directory, name, and extension of the file upon which the service is to operate. fnexpand returns a complete file specification for an incomplete input specification, supplying the current disk and directory as the path if not already present. The default disk and directory are provided by the routines getdisk and getddir.

```
* fnexpand  -  expand file name to full file specification (path+name)

      character*(*) function fnexpand (fname, disk, dir, name, type)
      character*(*) fname, disk, dir, name, type
      include      'global.def'
      integer      fp, fe, tp, te
      character*(MAXSTR) getdisk, getdir

      fe = index (fname, NULL)
      fp = index (fname(1:fe), ':')

      if (fp .eq. 0) then
         disk = getdisk()
      else
         disk = fname(1:fp)//NULL
      end if
      fp = fp + 1

      tp = fp
      te = index (fname(fp:fe), '\')
      if (te .eq. 0) then
         dir = getdir ()
      else
1        if (te .ne. 0) then
            fp = fp + te
            te = index (fname(fp:fe), '\')
            goto 1
         end if
         dir = fname(tp:fp-1)//NULL
      end if

      tp = index (fname(fp:fe), '.')
      if (tp .eq. 0) then
         name = fname(fp:fe)
         type = NULL
      else
         name = fname(fp:fp+tp-2)//NULL
         type = fname(fp+tp-1:fe)//NULL
      end if

      fnexpand = disk(1:index (disk, NULL) - 1) //
     &          dir(1:index (dir, NULL) - 1)   //
     &          name(1:index (name, NULL) - 1) //
     &          type(1:index (type, NULL))
```

```
        return
        end


  * getdisk  -  get default disk

        character*(*) function getdisk ()
        include  'global.def'
        include  'msdos.cmn'

        reg$ax = DOS$GETDISK
        call intrup (registers, 33)

        getdisk = char (ichar ('a') + mod (reg$ax, 256)) //':'//NULL

        return
        end


  * getdir  -  get default directory from default disk

        character*(*) function getdir ()
        include  'global.def'
        include  'msdos.cmn'

        reg$ax = DOS$GETDIR
        reg$dx = 0
        reg$ds = segment (getdir)
        reg$si = offset  (getdir)
        call intrup (registers, 33)

        if (getdir(1:1) .eq. NULL) then
           getdir = '\'//NULL
        else
           getdir = '\' // getdir(1:index(getdir,NULL)-1) // '\' // NULL
        end if

        return
        end
```

getfile is a directory search routine used in fbackup to return the next
file matching its input argument. The DOS wildcard characters are accepted,
although they aren't needed for this application. The current disk and directory
are also supplied if missing from the input string. The getfile routine is a
logical function and can be used in a while loop to process all files matching
a given pattern, which makes it useful for things such as directory listings.

```
  * getfile  -  get name of next file which matches pattern

        logical function getfile (pattern, name)
```

```
character*(*)   pattern, name
include        'global.def'
include        'msdos.cmn'
integer        NOMOFILES
parameter      (NOMOFILES = 18)
logical        equal
integer        dtaseg, dtaoff
character*(MAXSTR) buffer, lastpatt
save           buffer, lastpatt
data           lastpatt /NULL/

call getdta (dtaseg, dtaoff)
call setdta (segment (buffer), offset (buffer))

if (equal (pattern, lastpatt)) then
   reg$ax = DOS$GETFILE
   call intrup (registers, 33)
else
   lastpatt = pattern
   reg$ax = DOS$GETFILE1
   reg$ds = segment (pattern)
   reg$dx = offset  (pattern)
   reg$cx = 0
   call intrup (registers, 33)
end if

if (iand (reg$flags,1) .eq. 1) then
   getfile = .false.
   name(1:1) = NULL
   if (reg$ax .ne. NOMOFILES) call ioerr ('getfile: '//NULL)
else
   getfile = .true.
   name = buffer(31:43)
end if

call setdta (dtaseg, dtaoff)

return
end
```

The DOS call used by getfile is one of the older FCB-based routines and
requires that the disk transfer area (DTA) be defined prior to a read operation.
The getdta and setdta routines are used to set the DTA to the result string
address and set it back to its original address afterwards:

```
* getdta  -  get current disk transfer area

     subroutine getdta (dtaseg, dtaoff)
     integer  dtaseg, dtaoff
     include  'msdos.cmn'

     reg$ax = DOS$GETDTA
```

```
        call intrup (registers, 33)

        dtaseg = reg$es
        dtaoff = reg$bx

        return
        end


* setdta  -  set disk transfer area

        subroutine setdta (dtaseg, dtaoff)
        integer*2  dtaseg, dtaoff
        include    'msdos.cmn'

        reg$ax = DOS$SETDTA
        reg$ds = dtaseg
        reg$dx = dtaoff

        call intrup (registers, 33)

        return
        end
```

File closure is accomplished via fclose, which calls the MS–DOS file close service to perform the actual file closure, file length update, and file creation time and date. fclose then deallocates the unit, making it available for future allocations.

```
* fclose  -  flush buffer, close file, deallocate unit

        subroutine fclose (u)
        integer  u
        include  'global.def'
        include  'msdos.cmn'
        include  'iox.cmn'

        if (u.le.0 .or. u.gt.MAXOPEN) then
            call fputstr (STDERR, 'fclose: Invalid unit number'//EOL)
        else if (.not. alloc(u)) then
            call fputstr (STDERR, 'fclose: Unit not allocated'//EOL)
        else
            if (access(u) .ne. IOREAD) call fflush (u)
            reg$ax = DOS$CLOSE
            reg$bx = handle(u)
            call intrup (registers, 33)
            if (mod (reg$flags,2) .eq. 1) then
                call ioerr ('fclose: '//NULL)
            else
                alloc(u) = .false.
            end if
```

```
      end if

      return
      end
```

The I/O buffers associated with a unit are flushed by fflush, which is almost identical to its VMS counterpart:

```
* fflush  -  flush buffer associated with unit u

      subroutine fflush (u)
      integer u
      include 'global.def'
      include 'iox.cmn'

      if (bp(u) .gt. 1) call fputc (u, NEWLINE)

      return
      end
```

The falloc and fdealloc routines are required to maintain the external interface to the primitives, and are completely analogous to the VMS versions:

```
* falloc  -  allocate io unit

      integer function falloc (unit)
      integer unit
      include 'global.def'
      include 'iox.cmn'

      unit = 1
1 if (unit.le.MAXOPEN .and. alloc(unit)) then
        unit = unit + 1
        goto 1
      end if

      if (unit .gt. MAXOPEN) then
        unit = IOERROR
        call fputstr (STDERR, 'falloc: Open file limit exceeded'//EOL)
      else
        alloc(unit) = .true.
      end if

      falloc = unit

      return
      end
```

```
* fdealloc  -  deallocate a unit

    subroutine fdealloc (unit)
    integer  unit
    include  'global.def'
    include  'iox.cmn'

    if (alloc(unit)) then
       alloc(unit) = .false.
    else
       call fputstr (STDERR, 'fdealloc: Unit not allocated'//EOL)
    end if

    return
    end
```

That completes the generic MS–DOS-based primitives. The routines are written in standard Fortran except for the length of variable names and the use of $, so it should be easy to get them running with another compiler. There are four Lahey-supplied routines used in the I/O primitives that must be duplicated for any other compiler system:

```
intrup      !call DOS interrupt
segment     !get segment of a variable's address
offset      !get offset of a variable's address
iand        !bit-wise logical and
```

We did a benchmark of the Fortran I/O and MS–DOS I/O versions, measuring the time it takes v77 to process itself. The MS–DOS-based version is 40–50% faster than the Fortran-based system. Executable programs are about the same size for either system. However, the size of the MS–DOS-based version can be reduced considerably by eliminating wasted space in the ioerr error messages (about 1K) or by removing the output file backup feature, which is responsible for about half of the code in the primitives. Neither change would affect the speed significantly.

APPENDIX C

User Reference Guide

Documentation is an essential part of any program. The documentation of any program should always include some sort of description of the source code and the program organization as a reference for future programmers whose task it is to maintain the program. This is true even if that future programmer is you, because even the author of a program forgets details about a program's implementation over time. Writing good documentation requires much of the same discipline that is needed for writing good programs.

The main text of the book provides the program documentation for all of the software; this appendix provides a summary user reference guide to the complete programs in this book. The user reference material is written for the kind of people who will read this book—programmers—rather than for computer-illiterate users.

In the descriptions that follow, command arguments enclosed in brackets are optional. Commands for which both the input and output files are optional have a standard interpretation of file name arguments:

- If both names are given, the first is the input and the second is the output.

- If one file name is given, it is taken to be the input and the output is written to STDOUT.

- If no file names are given, the input is STDIN and the output is STDOUT.

Commands that accept escape sequences all recognize the same sequences. There are special sequences for the most common nonprintable characters, and a means of specifying any 8-bit unsigned integer value for a character is also provided:

Character	Escape Sequence
Blank	\b
Tab	\t
Null	\0
Newline	\n
Backslash	\\
Decimal encoded	\d000–\d255
Hex encoded	\h00–\hFF

change

Purpose: change words matching pattern.

Syntax: change pat1 pat2 [infile] [outfile] [-u]

Options: -u: case-insensitive match of pat1

Description: change accepts two patterns that may contain wildcard characters and substitutes pat2 for pat1 for each word matching pat1 in the input. A * in either pattern is treated as a wildcard and can match zero or more characters. In pat2, the text matched by the corresponding wildcard in pat1 is put in the substituted word. A ~ in pat2 causes the corresponding wildcard in pat1 to be deleted in pat2. For example,

```
$ change "*[*]*;*" "~~*"
```

would change the input

```
dua1:[tools.source]change.for
```

to the output string

```
change
```

Bugs: A word is any string not containing blanks.

detab

Purpose: replace tab characters by blanks.

Syntax: detab [infile] [outfile] [-ntab]

Options: -ntab: make tab stops equivalent to ntab blanks, where ntab is an integer (default = 8)

Description: detab replaces all tab characters in the input file with an equivalent number of blanks; the number of blanks is chosen so that the next character after the tab is in a column position that is a multiple of the tab stop size. For instance, if a tab appears in column 10 and the tab stop size is 8, then the tab is replaced by 6 blanks, and the character following the tab is in column 17 $((2 \times 8) + 1)$.

Bugs: no known bugs.

f

Purpose: compile Fortran source files.

Syntax: f infile [-options]

Options: -l: Produce listing file
-d: Produce debugger code
-p: Preprocess source file
-s: Save intermediate preprocessor output code
(preprocessed code is in file preptemp.lis)

Description: f compiles the source file by invoking the VAX/VMS Fortran compiler, with implicit none checking enabled, extended source format (source lines up to 132 columns wide), and array bounds and arithmetic overflow checking enabled. If the -l option is used the Fortran /list qualifier is used; if the -d option is present the /debug qualifier is used. If the -p option is present, the source file is preprocessed (see prep for a description of the preprocessor) and output onto the temporary file preptemp.for. The preptemp.for file is then submitted to the Fortran compiler.

Bugs: If -l and -p are both enabled, the listing file is created for the preprocessed code, in file preptemp.lis.

find

Purpose: find words matching pattern.

Syntax: find pat [infile] [outfile] [-u]

Options: -u: ignore case

Description: find searches its input for words matching the specified pattern, which may contain wildcard characters. Any lines containing a match are printed on the output. A * in the pattern is treated as a wildcard and can match zero or more characters.

Bugs: A word is any sequence of characters without blanks.

global_update

Purpose: update library with all files in a files list.

Syntax: global_update library fileslist

Options: see options for f command

Description: global_update executes the update command for all files named in the input files list (see description of pound for a definition of files lists).

Bugs: no known bugs (but see comments on f command bugs).

hashgen

Purpose: generate source files for initialized hash tables.

Syntax: hashgen [infile] [outfile] [-u]

Options: -u: convert input identifiers to uppercase

Description: hashgen is a utility for producing preloaded hash tables and produces two output files and a performance summary as output. The output files are a common block declaration file and a file containing data statements, whose names are derived from the name of the input file. For example, if the input file name is f77.hsh, the common block and data statement files are named f77table.cmn and f77data.def, respectively. If outfile is specified on the command line then the performance report is written to it; otherwise the report is written to STDOUT.

A simple language is used to define the hash table parameters and the initial table contents. The keywords are:

maxsymbol	length of namep, nextp, and parallel arrays
maxbuffer	length of buffer string storage area
hashsize	length of htable array
hashfunction	hash function number to be used:

Value	Hash Function Type
1,2	division (hashsize prime)
3,4	multiplication (hashsize 2^n)
5	Fibonacci (hashsize 2^n)

array	declare array parallel to hash table namep array

syntax:	array type name
valid types:	integer, real, logical, and string
name:	name of parallel array
!	comment (remainder of line is ignored)

The string array types are implemented by storing the (null-terminated) string value in buffer and assigning the array name to an array of integer string pointers in order to conserve space.

A file that specifies hash function 1, hash size 57, symbol table length 250, buffer size 5000, two parallel arrays, and two initial entries for the table might look like:

```
! example.hsh  -  example hashgen input file

    hashfunction = 1          !hash1
    hashsize     = 57         !57 is a good prime
    maxsymbol    = 250        !big enough
    maxbuffer    = 5000       !hopefully big enough

    array integer address    !storage location
    array real      value    !initialized value

    !name     address    value
    !----     -------    -----
    Thag       1452      10.75
    Lives       104      2.0E-10
```

All arrays must be declared before data begins. Values in data statements are assigned in the order in which the arrays were declared.

Bugs: The data statements must be included in a block data subprogram, and the block data subprogram must be referenced (via a Fortran external statement) in at least one program unit to inform the linker of its existence. Routines using the generated table must use the same hash function as that specified in the input file. The hashgen keywords cannot appear as names to be installed in the hash table.

image

Purpose: create an executable program from a library.

Syntax: image library program

Options: none

Description: image links a program and expects all of the modules necessary to link the program to be present in the library.

Bugs: no known bugs.

lexgen

Purpose: generate data statements for lexical scanner state tables.

Syntax: lexgen [infile] [outfile] [-u]

Options: -u: convert patterns to uppercase

Description: The input to lexgen is based on regular expressions. A regular grammar is a restricted class of mathematical grammars, and a sentence in such a grammar is a regular expression. Let A be the input alphabet, or the set of all allowed input characters. Then each element of A is a regular expression. If r and s are regular expressions and c_1 and c_2 are elements (characters) of A, then the following are also regular expressions:

$$rs \qquad r \text{ followed by } s$$
$$(r|s) \qquad r \text{ or } s$$
$$\{r\} \qquad \text{closure of } r \text{ (zero or more occurrences of } r)$$
$$c_1-c_2 \qquad \text{range of characters from } c_1 \text{ to } c_2$$

These rules can be applied to individual characters in the alphabet or to expressions built up from previous applications of the rules. Here are some examples:

$$\text{unsigned integer:} \quad [0-9]\{[0-9]\}$$
$$\text{signed integer:} \quad (+|-|)[0-9]\{[0-9]\}$$
$$\text{decimal number:} \quad (+|-|)([0-9]\{[0-9]\}.\{[0-9]\}\,|$$
$$\{[0-9]\}.[0-9]\{[0-9]\})$$

The last example accepts decimal numbers provided they have at least one digit, either before or after the decimal point. The expression $\{[0-9]\}$ accepts zero or more digits; the expression $[0-9]\{[0-9]\}$ accepts one or more digits.

The lexgen input file consists of a sequence of statements assigning integer token values to associated regular expressions. For example, the statement

```
42 = ( [a-z] | [A-Z] ) { [a-z] | [A-Z] | [0-9] | $ | _ ) }
```

specifies a regular expression that matches identifiers in VAX Fortran, and assigns the token 42 to strings matched by the expression. Blanks are ignored, but can be included in a regular expression by the escape sequence \b. All of the special characters (|){}[] can be obtained literally in an expression by preceding them with a backslash; in addition, any character can be obtained by a decimal or hexadecimal escape sequence such as \d032 or \h20 (both of which produce ASCII character 32, or blank). lexgen performs preprocessing on the input (see documentation for prep), so macros can be defined for the integer token values or for parts of regular expressions. For example

```
#define   letter   ([a-z] | [A-Z])
#define   digit    [0-9]
#define   $id      42

$id = letter { (letter | digit | $ | _ ) }
```

produces the same result as the previous example.

The output of lexgen is a series of data statements that initialize a transition table which recognizes the regular expressions in the input file. To use the lexical scanner, a prewritten routine named lexscan is provided to interpret the table. The lexscan routine should be modified by changing the routine name and changing an include statement to correspond to the file name specified as the output file for lexgen.

If an input string matches the regular expression specified in more than one token, the first token given in the input is used. For example, if the lexgen input contained

```
42 = ( [a-z] | [A-Z] ) { [a-z] | [A-Z] | [0-9] | $ | _ ) }
43 = print
```

the token 43 would never be returned by lexscan since the string print also matches the regular expression for identifiers.

The lexical analyzers generated by lexgen have only one character of lookahead and therefore cannot recognize some tokens in typical programming languages. For instance, in standard Fortran, a do keyword cannot be distinguished from identifiers like do100i without some lookahead. In such cases additional code is required in addition to the lexscan routine to perform lookahead.

Bugs: lexgen is somewhat slow and cannot produce lexical analyzers with more than 512 states.

match

Purpose: search input for lines matching regular expression.

Syntax: match reg-expr [infile] [outfile] [-u]

Options: -u: perform case-insensitive search

Description: match accepts the same syntax for regular expressions as that accepted by lexgen. The command

    $ match "([a-z]|[A-Z]|$|_){([a-z]|[A-Z]|$|_|[0-9])}" abc.txt

causes all identifiers in file abc.txt to be listed on STDOUT. match will also accept an option -u which causes the input file's lines and all characters in the regular expression to be converted to uppercase before searching, which makes the search case-insensitive. However, the lines of output are not converted to uppercase. The command

    $ match xyz.txt "hello" -u

degenerates to the level of most file searching programs.

Bugs: no known bugs.

pound

Purpose: generate strings from file names in a files list.

Syntax: pound "string containing #" [infile] [outfile] [-p]

Options: -p: process only lines beginning with #

Description: The input to pound is a files list, which is simply a list of file names, one per line. Blank lines and comment lines are ignored. A files list for the programs in Chapter 2 might be

```
! getting started

! command procedures:
        # f.com                !compile
        # update.com           !compile and insert into library
        # image.com            !link program
        # global_update.com    !files list version of update

! Fortran source
        pound                  !generate strings from files lists
        getargs                !get command line arguments
        stdargs                !apply standard defaults to arguments
        detab                  !replace tabs by blanks
        v77                    !translate VAX Fortran to Fortran 77
        fput77                 !output Fortran 77 source lines
```

Files lists may also "include" other files lists, so given a list for each chapter, a files list for this book might read

```
        #include intro.fil
        #include start.fil
        #include prims.fil
        #include strings.fil
        #include prep.fil
            .
            .
```

By convention, files lists have the extension .fil.

pound takes a pattern as a command line argument, and each occurrence of the character # in the pattern is replaced by the file names in the list. The command

```
$ pound "$ append #.for calcfiles.for/new" calc.fil aaa.com
```

creates a command procedure aaa.com that concatenates all of the files for
the calc program onto the file calcfiles.for, using the DCL append command. The pattern can also contain *escape sequences*, which are prefixed
by a backslash. Any ASCII code can be generated with escape sequences,
and special ones are provided for commonly used special characters, such
as \n for newline. Thus the command

```
$ pound "$ copy #.for [-.calc]* \n$ del #.for;" calc.fil aaa.com
```

generates two lines of output for each file name in calc.fil. It is possible
to create a files list of any directory with the DCL command

```
$ dir/noheader/notrailer/columns=1/versions=1
```

The # character also has a special meaning when it occurs as the first
character on a line in a files list. Files lists are generally used to document the organization of a program and show all of its components. The
components of programs fall into two categories: source files and other
files. The "other" category includes definition files, common block files, or
perhaps some documentation. The -p command line option causes only
lines beginning with # to be processed. The commands

```
$ pound "$ print #.for" calc.fil
$ pound "$ print #" calc.fil -p
```

generate print commands for all of the files in calc.fil, first for the Fortran
source files (for which the .for extension is given in the pattern argument)
and then for the "other" files.

Bugs: no known bugs.

prep

Purpose: general-purpose text file preprocessor.

Syntax: prep [infile] [outfile] [-d:name]

Options: -d:name   define name as a macro at startup

Description: prep is a simple computer language preprocessor with macro capabilities and conditional processing control. The language is similar to the standard C preprocessor language, with simplifications and minor deviations. The statements the preprocessor recognizes are:

```
#include filename
#define   NAME    replacement_string
#define   NAME(arg1,...argn)    replacement_string(arg1,...argn)
#undef    NAME
#clear
#quote    quote_char
#ifdef    NAME
#ifndef   NAME
#elsifdef NAME
#else
#endif
```

All of the preprocessor statements begin with the pound symbol, and all other input lines are scanned for macros specified in #define statements. The first form of #define is actually the same as the second form with no arguments; it can be used to declare symbolic constants as in

```
#define   NEWLINE   char(10)
#define   NULL      char(0)
#define   BETA      rval(4)
```

The #undef statement removes a macro definition; the #clear statement undefines everything.

The second form of #define is more powerful. It is something like a one-line function definition, with arguments. For example,

```
#define   incr(x)   x = x + 1
incr(i)
incr(stack(sp+OFFSET))
```

produces the output

```
i = i + 1
stack(sp+OFFSET) = stack(sp+OFFSET) + 1
```

prep preserves blanks in the input. Special characters such as NEWLINE can be included in a macro definition by using escape sequences, and macro definitions can be extended over one physical line by placing an ampersand at the end of a line. This allows multiple output lines from a macro expansion, as in

```
#define  skipblank(line,lp)  &
   do while (line(lp:lp) .eq. BLANK) \n&
      lp = lp + 1 \n&
   end do
```

No intervening spaces are allowed between the macro name and the opening parentheses of its arguments, to distinguish between the two forms of #define.

A special quote character can be used to prevent the expansion of a macro. By default, the character is the double-quote character, so that

```
the "skipblank(line,lp)" macro is real handy.
```

comes out literally as shown, except that the quotes are removed. The quote character can be changed with the #quote statement. If #quote is entered without any quote character, then quoting is disabled altogether.

The #if-related statements control the inclusion of lines in the output and processing of define statements. For example,

```
#define  BIGSTRINGS
#ifdef BIGSTRINGS
   #define  MAXSTR   255
   !big strings enabled
#else
   #define  MAXSTR   134
   !small strings enabled
#endif
```

would result in MAXSTR being defined to be 255, and the text comment "!big strings enabled" to appear in the output.

Bugs: The maximum size of the output text produced by a single line of input, after macro expansion, is 2048 characters.

shell

Purpose: provides I/O redirection and pipelines for DCL.

Syntax: shell [infile]

Options: none

Description: The shell provides the following operations on DCL command lines:

<file	Redirect standart input to file
>file	Redirect standard output to file
>>file	Append standard output to file
prog1 | prog2	Direct standard output of prog1 to standard input of prog2

If the shell is started without any file name arguments, it runs interactively, and the last 20 commands entered can be retrieved, edited, and resubmitted using the arrow keys. If file name arguments are provided on the shell command line, it processes infile as a script file, and the script file can contain any of the preprocessor commands (see prep).

The shell can be used on any DCL command, including the @ (command procedure execution) command. However, the shell does not process commands within command procedures.

The shell has four internal commands. The command

```
$ prompt  prompt_str
```

sets the shell prompt to the specified string. The prompt_str may contain escape sequences. The default prompt is $. The internal commands exit and lo terminate the shell; alternatively, the shell can be terminated by typing CONTROL/Z. While running the shell, the shell command itself is an internal command, and is only accepted if an input file name is provided.

Bugs: Typing CONTROL/C will stop an image executing in the subprocess, but it will not stop a command procedure. The shell may not work properly with commands that create independent subprocesses (e.g. the set host command won't work right unless the new process created invokes the shell).

spl

Purpose: compiler/interpreter for a simple programming language.

Syntax: spl [infile] [-lmt]

Options: -c: Calculator (interactive) mode
-l: Produce compiler listing
-m: Produce virtual machine code listing
-t: Trace machine state during execution

Description: spl is a compiler system that generates code for a virtual machine and interprets the generated code. If infile is provided on the command line with no extension, the default extension .spl is used. The following is a brief description of the language recognized by the spl compiler.

Source form: An spl program consists of a sequence of type statements and executable statements. Type statements may occur anywhere in a program. Executable statements consist of assignment statements, read and print statements, and multiline constructs.

All of the commands of prep are built into spl. An spl program consists of a sequence of logical lines. The following describes the syntax of logical lines:

Character context: A character appears in a character context if it is between the delimiters of a literal string, which are apostrophes (single quote marks).

Comments: The character ! indicates a comment except where it occurs in a character context. The comment extends to the end of the physical line. A comment is processed as though it were an end-of-line character.

Logical line separation: The character ; separates logical lines on a single physical line. Otherwise, the end-of-line character separates logical lines.

Logical line continuation: The character & as the last nonblank character of a line signifies that the logical line is continued on the next physical line. If a character context is being continued, the & may not be followed by a comment, and the first nonblank character of the next physical line determines the character position at which the continuation begins: if the first nonblank character is &, then the continuation begins at the character position immediately following the &; otherwise, it begins in column 1.

Blank lines: blank lines between logical lines are ignored. Blank lines may not occur between physical lines of a logical line.

The escape mechanism is also built-in for all character string operations. spl is case sensitive, that is, abc is not the same identifier as ABC. There is no predefined limit on the number of characters in an identifier, and all characters are significant.

Keywords: The following keywords are reserved (may not be used as identifiers):

```
integer      real        logical      if
else         while       repeat       until
read         print       end          and
or           not         true         false
```

Data types and type statements: There are four data types in spl: integer, real, logical, and character. One-dimensional arrays of any type are also supported. Type statements may occur anywhere in a program. There is a type keyword corresponding to each of the data types. There is no default typing in spl, so every identifier used must be declared except for the names of intrinsic functions, which are predeclared. The syntax of is of the form

```
type_keyword item, item, . . .
```

where an item is a scalar variable name or an array variable name followed by an integer constant in parentheses denoting the array size. For example,

```
integer   i, j, k(20)
character c, s(255)
```

Scalar variables of type integer, real, or logical are allocated one storage unit; arrays of these types are allocated one storage unit for each element. Characters are stored in character storage units separate from other types. Character strings are null-terminated by the compiler, so a scalar character variable is actually allocated two character storage units (one for the NULL). Storage is statically allocated and remains allocated throughout the execution of a program.

Control statements: spl statements are executed sequentially unless the order of execution is changed by control statements. spl has two types of looping constructs, a while construct

```
while condition
    statements
end while
```

which tests the condition before executing the body of the loop, and a repeat until construct, which tests the condition at the end of the loop:

```
repeat
    statements
until condition
```

spl also has a block-structured if construct:

```
if condition_1
    statements
else if condition_2
    statements
    .
    .
    .
else
    statements
end if
```

The else if and else clauses are optional. In all of these examples, condition is a logical-valued expression.

I/O statements: spl has a simple I/O capability that allows the user to read and write from STDIN and STDOUT. There is an intrinsic logical function readln that reads the next line from the input, returning true if the read was successful and false otherwise. The data in the input record can then be accessed with one or more read statements. For example, if the next input record contains three integer fields that are to be read into variables i, j, and k, it can be accomplished with

```
if readln()
    read i, j, k
end if
```

or the fields can each be read with separate statements:

```
if readln()
    read i
    read j
    read k
end if
```

A quoted string is expected for input to a character variable. If an attempt is made to read more fields from a record than are present, an error is reported. A call to the readln function is always required to get a new input line.

The list items in a read statement must be names of variables or array elements. In the print statement, the list items may be any valid expression of any data type. There is no implied record advance on the print statement, and lines must be terminated with NEWLINE. The variables in the preceding examples could be printed on one output line with the statement

```
print i, ' ', j, ' ', k, '\n'
```

or with

```
print i, ' '
print j, ' '
print k, '\n'
```

There is also no implied spacing or field width for output fields in the print statement, so spacing must be provided explicitly. In read statements, there is no implied field width, and any number of blanks can separate fields.

spl has a predeclared identifier input$ which is a character string holding the current input line. Thus the input can be copied to the output with the statements

```
while readln()
    print input$
end while
```

If spl is used with the shell, the standard input and output can be conveniently redirected to files.

Expressions: The following operators are allowed in arithmetic expressions:

```
arithmetic:    +    -    *    /    **
relational:    ==   <>   >    >=   <    <=
logical:       and  or   not
assignment:    =
```

There are no character operators; string manipulation may only be accomplished through intrinsic and user-written functions. Note that assignments are considered to be arithmetic expressions; this allows use of expressions like

```
while ((k = array(i)) > 0)
```

which assigns k to be the ith element of array before comparing it with zero, and

```
a = b = c = 0
```

which assigns all of the variables to zero. Assignments leave a result on the stack for use in an expression. The parentheses after a function name are required even if there are no arguments (in which case there is nothing between the parentheses).

spl Intrinsic Functions

r: real
i: integer
L: logical
s: string

Function(arguments)	Result	Description
sin(r)	r	sine of angle in radians
cos(r)	r	cosine of angle in radians
tan(r)	r	tangent of angle in radians
arcsin(r)	r	inverse sine
arccos(r)	r	inverse cosine
arctan(r)	r	inverse tangent
exp(r)	r	e^x
ln(r)	r	natural logarithm
float(i)	r	real conversion
int(r)	i	integer conversion
abs(r)	r	absolute value
iabs(i)	i	absolute value
index(s,s)	i	location of substring
ord(s)	i	integer conversion of first character
len(s)	i	dynamic string length
chr(i)	s	character conversion
cat(s,s)	s	concatenation
substr(s,i,i)	s	substring
eqs(s,s)	L	string comparison for equality
readln()	L	line input

Bugs: spl does not perform any run-time error checking.

update

Purpose: update object library from Fortran source file.

Syntax: update library sourcefile [-options]

Options: see description of f command.

Description: update compiles the specified source file and updates the specified library with the object code. If the object module already exists in the library, it is replaced; otherwise it is inserted. The object code file is deleted.

Bugs: no known bugs.

v77

Purpose: translate VAX Fortran programs to Fortran 77 source form.

Syntax: v77 [infile] [outfile] [-i]

Options: -i: perform file inclusion on INCLUDE statements

Description: v77 performs the following translations:

- Translates input to uppercase (except in character strings)
- Performs file inclusion (when -i option is enabled)
- Deletes all comments
- Inserts continuations as required to assure that all source text is within the 7th to 72nd columns
- converts loops of the form

        do i = 1, 10
          . . .
        end do

  to the standard form

        DO 7701 I = 1, 10
          . . .
        7701 CONTINUE

- converts loops of the form

        do while (condition)
          . . .
        end do

  to the standard form

        7701 IF (condition) THEN
          . . .
        GOTO 7701
        END IF

Bugs: The do statement in do...end do loops may not be continued. v77 can potentially produce incorrect results for programs that are tab-formatted or that contain character contexts extending over multiple source lines. v77 generates labels starting with 7701, so generated labels can conflict with preexisting ones in this range.

Index to Routines

Index